COURT AND POLITICS IN PAPAL ROME

This book attempts to overcome the traditional historiographical approach to the role of the early modern papacy by focusing on the actual mechanisms of power in the papal court. The period covered extends from the Renaissance to the aftermath of the Peace of Westphalia in 1648, after which the papacy was reduced to a mainly spiritual role.

Based on new research in Italian and other European archives, the book concentrates on the factions at the Roman court and in the College of Cardinals. The Sacred College came under great international pressure during the election of a new pope, and consequently such figures as foreign ambassadors and foreign cardinals are examined, as well as political liaisons and social contacts at court. Finally, the book includes an analysis of the ambiguous nature of Roman ceremonial, which was both religious and secular: a reflection of the power struggle both in Rome and in Europe.

GIANVITTORIO SIGNOROTTO is Professor of Early Modern History, Università degli Studi di Urbino, Italy.

MARIA ANTONIETTA VISCEGLIA is Professor of Early Modern History, Università degli Studi di Roma 'La Sapienza'.

CAMBRIDGE STUDIES IN ITALIAN HISTORY AND CULTURE

Edited by GIGLIOLA FRAGNITO, Università degli Studi, Parma

CESARE MOZZARELLI, Università Cattolica del Sacro Cuore, Milan

ROBERT ORESKO, Institute of Historical Research,
University of London

and GEOFFREY SYMCOX, University of California, Los Angeles

This series comprises monographs and a variety of collaborative volumes, including translated works, which concentrate on the period of Italian history from late medieval times up to the Risorgimento. The editors aim to stimulate scholarly debate over a range of issues which have not hitherto received, in English, the attention they deserve. As it develops, the series will emphasize the interest and vigour of current international debates on this central period of Italian history and the persistent influence of Italian culture on the rest of Europe.

For a list of titles in the series, see end of book

COURT AND POLITICS IN
PAPAL ROME, 1492–1700

EDITED BY
GIANVITTORIO SIGNOROTTO
AND
MARIA ANTONIETTA VISCEGLIA

CAMBRIDGE
UNIVERSITY PRESS

PUBLISHED BY THE PRESS SYNDICATE OF THE UNIVERSITY OF CAMBRIDGE
The Pitt Building, Trumpington Street, Cambridge, United Kingdom

CAMBRIDGE UNIVERSITY PRESS
The Edinburgh Building, Cambridge CB2 2RU, UK
40 West 20th Street, New York, NY 10011-4211, USA
477 Williamstown Road, Port Melbourne, VIC 3207, Australia
Ruiz de Alarcón 13, 28014 Madrid, Spain
Dock House, The Waterfront, Cape Town 8001, South Africa

http://www.cambridge.org

First published 2002

Printed in the United Kingdom at the University Press, Cambridge

Typeface Bembo 11/12.5 pt.   *System* LATEX 2$_\varepsilon$ [TB]

A catalogue record for this book is available from the British Library

ISBN 0 521 64146 2

CONTENTS

ABBREVIATIONS

AC	Archivio Capitolino, Rome
ADP	Archivio Doria Pamphili, Rome
AHNM	Archivo Histórico Nacional, Madrid
AGS	Archivo General, Simancas
AMAE	Archivo Ministerio de Asuntos Exteriores, Madrid
AMAEt	Archives du Ministère des Affaires Etrangères, Paris
APF	Archivio della Congregazione de Propaganda Fide, Rome
ARSI	Archivum Romanum Societatis Jesu, Rome
ASB	Archivio di Stato, Bologna
ASDMi	Archivio Storico Diocesano, Milan
ASF	Archivio di Stato, Florence
	Mediceo del Principato = MP
ASGe	Archivio di Stato, Genoa
ASL	Archivio di Stato, Lucca
ASM	Archivio di Stato, Mantua
ASMo	Archivio di Stato, Modena
ASP	Archivio di Stato, Parma
ASR	Archivio di Stato, Rome
AST	Archivio di Stato, Turin
ASV	Archivio Segreto Vaticano
ASVe	Archivio di Stato, Venice
BA	Biblioteca Angelica, Rome
BAV	Biblioteca Apostolica Vaticana
Barb. Lat.	Barberini Latini (ms.)
Vat. Lat.	Vaticani Latini (ms.)
Urb. Lat.	Urbinati Latini (ms.)
Ottob. Lat.	Ottoboniani Latini (ms.)
Chigi	Chigiani (ms.)

BL	British Library, London
BM	Biblioteca Marciana, Venice
BMC	Biblioteca del Civico Museo Correr, Venice
BNCVE	Biblioteca Nazionale Centrale Vittorio Emanuele, Rome
BNF	Bibliothèque Nationale de France, Paris
BNM	Biblioteca Nacional, Madrid
HHStA	Haus-, Hof- und Staatsarchiv, Vienna
DBI	*Dizionario Biografico degli Italiani*, Rome, Istituto dell'Enciclopedia Italiana, 1960– .

INTRODUCTION

GIANVITTORIO SIGNOROTTO AND
MARIA ANTONIETTA VISCEGLIA

Rome was defined during the early modern era as the *teatro del mondo* (theatre of the world) and *patria comune* (common homeland); these images expressed the awareness of a universalism that was not only religious in nature, but also a sign of cultural belonging and a recognition of an undisputed political centrality. The chapter on 'négotiation continuelle' in the *Testament politique* attributed to Richelieu, considered as a cardinal text of baroque politics, contains a warning that: 'we need to act the world over, near, far, and above all in Rome'.[1] In the city of the pontiffs, where power was manifested at the highest level, private citizens and delegations from institutional bodies and nations constantly strove to gain concrete advantages, prestige and authority. It was precisely for these reasons that Rome can be considered – to use a modern term – a *political laboratory*, a place where experiments were made with original ways of doing politics and where such ways were the subject of reflection and theorizing. The identification of the environments, the specific forms, the protagonists of the culture and political practices formulated in Rome still await a systematic reconstruction, despite the abundant written material on the subject, both Italian and international.

First, it must be said that it is still possible to benefit from the tradition of political and diplomatic studies that arose throughout the Protestant world after the work of Leopold von Ranke, who, on the premise that foreign policy was paramount, recognized the vitality and dynamic potential of papal Rome, even after the crisis of the sixteenth century.[2] On the other hand, the Catholic historiographical approach to the 'history of the popes' has constantly stressed the front-line role of the Holy See in European and world politics, but from a somewhat restricted

---

[1] A.-I. Du Plessis Cardinal de Richelieu, *Testamento politico e Massime di Stato*, ed. A. Piazzi, Milan, 1988, p. 301.
[2] L. von Ranke, *Storia dei Papi*, Florence, 1968 (the first German edition was in 1836).

point of view within the political and cultural climate of the *Kulturkampf*,[3] which was geared to the defence requirements of the papacy and was limited to the biographical perspective and the reconstruction of single papacies.

The revival of interest in the papal monarchy and papal state since the 1970s has marked a very clear change from those earlier approaches. This can only be understood by considering that a more wide-ranging discussion was by then in progress over the methods and interpretative categories of historical research, and that this debate was spurred by deep transformations in the general perception of politics and institutions. The discussion concerning the Papal Prince spearheaded by Alberto Caracciolo, Mario Caravale and Paolo Prodi between 1978 and 1983, which has remained a fundamental point of reference for subsequent studies, developed within a theoretical reflection on the state in the early modern era and on modernity.[4] The re-examination and reassessment of these themes (the state and modernity) over the last two decades has profoundly changed the very meaning of the conceptual categories used in studies on the formation of the papal monarchy. In the line of research initiated by Wolfgang Reinhard, the topic of modernization is of course not absent. However, as Robert Descimon recently emphasized, it is 'separated from the idea of progress'.[5] The interpretation put forward by the German historian places the emphasis on the question whether the relational categories of sociology are applicable to the papal oligarchy;[6] it sees the church as a social system characterized by an extraordinary capacity to endure over time.[7]

---

[3] L. von Pastor, *Storia dei Papi dalla fine del Medio Evo,* trans. by Angelo Mercati, Rome, 1931 (with different dates for the work's various volumes). Mercati's translation is based on the 1925 German edition. On the key issue of 'the lost victory of the Protestant Reformation and the vitality of the Catholic church', both in Ranke's work and in Catholic historiography, see the remarks by A. Prosperi, 'Riforma cattolica, Controriforma, disciplinamento sociale', in G. De Rosa, T. Gregory and A. Vauchez (eds.), *Storia dell'Italia religiosa. 2. L'età moderna*, Bari, 1994, pp. 12ff.

[4] M. Caravale and A. Caracciolo, 'Lo Stato Pontificio da Martino V a Pio IX', in G. Galasso (ed.), *Storia d'Italia*, vol. XIV, Turin, 1978; P. Prodi, *Il sovrano pontefice. Un corpo e due anime: la monarchia papale nella prima età moderna*, Bologna, 1982 (*The Papal Prince. One Body and Two Souls: The Papal Monarchy in Early Modern Europe*, Cambridge, 1987); A. Caracciolo, 'Sovrano pontefice e sovrani assoluti', *Quaderni storici*, 52, XVIII (1983), pp. 279–86.

[5] See R. Descimon, *Empirisme et méthode. Présentation à* W. Reinhard, *Papauté Confessions Modernité*, Paris, 1998, p. 10 (the volume contains a translation from German into French of some of Reinhard's essays that appeared between 1972 and 1982 and his complete bibliography).

[6] The reference is to W. Reinhard, *Freunde und Kreaturen. 'Verflechtung' als Konzept zur Erforschung historischer Führungsgruppen. Römische Oligarchie um 1600*, Munich, 1979.

[7] Recently W. Reinhard has again stressed the 'incredible social closure and narrowmindedness of the self-referential system of the holy Roman church from the Middle

Furthermore, the various analytical studies written from the perspective of historical sociology[8] have, with a few exceptions, fought shy of ambitious diachronic synthesis.[9] They have not produced any equivalent to recent studies on European diplomatic political history, which has become the subject of renewed interest over the last few decades. The major obstacles to a comprehensive discussion of Rome's role have derived, in part, from the legacy of the two historiographical traditions: on the one hand, Catholic apologetics and on the other, ideological Protestant prejudice of anti-curial origin.[10] But there has been a more serious problem: the diverse interests that inspired the choice of a pontiff can hardly be interpreted as unambiguous, especially from a 'modernity' viewpoint.

It is significant that nepotism – that most characteristic phenomenon of the papacy in the early modern era, which was of course kept dark by Catholic historiography – has been discussed more for the impulse that it gave to artistic production and its economic role[11] than for its sometimes decisive function in certain political contexts,[12] diplomacy and also religious debate.[13] In more recent historiography, furthermore,

Ages until the twentieth century – probably a fundamental reason for its endurance, which is almost unique in history': see 'Le carriere papali e cardinalizie. Contributo alla storia sociale del papato', in L. Fiorani and A. Prosperi (eds.), *Storia d'Italia. Annali 16 : 'Roma, la città del papa. Vita civile e religiosa dal giubileo di Bonifacio VIII al giubileo di papa Wojtyla'*, Turin, 2000, pp. 264–90.

[8] Analytical contributions, pursuing Reinhard's line but in an original way, to the reconstruction of the role of parental and patronage relationships in curial careers are P. Partner, *The Pope's Men. The Papal Civil Service in the Renaissance*, Oxford, 1990; R. Ago, *Carriere e clientele nella Roma barocca*, Rome and Bari, 1990; I. Fosi, *All'ombra dei Barberini. Fedeltà e servizio nella Roma barocca*, Rome, 1997.

[9] On the recruitment of cardinals over this very long period see C. Weber, *Senatus divinus. Verborgene Strukturen im Kardinalskollegium der frühen Neuzeit (1500–1800)*, Frankfurt am Main, 1996.

[10] See A. Lynn Martin's remarks in 'Papal Policy and the European Conflict, 1559–1572', *The Sixteenth Century Journal*, 11/2 (1980), 2, pp. 35–48, referring to N. M. Sutherland's *The Massacre of St. Bartholomew and the European Conflict, 1559–1572*, London, 1973.

[11] W. Reinhardt, *Kardinal Scipione Borghese (1605–1633). Vermögen, Finanzen und sozialer Aufstieg eines Papstnepoten*, Tübingen, Niemeyer, 1984; C. Robertson, *'Il Gran Cardinale'. Alessandro Farnese, Patron of the Arts*, New Haven and London, 1992.

[12] A purely political view of medieval nepotism was put forward by D. Waley, *The Papal State in the Thirteenth Century*, London, 1961. S. Carocci continues and supports this line of interpretation in *Il nepotismo nel medioevo. Papi, cardinali e famiglie nobili*, Rome, 1999, pp. 152–64.

[13] See, for example, the precise analysis by G. Fragnito, which demonstrates the substantial role of the 'spiritual' cardinals in persuading Parma and Piacenza to support Pier Luigi Farnese in 1545, inspired by their indifference to the territorial affairs of the papal state: 'Il nepotismo farnesiano tra ragioni di stato e ragioni di chiesa', in *Continuità e discontinuità nella storia politica, economica e religiosa, Studi in onore di Aldo Stella*, Vicenza, 1993, pp. 117–25.

Reinhard's functionalist approach, which sets two fundamental functions of nepotism – support (*Versorgungsfunktion*) and domination (*Herrschaftsfunktion*) – in the context of values and standards that are far removed from contemporary individualism and related to the concept of *pietas*, has favoured detection of the phenomenon's socio-cultural constants[14] over the reconstruction of specific situations in which, from the Middle Ages to the eighteenth century, it found expression. The topic of nepotism has had no better luck with historians interested in 'state building'; the efforts of the pontiffs – sovereigns without a dynasty – to bequeath power and wealth to relatives after their demise has not aroused such interest as 'Renaissance diplomacy' or the existence and development of the church's 'international relations'.[15] However, documentation relating to the activity of ambassadors in Rome, and the legacy of evidence from agents, papal nuncios and legations, gives a much more complete picture of endeavours (sometimes contradictory), simulations and dissimulations, where the concern to procure wealth and power for the *house* of the Pontiffs was just as important as the concern for the future of faith and European harmony.[16]

Lastly, we can assert that even the recent flurry of studies on the European courts has neglected that of the pontiffs.[17] Perhaps the most significant themes of current European historiography on the courts – the reconsideration of the relationships between court and state, no longer seen as separate worlds but as interwoven and interdependent spheres; the concentration on the symbolic aspects of politics, on ceremoniousness as a manifestation and at the same time a creation of sovereignty – have

---

[14] W. Reinhard, 'Nepotismus. Der Funktionswandel einer papstgeschichtlichen Konstanten', *Zeitschrift für Kirchengeschichte*, 86 (1975), pp. 145–85.

[15] P. Blet, *Histoire de la représentation diplomatique du Saint Siège des origines à l'aube du XIXe siècle*, Città del Vaticano, 1982.

[16] In this perspective see now G. Signorotto, 'Note sulla politica e la diplomazia dei pontefici (da Paolo III a Pio V)', in M. Fantoni (ed.), *Carlo V e l'Italia*, Rome, 2000, pp. 47–76.

[17] This lack of studies on the Roman court has been highlighted on many occasions: see A. Quondam, 'Un'assenza, un progetto. Per una ricerca sulla storia di Roma tra 1465 e 1537', *Studi romani*, 27 (1979), pp. 166–75; P. Hurtubise, 'Jalons pour une histoire de la cour de Rome aux XVe et XVIe siècles', *Roma nel Rinascimento* (1992), pp. 123–34 and, for a subsequent period, C. Weber, 'La Corte di Roma nell'Ottocento', in C. Mozzarelli and G. Olmi (eds.), *La corte nella cultura e nella storiografia. Immagini e posizioni tra Otto e Novecento*, Rome, 1983, pp. 167–204. W. Reinhard, 'Papal Power and Family Strategy in the Sixteenth and Seventeenth Centuries', in R. G. Asch and A. M. Birke (eds.), *Princes, Patronage and the Nobility. The Court at the Beginning of the Modern Age, 1450–1650*, London and Oxford, 1991.

recently begun to be applied also to Rome.[18] But there is still a lot of work to be done on the *household* of the pope, the court's financial administration, the matrimonial policy of the papal families and the network of relationships that linked them to the Italian ruling families and to European dynasties.

It is not our intention here to present a summary of previous research.[19] It is necessary to assess the contribution of the different historiographical approaches, and to acknowledge that a comparison with them remains inevitable, before we can adopt a different perspective. However we are not bound to accept the results of recent years, nor is it our intention to return, albeit with the support of today's methods and knowledge, to Ranke or Pastor.

We believe that what was happening within the Holy See cannot be understood without an accurate assessment of outside influences. On the other hand, any explanation based solely on the impact of external factors will be wholly unsatisfactory and inadequate with respect to the complexity of the situation in Rome. Hence the need to take a closer look at the papal court, the workings of the curial bodies (beginning with the College of Cardinals and the Secretary of State), while highlighting the informal contexts that took on political significance, and acknowledging that the dual nature of the pontiffs' authority and the well-known constitutional characteristics of their power, as compared to that of European monarchs, are fundamental assumptions.

Therefore attention to the particularly 'Roman' character of the political struggle, to the dynamics of faction, to the complexity of patronage relationships, to the basic ambiguity of friendship – themes central to many contributions in this volume – is continuously related to the 'physiology' of Roman politics and to the institutional particularity of curial structures – that is, the elective nature of sovereignty, the centrality of nepotism and the active presence of representatives of European and Italian states in the city and government bodies.

[18] See M. A. Visceglia and C. Brice (eds.),*Cérémonial et rituel à Rome (XVIe-XIX siècle)*, Ecole Française de Rome, 1997; M. A.Visceglia, 'Cerimoniali romani: il ritorno e la trasfigurazione dei trionfi antichi', in Fiorani and Prosperi (eds.), *Storia d'Italia. Annali 16*, pp. 111–70.

[19] Recent reviews of studies on court and curia in Roma in the modern age are: M. Pellegrini, 'Corte di Roma e aristocrazie italiane in età moderna. Per una lettura storico sociale della curia romana', *Rivista di storia e letteratura religiosa*, 30 (1994), pp. 543–602; M. A. Visceglia, 'Burocrazia, mobilità sociale e patronage alla corte di Roma tra Cinque e Seicento. Alcuni aspetti del recente dibattito storiografico e prospettive di ricerca', *Roma moderna e contemporanea. Rivista interdisciplinare di storia*, 3 (1995), pp. 11–55.

At the same time, we believe that a study of early modern European history from the Roman viewpoint may revive debate over the great traditional turning-points of the period. The change in the relationship between the Spanish crown and the papacy is as important as the victory at St Quentin for understanding the assumptions of 'Catholic Europe' and the intensity of its reactions in the following century. The modes and timing of the transition to the age of 'French dominance' are better understood by analysing the movements and political tendencies within the curia.

Considering that the level of current knowledge discourages any claim to exhaustiveness, we have decided to concentrate our attention within a limited period, from the beginning of the sixteenth century to the end of the seventeenth. There are two reasons for this choice. As appeared extremely clear to contemporaries, who have left us a precise picture of the court seen in this way, in the early modern age Rome was an open space, a meeting point for family ascents, a financial centre capable of mobilizing intense economic resources and a place of political decisions that interacted with the other centres of European politics. This dialectical and dynamic relationship between Rome and Europe became more rigid and weaker from the end of the seventeenth century to the early eighteenth century, changing the nature of the relationships between the court and the city and reducing the intermediary role that the Holy See had played in European political and diplomatic negotiations up to the peace of Westphalia. On the other hand, the decision not to undertake a diachronic synthesis left us free to study the chosen context in depth by drawing on the widest possible range of documentary sources. Hence the necessity for a more complex periodization, which could take into account the link between the important internal changes – the reorganization of the curia after the reform of Sixtus V, the bull of Gregory XV's conclave, the antinepotistic shift during the last decades of the seventeenth century – and those marked by the relationship between the papacy and international politics – the revival of Roman universalism in the period between the 1570s and the first decades of the seventeenth century, the unrest during the Barberini papacy, the setback of Westphalia and the difficult search for new harmonies in the second half of the seventeenth century.

The studies included here expand on aspects and episodes that demonstrate how the political way of doing things in the court and curia was projected externally, using different reference scales for nearby settings (the ancient states of the peninsula) and for those farther away. We are fully aware that in both directions the number of surveys is limited, but we hope that they constitute a good basis for renewing attempts at understanding this complex and problematic picture. It is nevertheless our opinion that a clarification of the relationship between the political institutions of Catholic Europe and Rome may help us to grasp the particularity of the *Ancien Régime*, in that it introduces us to its cultural horizon and to the particular interaction of religion and politics, both indispensable coordinates for discovering the hierarchy of interests and the decision-making criteria. Thus, by rejecting a generic approach, by looking beyond the stereotypes and taking detailed account of the historical events, we hope to have introduced a variable – an element of complication that is still largely neglected – into the 'general' histories and into those of individual countries.

This need to penetrate as far as possible into the mechanisms of politics at the court of Rome does not imply that we have neglected a parallel assessment of the spiritual authority of the pontiffs and of the perception of contemporaries and political observers during the period between the reorganization following the Italian Wars – coinciding with the Tridentine watershed – and the 'crisis of the European conscience'. Our investigations finish with the end of the seventeenth century, since the *età innocenziana* marked a significant turning-point in Rome with regard to all the paths that we have endeavoured to follow. In fact, the 'reforming' phase marked by the pontificates of Innocent XI and Innocent XII announced a new era for the church, which is also perceptible at the level of terminology. The definition 'court of Rome' – hitherto used interchangeably with 'curia' to indicate the persons in the service of the pope and the ecclesiastical government – was beginning to take on a negative meaning. At the same time, the Apostolic See was committed to acquiring a new image, extending its frontiers to include all Catholics. After the loss of territory in the struggle with the powers, this was the prerequisite for facing the still more difficult challenges that would come with the last tremors of the *Ancien Régime* and the onset of the contemporary world.

A TURNING-POINT IN THE HISTORY OF THE FACTIONAL SYSTEM IN THE SACRED COLLEGE: THE POWER OF POPE AND CARDINALS IN THE AGE OF ALEXANDER VI*

MARCO PELLEGRINI

Recently it has been suggested that we need to reconsider the ethos of the Renaissance cardinalate, taking that concept not so much in terms of generic morality but more narrowly in the sense in which it was used in the later fifteenth century, that is to say as the necessary point of intersection between legal *officium* and ethical *onus*.[1] In this perspective, the pontificate of Alexander VI Borgia (1492–1503) is of especial interest for the importance assumed in that period by what may be regarded as the factors leading to the decline of the Sacred College as an organ of government in the Roman church.

In the attempt to provide an historical interpretation of this process, it has been rightly pointed out that the exploitation of cardinalatial *dignitas* for purposes other than its institutional duties brought about its secularization. We find confirmation of this in the politicization of a conspicuous proportion of the Sacred College and in its domination by party politics, a phenomenon peculiar to the Renaissance age.[2] One might add that the later reform of the cardinalate, during the 'long century' when the Tridentine decrees were being applied to the structures of the curia, was obliged to concentrate on neutralizing the power of the cardinals at the level of temporal politics, as a necessary prelude to the bureaucratization of the Sacred College.[3]

---

* Translation by Mark Roberts.

[1] D. S. Chambers, 'What Made a Renaissance Cardinal Respectable? The Case of Cardinal Costa of Portugal', *Renaissance Studies* 12/1 (1998), pp. 87–108; M. Pellegrini, 'Da Iacopo Ammannati Piccolomini a Paolo Cortesi. Lineamenti dell'ethos cardinalizio in età rinascimentale', *Roma nel Rinascimento* (1998), pp. 23–44.

[2] J. A. F. Thomson, *Popes and Princes, 1417–1517. Politics and Policy in the Late Medieval Church*, London, 1980, pp. 57–77; M. Firpo, 'Il cardinale', in E. Garin (ed.), *L'uomo del rinascimento*, Rome and Bari, 1988, pp. 75–131; M. Pellegrini, 'Il profilo politico-istituzionale del cardinalato nell'età di Alessandro VI. Persistenze e novità', in the proceedings of the conference *Roma di fronte all'Europa nell'età di Alessandro VI*, now in press (a fuller version of the present essay).

[3] W. Reinhard, 'Struttura e significato del Sacro Collegio tra la fine del xv e la fine

The question is highly complex, and historians have not yet dealt with it in systematic and exhaustive terms. In summarily reconstructing here the juridical and institutional lineaments of the cardinalate in the time of Alexander VI, I take as my point of departure the widely agreed fact that the cardinals' *auctoritas* declined during the Renaissance.

From the very beginnings of the institution, in the eleventh century, what had governed the cardinals' code of behaviour, as vigilant *oculi Romanae Ecclesiae*, was constant deference to papal authority and to the honour of the church.[4] The principle of *libertas Ecclesiae* was never to be compromised by a cardinal's behaviour, in public at least. This meant in practice that no cardinal was ever to owe his obedience, his *debitum fidelitatis*, to any earthly sovereign other than the sovereign pontiff. The pope in his turn was held to his particular *officium*, concerning the discharge of which he could be judged and condemned; this amounted to the *bonum Ecclesiae*, the just government of Christendom in general and of the Roman church in particular.

In juridical and institutional terms, the Renaissance proliferation of cardinals whose capacity correctly to exercise the prerogatives of government in the church was considered irrelevant, may be taken to indicate the erosion of those prerogatives and their replacement by something quite different.[5] The origins of this process are to be sought in the early decades of the fifteenth century. After the crushing of those pretensions towards oligarchic government which had led the Sacred College down the slippery slope of the Great Schism,[6] the way was open for the restoration of the papal monarchy, from Martin V Colonna onwards.[7] This new historical context saw the cardinalatial dignity progressively absorbed into the sphere of supreme papal authority, and the gradual disappearance of every vestige of power independent of the latter. The old hierocratic notion of the indivisibility and universality of the sovereign pontiff's jurisdiction

---

del xvi secolo', in *Città italiane del '500 tra Riforma e Controriforma*, Lucca, 1988, pp. 257–65; N. Pellegrino, 'Nascita di una "burocrazia": il cardinale nella trattatistica del XVI secolo', in C. Mozzarelli (ed.), *'Familia' del principe e famiglia aristocratica*, vol. II, Rome, 1988, pp. 631–77; R. Tamponi, 'Il "De cardinalis dignitate et officio" del milanese Girolamo Piatti e la trattatistica cinque–seicentesca sul cardinale', *Annali di storia moderna e contemporanea*, 2 (1996), pp. 79–129.

[4] E. Pásztor, *Onus Apostolicae Sedis. Curia romana e cardinalato nei secoli XI–XV*, Rome, 1999, pp. 29–46.

[5] P. Prodi, *Il sovrano pontefice. Un corpo e due anime: la monarchia papale nella prima età moderna*, Bologna, 1982, pp. 169–89.

[6] M. Souchon, *Die Papstwahlen in der Zeit des grossen Schismas. Entwicklung und Verfassungskämpfe des Kardinalates, 1378–1417*, vols. I–II, Brunswick, 1898–9; E. Pásztor, *Funzione politico-culturale di una struttura della Chiesa: il cardinalato*, now in Pásztor, *Onus Apostolicae Sedis*, pp. 347–63.

[7] M. Miglio (ed.), *Alle origini della nuova Roma. Martino V*, Rome, 1985.

over the affairs of Christendom, both spiritual and temporal (*regimen totius mundi*), was updated by emphasizing the definition of the Roman church as a papal monarchy, according to the doctrinal coordinates expounded by Torquemada in his *Summa de Ecclesia*.[8] It followed that the essence of the cardinalatial dignity could consist only in participation, at a subordinate level, in the multifarious jurisdictional activities of the Vicar of Christ, the absolute sovereign of the church on earth.

It remained an open question how far it was legitimate for a cardinal to exercise his just prerogatives of *iudicium* and *consilium*. In the middle of the fifteenth century the jurist Martino Garati da Lodi dealt with the matter in his treatise *De cardinalibus*. He emphasized the unity of the Sacred College with the pope, together with whom it constituted – in the anthropomorphic vision familiar to medieval culture – *unum corpus*, with the pope as *caput*: the entire organism was the Roman church.

As for the *officium* of the cardinals, it was defined as 'gubernare totum mundum' together with the sovereign pontiff with whom the *fratres* of the Sacred College had a relationship of necessary institutional proximity. It is possible to discern, in writings of this kind, a constitutionalist tendency which sought to distinguish the model of ecclesiastical government from that of the contemporary secular principate, since it had become evident that this latter, especially in Italy, had opted for a 'tyrannical' exercise of authority.[9] Garati's scheme, on the other hand, proposes an aristocratic model for the conduct of ecclesiastical affairs, in which the Sacred College assumes the function of a senate, explicitly recalling the example of ancient Rome – just as St Peter Damian had done at the very beginnings of the cardinalate as an institution.

These are the juridical sources of a terminology destined to be widely used in the later fifteenth and earlier sixteenth century, in the face of an historical reality increasingly deaf to the constitutional aspirations of a certain number of curial humanists. Paolo Cortesi in his *De cardinalatu* refers to the Sacred College as *senatus*, and maintains that the sovereignty of the *respublica christiana* is vested jointly in the pope and cardinals, as expressed by the Romanizing formula he himself devised, *P.M.S.Q.* (*Pontifex Maximus Senatusque*, making use of the learned term *Pontifex Maximus* introduced by Nicholas V). Behind this erudite artifice lay

---

[8] T. M. Izbicki, *Protector of the Faith. Cardinal Johannes de Turrecremata and the Defense of the Institutional Church*, Washington DC, 1981, pp. 75ff.

[9] G. Soldi Rondinini, 'Per la storia del cardinalato nel secolo XV' (with an edition of the treatise *De cardinalibus* by Martino Garati da Lodi), Milan, 1973, pp. 60–1; G. Alberigo, *Cardinalato e collegialità. Studi sull'ecclesiologia tra l'XI e il XIV secolo*, Florence, 1969; A. Black, *Monarchy and Community. Political Ideas in Later Conciliar Controversy*, Cambridge, 1970.

a precise ideology, which we might call temperate in reference to the papacy, senatorial and princely in reference to the cardinalate.[10]

The association of the cardinals with the holiness of the papacy was, together with the vast riches they accumulated and their exalted social position, the aspect which most struck the collective imagination of the Renaissance. It engendered an almost mythical image of the cardinal, based on his privileged communion with the spiritual majesty of the pope and his pre-eminence in both the ecclesiastical and the terrestrial hierarchy. To cite a single example of how the cardinalatial dignity was then perceived throughout Christendom, the sermons of one of the most celebrated Italian preachers of the later fifteenth century, Bernardino da Feltre, show the cardinal as the bearer of extraordinary powers, enough to make him an allegory of Divine grace.[11]

It is interesting to note how such literary texts show the cardinalate attaining to the maximum degree of respect at the very moment when the cardinals' real *auctoritas* was entering on an irreversible decline. During the fifteenth century it became clear how the conflict of powers that had opened between the papacy and the Sacred College was to be resolved, following the enormous growth in the cardinals' importance within the structure of the papal court during the Avignon period.[12] In the final analysis, the only one of the cardinals' original prerogatives destined to remain truly undisputed in later centuries was that of electing the new pope, and the only time when the Sacred College could be said fully to enjoy the *plenitudo potestatis* was during a vacancy of the Apostolic See: 'potestas papae remanet in Collegio papa defuncto', according to an old adage that was still current.[13]

In the later fifteenth century, it was precisely the electoral function of the College that offered the opportunity for an interesting attempt to reassert its nature as a sovereign body. At that time an apocryphal story was in circulation which, figuratively speaking, answered 'yes' to the question whether the cardinalate was founded on *ius divinum*, based

[10] I. Kaianto, 'Pontifex Maximus as Title of the Pope', *Arktos. Acta Philologica Finnica*, 15 (1981), pp. 37–52; D. Cantimori, 'Questioncine sulle opere progettate da Paolo Cortesi', in *Studi di bibliografia e storia in onore di Tammaro De Marinis*, vol. 1, Verona, 1963, pp. 278–9; G. Ferraù, 'Politica e cardinalato in un'età di transizione. Il "De cardinalatu" di Paolo Cortesi', in S. Gensini (ed.), *Roma capitale (1447–1527)*, Pisa, 1994, pp. 519–40.

[11] Bernardino da Feltre, *Sermoni*, ed. C. Varischi, Milan, 1964, vol. 1, pp. 168–9.

[12] Not until the early fourteenth century was the rule established, by the expert canonist cardinal Jean Lemoine, that the pope should avail himself of the *consensus fratrum* in deciding *res arduae* (H. Jedin, *Storia del concilio di Trento*, vol. 1, Brescia, 1973, p. 72).

[13] W. Schürmeyer, *Das Kardinalskollegium unter Pius II*, Berlin, 1914 (reprint Vaduz, 1965), p. 90. On this question in general, cf. L. Spinelli, *La vacanza della Sede apostolica dalle origini al Concilio tridentino*, Milan, 1955.

on the *ius divinum* that the Bishop of Rome possessed as successor to
Peter.[14] According to this legend, St Peter wished to recreate in Rome
the community of the apostles as it had been when he used to consult it in
Jerusalem, before the individual members dispersed to preach the Gospel
throughout the world. The Vicar of Christ therefore founded at Rome
a college of twenty-four priests and deacons chosen by him, fixing the
number on the basis of the twenty-four Elders of the Apocalypse; under
Pope Sylvester these apostolic consultants became known as cardinals,
as they were the *cardines* (hinges) of the Roman Church. St Peter himself recognized their right to participate in the choice of future Vicars
of Christ when he submitted his designated successor, Clement, for approval by the senate of the Roman church. The senate, however, rejected
Clement, elected Linus instead, and declared that the procedure adopted
by Peter had been mistaken in that, by legitimating a system whereby
the primate adopted his own successor, it would impede the just government of the Roman church, which ought to be collegial. According
to the legend Peter, displaying rather more humility than many of his
successors, bowed to the opinion of his brethren in the proto-college,
withdrew his support from Clement and recognized the election of
Linus.

This remarkable story, still circulating in the early sixteenth century
when it was recorded by the papal master of ceremonies, was evidently devised with the intention of safeguarding the cardinalate's *ius
divinum*, using a philosophical argument based on the thesis, derived
from Aristotle, that the judgment of the many must be superior to that
of one, thereby establishing collegiality as the most suitable means of
governing the Roman church. Once the conditions that gave rise to
this story had disappeared, not many decades after its invention, the
pious legend became confused with many other tales circulating in
Rome concerning the age of the martyrs and of the sainted popes,
and it was soon pushed into the background, if not subjected to actual
censure.

As the circulation of such tales demonstrates *a contrario*, the pontificate
of Alexander VI represented the waning of the medieval cardinalate. From
this period dates a lapidary phrase uttered by the Venetian ambassador to
Rome, which epitomises the process just described and its conclusion in
the cardinals' loss of every autonomous political and jurisdictional power

---

[14] The legend was inserted by Cristoforo Marcello in his heavily reworked edition, published in 1516, of the treatise on the ceremonies of the Roman court compiled under
Innocent VIII by the Bishop of Pienza, Agostino Patrizi Piccolomini: cf. M. Dykmans,
L'œuvre de Patrizi Piccolomini ou le Cérémonial papal de la première Renaissance, vol. I, Città
del Vaticano, 1980, p. 38.

in the face of the increasing papal absolutism of the modern age: 'the cardinals without the pope can do nothing'.[15]

The results of the fifteenth-century struggle for power between cardinalate and papacy would only become apparent in the long term, that is to say by the second decade of the sixteenth century. Under Alexander VI, what especially struck contemporaries was rather the fragility of the power-base of a pope known to have been simoniacally elected. The problem came dramatically to the fore in 1494–5, on the occasion of Charles VIII's invasion of Italy, when the possibility was mooted of a Gallican council on Italian soil, to condemn and depose Alexander VI.[16] This project, nursed by the anti-Borgia faction amongst the cardinals, collapsed on the very brink of success, because Charles VIII refused to involve himself in a reform of the church which would distract him from his conquest of Naples.[17]

The tribulations of the Borgia pontificate may be interpreted as a resurgence of the problems which the healing of the Western Schism, thanks to an action external to the Roman curia, had smothered rather than resolved, with the elevation at Constance of Martin V. Once the unity of the church had been regained, there remained the problem of whether the function of *auxilium et consilium* exercised by the Sacred College might represent a constitutional restraint on the will of the sovereign pontiff, or even a brake on the reconstruction of the papal monarchy which the fifteenth-century popes had embarked on without making provision for adequate legitimation.

After the decisive blow inflicted by Pius II Piccolomini on conciliarism by his constitution *Execrabilis* of 1460, the pontificate of Paul II Barbo was especially fruitful in pro-papal juridical theorizing, which was first put into practice after the election in 1471 of Sixtus IV della Rovere, who is regarded as the first real pope-king of the Renaissance.[18] However, the

---

[15] E. Albèri (ed.), *Relazioni degli ambasciatori veneti al Senato*, vol. VII, Florence, 1831, p. 5 (P. Capello, 1500).

[16] P. De Roo, *Material for a History of Pope Alexander VI*, Bruges, 1924, vol. III, pp. 407–20, 431–4; E. Vecchi Pinto, 'La missione del card. Francesco Piccolomini legato pontificio presso Carlo VIII (ottobre–novembre 1494)', *Archivio della Società Romana di Storia Patria*, 68 (1945), pp. 97–110.

[17] P. de Commynes, *Mémoires*, ed. J. Calmette and G. Durville, vol. III, Paris, 1925, pp. 87ff. Commynes exaggerates the number of cardinals available to the king of France, asserting that Charles VIII could rely on no fewer than eighteen.

[18] G. B. Picotti, 'La pubblicazione ed i primi effetti della "Execrabilis" di Pio II', *Archivio della Società Romana di Storia Patria*, 37 (1914), pp. 5–56. The ecclesiological implications of Pius II's ban were explored in Lelli's anti-conciliarist treatise *Contra Supercilium* (1464), republished in J. B. Sägmüller, *Zur Geschichte des Kardinalats. Ein Traktat des Bischofs von Feltre und Treviso Theodoro de' Lelli über das Verhältnis von Primat und Kardinalat*, Rome, 1893; W. Ullmann, 'The Legal Validity of the Papal Electoral Pacts',

subsequent election of Innocent VIII Cibo in 1484 marked a pause in the onward progression of the papal monarchy in relation to the authority of the cardinals, owing the pope's deference to his patron and leading elector, Cardinal Giuliano della Rovere (nephew to Sixtus IV, and the future Pope Julius II) and to the party of cardinals led by him.

This was the unresolved situation inherited by Alexander VI in 1492. At the time of his enthronement, while the new, monarchical, ecclesiology had reached an advanced stage at the papal court, the collegial approach to the government of the Roman church remained, at least to an extent, dominant in the minds of his brother cardinals and collaborators. The assumption that the papal *suprema potestas* was not to be used in *res arduae* without the consent of the College would have supplied the anti-Borgia faction among the cardinals with sufficient justification for constituting itself as *sanior pars Ecclesiae* and summoning a council to judge the pope.[19]

The rumblings erupted at a very delicate moment, when the King of France appeared in person at the gates of Rome as the political and military enemy of the Borgia pope, and declared himself ready to transfer the contest to the ecclesiastical level, being assured of the support of a number of cardinals – anything from three to eight. This would have reopened the conflict between the papacy and France, which went back to the methods used to put an end to the Great Western Schism only forty years previously. It had not been until the reign of Nicholas V Parentucelli that the antipope Felix V, the former Duke of Savoy elected by the council of Basle, had agreed to abdicate; the operation was mediated by the French king, who, as protector of the council, guaranteed the agreements by which the Schism was healed.[20]

Such was the background to the events of 1494–5. It then seemed possible that, with the essential assistance of Charles VIII in his double capacity as advocate of the Gallican church and arbiter of the Roman church, a group of dissident cardinals, led by an old adversary of the Borgia such as Giuliano Della Rovere, might succeed in bringing Alexander VI to trial,

now in W. Ullmann, *The Papacy and Political Ideas in the Middle Ages*, London, 1976, chap. xv, pp. 258–60. For an overview see P. Richard, 'La monarchie pontificale jusqu'au Concile de Trente', *Revue d'Histoire Ecclésiastique*, 20 (1924), pp. 413–56.

[19] A. Landi, *Concilio e papato nel Rinascimento (1449–1516). Un problema irrisolto*, Turin, 1997. The right of the Sacred College in an emergency to summon a council for the reform of the church, affirmed by Ailly and Gerson, was never condemned by the Holy See, among other reasons because it received authoritative support from celebrated canonists such as Zabarella and Tudeschi (Panormitanus).

[20] N. Valois, *La crise religieuse du xvme siècle. Le pape et le concile (1418–1450)*, vol. II, Paris, 1909, pp. 327–58; H. Müller, *Die Franzosen, Frankreich und das Basler Konzil (1431–1449)*, vols. I–II, Paderborn, 1990.

with a view to deposing him and replacing him with an antipope, who would very probably be Della Rovere himself. The principal accusation would have been simoniacal election, which was the most unanswerable of all, and was dusted off *ad hoc* by the dissident cardinals.[21]

The most prominent supporter of the conciliarist solution at that time in the College was the Cardinal of Naples, Oliviero Carafa, one of the principal members of the group known as the 'cardinali vecchi' – 'old cardinals'.[22] Having lain low for political reasons during the events of 1494–5, Carafa came into prominence during the tribulations of the succeeding years, when he even tried to protect Savonarola when the latter was planning to call a Gallican council to depose the Borgia pope.[23] While such plots were a-brewing, even after the condemnation and burning of Savonarola, the Neapolitan cardinal's constitutionalist vision had a second and unexpected airing in the early summer of 1497. After the untimely death of the Duke of Gandìa, Alexander VI – guilt-ridden and needing time to prepare his revenge against his sons' murderers – promoted the reform of the Roman curia and entrusted the task of drawing up the programme of reform to two of the most prestigious 'old cardinals', Carafa and Costa.[24]

In order to plan a reform of the Roman church which would extend not only to the customs of the court but also to the government of the state and the care of sacred edifices (including the construction of a dome for St Peter's), Alexander VI established on 19 June 1497 a deputation of six cardinals, two for each of the three ecclesiastical orders. In its early days the commission acted vigorously: it met every morning in the Apostolic Palace and synthesized the projects for curial reform already prepared by the fifteenth-century popes, from Martin V to Sixtus IV. At the same time, opinions were requested on irregularities in the workings of curial offices, especially the Chancery. On the basis of these data the cardinal commissioners drafted a number of proposals for reform; two of the most important drafts, those of Carafa and Costa, have come down to us. From them, decrees were to be drawn which would then become articles in the papal constitution with which Alexander VI intended to promulgate his reform of the church *in capite*.

In the first place it was decided to regulate the behaviour of cardinals. Their annual income from benefices (which were not to include

[21] F. La Torre, *Del conclave di Alessandro VI papa Borgia*, Florence, Genoa and Rome, 1933, pp. 122–3.

[22] Cf. the entry by F. Petrucci in *DBI*, vol. XIX, pp. 588–96.

[23] R. De Maio, *Savonarola e la curia romana*, Rome, 1969, pp. 133–46.

[24] L. Célier, 'Alexandre VI et la réforme de l'Eglise', *Mélanges d'Archéologie et d'Histoire de l'Ecole Française de Rome*, 27 (1907), pp. 65–124.

more than one bishopric) was to be limited to 6000 ducats; their sumptuary expenditure would be reduced, and each cardinal's *familia* would be restricted to eighty members. These severe regulations were followed by extremely rigorous rules for the conduct of the conclave, which would have made simoniacal election impossible. Next, the cardinal commissioners went on to consider the more controversial aspects of the church's government, in both the temporal and the spiritual sphere, and to examine the exercise of the papal *suprema potestas*.

At this point the understanding between Alexander VI and the reforming cardinals broke down. By early July it was evident that the enterprise had become a struggle between the sovereign pontiff and the senate of cardinals, concentrated no longer on the practical issue of reforming the Roman court but on the exercise, and even the very essence, of supreme ecclesiastical authority. Alarmed at the prospect of having his own powers as the monarch of Christendom curtailed by a group of zealous cardinals bent on settling old scores, Alexander VI set about sabotaging the work of his own commission.

The convulsions of the Roman church during the pontificate of Alexander VI demonstrated the vitality of an ideal that was not extinguished by Charles VIII's abandonment of Gallican conciliarism, since it was revived in 1498–9, this time under the aegis of a hypothetical antipapal coalition between Ferdinand the Catholic and Maximilian of Habsburg which never came into effect.[25] The outbreak of the famous *conciliabulum* of Pisa–Milan in 1511 – most ironically, while Giuliano Della Rovere was on the throne of St Peter – shows how some members of the Sacred College were ever open to schismatic solutions. Enjoying the much more decided support of the French king, Louis XII, the dissident cardinals came out into the open, assuming the role of *senior pars Ecclesiae* in order to impose an antimonarchical reform on the church.[26]

The ringleader of this Gallican *conciliabulum* – who seems even to have been elected antipope, taking the name of Martin VI – was the Spanish cardinal Bernardino Carvajal, who had been a favourite of Alexander VI.[27] This suggests that under the Borgia pope, the conciliarist hypothesis had been surreptitiously supported by some, not only in the Sacred College but even in the Apostolic Palace – especially if it is true that a

[25] Jedin, *Storia del Concilio di Trento*, vol. I, p. 50.
[26] W. Ullmann, *Julius II and the Schismatic Cardinals*, now in Ullmann, *The Papacy and Political Ideas*, chap. XVI.
[27] H. Rossbach, *Das Leben und die politisch-kirchliche Wirksamkeit des Bernardino Lopez de Carvajal*, Breslau, 1892; N. H. Minnich, 'The Role of Prophecy in the Career of the Enigmatic Bernardino Lopez de Carvajal', in M. Reeves (ed.), *Prophetic Rome in the High Renaissance Period*, Oxford, 1992, pp. 111–20.

defence of it was written by one of the most brilliant canonists and curial bureaucrats of the Sacred College, Gian Antonio Sangiorgio.[28]

Alexander VI's policy of towards the cardinalate is to be seen in the light of these constitutionalist tensions and the new schismatic threats which they implied. The 'carnal' desire to promote the careers of his relatives and children was certainly very much alive in Alexander, but his main aim was to forestall any attempt to depose him by a hostile faction of cardinals.

Alexander VI was not the first fifteenth-century pope to alter the composition of the Sacred College by means of extensive and frequent promotions, so as to tip its internal balance in his own favour and thus protect himself from the danger of schism. There was the recent example of Sixtus IV, who raised to the purple an unusually high number of his followers who, as often as not, were relations of his. They were selected not only on the basis of *pietas erga parentes* and of ensuring faithful collaborators, as has been said;[29] Sixtus was also anxious to prevent a resurgence of conciliarism, which he had to deal with on at least two occasions.[30] Linked to this was the need to break up the cohesiveness of the Sacred College and so weaken its ability to resist the decisions which the imperious pontiff tended to expound, rather than propose, in Consistory.[31] The new appointments made by Sixtus IV were crowned with full success *post mortem*: the party of his creations (known as the 'Sistine cardinals' and led by his nephew Giuliano Della Rovere)[32] dominated the conclave of 1484 and secured the election of one of its own members, the Cardinal of Molfetta, Giambattista Cibo, as Innocent VIII.

Under Sixtus IV the relationship between cardinalate and papacy shifted decisively in favour of the latter, thanks to a new weapon, or one used with unprecedented consistency: the numerical expansion of the Sacred College under the close supervision of the pope and his trusted advisers. As a corollary to his policy towards the cardinalate, intended to consolidate the monarchical configuration of the Roman church and its base in Italy, Sixtus IV inaugurated in grand style the practice of promotions to the cardinalate as pledges of alliance with

[28] Jedin, *Storia del Concilio di Trento*, vol. I, pp. 110–15, especially p. 111.

[29] W. Reinhard, 'Nepotismus. Der Funktionswandel einer papstgeschichtlichen Konstante', *Zeitschrift für Kirchengeschichte*, 86 (1975), pp. 145–85, p. 164.

[30] L. von Pastor, *Storia dei papi*, vol. II, Rome, 1961, pp. 518–24, 551–8; Jedin, *Storia del concilio di Trento*, vol. I, pp. 37–8, 50–2, 92–5.

[31] G. B. Picotti, *La giovinezza di Leone X, il papa del Rinascimento*, Milan, 1928 (facsimile reprint Rome, 1981), pp. 179ff. For a controversial presentation of Sixtus IV's nepotism and autocratic rule see I. Ammannati Piccolomini, *Lettere (1444–1479)*, ed. P. Cherubini, Rome, 1997, vol. III, pp. 1489–90, 1622–3.

[32] C. Shaw, 'A Pope and his *Nipote*: Sixtus IV and Giuliano della Rovere', *Atti della Società Savonese di Storia Patria*, n.s. 24 (1988), pp. 233–50.

secular sovereigns, especially Italian ones.[33] This was a practice which, by opening the doors of the Sacred College to an important nucleus of cardinal-princes, diminished the spiritual authority of the cardinalate as a whole and aggravated the tensions and inequalities within it.

Alexander VI followed the same path, perhaps even more systematically than Sixtus IV, but resorted to devious expedients on account of the fragility of his power-base, which – especially at first – depended almost entirely on the support of the party led by his leading elector, Ascanio Sforza.[34] The figures clearly show a similarity of aims and methods: Sixtus IV created thirty-four cardinals in eight promotions, during a reign of thirteen years, of whom no fewer than six were nephews of his; Alexander VI created forty-three cardinals in nine promotions, during a reign of eleven years; seventeen cardinals were fellow Spaniards, including five of the pope's relations.[35]

The main difference in the selection criteria of the two popes is that Sixtus IV was more devoted to his own relatives; Alexander VI, while not neglecting his sons and nephews, preferred to raise to the purple his own Catalan followers, often of modest social extraction, whose loyalty had been tested by long years of service in his *familia* when he was a cardinal. In any case, these two pontiffs made more cardinals than any others throughout the fifteenth century. Their record was exceeded only by Leo X Medici in 1517, who once promoted thirty-one cardinals at a single stroke, following the suppression of Cardinal Petrucci's conspiracy.[36]

Leo X also copied one epoch-making novelty introduced by Alexander VI: he demanded huge sums of money in exchange for a red hat. This practice, universally condemned as simony but tolerated because it suited both parties, made its first appearance in September 1493, when the Borgia pope created twelve new cardinals at once, requiring from most of them a contribution which was negotiated case by case, starting from a minimum of 15,000 ducats. It is known that red hats were also exchanged for cash at the promotion on 28 September 1500.[37]

Later, the price of the cardinalatial dignity rose: the oblation requested by Leo X from the new creations in 1517 started at 25,000

[33] M. Pellegrini, 'Ascanio Maria Sforza: la creazione di un cardinale "di famiglia"', in G. Chittolini (ed.), *Gli Sforza, la Chiesa lombarda, la corte di Roma*, Naples, 1989, p. 216, n. 6.

[34] M. Pellegrini, 'Ascanio Maria Sforza. La parabola politica di un cardinale-principe del rinascimento', forthcoming, Istituto Storico Italiano per il Medio Evo, Rome.

[35] De Roo, *Material for a History of Pope Alexander VI*, vol. II, pp. 314–26; vol. III, pp. 395–407.

[36] F. Winspeare, *La congiura dei cardinali contro Leone X*, Florence, 1957, pp. 175–9.

[37] J. Burchardus, *Liber notarum,* ed. E. Celani, Città di Castello, 1906, vol. II, pp. 242ff.

ducats per head. It is impossible to exaggerate the importance of this late-fifteenth-century extension of venality to the cardinalate. It ended by turning the dignity into a purchasable commodity that could be attained by a strategy of curial advancement and financial investment: a decisive step towards the Italianization of the Sacred College.[38]

Personal or family riches thus became primary requisites for candidates to the purple. Complementary to that criterion was the tendency, in which Alexander VI followed Sixtus IV, to bestow red hats on members of great aristocratic families, or reigning houses, who were provided with massive funds. Most of the cardinal-princes created by the Borgia pope were Italians (Grimani, Cornaro, Este, Aragona, Tivulzio, Fieschi, Soderini), but several were foreigners of royal blood (Frederick Casmir of Poland, Philip of Luxembourg, Amanieu d'Albret) or royal ministers (John Morton, Georges d'Amboise, Guillaume Briçonnet, Thomás Bakócz, Melchior von Meckau).

This latter component also demonstrates the marked antischismatic tendency in the Borgia pope's handling of the cardinalate: he deliberately rewarded those European monarchs who had shown their willingness to support him against conciliarist plots encouraged now by the King of France, now by the King of Spain. With the 'Catholic Monarchs' in particular – who were granted that title by Alexander himself – the pope had a somewhat ambiguous relationship. This is confirmed by the fact that none of the many Spaniards who received red hats could be said to have been a creature of the Spanish king, with the possible exception of Carvajal. The party of the Spanish cardinals, or rather the Valencian and Catalan cardinals, was in essence the Borgia party: their common language and geographical origin helped to bind them together and to close their ranks against rival groupings. Their subjection to the Catholic Monarchs – the sovereigns of the nation to which they belonged – was merely nominal; in matters of international politics the group was more in sympathy with the objectives of Louis XII of France than with those of Ferdinand the Catholic.

Interestingly, the peculiarity of Borgia party of cardinals tended to shift from anagraphical to cultural grounds. Since the nucleus of opposition to Alexander VI was the group of 'old cardinals', who had almost all been his rivals while he himself was a cardinal,[39] the pope's many promotions

---

[38] P. Partner, *The Pope's Men. The Papal Civil Service in the Renaissance*, Oxford, 1990, pp. 76ff. For general observations on this question see M. Pellegrini, 'Corte di Roma e aristocrazie italiane in età moderna. Per una lettura storico-sociale della curia romana', *Rivista di storia e letteratura religiosa*, 30 (1994), pp. 543–602.

[39] One of its leaders was the future Pius III, for whom cf. A. A. Strnad, 'Francesco Todeschini Piccolomini. Politik und Mäzenatentum im Quattrocento', *Römische*

came to form a party of some twenty 'young cardinals', respectful of his personal authority. Most, but not all, were Catalans; among those who were not were the Romans Giuliano Cesarini and Alessandro Farnese (the future Pope Paul III).

Owing to their relative youthfulness, and especially because they owed nothing to the traditional mechanisms of ecclesiastical promotion and cooption into the Sacred College, the 'young' militants of the Borgia party, and especially the Catalans, embraced a radically different ethos from the traditional curial code of behaviour. More than the *salus Ecclesiae*, their priority was the survival of their own group, which was linked to the fortunes of the house of Borgia by a double thread, pending the decisive event of Alexander's death. This was the reason for their readiness to employ any means to help the house of Borgia retain power, an attitude that we might well term 'Machiavellian'; the term does not seem improper if we remember that Machiavelli's political education coincided with certain experiments in the secularization of politics at the very heart of European Christendom, in the *penetralia* of the Apostolic Palace.[40]

Apart from individual tragedies which contributed to the Borgia *légende noire*, the collusion between the Borgia party of cardinals and Alexander's machinations on behalf of his family emerges clearly from one of the episodes which earned the greatest contemporary obloquy for the Borgia clan. This was when the duchy of Benevento and the cities of Terracina and Pontecorvo were subtracted from the Patrimony of St Peter and granted in fief to Giovanni Borgia, Duke of Gandìa, the pope's son.[41] Even more notorious is the collaboration of the Borgia cardinals in the creation of a principality in Romagna for Cesare Borgia, and Cesare's unsuccessful attempt to preserve it after his father's death, impeding its reversion to the church.[42] These were the most extreme manifestations of subjection to the Borgia cause on the part of a large group of cardinals that was nevertheless destined to disperse on the death of its founder. More normally,

Historische Mitteilungen, 8–9 (1964–6), pp. 101–425. For another cardinal belonging to this party, cf. G. Soranzo, 'Giovanni Battista Zeno, nipote di Paolo II, cardinale di S. Maria in Portico (1468–1501)', *Rivista di storia della Chiesa in Italia*, 17 (1962), pp. 249–74.

[40] Some of the enormities committed by Borgia cardinals against their own brethren (such as the poisoning of Cardinal Michiel so that the pope could seize his patrimony) are recorded in P. Villari (ed.), *Dispacci di Antonio Giustinian*, Florence, 1876, vol. I, pp. 59–61, 411–12, 474–5; vol. II, pp. 342–3, 351.

[41] L. von Pastor, *Storia dei papi*, vol. III, Rome, 1932, pp. 428–30.

[42] M. Mallett, *The Borgias. The Rise and Fall of a Renaissance Dynasty*, London, 1969, pp. 242–52; C. Shaw, *Julius II*, Oxford, 1993 (Italian translation: *Giulio II*, Torino, 1995, pp. 132–6; 147–8).

if the Borgia pope's creations helped to consolidate his fragile monarchical power, it was by acquiescing in the shift of the decision-making process away from the Sacred College and towards the restricted circle of papal advisers.

In the late fifteenth century the fact that the Apostolic Palace was far distant from the centre of Rome, while the cardinals' ever more magnificent residences tended to be concentrated in the lively and flourishing area around the Campo Marzio, assumed more than topographical importance. This dualism was further accentuated around 1458–9 by Pius II, during his struggle with the cardinals who had opposed his election. Aiming to deprive his enemies of their power to decide which petitions (or supplications) should be presented to the pope, Pius II confined this function to his domestic referendary, who thus became the only person answerable to the Tribunale della Segnatura. This reform of the procedure, snatching it from the grasp of the cardinals and awarding it to a lower functionary who enjoyed the pope's trust, put an end to the recommendations which the cardinals were accustomed to make as they personally conveyed documents to the pope. This practice had represented a considerable source of income to the cardinals, money which was now diverted into the pontiff's private treasury – what was later to be known as the 'scarsella di Nostro Signore' (Our Lord [the Pope's] purse)'[43] – in the form no longer of *sportule* and *propine* (kickbacks) but of chancery taxes and *compositiones* (datary taxes). At the same time, Pius II granted two of his domestic secretaries the exclusive power of approving in advance the drafts of briefs to be submitted to the pope, still with the idea of extirpating practices which had been stigmatised as simoniac, and which cardinals and curial dignitaries had used to enrich themselves.[44]

After the death of Pius II the superintendence of the Tribunale della Segnatura became once again a cardinal's prerogative reserved for 'cardinal prefects'; but they were part of the *familia* of the Apostolic Palace and were quite different from the ordinary curial cardinals. Under Innocent VIII the Segnatura was divided into two branches, 'Grace' and 'Justice', each under a cardinal-prefect; Alexander VI maintained this division which was to be perfected by Julius II.[45] In the last analysis all these

---

[43] This was something different from the Apostolic Chamber, which remained under the control of the cardinal-chamberlain: cf. N. Storti, *La storia e il diritto della Dataria apostolica dalle origini ai nostri giorni*, Naples, 1969, pp. 63ff. Cf. M. Rosa, 'La "scarsella di Nostro Signore": aspetti della fiscalità spirituale pontificia nell'età moderna', *Società e storia*, 38 (1987), pp. 817–45.

[44] E. S. Piccolomini (Pius II), *I Commentarii*, ed. L. Totaro, Milan, 1984, vol. I, pp. 258–9. For an overview of the situation prior to these reforms see E. Pitz, *Supplikensignatur und Briefexpedition an der römischen Kurie im Pontifikat Papst Calixts III.*, Tübingen, 1972.

[45] B. Katterbach, *Referendarii utriusque Signaturae*, Città del Vaticano, 1931, pp. XIV, 54–70.

must be regarded as phases in a lengthy process, characteristic of the Roman curia as restored in the fifteenth century; its beginnings may be traced to the foundation of the college of referendaries by Eugenius IV Condulmer. The principle behind its development was the desire to deprive the Apostolic Chancery of its wide latitude in the emission of papal documents; this latitude was in fact removed from the direct influence of the cardinals and awarded to functionaries of the Apostolic Palace who – at least in theory – always acted *in praesentia papae*.[46]

The great power wielded by Alexander VI's domestic functionaries aroused not a few protests from the Roman curia itself. An especially vehement protest came from the Masters of the Registry, who in 1497 accused Alexander VI's datary, Giambattista Ferrari (Bishop of Modena, and a future cardinal), of arbitrarily disposing of supplications which ought to have been presented to the pope, treating them like they were 'scripturae macellariorum' ('butchers' bills', i.e. worthless).[47] The extension of the papal datary's bureaucratic functions during the pontificate of Alexander VI is witnessed by a document, dating from that time and the oldest in our possession emanating from the papal datary, listing the matters to be handled by the datary's office and the various charges to be levied.[48]

Not only with regard to administration, but also – and even more – to politics and diplomacy, the later fifteenth century saw ecclesiastical government being increasingly concentrated in the hands of a small palace committee, consisting of the pope and a few close advisers.

The modifications to the structure of curial government during the fifteenth century were consolidated under Sixtus IV, whose approach was continued after some initial hesitation by Innocent VIII.[49] Following papal innovations in the second half of the fifteenth century, the Sacred College's opportunities for direct personal consultation with the pontiff were reduced to the temporary commissions or congregations, consisting of a handful of cardinals, appointed by the pope to examine a specific problem and report on it in Consistory.[50]

The principal institutional consequence of this adoption by fifteenth-century popes of an autocratic style of government, comparable to the

---

[46] W. von Hofmann, *Forschungen zur Geschichte der kurialen Behörden vom Schisma bis zur Reformation*, Rome, 1914, vol. I, pp. 56–161.

[47] M. Tangl, *Die päpstliche Kanzleiordnungen, 1200–1500*, Innsbruck, 1894 (reprint Aalen, 1959), pp. 386–412.

[48] L. Célier, *Les dataires du XVme siècle et les origines de la Daterie apostolique*, Paris, 1910, pp. 56–70, 103–16. The 'rates' are given on pp. 152–5.

[49] For a concise exposition of these changes see M. Pellegrini, 'Curie (xv.me siècle)', in P. Levillain (ed.), *Dictionnaire historique de la papauté*, Paris, 1994, pp. 518–21.

[50] Examples in W. Schürmeyer, *Das Kardinalskollegium unter Pius II*, pp. 46–75.

Italian 'tyrannies' of the time, was that the sovereign pontiff's chief collaborator in temporal affairs was now the *secretarius domesticus*, a trusted minister who supervised diplomatic correspondence and the preparation of briefs, rather like a modern secretary of state. At the end of the fifteenth century the role was not yet detached from the papal *familia*; but Innocent VIII took a decisive step in that direction by recognizing the primacy of the domestic secretary within his administrative entourage and placing him at the head of the college of the Apostolic Secretariat, which had been reorganized and rendered purchasable.[51] The domestic secretary was flanked by a small group of palace cardinals (*cardinales palatini*), the pope's private counsellors, for the most part his nephews or at any rate his own creations, who lived in the Apostolic Palace and enjoyed daily personal contact with him.

There was also a small handful of high curial officials, all members of the *familia papae*, resident in the Vatican and therefore distinct from the numerous officials of the Holy See who resided in the centre of Rome: the datary; the cardinal prefects of the Segnatura; the domestic referendaries, who were consulted especially in spiritual matters; a few particularly trusted chamberlains or *cubicularii*; one or two financial experts, including possibly the pope's banker and his secret treasurer; finally, the 'lay nephew' of the pope, who was generally appointed 'Gonfalonier of the Church', a position which included the functions of minister of war and overseer of the temporal affairs of the Holy See, and involved the *de facto* control of the more important fortresses in the papal states, in competition with the Cardinal Chamberlain. This extremely sensitive post, which made the lay nephew the coordinator of the papacy's Italian policy, was held under Callixtus III and Sixtus IV by their respective nephews, Pedro Luis Borgia and Girolamo Riario. Alexander VI entrusted it to one of his lay sons: first to Giovanni Borgia, Duke of Gandìa, and then, after Giovanni's murder, to Cesare, who duly renounced his cardinal's hat.

The executive branch of the papal government was the palace circle – the real *consilium pontificis*, although it was never actually called so out of deference to the institution of the cardinalate. In comparison, the Sacred College seemed no more than an appendix to a decision-making structure that was hostile and inaccessible to the cardinals. Fragmented and riven with contradictions, the Sacred College under Alexander VI experienced all the trials and tribulations of an age of transition: a structural transformation, difficult for those most affected to understand, which reduced some cardinals to penury and engendered conflict. While

[51] P. Richard, 'Origines et développement de la Secrétairie d'Etat apostolique (1417–1823)', *Revue d'Histoire Ecclésiastique*, 11 (1910), pp. 56–72.

the causes of this impoverishment and loss of political authority were not clear, its repercussions were: they were reflected in the dynamics of internal groupings which gave rise to new informal hierarchies of patronage, and shaped the factions which appeared among the cardinals.

Weakened by an enlargement which reduced each individual's share in the division of incomes and benefices, and further weakened by a policy of promotions that was entirely alien to its corporate interests, the Sacred College suffered from an ever-increasing internal imbalance. Whereas some of its members enjoyed unparalleled riches and prestige, many others found it increasingly difficult to finance the extravagant lifestyle dictated by an ever more aristocratic interpretation of a cardinal's *dignitas*, in line with the prevailing tendency among Italian and European elites.[52] The 'poverty' lamented by some of the cardinals was certainly relative, but it was no less shameful than the penury suffered by many nobly born persons in Italian cities who had fallen on hard times and become *pauperes verecundi*, so that they had surreptitiously to beg for alms.[53] The situation of the poorer cardinals was aggravated in the fifteenth and sixteenth centuries by the increasingly competitive lavishness indulged in by their richer brethren, especially as regards the size of their *familiae*.[54]

The widely differing financial circumstances of the cardinals, and the shadow of poverty falling on some of them, exacerbated the tendency of the Sacred College to fragment into networks of clientage which modified the traditional dynamics of its internal factions. Fed by numerous benefices which could not be conferred or redistributed without the permission of local sovereigns, the networks that criss-crossed the Sacred College like spider's webs tended to look outside Rome for support, to the great ones of the earth. And it was in the interest of all these great ones to spend money in order to penetrate the ever-shifting factions amongst the cardinals, seeking thereby to influence the policies of the Roman church and the papal elections.

An organic link between cardinals and kings had been established at the time of the Avignon papacy, when some cardinals indubitably looked

---

[52] D. S. Chambers, 'The Economic Predicament of Renaissance Cardinals', *Studies in Medieval and Renaissance History*, 3 (1966), pp. 289–313; A. V. Antonovics, 'A Late Fifteenth Century Division Register of the College of Cardinals', *Papers of the British School at Rome*, 35 (1967), pp. 87–101; D. Hay, 'The Renaissance Cardinals: Church, State, Culture', *Synthesis*, 3 (1976), pp. 35–46.

[53] An example of a 'poor cardinal' at this time is Gian Giacomo Schiaffenati, a native of Lombardy but an adversary of the Dukes of Milan and for that very reason condemned to financial hardship: cf. R. Bizzocchi, *Chiesa e potere nella Toscana del Quattrocento*, Bologna, 1987, pp. 125–31.

[54] G. Fragnito, 'Cardinals' Courts in Sixteenth-Century Rome', *The Journal of Modern History*, 65 (1993), pp. 26–56.

after the diplomatic interests of secular sovereigns who urgently required a mediator in the allocation of major benefices, which took place in Consistory.[55] In this capacity the cardinal was known as *ponens* or *promotor* or *relator*, since his task was to propose a candidate and vouch for his qualities; but in ordinary conversation his activities were assimilated rather to that *tuitio* which curial cardinals traditionally accorded to religious orders or needy clerics.[56] This protectoral function, modelled on a relationship long recognized in canon law and based on trust between a cardinal and a sovereign, earned the former a reward which usually took the form of ecclesiastical benefices in the royal gift, awarded either to the protector himself or to other cardinals in his circle.

This situation continued throughout the fifteenth and into the sixteenth century, when the more politically fortunate cardinals were accustomed to accumulate, with the support of their sovereigns, emoluments and benefices amounting to many times the average patrimony of their brethren.[57] Such riches were for the most part spent on luxuries and artistic patronage, intended to emphasize the distinctions of rank that originated in differences of wealth; but a not inconsiderable portion was used to construct an immaterial 'edifice' consisting of *reputatione* and *dependentie*. In other words, the richer and politically better-off cardinals were able to dispense incomes and favours to their indigent brethren, patronizing them in a way that increased their own personal authority and that of the sovereigns whom they represented – all the more so because on special occasions, such as conclaves, princes were accustomed to give their cardinal emissaries money to strengthen the networks of dependency they had created around themselves. In these circumstances, the link with a secular power became a trump card in the hand of any cardinal who, able to count on a group of supporters, nursed an ambition in the conclave. At the conclave of 1484, such an attempt was made by Giuliano della Rovere, who for this purpose dug deep into his own pocket, which had been well filled by his uncle Sixtus IV and the French king; another was made in the conclave of 1492 by Ascanio Sforza, who used not so much his own funds as those of his candidate, Roderigo Borgia, who had acquired an enormous fortune by the favour of his uncle Callixtus III Borgia and of the Spanish crown, and used it to ensure his own

---

[55] H. Fokcinsky, 'Conferimento dei benefici ecclesiastici maggiori nella Curia romana fino alla fondazione della Congregazione concistoriale', *Rivista di Storia della Chiesa in Italia*, 35 (1981), pp. 334–54.

[56] J. Wodka, *Zur Geschichte der nationalen Protektorate der Kardinäle an der römischen Kurie*, Innsbruck and Leipzig, 1938, reprinted 1967, pp. 4–6, 29.

[57] For the richest cardinal in the early years of Alexander VI see M. Pellegrini, 'Ricerche sul patrimonio feudale e beneficiario del cardinale Ascanio Sforza', *Archivio Storico Lombardo*, 122 (1996), pp. 41–83.

election. It is noteworthy that in each case the cardinal who determined the outcome of the election did not himself seek the tiara, but managed to impose his favourite, and is thus to be regarded as a pope-maker rather than an aspirant to Peter's throne. Each of them calculated, mistakenly, that his own eventual election would be ensured by the assistance of the pope he created.

Another result of these struggles for power was that in the fifteenth century, the pope and the Sacred College contended for control of relations between sovereigns and the Roman curia. The contradiction between financial dependence on a secular power and the ideology of *libertas Ecclesiae* was at the base of the fifteenth-century conflict between papal authority and the cardinalate over the exercise of 'protective' functions.

The protectorship of lay rulers was prohibited by various reforming papal constitutions in the fifteenth century, some of which were never officially promulgated.[58] Mindful that alliances with secular sovereigns had represented the great strength of the Avignonese cardinals in their struggle with the papacy, the popes of the fifteenth-century restoration did not hesitate to forbid such activities even though their veto flatly contradicted the facts of the situation.

The earliest reforming provisions of this kind, drawn up by Martin V in 1425, were accompanied by a reminder of the canonical definition of the cardinals as *assistentes papae*: as strenuous and disinterested defenders of the honour of the church, they were to approach the powerful not as advocates but as judges. The idea that *ecclesiastica libertas* meant the absence of secular constraints on the *consilium* given by cardinals to the pope recurs in all the schemes for curial reform devised in the course of the century, including the draft reform of 1497. That document, drawn up by Cardinals Costa and Carafa, censured both protectorship and attendance at courts and chancelleries by members of the Sacred College. Reflecting an attitude already prevalent at the papal court in the time of Alexander VI, it denied that cardinals could properly be 'interested in affairs of state', to borrow the excellent self-definition of Cardinal Soderini.[59]

However, under the second Borgia pope times were changing; a structural alteration was taking place, encouraged by a pope who during his long years as a curial cardinal had acted as protector of the kingdoms of

---

[58] L. Célier, 'L'idée de réforme à la cour pontificale du Concile de Bâle au Concile du Latran', *Revue des questions Historiques*, 86 (1909), pp. 418–35; H. Jedin, *Proposte e progetti di riforma del Collegio cardinalizio*, now in Jedin, *Chiesa della fede Chiesa della storia*, Brescia, 1972, pp. 156–92.

[59] K. Lowe, *Church and Politics in Renaissance Italy. The Life and Career of Cardinal Francesco Soderini, 1453–1524*, Cambridge, 1993, pp. 46–52; the quotation is on p. 50.

Spain and proved himself a flexible and experienced negotiator. The legitimization of the cardinals' protectorship was based on the right of Christian *nationes* to be represented at the Holy See and before the sovereign pontiff. This principle, associated with the cardinalatial dignity, had achieved positive recognition in the conciliar period, when the assembly of Constance declared that the *nationes* should be permanently represented at the Roman curia: a reform which would have transformed the Sacred College into a kind of universal parliament of the Western church, in which the *protectio* of the Christian *nationes* would have been exercised by constitutional prerogative and, more importantly, without charge.[60]

Although after the post-conciliar restoration the popes took care not to put any such proposal into effect, they accepted without too much reluctance that in exceptional circumstances certain cardinals might 'protect' some nation or prince. However, protectorship was never to mean that a cardinal should depend on any secular authority.

Thus circumscribed, in the fifteenth century the cardinals' political 'protectorship' went underground; though still illegal, the institution went from strength to strength, since the popes themselves found it convenient. It effectively extended the influence of the Sacred College by means of agreements with secular sovereigns.

The cardinals' protectorship discovered new possibilities within a curial negotiating framework strongly influenced by the autocratic tendency of papal government, especially in foreign policy. With his role of introducing and assisting ambassadors at private audiences, and his opportunities for direct and informal contacts with the pontiff and his entourage, the cardinal-protector in his political guise could be said to be a product of the Renaissance development of Italian and European diplomacy, centred on the court of Rome.[61] It is no coincidence that the earliest precursors of that institution were cardinals sponsored by those powers which traditionally held a privileged relationship with the papacy: the kingdom of France, the Empire, and, in the course of the fifteenth century, certain Italian states which developed close relations with the Apostolic See, such as the Duchy of Milan.[62]

Whenever controversies became particularly bitter, the pope himself preferred to speak directly to the diplomatic representatives of the powers

---

[60] H. Jedin, *Concilio episcopale o parlamento della Chiesa? Un contributo all'ecclesiologia dei concili di Costanza e Basilea*, now in Jedin, *Chiesa della fede Chiesa della storia*, pp. 127–55.
[61] G. Mattingly, *Renaissance Diplomacy*, Baltimore, 1955, pp. 91–118.
[62] Cf. in this connection the observations of J. Vincke in his review of Wodka's *Zur Geschichte der nationalen Protektorate* in *Zeitschrift der Savigny-Stiftung für Rechtsgeschichte, Kanonistische Abteilung*, 28 (1939), pp. 516–20.

concerned, assisted by a few trusted advisers. This led to a double procedure whereby real political negotiation took place at a private audience
(*udienza*) between the pope and the resident *oratore*, while the public
Consistory, to which ambassadors were admitted by right together with
the cardinals, was a purely ceremonial occasion.

All this tended to legitimize, in practice if not yet in theory, the tendency for cardinals in a relationship of trust with princes to become the
latters' political representatives. As regards the Italian states, the whole
subject of cardinal-protectorship was complicated by extra-institutional
factors, since the performance of such functions was gradually facilitated
by the admission into the Sacred College of members of ruling houses.
The first of these was Francesco Gonzaga in 1461; before the end of the
century he was followed by Aragon, Foscari, Sforza, Este and others. For
cardinal-princes, diplomatic activity was a natural consequence of the
degree of sovereignty which they enjoyed in their own states by virtue
of their rank.[63]

Alexander VI's action decisively overstepped the tight network of ruling families who, by dominating the world of Italian politics, could boast a
closer connection with the governing apparatus of the Roman church.[64]
Shortly after his coronation the Borgia pope anxious to consolidate his
own monarchic authority, acknowledged the existence of this controversial institutional figure (which had already made a nominal appearance in 1485, in the person of Cardinal Balue, Protector of France)[65]
by officially introducing the term *cardinalis protector* in relation to the
kingdom of England and the Empire.[66] This was, however, a strategic move, mainly intended to restrict the influence of those European

---

[63] An illustrious example of a Renaissance Italian cardinal prince is Francesco Gonzaga as
described by D. S. Chambers, *A Renaissance Cardinal and His Worldly Goods. The Will
and Inventory of Francesco Gonzaga (1444–1483)*, London, 1992. The first of the Italian
cardinal-princes of the later fifteenth century, he made a precise statement of his own
protective functions with regard to the family's political and ecclesiastical affairs: cf.
D. S. Chambers, 'A Defence of Non-Residence in the Later Fifteenth Century:
Cardinal Francesco Gonzaga and the Mantuan Clergy', *Journal of Ecclesiastical History*,
36 (1985), pp. 605–33.

[64] A. Prosperi, ' "Dominus beneficiorum": il conferimento dei benefici ecclesiastici tra
prassi curiale e ragioni politiche negli stati italiani tra '400 e '500', in P. Prodi and
P. Johanek (eds.), *Strutture ecclesiastiche in Italia e in Germania prima della Riforma*,
Bologna, 1984, pp. 73–9.

[65] H. Forgeot, *Jean Balue, cardinal d'Angers (1421?–1491)*, Paris, 1895, mentions (p. 238)
a payment to the cardinal of 2,000 *livres de Tournai* as his annual salary for protective
services to the kingdom of France.

[66] J. Schlecht, *Pius III. und die deutsche Nation*, Kempten and Munich, 1914, pp. 46–48;
W. E. Wilkie, *The Beginnings of the Cardinal Protectorship of England: Francesco Todeschini
Piccolomini, 1492–1503*, Fribourg, 1966; reprinted as chap. 1 of Wilkie, *The Cardinal
Protectors of England: Rome and the Tudors before the Reformation*, Cambridge, 1974.

powers with which Alexander VI had somewhat mixed relations at the beginning of his reign. He thus set in motion a powerful secularizing influence on the relations between papacy, cardinals and princes. On the more general ecclesiastical level, however, Alexander VI – probably confirming a tendency already begun by his predecessor Innocent VIII – was attempting to neutralize a wave of anti-Roman feeling such as was always threatening from the German-speaking world. Proof of this is the fact that the first cardinal to assume the official protectorship of both the German and the English nation was an old partisan of the Empire, the Cardinal of Siena Francesco Todeschini Piccolomini, nephew of Pius II and the future Pope Pius III. No cardinal-protector was granted initially to the king of France; but he could continue to avail himself, as had been done for decades, of the unofficial protection of the cardinal-diplomats whom he had introduced into the Sacred College for that very purpose.[67]

Like other bones of contention, the cardinal-protectorship of nations and princes was regulated on the basis of a voluntary (*gratiosa*) concession by the pope: although late, its institutionalization subordinated it more completely, on the juridical level, to the papal authority. If proof is needed that such provisions met the political requirements of the Renaissance church, we need only recall that Alexander VI's line would be pursued on a larger scale by Julius II, and that in the Counter-Reformation the cardinal-protectors would assist in the *aggiornamento* of relations between the papacy and the Catholic powers.[68]

On the other hand, the way was open for new factions in the Sacred College, which took a somewhat different approach to the world of secular politics, and were more openly attuned to the power-game of European diplomacy. As late as 1490, at the time of the admission to the Sacred College of Giovanni de' Medici (the future Pope Leo X), we find the terms 'guelf' and 'ghibelline' used, curiously, to indicate the two factions of cardinals then disputing the hegemony of the College, one led by Giuliano Della Rovere and the other by Ascanio Sforza, looking respectively to Naples and to Milan: these were the forces which disputed control of the papal election at the conclave of 1492.[69]

With the opening of a long series of Italian wars, provoked partly by the temporal policies of Alexander VI, Italy saw the collapse of the

---

[67] For an example see C. Samaran, *Jean de Bilhères-Lagraulas, cardinal de Saint-Denis. Un diplomate français sous Louis XI et Charles VIII*, Paris, 1921.

[68] Wodka, *Zur Geschichte des nationalen Protektorates*, pp. 9–10, 37–8; A. V. Antonovics, 'Counter-Reformation Cardinals: 1534–1590', *European Studies Review*, 2 (1972), pp. 318–19. Cf. also Poncet's chapter in this volume.

[69] Picotti, *La giovinezza di Leone X*, pp. 189–92.

interstate system which for over half a century had regulated the political orientations of the factions of cardinals. The structure of the College changed after the death of Alexander VI in 1503, when the factions acquired entirely new names that were to remain in use for many years. With the demise of the pro-Milanese and pro-Neapolitan parties, the scene was dominated by the 'Gallican' faction, which included the Borgia cardinals and many pro-French Italians. It was opposed by the cardinals who were *partiales* for the Empire: a group which for political and dynastic reasons was joined by the supporters of the king of Spain, at least in the early decades of the sixteenth century.[70] And it was this second faction which was to prevail, installing on the throne of Peter Cardinal Francesco Todeschini Piccolomini, who had been cardinal-protector of the German nation at the papal court. This was already, *in nuce*, the structure of the early modern conclave, reflecting the pressure exercised by the great monarchies which were disputing the hegemony of Catholic Europe.[71]

---

[70] T. Gar, 'Lettera dell'imperatore Massimiliano I ai suoi oratori presso la corte di Roma (MDIII)', *Archivio veneto*, I (1871), pp. 84–95.

[71] J. B. Sägmüller, *Die Papstwahlen und die Staaten von 1447 bis 1555 (Nikolaus V bis Paul IV). Eine kirchenrechtlich-historische Untersuchung über den Anfang des Rechts der Exclusive in der Papstwahl*, Tübingen, 1890, pp. 77ff.

COURT AND CITY IN THE CEREMONY OF THE *POSSESSO* IN THE SIXTEENTH CENTURY

IRENE FOSI

INTRODUCTION

'Cerimonia nihil aliud est quam honor debitus Deo aut hominibus propter Deum.'[1] With this concise formula, jurists and Masters of Ceremonies of the papal court summed up both the deeply felt value and the twofold meaning, political and religious, of the complex of rules they followed, in public and in private, on all solemn occasions.[2] Previous historians have taken little interest in analysing ceremony – a complex and elaborate system inseparable from the nature of the authority it exalted – as a key to changes in the way power was expressed.[3] Even Paolo Prodi, in his stimulating book on papal monarchy, though interested in such sources, handled them gingerly; indeed he emphasized the difficulty of detecting 'changes in the symbols and ceremonies, whose basic fonction in the process of the legalisation of power is to appear immutable'.[4] But now the historiographical ground has shifted; one can no longer shrug off the findings of anthropology and sociology. Deciphering symbolism has become a crucial tool for comprehending the essence of princely power, or, here, of pontifical power, as expressed both in court and outside it, in diplomacy, in the city, in *feste* and in ceremonies.

* I am grateful to Thomas V. Cohen for the translation and comments on this paper and to Simon Ditchfield for his suggestions.

[1] BAV, Vat. Lat., 12285, f. 63v. The *cerimonieri* in their writings often reaffirmed the function of ceremony as not only a serviceable instrument for human communication but also an act owed to those who served the church.

[2] I follow here the definition of ceremony proposed by S. Bertelli and G. Calvi, 'Rituale, cerimoniale, etichetta nelle corti italiane', in S. Bertelli and G. Crifò (eds.), *Rituale, cerimoniale, etichetta*, Milan, 1985, p. 11.

[3] M. G. Constant, 'Les maîtres de cérémonies du XVIe siècle. Leurs diaires', *Mélanges d'Archéologie et d'Histoire*, 1–3 (1903), p. 229.

[4] P. Prodi, *The Papal Prince. One Body and Two Souls: The Papal Monarchy in Early Modern Europe*, Cambridge, 1987, p. 45.

Compared with those of other courts in Italy and Europe, Rome's rituals, jealously guarded by its assiduous Masters of Ceremonies, touchy defenders of tradition, might seem imbued with repetition and immobility. But a diachronic analysis of those gestures and symbols fundamental to ceremony, in its function as legitimation of power, reveals the significance that the pope, at various times and places, attached to this symbolic apparatus.[5] What emerges from such a study is the theme of sovereignty, embodied in ceremonies and liturgy at key events like the cavalcade to take *possesso* of the Lateran or the Corpus Christi procession.[6] Until now, it is the art historians who have studied the many solemn ceremonies fostered by pontifical ritual – identified with the very life of the church – and who have stressed the political significance of Renaissance and baroque Roman *feste*.[7] For other states – the French and English monarchies especially, but lately also the states of the Holy Roman Empire[8] – the study of ceremonies has furnished a key for reading the whole evolution of the apparatus of state, the change in the figure of the sovereign, and external perceptions of such transformations. So far it can hardly be said that the same attention has been given, except in passing, to the transformations of the papal monarchy, a polity too often seen as monolithic and immobile. Both anti-Roman polemical histories and the observations of curious travellers of the seventeenth and eighteenth centuries, their eyes caught by the pomp of a court that often seemed to veil with splendour its irreversible political weakness, may

[5] The invitation to historians to consider 'spectacles and pageantry as an integral part of power and politics themselves' was formulated by D. Cannadine, who remarked that the study of ceremony was still a field reserved above all to sociologists and anthropologists: in D. Cannadine and S. Price (eds.), *Rituals of Royalty: Power and Ceremonial in Traditional Societies*, Cambridge, 1987, p. 6.

[6] Prodi, *The Papal Prince*, pp. 42ff., emphasizes the political function of the *possesso* as propaganda for the popes of the late Middle Ages. M. A. Visceglia, 'Rituali religiosi e gerarchie politiche a Napoli in età moderna', in P. Macry and A. Massafra (eds.), *Fra storia e storiografia. Scritti in onore di Pasquale Villani*, Bologna, 1994, pp. 587–620, offers an analysis of the evolution of the Corpus Christi ceremony and of its political meaning in sixteenth-century Naples.

[7] M. Fagiolo and M. L. Madonna, *La festa a Roma*, 2 vols., Roma, 1997, provides a rich and up-to-date bibliography on pp. 587–620.

[8] For France, see the remarks by C. Klapisch-Zuber, 'Rituels publics et pouvoir d'état', in *Culture et idéologie dans la genèse de l'Etat moderne: Actes de la table ronde organisée par le Centre National de la Recherche Scientifique et de l'Ecole Française de Rome (Rome 15–17 octobre 1984)*, Rome, 1985, pp. 135–44. For the German-speaking lands, see, in general, M. Edelman, *Politik als Ritual. Die symbolische Funktion staatlicher Institutionen und politischen Handelns*, Frankfurt/Main, 1990, and the more recent J. J. Berns and T. Rhan (eds.), *Zeremoniell als höfische Ästetik in Spätmittelalter und frühen Neuzeit*, Tübingen, 1995; B. Stollberg Rilinger, 'Höfische Öffentlichkeit. Zur zeremoniellen Selbststellung des brandenburgischen Hofes vor dem europäischen Publikum', *Forschungen zur brandenburgischen und preussischen Geschichte*, n.s., 7 (1997), pp. 145–76.

have infused our notion of the past with earlier impressions of sclerotic immobility. Recent studies that view the 'system' of papal ceremonies as part of a comprehensive political language have helped to conjure away the old adage that 'la cour de Rome ne varie jamais'.[9] In fact, even the papal monarchy, in the course of the fifteenth and sixteenth centuries, took on the lineaments of a political, bureaucratic organism, a court whose sovereign's power was shaped by the dual nature of the papacy.

The ceremonial of coronation and of the *possesso* caught the eye of historians at an early stage, above all in connection with particular issues, such as the curious affair of Pope Joan.[10] More recently, studies with a strong anthropological coloration have attempted to detect cases of sacred rituals of power in western Europe.[11] If analysed accordingly, as a manifestation of power and grandeur, ever closer in spirit to the triumphal entries of contemporary temporal sovereigns, and as one of the most elaborate of expressions of Renaissance theatre, the *possesso* ceremony invites a political reading.[12] In their sixteenth-century rearrangement, the fragments of this ceremony – already a theological metaphor in the Middle Ages – bear witness to a new representation of power, as political action and as propaganda. Thus, while 'it is not particularly helpful to ask whether the increasing magnificence of papal ritual in our period reflected an increase in papal power or compensated for a decrease in it'[13] there is nonetheless reason enough to ask via what symbols and metaphors power

---

[9] M. A. Visceglia, 'Il cerimoniale come linguaggio politico. Su alcuni conflitti di precedenza alla corte di Roma tra Cinquecento e Seicento', in C. Brice and M. A. Visceglia (eds.), *Cérémonial et rituel à Rome (XVIe–XVIIe siècle)*, Rome, 1998, pp. 117–76.

[10] A. Boureau, *La papesse Jeanne*, Paris, 1988. The author analyses in detail the ceremony of the *possesso*, both its formal and its substantial evolution, in the context of early medieval Rome, and especially in the European setting that saw the definitive affirmation of papal power. For a more detailed study of the ceremony and its relationship with the city see M. Boiteux, *Rome, espace urbain et ses représentations*, Paris, 1992.

[11] S. Bertelli, *Il corpo del re. Sacralità del potere nell'Europa medievale e moderna*, Florence, 1995.

[12] F. Cruciani, *Teatro nel Rinascimento, Roma 1450–1550*, Rome, 1983, p. 313. For French royal entries and the relations of city and king, cf. R. Strong, *Art and Power: Renaissance Festivals 1450–1650*, Woodbridge, Suffolk, 1984; L. M. Bryant, *The King and the City in the Parisian Royal Entry Ceremony: Ritual and Art in the Renaissance*, Geneva, 1986; R. Giesey, *Cérémonial et puissance souveraine: France, XVe–XVIIe siècles*, Paris, 1987; M. Weintraub, 'Civilizing the Savage and Making a King. The Royal Entry Festival of Henry II (Rouen 1550)', *The Sixteenth Century Journal*, 29 (1998), pp. 465–594. For the reception of the European model in Italy, see B. Mitchell, *The Majesty of the State: Triumphal Progresses of Foreign Sovereigns in Renaissance Italy*, Florence, 1986.

[13] P. Burke, 'Sacred Rulers, Royal Priests: Ritual of the Early Popes', in Burke, *The Historical Anthropology of Early Modern Italy. Essays in Perception and Communication*, Cambridge, 1987, p. 182.

communicated and imposed its presence, both at the centre of the state and on the periphery.[14]

What, then, at this time, were the symbolic elements that, in the solemn, resplendent language of ceremony, defined the components of temporal and spiritual power? A comparison, at several points during the sixteenth century, of a ritual such as the procession for the *possesso* of the Lateran, helps uncover important changes: in the ever more universalistic conception of papal power, and in the delicate relations between the pope and his court, on the one hand, and the city and its inhabitants on the other. For example, in the course of the sixteenth century the symbolism of justice not only changed shape and connotation, but also up-staged or blurred older papal themes such as military force, liberality and magnificence. At the end of the sixteenth century, by which time papal power was consolidated in the city, by now merely the seat of the curia and court, the *popolo romano* and its representatives were definitively marginalized and the baronage were relegated to a walk-on role. Thus the ceremony of the *possesso* served to represent and impose pontifical sovereignty not only on the city of Rome but also, as a model readily exported, on the periphery of the state. Similarly, the rules elaborated in treatises on the ceremonial entries of papal legates into their appointed provinces can be read as an attempt to represent and reproduce, by visual means, a state power that rested above all on the exercise of distributive justice and of grace in a periphery where relations with local elites and local institutions were often both delicate and tense. Furthermore, by parsing the symbolism of hierarchic structures we can demonstrate how the ever more orderly cavalcade addressed the city and its officials and citizenry less and less, and foreign powers more and more. As it did so, it took on a universalistic triumphalism, as befitted the reaffirmation of Catholic supremacy after the Reformation.

We shall now consider three moments that throw light on these changes: first, the Renaissance papacies of Julius II and Leo X, which differed sharply in their symbolism, the former exalting war, the latter peace; secondly, the election of Paul III Farnese, celebrated with a *festa* that hailed the *romanità* of the pontiff and the virtue of nobility; finally, the *possesso* of Sixtus V in 1585, a perfect synthesis of the project of discipline and control, not only of the city and its institutions, but of all society.

---

[14] For an analyis of the ceremonies of the *ingresso* of papal legates, which were also filled with political symbolism, see my essay 'Parcere subiectis, debellare superbos: l'immagine della giustizia nelle cerimonie di possesso a Roma e nelle legazioni dello Stato Pontificio nel Cinquecento', in Brice and Visceglia (eds.), *Cérémonial et rituel à Roma*, pp. 89–115.

THE MOMENTS OF PAPAL ENTHRONEMENT:
CORONATION AND *POSSESSO*

In the papal monarchy, after the solemn, hidden moment of election in the conclave, came two fundamental rites of passage that initiated and sanctioned the new functions of the pontiff. Ceremony here was articulated in several phases. In each of them, there figured diverse symbols of the victor's new, twofold power; even the colours of the vestments, white and red, took on a symbolic value. First came the coronation. Taking place in Saint Peter's, it was spatially defined. There, the cardinal-electors still played a fundamental role, as they had in the conclave. The newly elected pontiff was robed in white raiment, and for the first time called by his newly chosen name. Then, with the symbols of his power – throne, crown and the *baldacchino* – he was carried on his litter out of the church. The ceremony betokened a break with the past; moreover, the places where the new pope had lived – his palace, his conclave cell – were put to ritual sack. With the election of Julius II, the ceremony of coronation was first separated, *de facto*, from that of the *possesso*; this division of the two fundamental moments would, however, be made official only under Gregory XIV, in 1590.[15]

Very different was the significance of the ceremony of *possesso*. This term, which, under Eugenio IV in 1471 replaced *processione*, indicated the pope's solemn cavalcade, after his coronation in Saint Peter's, across the city to take possession of the basilica of Saint John Lateran, his episcopal seat. With this, the ceremony of his enthronement was complete. After the Middle Ages, these two ceremonies grew ever more distinct in symbols and gestures. Indeed, even the route was inverted: in the Middle Ages, the pope had been elected at the Lateran and had then walked to Saint Peter's. In the sixteenth century, the route of the solemn cavalcade traversed the city, passing its most important sites, which were thus re-founded and resacralized by the presence of pope and court. In an epoch thoroughly imbued with the recovery and re-use of classical culture, the symbolic places of past Roman glory assumed new vitality thanks to the presence of the church. The *possesso*, therefore, took on the coloration of an ancient triumph or a nuptial parade – not unlike those of contemporary monarchs – to be consummated in the mystical marriage of the pope with 'his' episcopal church. The route – the Via Sacra or Via Papalis – began at St Peter's and went to Castel Sant' Angelo, then to the Ponte Sant' Angelo, via Monte Giordano and Piazza Navona. From here the Via Sacra

---

[15] F. Cancellieri, *Storia de' solenni possessi de' sommi pontefici detti anticamente processi o processioni dopo la loro coronatione dalla Basilica Vaticana alla Lateranense dedicata alla Santità di N. S. Pio VII P. O. M.*, Rome, 1802, p. 128.

reached S. Marco and then took in the most important sites of ancient Rome: the Forum, the Arch of Constantine and the Colosseum, and came to the Lateran passing through the old churches of S. Clemente and SS. Quattro Coronati on the Caelian Hill.

On the model of ancient Roman triumphs, the processional route was marked by four fundamental moments. First came the *exitus* from the Vatican, where the pope had been crowned. Then came the *ascensus* to the Capitoline Hill, a sacred place symbolizing the power of the citizens. In reality, until 1565, the papal procession merely skirted the Campidoglio, for the piazza was still under construction, implementing Michelangelo's grand design. The crossing of the Campidoglio often brought out the tensions in the never-easy relations between the Roman municipality and the popes, especially from Julius II down to Sixtus V. The whole of the sixteenth century bore witness to the progressive reduction in the powers of the urban magistrates, who fiercely defended their privileges and their jurisdictions, especially in the sphere of justice. In moments of tension between the two powers – papal and civic – as for instance under Pius V (1565–1572), the civic magistrates did not stand waiting for the papal cavalcade to pass the Campidoglio, but went 'on their own account' to the Lateran basilica. Two decades later, at the election of Sixtus V, to drive home the submission of the municipality to the curia, the papal arms, significantly, were posted at the entrance to the Capitoline square.[16] The third phase of the march was especially resonant: the *triumphus* of the New over the Old Testament. The superiority of Rome over Jerusalem was symbolized in the pope's encounter with the Jewish community's representatives, who under the Arch of Titus, conqueror of Jerusalem, offered the pope the Mosaic laws.[17] In the earlier years of the sixteenth century this meeting, which publicly sanctioned the pontiff's power over the Roman Jews and emphasized his contempt for their law, had taken place at Monte Giordano and on Ponte Sant'Angelo; later it was fixed at the symbolic arch.[18] The final step was the *introitus*, the entry into the Lateran basilica, where the pope received the two keys, symbols of his temporal and spiritual power. Unlike the coronation, after the sacred rites in St Peter's which opened outwards, concluding with a benediction, the

---

[16] L. Spezzaferro and M. L. Tittoni (eds.), *Il Campidoglio e Sisto V*, Rome, 1989.

[17] C. L. Stinger, *Renaissance Rome*, Bloomington, 1985, pp. 54–5, explains the several functions of this 'curious rite' and remarks that 'In performing a similar act, the popes thereby emulated a Roman precedent for imperial government' (p. 54).

[18] In the *possesso* of Leo X, the meeting with the Jewish Roman community took place at Castel Sant' Angelo: Cruciani, *Teatro nel Rinascimento*, p. 395. For the symbolic meaning of the meeting between the pope and the Jews in the *possesso*, see A. Prosperi, 'Incontri rituali: il papa e gli ebrei', in *Storia d'Italia*, Annali 11: C. Vivanti (ed.), *Gli Ebrei in Italia*, Turin, 1996, pp. 508–10.

distribution of coins to the populace, and a banquet under the public eye, the ceremony of *possesso* turned inwards, for it ended inside the basilica, excluding the faithful and the city.

In the Middle Ages, quite different rites had marked the stages in the ceremonial of enthronement. Then, the newly elected pontiff had been clothed in a pontifical mantle, mitred, and led to the altar, and there adored and blessed. Then, re-clothed in royal robes, he was led to the marble throne and once again adored. Finally came the crowning with the tiara. The procession then went towards the episcopal church where the keys and the ferule, symbol of the sceptre given to Pope Silvester by Constantine, were received. The medieval Lateran ceremonies had always featured chairs. The first, at the door, was the *sedia stercoraria* (the 'excremental chair', with a hole in the seat), that may have had a humbling function, signalling the earthly origin of the newly elected pope.[19] The last, a double porphyry seat inside the church, symbolized the power to govern. The rituals connected with these seats were all rites of passage: standing next to the *sedia stercoraria*, the pope showered coins upon the populace and by his very largesse made an explicit and very traditional claim to legitimate authority.[20] In the double chair of porphyry – a stone which explicitly symbolized the Roman imperial dignity – he had to sit at once, and received various symbols of power such as like the keys of the Lateran basilica and palace. Thereupon he acquired the decisive sanction of his power, the *plenitudo potestatis*, and became the *Vicarius Christi*. At the end of the ceremony, the Lateran clergy kissed the pope's feet and the new *Vicarius Christi* was allowed to pray in the *Sancta Sanctorum*. The ritual was concluded by a banquet. Most of these rites vanished at the beginning of the pontificate of Leo X (1513–21), as they were no longer fitting expressions of the essence of papal power, which was by then much stronger than it had been in the later Middle Ages.

The procession that accompanied the pope on the way to his episcopal seat became more sumptuous and had to follow a very precise, hierarchical order which the curia imposed on the city: the latter played an ever shrinking role in a *mise en scène* in which the pontiff and his court had become the principal actors. But this well-ordered hierarchical arrangement was a late, hard-won achievement. If we compare accounts of early

---

[19] Another current interpretation was that it served to ascertain the maleness of the pope as a deacon explored under the papal garments. His exclamation 'Habet!' could have been read as serving to stave off deception and to avoid repeating the legendary misadventure of Pope Joan. For the meaning of this medieval ceremony see Boureau, *La Papesse Jeanne*, pp. 53–115. For a different interpretation of the changed ritual see A. Paravicini Bagliani, *Il corpo del papa*, Turin, 1994, pp. 49–50.

[20] He exclaimed: 'Gold, silver are not mine; what I have I give to you': Stinger, *Renaissance Rome*, p. 54.

sixteenth-century *possessi*, such as the solemn and wonderfully rich and theatrical *possesso* of Leo X, with the cavalcades of Sixtus V or Clement VIII (1592–1605), we find that the organization of the parade was quite different. Throughout this evolution the parade continued to reflect the tensions between the city's hierarchies – especially the frictions between the powerful baronial houses and the pontiff – but also the internal rivalries of the baronial class and tensions between the pope and the urban magistrates, Senators and Conservators. More generally, the procession became ever more a mirror of European politics, marked in Leo's time by the Italian wars, and later by the French Wars of Religion and the Catholic campaigns of religious reconquest.

Nevertheless, the *possesso* also kept its character as a *festa* for the faithful, the foreign *nationes* resident in Rome, and the entire city. The procession had to manifest hierarchy, precedence and order. By the end of the sixteenth century it had assumed the following form. At its head marched the cavalry, the lancers, followed by the households and mace-bearers of the cardinals, and the apostolic standard-bearers. The thirteen *caporioni*, the heads of Rome's *rioni* (districts), marched before their standard-bearers. Gentlemen in black velvet led the richly caparisoned pontifical mares. Then followed a swarm of servants and papal chamberlains, and behind them the Roman barons with the ensigns of their ancient houses. After these came the musicians and singers of the papal chapel. Behind them paraded the principal vassals of the church, the ambassadors, the urban clergy and the Conservators – chief magistrates of the *popolo romano*. Then came the pope himself, dressed in white, on horseback, and sheltered by a baldaquin held aloft by eight nobles – under Sixtus V this privileged sacral ministry was bestowed on emissaries from Japan. Next in line of march came the Swiss guards, and then the cardinals robed in red, in order of seniority. The light cavalry brought up the rear. This, schematically, was the parade order of Sixtus V, the template for later ceremonies and an emblem for an altered conception of the pope's power, of his universal claims, and of the task of governing the church's state.

Urban space, for the duration of the sixteenth and seventeenth centuries, was not only the backdrop for the theatricals of sumptuous ceremonies, but also their history-laden foil. Accordingly, the papal monarchy always used the *possesso*, its first self-declaration, to vaunt a distinctive political message linked to the person of the newly elected pontiff, who often wished to appear the antithesis of his predecessor. In most other European monarchies, such as the French, ceremonies tended to exalt the unity and continuity of the realm in the person of the sovereign.[21]

---

[21] M. Renlos, 'La place de la justice dans les fêtes et cérémonies du xvie siècle', in J. Jacquot (ed.), *Les Fêtes de la Renaissance*, vol. iii, Tours, 1975, pp. 71–80.

The new pope, by contrast, deployed his ceremony of the *possesso* to manifest the caesura with his predecessor and the negation of his policies. He therefore tended to celebrate and exalt, above all, his own person, rather than the power he represented. Meanwhile, participation in the procession was, for all participants, the most explicit way to lay claim to their own roles in society, secure their privileges, and parade their expectations from the new pope. In this dialogue between urban powers, foreign ambassadors, *nationes* in Rome, the nobles and the pope, the ephemeral apparatus – the triumphal arches and the inscriptions put up as back-drops to the ceremony – also played its part. These were more than mere rhetorical celebrations of the pope, his family and the church; they also expressed the bases of a political programme as expounded in the solemnities. These symbols therefore reflect the expectations of those who paid for them, and express a dialogue between tradition on the one hand, and on the other, adaptation to present conditions, and to the political and religious exigencies of the sixteenth-century church.

Though the sixteenth century seems to recycle fragments of earlier ritual discourses that readily bore multiple readings, the conservatism of its ceremonies is illusory. Although the Masters of Ceremonies, as they often grumbled in their *Diarii*, put up a stalwart resistance, innovations crept in, sometimes imperceptibly, aspiring to bend standard forms so as to engender symbols of the political programme of the new pope. Other sources help to trace this change in the meaning of the enthronement ceremony. Iconography is a precious source. The apparatus of decorations, triumphal arches and laudatory inscriptions illustrates the changes in this ceremony, from early Renaissance to mid-baroque, and helps to link them with events in European politics and religion in which the pontiff was a protagonist. Also important are printed accounts, which were often commissioned by the pope's kinfolks, members of his regional 'nation', or rich merchants and bankers fishing for protection, honours and economic leverage in exchange for propaganda flattering the new pontiff. The writings of masters of the genre, such as (in the seventeenth century) Giovanni Briccio an Antonio Gerardi, were intended for circulation not only in the courts of Italy, but also in those abroad.[22] These accounts, especially when printed and distributed in the course of the seventeenth century, served the needs and desires of a wide and varied public, no longer made up only of academics and the learned.[23] Readers must have been fascinated by the words, conceits, and contrasting ideas and images that blazoned such splendid solemnity and pomp. But such rhetorical

---

[22] L. Rossi, 'Bricci, Giovanni', in *DBI*, vol. xiv, pp. 220–2.
[23] L. Nussdorfer, 'Print and Pageantry in Baroque Rome', *The Sixteenth Century Journal*, 29 (1998), pp. 439–64.

constructions often concealed the reality; in these descriptions it is hard to find images of disorder, offences against good ceremonial order or the rupture of hierarchical schemes painstakingly prepared and defended. Therefore a reading of such texts must be combined with perusal of the *Avvisi*, brief notices of Roman events that circulated throughout Europe and did recount odd twists and mishaps and retail stories of disorders and brawls arising during the solemn procession. For example, an *avviso* of 2 November 1555 reported:

> when the pope went last Monday to San Giovanni, accompanied by all the court, and the soldiers, and the whole *popolo*, to take *possesso* of his bishopric according to the ancient customs, a bit of a brawl broke out between Papirio Capisuccha [Capizucchi], who was leading some of the mercenaries, and some toughs from the *Rioni* of Ponte and Trastevere. Precedence was the issue, and things got rough, and Papirio came out of it wounded with a stab in the thigh. Also injured were fifteen or twenty on one side or the other. And blood would have really flowed, had not the cavalry got in between, and Cardinal Caraffa came running up when the fight started, in his cardinal's robes, and, hat in hand, rushed into the thick of it, and by his authority and presence calmed it all down, and nothing else came of it.[24]

The Masters of Ceremonies passed over such things in silence, or condemned them; the celebratory reports, which, in the seventeenth century, were actually printed before the event, ignored them, while prudish diarists were scandalized.[25]

A MILITARY TRIUMPH: THE *POSSESSO* OF JULIUS II (1503–1513)

On 26 November 1503, Julius II was crowned; on 5 December, he took possession of the Lateran. The pope, crowned with the tiara, 'with seven pounds, or nearly, of precious stones' made a visible show of his power and sovereign strength in the urban procession.[26] The coronation gave rise to the first of many frictions with the Master of Ceremonies, since the pontiff refused to don the traditional raiment, intrinsically linked to the meaning of the solemn occasion.[27] The temporal separation of the *possesso*

---

[24] BAV, Urb. lat., 1038, 98. I am grateful to T. Cohen for pointing this document out to me.

[25] G. Gigli, *Diario romano*, ed. G. Ricciotti, Rome, 1958, p. 263.

[26] Cruciani, *Teatro nel Rinascimento*, p. 314.

[27] J. Burchard, *Diarium, sive rerum urbanarum commentarii (1483–1506)*, ed. L. Thuasne, Paris, 1885, pp. 308–9; Cancellieri, *Storia de' solenni possessi*, pp. 55–60. Cf. also Cruciani, *Teatro nel Rinascimento*, pp. 294–6, for the affirmation that Julius II was the first to separate the ceremony of the coronation from that of the *possesso*.

from the coronation allowed Julius II to prepare the former with all the care that his political programme required. Its symbolism quite openly took its inspiration from the theme of victory, in order to exalt the pope's warlike nature and above all to draw citizenry and foreign observers alike into his political designs for the *renovatio imperii*. Among the protagonists were the Roman barons, represented by Giulio Orsini and Marcantonio Colonna, custodians of the procession and guardians of a well-ordered entry into the Lateran. Their presence, not only in the parade but also in that particular urban space, expressed the continuity of their sway over the town. The basilica and the adjacent hospital and confraternity of San Salvatore ad *Sancta Sanctorum* were both places traditionally controlled by the Roman nobility. Sixteenth-century papal intervention in this sector of the city and in its places of worship was linked with a campaign, albeit not always forceful or coherent, to control and undercut the political authority of the barons and other nobles. This represented the desire to reappropriate a part of town which since the Middle Ages had been peripheral to the location of curial power.[28] The new city planning and Domenico Fontana's reconstruction of the apostolic palaces there, in the reign of Sixtus V, would in time solemnize and affirm papal power in the Lateran area.[29]

The order of Julius II's procession, and above all its splendour, were calculated to underline the distinct inferiority of the representatives of the Capitoline magistracies. They took part according to a long-established order, but, as Burchard remarks in his account, they were seen more and more as an element of disorder, potential enemies who could easily upset the delicate, careful equilibrium of hierarchies and rhythms. Papal majesty was announced by the baldaquin of the Sacrament, a symbolic apparatus that exalted and protected the holiness of the eucharist, and was also the gift of the sovereign's subjects. But, as the Master of Ceremonies observed, the Romans carried this sacred symbol 'in a pacific, tranquil way' only because of the award money the pontiff had promised them. His words here underline the desire to sharpen the distinction, already strong, between the people and the court. The sumptuous vestments and the splendid apparatus, in Burchard's description of the procession, contrast with the clothes of the servants of the *caporion*, 'badly dressed, on foot'. He adds

[28] The identity of the civic nobility was reflected in its sway over certain zones of the city, like the Lateran: P. Pavan, 'La Confraternita del Salvatore nella società romana del Tre–Quattrocento', *Ricerche per la storia religiosa di Roma*, 5 (1984), pp. 81–90.

[29] For the multiple problems linked with the urban and architectural planning of the area around the Lateran basilica, see the contributions in M. Fagiolo and M. L. Madonna (eds.), *Sisto V*, vol. I, *Roma e Lazio*, Rome, 1992, and especially the second section, 'L'urbanistica e gli interventi architettonici', pp. 395–640. See also J. Freiberg, *The Lateran in 1600: Christian Concord in Counter-Reformation Rome*, Cambridge, 1995.

testilly that 'By fault of the Romans, the order of the procession was not good, because some of them, badly dressed, carried it [the eucharist] to Saint Peter's without a mule'.[30] Order and disorder are juxtaposed: the Master of Ceremonies tends in his detailed account to cut out all those contrasting features that seemed at loggerheads with the traditions of which he was the jealous guardian. Likewise, the 'sorry behaviour' shown by the Roman people, deplored by a later Master of Ceremonies, Paride De Grassi, in his description of the 1507 triumph of Julius II, under-scored their marginal role in the ceremonies. The inhabitants of Rome, in his eyes, were better suited to those bloodthirsty, turbulent activities which Erasmus defined as 'beastly games' than to papal festivals, ever more elaborate, sumptuous, and aloof.

While in the *possesso* Julius II still felt trammelled by formal order and the customs imposed by codes of ceremony, his triumphal entry into Rome in 1507, after the reconquest of Bologna, allowed him to make a political point via a *festa*. As observers from other Italian courts were quick to note, the themes of war and victory suffused the symbolism of his triumphal arches, underscoring his military triumph, his rebuilding of the territory of his state, and his reinforcement of papal sovereignty.[31] In Julius's pontificate there was no room for symbols of power linked to peace, abundance or justice, notions tied to projects of internal pacifica-tion. For him it was foreign policy that defined sovereignty and endowed it with force and legitimacy, as did the explicit, pragmatic restoration of classical antiquity. However, it is true that Julius II made the reorganiza-tion of justice a cornerstone of his internal policies. The concentration of all the courts of justice on the Via Giulia, had it come to pass, would have meant not only a reorganization of urban space, but also an end to the fragmentation and overlapping jurisdictions of the numerous Roman law courts.[32] But, above all, he wanted to annihilate the authority of the Capitoline courts and impose the justice of papal tribunals on everyone.[33]

---

[30] Cruciani, *Teatro nel Rinascimento*, p. 315.

[31] The same themes of military victory are predominant in the coins and medals struck during Julius's pontificate: *Numismata Pontificum Romanorum praestantiora a Martino V ad Benedictum XIV per Rodolphinum Venuti Cortonensem illustrata*, Rome, 1744, pp. 47–54; E. Martinori, *Annali della Zecca di Roma: Alessandro VI, Pio III, Giulio II*, Rome, 1918, pp. 35–92. See also Stinger, *Renaissance Rome*, pp. 235ff.

[32] For the project for the great palace of the law courts, see C. L. Frommel, *Der römische Palastbau der Hochrenaissance*, vol. 1, Tübingen, 1973, pp. 93, 143. The project stirred up a great deal of tension with the Florentine colony in Rome, who lived mainly in the *Rione Ponte*, for they feared that the premises where they held the meetings of their confraternity would be razed: I. Fosi, 'Il consolato fiorentino a Roma e il progetto per la chiesa nazionale', *Studi Romani*, 37 (1989), pp. 50–70.

[33] In this connection it is worth examing the minutes of meetings of the Capitoline council, in which the civic nobility's outrage at papal policies is clear: AC, *Camera Capitolina*, Cred. I, t. 21.

Yet, as symbol, even the reorganization of justice had to yield to foreign policy.

In Julius' reign, the use of history and the classics evolved in several directions. On the one hand, the pope himself, attentive director of and actor in his own festivals and triumphs, energetically embraced classic forms of political propaganda, such as triumphal arches and backdrops with statues of Roman emperors, to emphasize his political and military power.[34] Meanwhile, distinct from the pope's adaptive, pragmatic use of the past, there was the immobile inheritance of the antique, solemnly and proudly expounded in the *feste* of the Roman people. Carnival, and the *Testaccio* and Agone games, also presented a reawakened classicism, harking back to a lost past and imbued with nostalgia, as is especially evident in the heartfelt, lively descriptions of the patrician Marcantonio Altieri in his *Nuptiali*.[35]

LEO X: THE TRIUMPH OF THE AGE OF GOLD (1513–1521)

If we are seeking to trace how a new pontiff might use his early ceremonies to affirm, explicitly or implicitly, his will to reverse the policies of his predecessor, the contrast between the *possessi* of Julius and Leo X is, for the early sixteenth century, among the sharpest. Giovanni de' Medici's deliberate propaganda campaign to exalt the return of an Age of Gold after the wars of the della Rovere pope also expounded a different vision of sovereignty. For this son of Lorenzo the Magnificent, the constituents were no longer force and military victory, but *liberalitas*, patronage and justice. The staging of his *possesso* and the accompanying political message transported the legend of Lorenzo and the Medici to Rome and emphasized that city's ancient ties with Florence.

Peace, the premise of the Leonine Age of Gold, would now be attained through the intelligent exercise of justice and grace; these, in a pacified world, would manifest papal force and sovereign power. Turning his back on his predecessor's undermining of the Capitoline magistrates, Leo X at once proposed conciliation. But only in appearance did he restore their privileges, which in fact were destined to shrink sharply under Giovanni de'Medici's centralizing pressure.[36] Justice and its symbols thus became the emblem of a deeper political project that, though presented in terms opposite to those of the recent past, in fact followed the same plan of

---

[34] The pope's project of *renovatio imperi* was supported by a rich and articulated humanistic propaganda that presented the pope as Caesar: Stinger, *Renaissance Rome*, pp. 238–46.

[35] Cruciani, *Teatro nel Rinascimento*, p. 335, refers to this famous work by Altieri (*Nuptiali*, ed. E. Narducci, Rome, 1873).

[36] Documentation in G. B. Fenzonio, *Annotationes in Statuta sive ius municipale Romanae Urbis*, Rome, 1636, pp. 670ff.

affirming and reinforcing sovereignty. The antithesis emphasized by the procession is thus only apparent. The campaign to reinforce papal power had remained constant ever since the return of the popes from Avignon; only the forms and modulations differed and contradicted one another, from one pontificate to the next. Why, then, was there such a wish to underline political discontinuity? It was in fact the non-hereditary nature of the monarchy that ensured this emphasis on the person of the newly elected pope and again and again exalted his individual qualities, his place of origin, and his family, all traits often chosen precisely because they contrasted with those of his predecessor. The logic of pontifical elections, no longer distorted by the strife of noble and civic factions, now instead reflected the forms and balances of international affairs. Therefore the person, and his representation as an individual and member of a family, overshadowed the portrayal of institutions. With Leo X the personal and the political were combined. Thus, his 1513 *possesso* reflected new and very different political realities while his ceremony mirrored the papal monarchy's ongoing campaign for ascendancy over the municipality and the nobility – massively and turbulently present in the parade – the grandeur of the *festa* aimed to celebrate the triumph of Medici power in Rome.

The chronicles of Leo's *possesso* describe in rich detail the collective festival of the Florentine 'nation' in Rome. The most prominent members of the mercantile oligarchy (who, as victims of the struggle between the pope and Florence occasioned by Julius' *conciliabolo* – mini-council – at Pisa, had in the preceding reign suffered extortion and persecution) appeared in well-marshalled force.[37] The solemnity of the occasion was expressed by triumphal arches exalting such traits of sovereignty as artistic patronage, *liberalitas*, peace and justice. At the same time, this festive celebration of the Florentine 'nation' had its fault-lines, traceable to conflicts internal to the court, as various inchoate parties seized the chance to stake a claim to future policies and practices.[38] Paride De Grassi wrinkled his fastidious nose at these disturbing elements, that surfaced especially at the portentous moment of the hotly contested distribution of money.[39] This gesture repeated the ritual of the *sparsio*, which took place both at precise spots along the route of the lustral parade and inside the Lateran

---

[37] For a more detailed examination of the relations between the pope and the Florentine colony of 'mercatores Florentini Romanam curiam sequentes', see my 'Il consolato fiorentino' and 'Pietà, devozione e politica: due confraternite fiorentine nella Roma del Rinascimento', *Archivio storico italiano*, 149 (1991), pp. 119–61.

[38] The massive participation of the Florentine 'nation' in the installation of Leo X reflected the real power of the pope's fellow Florentines. But it also became a model that was applied again at the elections of Clement VIII and, above all, of Leo XI, in 1605. See Cancellieri, *Storia de' solenni possessi*, pp. 154–67.

[39] Ibid., pp. 63–4.

basilica itself.[40] This infringement of the rules of ceremony probably betrayed both fear of the usual violence that broke out in the scramble for the coins and the growing desire to insulate the papal rites from unacceptable external contamination. The distribution of newly minted coins stamped with the image of the new pope not only vaunted his *liberalitas*, but also signalled the diffusion to court and people of his sacred self, in effigy. As for *liberalitas*, its symbols recurred in the coins themselves: they showed an allegorical woman pouring from a cornucopia, amidst books and musical instruments. The theme, under Leo X, was continually evoked by the ostentatious magnificence that marked his whole reign.[41]

Thus, in the early sixteenth century, the ceremony of the *possesso* still seemed fragile. It was violated by struggles among the courtiers that threatened to profane the rite in the streets and to project the image of chaos or disorder in the papal court, or worse, risked carrying these troubles into the Lateran itself. Moreover, the fear of disorders pervaded the diary of the Master of Ceremonies, who doubted the capacity of the representatives of the *popolo romano* to quell dangerous interference with a ceremony that he thought would be better made more aloof from the city. The records of the Masters of Ceremonies stigmatize the populace, stressing their greed and lack of discipline and the uncouthness of their behaviour, further reflected in their indecorous or vile attire. At the cavalcade of 1513 it was only a promise by the Conservators and *caporioni* to hand out more coin than usual that averted the seizure of the baldaquin, and the papal horse and chair ('raptum baldachini et equi ac sedis papalis'). Such violent breaches of curial arrangements had by then become commonplace. This expression of ritual violence, justified not so much by an unlikely 'right of sack' (*ius spolii*) as by a wish to appropriate souvenirs charged with sacral aura, had always been past of the day's events.[42] But in the sixteenth century, the words of the Masters of Ceremonies betrayed a growing aversion to all forms of violence, and a desire to dominate and to withdraw ever further from the urban context, in order to endow the rite with absolute values and functions and a universal message.[43] The Master

---

[40] This act seems to have meant not so much a reconciliation of the pope and his subjects as a symbolic change of status. See Bertelli, *Il corpo del re*, p. 100.

[41] *Numismata Pontificum Romanorum*, pp. 55–60: 'Liberalitas pontificia: mulier quae supra aliquot volumina cornu copia fundit, libris circumdata, musicisque instrumentis'. It is worth noting the different representation of the same concept of *liberalitas* in the coins and medals of Sixtus V: ibid., pp. 156–74.

[42] Bertelli, *Il corpo del re*, p. 97.

[43] Some aspects of the evolution of the papal state during the Cinquecento can be interpreted using Elias's notion of the 'monopoly of violence': N. Elias, *Über den Prozess der Zivilisation*, vol. II, *Wandlungen der Gesellschaft. Entwurf zu einer Theorie der Zivilisation*, 2nd edn, Frankfurt, 1980.

of Ceremonies seemed increasingly unable to control the violent distur-
bances that took place inside the Lateran basilica. In this sacred space, the
canons, at heart churchmen second and noble Romans first, ransacked
everything the pope left behind, not only in order to appropriate sacred
value, but also, in a disordered but decisive way, to retrieve a space of
their own which they felt was being increasingly pervaded by the papal
presence, and not only during the cavalcade.[44]

In his history of the *possesso*, Cancellieri, reporting the words of the
Master of Ceremonies Francesco Mucanzio, notes how the last proper
ceremony, which he calls a 'processo', was Leo X's; thereafter the pope

> abandoned his sacred garments and his mitre, in which he had ridden, and
> also the rituals of carrying the Holy Eucharist in procession, and accepting
> the Law of the Jews as he passed before them, and scattering coins in the
> street, and seating himself in the Lateran on the *sedia stercoraria* and on the
> chairs of porphyry, girding himself with the keys, the seals and the musk,
> and holding a banquet. So it is no wonder that, after all these changes, it
> is no longer called Processo or Processione, but Possesso.[45]

Here the Master of Ceremonies simultaneously notes a turning-point
and remarks on the danger of disorder caused by the dislocation of old
traditions that have not been replaced by any sure, well-defined ritual.

FESTE FOR A ROMAN POPE: PAUL III (1536–1549)

The election of Paul III Farnese in 1536 opened a parenthetical period of
reconciliation by re-establishing the bond between the city and the court.
The pope, who belonged to a family of the Roman military nobility,
solemnized his election in the company of the Capitoline magistrates and
the young Roman knights. In this meeting, the positions were reversed.
It was not the pope who crossed Rome to reach the Lateran – he never
moved at all – but the nobility who came to visit him and to display
themselves in a chivalrous joust:

> Finally . . . thirty-two barons and Roman gentlemen, some of the noblest
> of all the city, came out, all riding the most handsome jennets, dressed with
> great pomp, in varied and novel livery, cloth of gold, and silk of diverse
> colours, and each of them had a page in the same livery on another horse
> just as finely furbished, and each carried a shield in the Moorish fashion,

---

[44] The restoration of the Lateran palace, much vaunted by De Grassi, assumes a precise
meaning as a public demonstration of the desire to restore papal dominion over an
area that had became marginal both to the Vatican and to the architectural, social and
commercial centre of Renaissance Rome: Cancellieri, *Storia de' solenni possessi*, p. 64.

[45] Ibid., p. 120, n. 3.

and the lords with their lances first put in an appearance in the very square of Saint Peter's, where they ran courses and jousted, and put on other displays of knightly horsemanship, and rested their horses, threw the lance, and took shots at targets with certain gilded balls, which they call *caroselli*, in the most handsome order, proceeding in pairs, in fours, in sixes. Finally, they broke into two squadrons, and, sometimes fleeing, sometimes pressing forward, they attacked one another in a most pleasing, joyful battle. Their games being done, they knelt before his Beatitude, who was watching from a window, and then went off to joust in other places in the city.[46]

This spontaneous tourney among the young Roman nobles was a restaging of an ancient game displaying military *virtù*, force and wealth. It had not been taken over by the pontifical court. On this occasion, the triumphal arches gave way to floats, and the allegories the Roman people offered to the pope put forward a reading of current events intended to influence the course of papal policies:

> On 29 October, the Roman people, with all its most illustrious barons, and with the gentleman citizens, and the other officials, went off to the Campidoglio . . . with the greatest pomp, to visit and revere his Beatitude. They carried an infinite number of blazing torches, which made a wonderful sight, and went with trumpets and other sounds before them, set in good order by their marshals, *caporioni*, constables and other officials, and last came the lord Conservators and the barons of the famous houses. They brought with them three triumphal cars, each drawn by four extremely beautiful war horses festooned with fine horse-cloths reaching to the ground in the proudest fashion. The first float was Rome in Triumph, with many wonderful devices of warriors, prisoners, and other figures who represented all the virtues of his Holiness. The second was the float of the church, in the form of a triangle with certain niches, wherein stood Peace, Abundance and Charity, and other pretty symbols. The third was [the float of] Faith, with many priests around it, and other chimeras, all of which stood for the triumph of the church.[47]

On this occasion, the Roman people became once again the protagonists, expressing their wish to reappropriate a festival that had fallen into the hands of the curia and its Masters of Ceremonies and, above all, of the Florentines and their powerful merchants. Peace, Abundance and Charity rode the float of the church, as if to say that resolving the knotty problems of the Reformation and the pacification of *Christianitas afflicta* would ensure good governance in the state.

[46] Cruciani, *Teatro nel Rinascimento*, p. 536, quoting G. Fantini, *Successi di Roma, et di tutta Italia . . .*, Rome, 1542.
[47] Ibid., p. 535.

A new pope's origins had a good deal to do with defining the stages in and gestures of his *possesso*. Describing the cavalcade that left Saint Peter's 'in a way as splendid and solemn as the world could ever imagine', Girolamo Lunadoro, in the seventeenth century, recorded that two triumphal arches were always erected in the honour of the pope along his route. One was in the Campo Vaccino, as the Forum then was called; another by the Orti Farnesiani, on behalf of the Farnese Dukes of Parma and Piacenza; and a third, 'if the pope is Roman', on the Campidoglio. At this last,

> the urban militia of the Roman people are seen drawn up in formation with their insignia, and the Senator of Rome humbles himself in his robes of office with a chain of gold round his neck and a sceptre of ivory in his hand, accompanied by the *Conservatori* and other officials of the Capitoline courts. He offers and promises to the pope, in a short Latin oration, the fidelity and obedience of the Roman people, and His Holiness answers him with the usual formulas.[48]

By the middle of the seventeenth century, this ritual was already void of all political significance, and the original tension and scorn of the Masters of Ceremonies had been placated by the eclipse of civic claims and by affirmations of pontifical power. The luxury and magnificence of the costumes worn by the Roman magistrates disguised the fact that, in reality, they had been reduced to supporting players in a well-choreographed *festa*, offered by the pope to the populace, the ambassadors of the European courts, and the ever-swelling ranks of knights and gentlemen sojourning in Rome.

THE TRIUMPH OF ORDER: SIXTUS V (1585–1590)

The 'most solemn procession of the cavalcade' evolved gradually from a symbolic act into a real 'possession' of the Lateran church, emphasizing among other things, papal control over the city and the new power of the vicar of Christ in his episcopal role. Accordingly, by the late sixteenth century the festival aimed to project the image of the triumphant universal church. Symbols of military victories were no longer acceptable; nor were pompous, ephemeral celebrations of a precarious peace. The aim was rather to exalt the power and universalism of a papal monarchy and of a church revitalized by the council of Trent. This semantic metamorphosis reflected real changes in political realities. The first serious break in the

---

[48] *Della elezione, coronazione e possesso de' romani pontefici. Trattato del cav. Lunadoro accresciuto e illustrato da Fr. Antonio Zaccaria*, Rome, n.d., pp. 103–4.

style of the Renaissance papacy came with the enthronement rites of Pius V. An *Avviso* of 19 January 1566 is eloquent. It reports:

> on Saint Anthony's day, the day of pope's birth, he was crowned amidst such a crush of people that it was estimated that in St Peter's square were more than thirty thousand men. He did not throw money, but gathered all the poor in the Campo Santo, and then made them come out through a door and had each one given three *julii* . . . The meal was sumptuous and royal, but not extraordinary. There was a little music, but not such a crush of people as to cause confusion. His Holiness ate so lightly that he might have been in a refectory of friars . . . His Holiness in these beginnings has given such a sample of his mildness and liberality that his austerity, which was one feared, was more likely a matter of his character, and the office [of chief inquisitor] that he held, than of his nature, which promises all sorts of sweetness and clemency.[49]

Austerity and well-regulated charity did not exclude liberality; the rejection of useless pomp, considered contrary to the image Rome wished to project at a time of great tension with the Protestant world, would two decades later set the model for Sixtus V.

The antithesis we noted in the pontificates of the early years of the sixteenth century is still there at the century's end. But now the terms of reference are entirely different, and the symbolism of power has become far more elaborate, especially under Sixtus V. The Peretti pope was keen to distinguish himself starkly from the muddled policies of his weak predecessor, Gregory XIII (1572–85), and rather to follow the model of Pius V. Histories have made this amply clear, both contemporary sources and later historiography, often guilty of bias in his favour.[50] The intent to use the ceremony of coronation and *possesso* as a political act is unmistakable; its precise message was a political platform that aimed to strengthen temporal power, above all by establishing 'good justice'.

It was Sixtus himself who planned the ceremony of his cavalcade. A proclamation by the Governor of Rome, who was by this time the most powerful judicial authority in the city, laid down the rules for the orderly deployment of the procession.[51] This decree contained in a nutshell the entire programme of public order that the pope would try to realize in his reign. It fixed the schedule for the departure and the meeting-places

---

[49] BAV, Urb. Lat., 1044, 172v–173r.

[50] For the use of imagery, and for the historiography of Sixtus, see my 'Justice and its Image: Political Propaganda and Judicial Reality in the Pontificate of Sixtus V', *The Sixteenth Century Journal*, 24 (1993), pp. 75–95.

[51] *Ordini da osservarsi nella cavalcata il giorno del Possesso in San Giovanni dalla Santità di N. S. Sisto V, per evitare scandali*; quoted in Fagiolo and Madonna (eds.), *La Festa*, pp. 170–2. Cancellieri, *Storia de' solenni possessi*, pp. 21–5.

of the pope and the various dignitaries and officials who had a part to play; it warned against allowing quarrels over rank and precedence to surface. Excessively lavish display was to be avoided, and costume was to be 'moderate, noble, but not vain'. Abuses and the display of useless luxury would be punished by loss of both honour and employment. All concerned were to abstain from causing scandal by brawls and quarrels; a special warning was addressed to the nobility, who too often in the past had violated the rules of the ceremony by conduct unbecoming their station. A pacified city and a tamed nobility were to serve as spectators for a parade that would in its symbolic progress expound the pontiff's complete conquest of his city.

It was the pope himself who laid down the punishments for breaking the rules. His plans and warnings, seconded by the Masters of Ceremonies, eloquently express a desire to communicate a papal resolution that looked well beyond the rules in question:[52]

> He did not wish for coins to be thrown in the *piazza* to the Plebeians, because often people were killed, and because he also thought that this was not a true almsgiving, but a prodigal waste, since the vagabonds and tricksters, who put on a show of being poor, and are of robust body, join with violence in the fray, and collect all the money, and the true poor, weak, ill, lame, and old get none of this profusion of money; so he had it distributed to the true poor, by the houses [of religion] and the hospitals. Furthermore, he did not want to put on the usual regal feast, considering it a boastful waste, all the more so because in Rome there was a dearth of victuals.[53]

Liberalitas is no longer identified with the disorderly distribution of money, but with well-regulated charity: the ritual value of an ephemeral gesture, destined to die with the ceremony itself, no longer satisfied its protagonist.

The desire to leave other, more solid testimonials to the foundations of his pontificate impelled Sixtus V to transfer the exaltation of symbols of his power from the ceremony to monuments and iconography, which were surer routes to a more solid and durable remembrance of his reign. Thus *liberalitas*, charity, abundance and justice would be definitively consecrated in the frescoes of the Salone Sistino in the Vatican Library, in the Lateran palaces, and on his own tomb in Santa Maria Maggiore, not to mention the many coins and medals struck during his five-year

---

[52] The lamentations of the Masters of Ceremonies is a topos in their *Diarii*. On the quarrel among several cardinals during the *possesso* of Clement VIII, over whether the pope should kneel before Cardinal Colonna, archpriest of the Lateran, who would be offering him the cross to kiss, see Cancellieri, *Storia de' solenni possessi*, p. 155.

[53] Ibid., p. 121. The passage in question refers to the *possesso* of Sixtus V.

reign.[54] No triumphal arch bedecked his lustral line of march, while on the Campidoglio the pontifical emblems held sway. The symbolic force of this act was eloquent: to refuse the customary decorations put up by the Roman magistrates was 'to refuse the act of fealty ... this desire to conceal the visible presence implies the negation of its power; this, perhaps, is the first public declaration of Sixtus V's plan for the concentration of his power'.[55] Thus, with Sixtus V, the *possesso* 'becomes a demonstration of power'[56] within the framework of a new urban scenography that aimed a polemical riposte at the heretics' calumnies. Just as the ambassadors of the Italian states had been swift to note Julius II's exaltation of military force, so even the Japanese envoys, participant observers, understood at once the message that church and sovereign claimed universal power.[57]

To conclude: in the sixteenth century, once the last Italian wars had petered out, the reconstruction and reinforcement of the papal state imposed a new language on both the centre and the periphery of its territory. The procession to possess the Lateran, as it became encoded through this century, assumed an ever more universal cast. Its symbolic language no longer addressed the city, for its magistrates had been bridled by the superior authority of the popes; rather, it proclaimed to all the triumphant universal power of the Catholic church. In the next century the communal institutions of the city would again participate, laying out great sums on ephemeral displays. From the end of the sixteenth century, however, the ceremony was part of a *festa* offered to the world by the papal court, at the magistrates' expense, for which the city was merely the frame.[58] Like

---

[54] The rejection of a ceremony based entirely on externals appears in several *Diarii*: Cancellieri, *Storia de' solenni possessi*, pp. 124–5. Nevertheless, self-celebration did enter the picture; it imposed Sixtus' personal symbol (a lion on a mountain, holding a pear branch in its paw) unmediated by symbols or metaphors adapted from antiquity or the Old Testament. For Sistine symbolism see J. Typhotius, *Symbola divina et humana pontificum, imperatorum, regum*, vol. III, Prague, 1603, pp. 34–5.

[55] Boiteaux, *Rome, espace urbain*, p. 363.

[56] G. Labrot, *Un instrument polémique: l'image de Rome au temps du schisme, 1534–1667*, Paris, 1978, p. 480.

[57] Among the many contemporary reports of the visit of the Japanese ambassadors, see P. Mejetto, *Relazione del viaggio e arrivo dei prencipi Giapponesi a Roma*, Rome, 1585; G. Gualtieri, *Relazioni della venuta degli ambasciatori Giapponesi a Roma fino alla partita di Lisbona*, Rome, 1586.

[58] In 1623, for example, Urban VIII (1623–44), after a struggle, finally yielded to the prayers of the Capitoline magistrates to be allowed to offer him honours for the *possesso*: Gigli, *Diario*, p. 80. For the relations between the Barberini pope and the Campidoglio see L. Nussdorfer, *Civic Politics in the Rome of Urban VIII*, Princeton, NJ, 1992. The celebrations of the Roman pope Innocent X (1644–55) were even more solemn. In their good order they seem to repeat the 'allegrezze' of the Roman people on the election of Paul III. On the staging of this *festa* see M. Fagiolo dell'Arco and S. Carandini, *L'Effimero barocco. Strutture della festa nella Roma del 600*, vol. I, Rome, 1977, pp. 131–6.

other ceremonies, the *possesso* aimed to represent political harmony, or at least to mask tensions. The repetition of ritual gestures served to present a power that was harmonious because subject to a rigid hierarchy.[59] The growing emphasis on justice as a unifying principle showed there as well. Pontifical authority aimed to show its power through a representative whose calling was, above all, to be a just judge.[60]

[59] E. Muir, *Ritual in Early Modern Europe*, Cambridge, 1997, pp. 229–68. The author does not, however, consider the ceremonies of papal enthronement.

[60] This idea is amply theorized in many sixteenth- and seventeenth-century treatises, most of them still unpublished, that are dedicated to the tasks of the legates and governors of the papal state. See for instance BAV, Chigi, Q. I. 12, ff. 150r–191v; Vat. Lat., 10446, ff. 123r–159r; ASV, Fondo Bolognetti, vol. 156, 73r–86v.

'ROME, WORKSHOP OF ALL THE PRACTICES OF THE WORLD': FROM THE LETTERS OF CARDINAL FERDINANDO DE' MEDICI TO COSIMO I AND FRANCESCO I

ELENA FASANO GUARINI

The expression 'Rome, workshop of all the practices of the world'(that is to say, of political negotiations and manoeuvre as well as of recommendations, plots and intrigue) is found in a letter sent on 13 March 1579 by Cardinal Ferdinando de' Medici to his elder brother Francesco, second Grand-Duke of Tuscany. The letter forms part of an extensive body of correspondence, still largely unexplored,[1] which is of great interest partly on account of the vast canvas of Rome it depicts, providing valuable information on affairs in the city, but even more so by virtue of its nature as a witness to the late sixteenth-century papal court. For Ferdinando was a shrewd and acute observer of the world of Rome under the three pontificates of which he was an eye witness: those of Pius V, Gregory XIII and Sixtus V. Descriptions of this world filled the letters he wrote almost twice a week to his father Cosimo I and his brother Francesco, dwelling in particular on the aspects that concerned them most directly, such as the relationships at court and in the College of Cardinals, the political and social rules of behaviour followed in this *milieu* and the nature of its 'practices'. This article seeks to shed light on Ferdinando's experience and testimony and highlight the image of Rome as the focal point of the 'political activity' that took shape in this setting. First, however, it is germane to delineate the figure of the cardinal and future grand-duke, the circumstances of his removal to Rome and the role he fulfilled there.

Ferdinando, born in 1549, was the fifth son of Cosimo I and fourth among those who survived beyond early infancy. His life underwent a

---

[1] ASF, MP, 5085, 5087, 5089, 5090, 5091, 5092. This letter is in 5089. The papers, still unpublished, are due to be printed shortly by the Istituto Storico Italiano per l'Età Moderna e Contemporanea. For a first study, cf. S. Calonaci, 'Ferdinando dei Medici: la formazione di un cardinale principe', *Archivio storico italiano*, 154 (1996), pp. 635–90; idem, ' "Accordar lo spirito col mondo". Il cardinal Ferdinando de Medici a Roma durante i pontificati di Pio V e Gregorio XIII', *Rivista storica italiana*, 112 (2000), pp. 5–74.

brusque shift at the end of 1562.[2] His mother Eleanor of Toledo, as well as two of his brothers, Giovanni, already appointed cardinal in 1560 and Archbishop of Pisa in 1561, and Garzia, succumbed to malarial fever. Ferdinando thus became the second in order of succession to the throne. At the same time he found himself the designated heir of the cardinal's hat which Pius IV had already granted to Giovanni, as a token of gratitude for support received from Cosimo on the occasion of his election to the papacy and subsequently of the resumption of the Council of Trent. We will not pursue the sequence of events that led to the transmission of that hat to Ferdinando. Suffice it to say that this event came to pass despite the opposition of such figures as Cardinal Michele Ghislieri who, in the Consistory, refused to sign the bull on account of the nominee's tender age, considering it to be in conflict with canonical norms and against the spirit of the Council of Trent.[3] But it is interesting to note that Ferdinando's appointment was part of an extremely limited and thoroughly political promotion, which was not in harmony with the proposals to reform the College of Cardinals that Pius IV himself cherished. Only one other name was put forward in addition to the son of the Duke of Florence and Siena, that of the twenty-two-year-old Federico Gonzaga, brother of the Duke of Mantua and nephew of Cardinal Ercole.

As with Giovanni, the appointment was not followed by immediate transfer of the adolescent cardinal to Rome. It was not until two years later, in May 1565, that Ferdinando undertook a first brief journey to receive the title of absent cardinal deacon of Santa Maria in Domnica. On that occasion he was escorted by authoritative figures expert in the ways of the court and the Roman curia, such as Cardinal Giovanni Ricci, the ambassador Averardo Serristori, Angelo Niccolini, himself promoted to the rank of cardinal, and Ugolino Grifoni.[4] Still under the guidance and tutelage of Angelo Niccolini and other trusted figures in the entourage of Cosimo I – Serristori, Bartolomeo Concini, Nofri Camaiani – he then took part in the conclave that followed the death of Pius IV, on 20 December of that same year. Although Alessandro Farnese, leader of the faction that opposed the Medici family, was forced to relinquish his personal ambitions, the conclave ended with the defeat of the Medicean candidates and the election of a candidate proposed and championed by the Farnese, Michele Ghislieri (Pius V), who, as a cardinal, had strongly challenged the promotion of Ferdinando. Given the unfavourable climate

---

[2] On Ferdinando I cf. the entry by myself in *DBI*, vol. XLVI, to which I refer for the information presented below, unless otherwise indicated.

[3] R.Galluzzi, *Istoria del granducato di Toscana sotto il governo di casa Medici*, Florence, 1781, vol. II, pp. 47–8; Calonaci, 'Ferdinando dei Medici', pp. 638–50.

[4] On these men cf. F. Diaz, *Il Granducato di Toscana. I Medici*, Turin, 1976, *passim*.

of the new pontificate, it was thought best to keep Ferdinando, who was still quite young, in Tuscany.

It is not easy to determine how Ferdinando was coached to prepare him to exercise the functions to which he was destined by virtue of his title. However, he certainly did not undergo a traditional mode of training. Whether on account of the fragility of his vocation or perhaps because his family desired to leave open the door to a possible succession, in matters ecclesiastical he did not go beyond the diaconate. Unlike his brother Giovanni, he was not awarded the archbishopric of Pisa, which instead went to Angelo Niccolini in 1565. In any case, although he showed a precocious interest in collector's items and antiquities, following in his father's footsteps,[5] Ferdinando was known to prefer hunting and the outdoor life to study. In 1565 his preceptor Ludovico Beccadelli described him as 'very child-like and helpless', 'not wont to devote himself to the world of letters'. Indeed, his limited familiarity with the basics of the liturgy and of communication among cardinals also emerges clearly from the recommendations addressed to him by his mentors. Thus on the occasion of his first journey to Rome, Serristori urged him to learn the liturgy of the mass by heart, as the cardinals used to mumble the words to themselves in unison with the priest.[6] Again in 1568, when longer stays in Rome were anticipated, the Medici agent in Rome, Lodovico Ceresola, exhorted him to learn the rudiments of Latin: 'Two words of Latin that Your Grace may pronounce in the Consistory will be worth more than the hundred uttered by the most solemn-minded and highly accomplished of your devoted orators and servants.'[7] But Ferdinando's education in this sphere apparently remained incomplete: five years later, in Rome, he once more took up the study of Latin 'to confound the envious and the spiteful', and in 1578 he was still practising with his tutor, Piero Angeli da Barga, during their outings 'in the carriage'.[8]

However, Ceresola and the other Medici agents in Rome were not merely concerned with exhorting Ferdinando to persevere with his studies. The letters he received[9] from Rome offered a vivid commentary on political affairs in the city and events at the curia. News on promotions to the cardinalate, rumours – at times reported with barely concealed irony – on measures to implement the Council of Trent ('they attend

[5] P. Barocchi and G. G. Bertelà (eds.), *Collezionismo mediceo. Cosimo I, Francesco I and cardinal Ferdinando*, Modena, 1993, p. XI and *passim*.
[6] Letter to Francesco de' Medici, Rome, 22 March 1656, ASF, MP, 3472.
[7] Letter to Ferdinando, Rome, 26 April 1568, ibid., 5096A.
[8] Letter from Ferdinando to Francesco, 12 January 1573, ibid., 5085, and 8 October 1578, ibid., 5089.
[9] Cf. in particular ibid., 5096 and 5096A (letters to Ferdinando, 1563–9).

to no other matter than that of reforming the world'),[10] descriptions of baptisms of Jews and solemn abjurations by victims of the Inquisition,[11] were interspersed with comments on the pontiff's attitude towards the Spanish monarchy, or on the movements of Turkish troops, which were followed with considerable apprehension in Rome.[12] Often the letters would be accompanied by anonymous *avvisi* or notices drawn up in Rome or originating from Vienna or elsewhere. His correspondents also wrote at length on the network of relationships at court and in the curia, conflicts among factions of cardinals, the pontiff's relations with various cardinals, the most 'regal banquets' held in the 'vineyards', 'gardens' and grounds in the surroundings of the city. Ferdinando thus gradually became familiar with the customs and lifestyle of the Roman court. He acquainted himself with its protagonists and learned to identify friends and foes. He was instructed on how to fight against the most dreaded opponent, old Alessandro Farnese, whose tremendous power appeared to play a crucial role in defining the balance among the various forces within Italy, and therefore in preserving the Medicean state. Ferdinando acquired a feel for allegiances and alliances. It thus behoved him – wrote Ceresola, in one of his letters, composed on the occasion of a passing visit by Cardinal Morone from Florence – to cultivate the latter with 'every type of compliment and homage, if for no other reason than to give these Farnesians something to cudgel their brains about', and obtain support against them.[13] The advice imparted to the prince thus did not pertain merely to study, but also to rules and code of behavior. It would be fitting to send Cardinal Carafa and Cardinal Della Chiesa some 'gold brocade and lining for their vestments', so ran another letter from Ceresola, which sheds light on the social stratification of the College of Cardinals. Such an act, worthy of the 'beneficence, grandeur, munificence' of the Medici, would please the pontiff, because the two cardinals, only recently elected, were poor and were 'his creatures: it would thus be money well spent, even more so than "giving one in order to get a hundred"'.[14] Meanwhile,

---

[10] Letter from Alessandro Mola, 1 November 1566, ibid., 5096. Cf. also letter from Lodovico Ceresola, 19 July 1566, ibid.

[11] Letters from Ceresola, 7 June 1566 and 23 June 1566, ibid.

[12] Cf. e.g. letter from Ceresola, 31 May 1566, ibid.

[13] Letter of 26 April 1568, ASF, MP, 5096A. On Farnese see also letter from Ceresola, 4 November 1566, ibid., 5096.

[14] Letter 26 April 1568, ibid., 5096A. Antonio Carafa and Giovan Paolo Della Chiesa had been elected during the second promotion of Pius V (24 March 1568): cf. C. Eubel and G. Van Gulik (eds.), *Hierarchia catholica Medii Aevi*, vol. III, Münster, 1910, p. 48. On the increasing divergence between 'rich' and 'poor' cardinals in the middle of the sixteenth century cf. G. Fragnito, 'Vescovi e cardinali tra Chiesa e potere politico', *Società e Storia*, 412 (1988), pp. 644 and 647; G. Fragnito, 'Cardinals' Courts in Sixteenth

the young cardinal was beginning to receive a steady stream of petitions and requests for protection and support. Though far from Rome, he was beginning to learn the exercise of patronage, to which he was destined by his rank.[15]

Ferdinando finally removed to Rome in January 1569. Relations between the Medici (Cosimo I and his son Francesco, to whom Cosimo had yielded a share in the government of the state in 1564) and Pius V had substantially improved. The pontiff was preparing to bestow on Cosimo I the title of Grand-Duke of Tuscany, satisfying an ambition that Cosimo – who had been made Duke of Florence by Charles V in 1537 and had also been invested with the dignity of Duke of Siena by Philip II in 1557 – had cherished for years.[16] The new title would guarantee Cosimo an honorific pre-eminence in Italy, a matter of the utmost significance at a time when honour and precedence were very serious things, as testified by the conflict that had arisen between the Medici and the Este at the beginning of the 1540s and was still unresolved.[17] His pre-eminence would consolidate the international prestige of his dynasty, favouring his ambitious matrimonial policy. Above all, it would help legitimize a dominion whose legal foundations remained equivocal, based as they were first on the acquisition of supremacy over a city, Florence, that claimed to be free, and secondly on the feudal tenure of Siena. No less important than the grand-ducal title was the fact that it made reference to Tuscany rather than, as previously, to two distinct cities. Thus the title became the

Century Rome', *Journal of Modern History*, 65 (1993), pp. 26–55. For a comparison with the first half of the seventeenth century, cf. M. A. Visceglia, '"La giusta statera de' porporati". Sulla composizione e rappresentazione del Sacro Collegio nella prima metà del Seicento', *Roma moderna e contemporanea*, 4 (1996), pp. 167–211.

[15] On patronage in Rome in the sixteenth and seventeenth centuries cf. W. Reinhard, *Freunde und Kreaturen. 'Verflechtung' als Konzept zur Erforschung historischer Führungsgruppen. Römische Oligarchie um 1600*, Munich, 1979; W. Reinhard, 'Papal Power and Family Strategy in the Sixteenth and Seventeenth Centuries', in R. G. Asch and A. M. Birke (eds.), *Princes, Patronage and the Nobility. The Court at the Beginning of the Modern Age (1450–1650)*, London-Oxford, 1991, pp. 239–356; M. A. Visceglia, 'Burocrazia, mobilità sociale e patronage alla corte di Roma tra Cinque e Seicento. Alcuni aspetti del recente dibattito storiografico e prospettive di ricerca,' *Roma moderna e contemporanea*, 3 (1995), pp. 11–55.

[16] D. Marrara, *Studi giuridici sulla Toscana medicea. Contributo alla storia degli Stati assoluti in Italia*, Milan, 1965, pp. 3–56; A. Contini, 'Aspects of Medicean Diplomacy in the 16th Century', in D. Frigo (ed.), *Politics and Diplomacy in Early Modern Italy. The Structure of Diplomatic Practice, 1450–1800*, Cambridge, 2000, pp. 49–94.

[17] L. Mannori, *Il sovrano tutore: pluralismo istituzionale e accentramento amministrativo nel principato dei Medici (secc. XVI–XVIII)*, Milan, 1994, pp. 81–3. For general picture see M. A. Visceglia, 'Il cerimoniale come linguaggio politico. Su alcuni conflitti di precedenza alla corte di Roma tra Cinquecento e Seicento', in *Cérémonial et rituel à Rome (XVIe–XIXe siècle)*, Rome, 1997, pp. 117–76.

focus of the overt interests of Cosimo I as well as the more covert, but no less far-reaching, designs of the pontiffs. For Pius IV and later for Pius V it was an opportunity to appropriate (or reappropriate) high-level jurisdictional powers, and also arbitral powers within an international framework which would be prominent in their actions during the second half of the Cinquecento.[18] A chance, in other words, to reiterate and consolidate the centrality of Rome.

Through Ferdinando's removal to Rome the Medici offered Pius V a testimony of their gratitude and trust, and paid homage to him, respecting his desire – in conformity with the post-Tridentine climate – that cardinals should reside in Rome. But they also gave visibility to their lineage in the papal capital, far more impressively than by previous symbolic enterprises such as the restoration of the Medici church of the Navicella in 1566, or the representation on its ceiling of a heraldic lion – a ruse to associate the name of Ferdinando with that of the first Medici pope and the memory of his city of origin.[19] Ferdinando himself reminded his father in 1570 that one of the main reasons for sending him to Rome had been 'that I should become known amongst men and that I should be to Our Holiness a shining witness of your devotion and that of our entire house towards His Beatitude'.[20]

Such attitudes, it need hardly be added, represented a generalized political tendency. During the Cinquecento the powers of the College of Cardinals had been eroded by the new papal centralism and by the growing control of sovereigns over the highest ranks of the church. But this period had also seen an increase in prestige of those cardinals who were also princes; and Italian dynasties had attached increasing importance to having one of themselves in the Consistory. In 1598, in his treatise *Del cardinale*, Fabio Albergati was to celebrate the excellence of those who combined in their person the prince and the cardinal, uniting virtues of government with elevated spiritual qualities. Being superior to the other cardinals, only for the sake of 'humility' should the cardinal-prince stoop to equality with them, thereby restoring beyond natural differences, the conditions of equality (or parity) which alone could ensure a perfect 'friendship' between them.[21] It was unthinkable that the prince-cardinals, whose ranks featured such names as Farnese, Este and

---

[18] P. Prodi, *Il sovrano pontefice*, Bologna, 1982, pp. 297–344.

[19] S. Butters, *Le cardinal de Médicis*, in A. Chastel and P. Morel (eds.), *La Villa Médicis*, vol. II, Rome, 1991, pp. 170–98.

[20] Letter to Cosimo I, 7 April 1570, ASF, MP, 5085.

[21] F. Albergati, *Del Cardinale*, Rome, 1598, pp. 3–4, 159, 163 (the treatise is dedicated to the newly elected cardinal, Prince Odoardo Farnese). Cf. Visceglia, 'Il cerimoniale', pp. 146–7.

Gonzaga, should not include a Medici; and like the others, he must reside in Rome.

To the task of representing his lineage at court and in the city Ferdinando dedicated great energy and commitment. Although initially excluded from the most confidential negotiations, conducted by more experienced men,[22] he assiduously pursued the question of the title, as is revealed by his letters. This issue did not end with the solemn coronation of Cosimo in Rome, which took place on 5 March 1570, but continued up to his recognition by the Empire and subsequently by Spain and the Italian states, in 1576. Ferdinando also addressed the no less vexed question of the precedence between the Medici and the Este houses. Against a still-fluid backdrop of international relations, wherein institutional procedures often existed side by side with tacit parallel channels of interaction, the younger brother of Francesco often furnished a respected buttress for the diplomacy of the grand-duchy. He directed the family's matrimonial strategies. He protected and expanded its clientage. He concerned himself with consolidating the power of his lineage and transmitting the image of its magnificence, rivalling the pomp and circumstance of the other Italian princely families.

According to the biography by Pietro Usimbardi, his secretary in Rome and then in Florence during the first years of his grand duchy,[23] Ferdinando's transfer to the papal city was also a response to another, more personal concern which is no less interesting from our point of view. Here too we find the observation that Ferdinando, though 'well-mannered and disciplined in his boyhood with his brothers', had not reached the same level of accomplishment through his studies: indeed, he at first seemed 'somewhat dull-witted', or at least lacking the will to apply. Indeed if Cosimo I, once the conflict with Pius V had been resolved, decided that his son should reside in Rome, this was because 'he esteemed that the time had come to uproot Ferdinando from domestic idleness and send him to the discipline of the Roman court'.[24] Recent historiographical debate on the concept of 'discipline' and its forms in the age of 'confessionalization'[25] helps us to grasp the sense of these words. They coherently express the central value that Usimbardi, a 'provincial' from Colle Valdelsa who had himself been educated in

[22] Such as Ugolino Grifoni, letters in ASF, MP, 515, 533–5, 541, 541a, 542, 546, 548, 552; Bartolomeo Concini and also Ferdinando's secretary, Pietro Usimbardi.

[23] G. E. Saltini (ed.), 'Istoria del gran duca Ferdinando I scritta da Piero Usimbardi', *Archivio storico italiano*, s. IV, 6 (1880), pp. 365–410.

[24] Ibid., pp. 371–2.

[25] P. Prodi (ed.), *Disciplina dell'anima, disciplina del corpo e disciplina della società tra medioevo ed età moderna*, Bologna, 1994.

Rome,[26] attributed to that prolonged stay as part of the grand-duke's training. In Rome – so his secretary-biographer suggests – Ferdinando acquired knowledge and internalized rules that would become second nature to him and guide him throughout his life. But as far as the actual contents of that 'discipline' are concerned, Usimbardi has little to say. Far more is revealed by the lengthy and respectful letters Ferdinando wrote to his father right up to the death of the latter (1574), and to his brother, in a not infrequently polemical tone, up to September 1587, when Francesco fell gravely ill and Ferdinando returned to Florence to succeed him on the grand-ducal throne, an eventuality he had long contemplated.

The letters paint a vast fresco of eighteen years at the papal court. Their pages offer an array of themes, such as devotional practices and commitments at the curia, presences at the College of Cardinals and the court, antiquarian and archaeological interests and patronage practices, plans for increasing his personal and family estate, scenes from his personal life. But the 'political' interest consistently predominates. In Ferdinando's eyes, the pontiff was the potential arbiter of international questions and equilibria far more than the spiritual head of the church. His letters speak of promotions, factions and allegiances among cardinals, consistories and conclaves in terms suggesting he saw these as political events. From the vantage point of Rome Ferdinando then cast his glance beyond the city and looked to Italy and Europe, to relations between Spain, France and the papacy, to the 1575 events in Genoa and those of 1580 in Portugal, to the religious wars in France and the situation in Flanders, to the leagues and plans for leagues against the Turks. Equally 'political' were the behavioural models he adopted on the basis of his experience, contrasting them with the customs and habits of his brother Francesco and displaying a brashness that grew more brazen over time.

Yet 'political' is an anachronistic term if applied, in the early modern age, to mean bargaining and negotiating and making decisions in this way. It is more helpful to investigate the vocabulary used by the young cardinal and his mental and moral categories. We will begin by considering his lifestyle and the requirements he expressed in this regard. The road will be long, but useful in showing how these categories actually took shape and operated.

In the light of these observations, it comes as no surprise that a considerable portion of Ferdinando's correspondence, particularly in the

---

[26] M. Fantoni, 'Dalla provincia alla capitale: gli Usimbardi di Colle alla corte medicea', in P. Nencini (ed.), *Colle Val d'Elsa: diocesi e città tra '500 e '600*, Castelfiorentino, 1994, p. 121; M. Fantoni, *La corte del granduca. Forme e simboli del potere mediceo fra Cinque e Seicento*, Rome, 1994, pp. 144–5.

early stages, is concerned with the substantial expenses needed to surround himself with adequate decorum. As far as we know, he was not
among those cardinals who divided up 'the church as property' among
themselves, to borrow a phrase from Barbara McClung Hallman.[27] According to data published by Jean Delumeau, the benefices belonging to
Ferdinando that were taxed for the 1571 *donativo* amounted to 4,688 *scudi*.
He was thus still far from the position achieved by Alessandro Farnese
(16,750 *scudi*) and Luigi d'Este (19,665), his most immediate and constant terms of comparison and models, or by Giulio della Rovere (16,267
scudi) and Marco Sittich d'Altemps (14,124).[28] Rather, Ferdinando de'
Medici was among those who owed their wealth to family support. Yet
even the latter was limited. Probably court ideology held little sway not
only in his native city, mindful of its republican past, but even over its
sovereigns, whose energies were still directed towards finance, commerce
and industry. In the Florence of Cosimo I and Francesco I the court was
a relatively small-scale establishment, less extensive than the Renaissance
cardinals' courts, which at times had as many as 300–350 members;[29]
indeed, it was smaller than the retinue that travelled to Rome with the
young cardinal (300 individuals and 180 horses). The Florentine court
numbered 168 in 1564, at the time of Francesco's promotion to head
of state; 233 at the beginning of Ferdinando's grand duchy. Court
ceremonial was still erratic, and its seat, prior to the transfer to
Palazzo Pitti, was unprepossessing.[30] It was thus by no means easy for
Ferdinando to make a convincing case for the extravagant expenses of
the lavish lifestyle his role demanded. His initial appanage of 24,000 gold
scudi was raised by his father to 36,000 in 1572, yet this was still far
from sufficient to compete with the 60,000 *scudi* which, according to the
figures reported by Jean Delumeau, both Alessandro Farnese and Luigi
d'Este received in 1571.[31] This explains why, two months after his arrival,

[27] B. McClung Hallman, *Italian Cardinals, Reform and the Church as Property, 1492–1563*,
Berkeley and Los Angeles, 1985, pp. 14 and 134–68.

[28] J. Delumeau, *Vie économique et sociale de Rome dans la seconde moitié du XVIe siècle*,
Paris, 1957, pp. 452–3. On the revenues of Alessandro Farnese and Luigi d'Este, cf.
respectively, the entries by S. Andretta in *DBI*, vol. XLV, pp. 52–65, and P. Portone,
ibid., vol. XLIII, pp. 383–90.

[29] G. Fragnito,' "Parenti" e "familiari" nelle corti cardinalizie del Rinascimento', in
C. Mozzarelli (ed.), *"Famiglia" del Principe e famiglia aristocratica*, Rome, 1988,
pp. 568–9 and 581–2; M. Völkel, *Römische Kardinalhaushalte des 17. Jahrhunderts. Borghese – Barberini – Chigi*, Tübingen, 1993, pp. 50–1.

[30] Fantoni, *La corte del granduca*, pp. 24–31.

[31] In addition to the entry on Ferdinando I in *DBI*, cf. G. Pieraccini, *La stirpe dei Medici
di Cafaggiolo*, Florence, 1925, pp. 283–304. For Alessandro Farnese and Luigi d'Este cf.
Delumeau, *Vie économique et sociale*, p. 452, where however the revenues of Ferdinando's
estates are not documented.

Ferdinando provided Francesco with a painstakingly detailed account of the expenses he had incurred to clothe his 'familia' and himself, to purchase wine for his own table and feed his retinue, to procure an adequate stock of firewood as well as hay and fodder for the horses. The extent of such expenses clarifies why Ferdinando found it necessary to ask for an advance on his appanage.[32] The debts he rapidly accumulated became a constant grievance, and a persisting source of friction with his brother.[33]

Ferdinando did not forget to acquaint his father with the specific needs of a cardinal's court, and after his arrival in Rome he sent requests for financial support in order to restore Palazzo Firenze, an inadequate and ramshackle dwelling, 'almost all very old and shored up with props'. Life as a cardinal required a large and comfortable palace: not merely an 'honourable' personal suite, but also rooms for visitors, lodgings for the whole of his retinue 'so that at the touch of a bell my servants can be ready at once to do me honour', and stables for the master's horses and those of the servants.[34] Palazzo Firenze, restored, extended and decorated with paintings that extolled the worldly glory of the prince and his noble line rather more than his distinction as a cardinal, would continue to be Ferdinando's main dwelling in the city. In the mid-1570s (when, following his father's death, Ferdinando had a disposable income from his estates amounting to 80,000 *scudi*, which was still insufficient to stave off debts but enabled him to cultivate more lofty ambitions) he also acquired Villa Medici, which had previously belonged to Cardinal Giovanni Ricci, with its outstanding collection of antiquities. Even this was hardly a rival to the numerous villas and gardens that were a 'testimony in stone' to the grandeur and pageantry of such great patrons of the arts as Cardinals Farnese and Este;[35] but it did contribute to enhancing the status of his dynasty. The frescoes painted here by Jacopo Zucchi around the mid-1580s aptly express how Ferdinando, encouraged by further deaths (that of Francesco I's only legitimate son occurred in 1582), was gradually coming to realize his destiny. According to the most recent interpretations, the astrological symbolism and political emblems

---

[32] Letter to Francesco, 4 March 1569, ASF, MP, 5085, and note.
[33] Cf. e.g. letter to Francesco, 16 February 1576, ibid., 5089. But fruitful investments (in venal offices) are mentioned in the report from Rome by Antonio Tiepolo, 1578: see E. Albéri, *Relazioni degli ambasciatori veneti al Senato*, s. II, vol. IV, Florence, 1847, p. 247.
[34] Letter to Cosimo I, 4 March 1569, ASF, MP, 5085.
[35] On Farnese's intention to assert his status 'through fine buildings', and the construction work financed and promoted by the Farnese even after the Council of Trent, cf. C. Robertson, *"Il Gran Cardinale". Alessandro Farnese, Patron of the Arts*, New Haven and London, 1992.

embodied a veiled allusion to a future sovereign behind the figure of the cardinal-prince.[36]

Ferdinando's early letters also depict the glittering social occasions that were one of the causes of his soaring expenses: meetings, tables laid for sumptuous banquets and illustrious guests. There emerges a vision of the papal court – one might even say a philosophy of courtly life in Rome – which, although echoing *topoi* in the numerous treatises of the time, seems to reflect above all his personal experiences and reflections. In Ferdinando's eyes, the world of Rome seemed ambivalent, yet fluid and malleable: centring on specific focal points (first and foremost, on Alessandro Farnese), but not divided by rigid barriers; mutable, but for that very reason manageable and perhaps conquerable. In Rome, so the cardinal wrote to his princely brother, interests and inclinations change and bend like reeds in the wind. It is not easy to recognize true 'friends', and therefore one must 'take with one's hands that part of their benevolence which men are willing to hand over, and seek with dissimulation, response and flattery to coax out the rest'.[37]

Hence the need to establish advantageous relations with those who wielded power and showed themselves well disposed towards the Medici, to assist the relatives and protégés of any minor cardinals who might seek their favour,[38] and distribute secret subsidies to impoverished cardinals. Such moves – wrote Ferdinando – were not designed 'to buy votes . . . but to help individuals pleasing to the pope'.[39] It was meet and fitting to act towards all persons – not excluding those who espoused the Farnese cause – with 'courtesy and honor . . . showing that one had and wished to have all of them as friends and refraining from certain manifestations which here are universally offensive'; 'friendship and trust should be displayed to all'.[40] These modes of behaviour, together with a house open at all times, were the tools with which to achieve success on the Roman stage, so that 'others' intent to see me ridiculed at court may turn into our own laughter'.[41]

[36] P. Morel, 'La Villa Médicis', in Chastel and Morel (eds.), *La Villa Médicis*, vol. III, pp. 118ff., 164ff.

[37] Letter to Francesco, 26 February 1569, ASF, MP, 5085. 'Dissimulation' is a recurrent term in Ferdinando's letters. On its relevance in baroque political language, cf. R. Villari, *Elogio della dissimulazione. La lotta politica nel Seicento*, Rome and Bari, 1987.

[38] Letters to Francesco, 5 and 10 February 1569, ASF, MP, 5085.

[39] Letter to Cosimo I, 1 June 1570, ibid. The 'poor cardinals' were Benedetto Lomellini, Giacomo Simoncelli and Innocenzo Del Monte. In contrast to the approach later adopted by Francesco, Cosimo consented to the distribution.

[40] Letter to Francesco, 14 March 1569, ASF, MP, 5085.

[41] Letter to Cosimo I, 26 February 1569, ibid.

One year later the cardinal had reason to feel most satisfied with his achievements: his familiarity with the cardinal-nephew Michele Bonelli aroused the envy of those who bore him a grudge.[42] Reading between the lines of Ferdinando's desire to 'live like a cardinal', of his requests for financial help addressed to his father and his brother and his thirst for 'friends', one senses in his letters the specific intent to create a new focus group within the College of Cardinals and at court, one that would rally opposition against the Farnesian camp. This plan, he believed, represented a fundamental interest of the house of Medici, and he frowned on his brother's indifference to Roman intrigue. 'I contrive to make friends and consolidate relations with old ones', Ferdinando wrote to his brother in 1577, at a time when rumours were rife of an imminent conclave when Farnese might again be a candidate for the papal tiara. 'It is helpful and enhances your reputation' – Ferdinando wrote – 'to have as much support as possible in this college, because without this I would benefit little – indeed inadequacy in this regard would bring all my efforts to nought'.[43] For it was 'friends' who loaded the dice in dealings among cardinals, and thereby the possibility of conducting productive 'practices' in Rome.

The term 'practices' is recurrent in Ferdinando's letters. In the political jargon of the Cinquecento the term assumed a number of different meanings. A glance at the historical examples supplied by the best-known dictionaries – the *Dizionario del linguaggio storico e amministrativo* by Guido Rezasco (1881) and the *Dizionario della lingua italiana* by N. Tommaseo and B. Bellini (1869) – suggests that to sixteenth-century authors 'practice' designated the actions involved in diplomacy, arranging, bargaining, negotiating. 'You will find yourselves in a place where two things are managed', wrote Machiavelli, 'war and practices.' 'While practices for peace are being undertaken', observed Francesco Sansovino in his *Concetti politici* (1588), 'it is necessary to be cautious and circumspect and know how to guard against the trickery that the enemy may set afoot.' Negotiation, bargaining, manoeuvering, in other words, between states and official centres of power, conducted overtly or covertly, but legitimate and pertaining to the public sphere. Yet there is also mention of private 'practices', for instance concerning marriage or kinship relations. In the private sphere the term could mean a secret 'friendship or association'. In the pejorative sense, it could refer to the entreaties, recommendations, scheming, intrigue or 'worse matters' that might be undertaken in order to procure a public office. Towards the end of the century Bernardo

---

[42] Letter to Cosimo I, 6 January 1570, ibid.
[43] Letter dated 21 December 1577, ASF, MP, 5089.

Davanzati's translation of Tacitus' *Annals* appears to hint at a slightly different connotation, one of illegality: the laws can be 'perverted by force, practices, money'. At times the meaning of the word may not be too far removed from 'plot': 'those friendships that one may note amongst the reprobate, the purpose of which is to cultivate evil designs', wrote Gelli in *Circe*, 'are more appropriately called practices and plots than friendships'.[44]

A twofold semantic force can also be discerned in Ferdinando's letters. Noble and clear is the 'parley and practice of the League that Your Holiness is effecting among all Christian princes against Infidels';[45] legitimate, although secret, the 'practice' Ferdinando wove in 1579 to bring the Venetian ambassador before the pope in anticipation of a recognition of the grand-ducal title.[46] But 'Farnese's practices' during the exhausting wait for the death of the aged Gregory XIII, amid general dread that Farnese would be elected to the papacy, were quite a different matter: they justifiably aroused 'widespread and proportionate anxiety and fear' in Rome.[47] Likewise, quite a different matter were the 'artifices and practices', the occult 'practices about which everyone is outraged' which seemed to be paving the way for the election of Giacomo Savelli, a protégé and ally of Farnese's.[48]

It would thus appear that Ferdinando's experience at court in Rome, the 'discipline' he learned thereby, was a blend precisely of these two types of 'practices', which at that time were not altogether distinct, and may in fact have been complementary. The way they are intermeshed in his letters not only highlights his idea of the centrality of Rome, but also his – quintessentially sixteenth-century – vision of 'politics'. The papal court, the College of Cardinals, the curia – all these presented themselves to him first and foremost as dazzling venues where the myriad strands of private 'practices' were entwined, and, through patronage, clientage relations and alliances were forged and deals struck. But in Rome he also discovered the dimension of great political negotiations and international strategies. Nor did he fail to reflect on the connections linking these two spheres, instructing his brother, the grand-duke, on tactics and strategy.

[44] On the meaning of the term cf. E. Fasano Guarini, ' "Congiure contro alla patria" e "congiure contro ad uno principe" nell 'opera di Niccolò Machiavelli', in Y. M. Bercé and E. Fasano Guarini (eds.), *Complots et conjurations dans l'Europe moderne*, Rome, 1996, pp. 29–32.
[45] Letter to Francesco, 23 January 1573, ASF, MP, 5085.
[46] Letter to Francesco, 7 January 1575, ibid., 5089.
[47] Letter to Francesco, 13 December 1577, ibid.
[48] Letters to Francesco, 18 January 1575 and 4 February 1575, ibid.

The two different meanings of the term 'practices' and the two different levels of political activity they presuppose can be found in the letter dated 13 March 1579, mentioned at the beginning of this chapter. By 1579 Ferdinando had acquired a solid ten-year grounding in Roman 'discipline' and did not hesitate to point out the contrast between the methods and customs typical of the papal court and the criteria adopted by Francesco in the relative isolation of the Tuscan court. The items on the agenda were, once again, Farnese's evident aspiration to the tiara and the need to reinforce the pro-Medici grouping as a bulwark against the Farnesian cohort. But Ferdinando broadened the horizon to include the entire sweep of grand-ducal policy towards Spain and Rome. This picture offered him scope for inferring the criteria that should guide him and his brother in building up a network of 'friends'. There would be no cause for concern 'if riding the crest of Spanish fortunes were a matter which Your Highness could pursue with total confidence'. But it could not be disregarded that there had been 'signs of a less than sincere disposition in that Majesty'. Further, there was some risk that the intents of princes might be swayed or indeed overturned by 'either the accidents of common things or the inclinations and passions of councillors and ministers who deal with their affairs'. The cardinal-prince then proceeded to draw a distinction between the ambivalence of the distant Spanish court and the closeness and crucial relevance of the anomalous Roman chessboard:

> And if, as affirmed by well-versed opinion and experience, Rome were not the workshop of all the practices of the world, so that it is appropriate for all states, but in particular those that are close and contiguous, to be on good terms with this court, which is driven more by the impetus of passions and by the unbridled whims of those who hold its reins than by any hereditary reason of state, then I would not so importunately have reminded Your Highness that we have but small leverage there and that it would be expedient to win men's souls through acts of courtesy, not only on account of these difficult times but above all with a view to the lustre and good repute that a Prince acquires by wielding authority there, enabling him to prevent and divert disagreeable matters and obtain those that one desires.

Hence the recurrent proposal to ease the 'poverty and need' of some cardinals – albeit without making them into 'salaried men . . . , and without any fixed obligation' – as they might provide an opportunity for outmanoeuvring the popes themselves. If the grand-duke was of the opinion, as he had already specified to Ferdinando, that such a procedure would be 'an indignity for him', then Ferdinando would in any case spare no effort to do his part to the best of his ability, 'with blandishments and other tokens, so that I may be ever at the ready to serve Y. H. and support every wish of yours and serve as stated'.[49]

As testified not only by his letters but also by the *avvisi* and reports on the popes and the Roman court over these years, the network of Medici 'friends' expanded over time. Ferdinando became one of the poles of the conflict-ridden world of Rome. Two such poles were mentioned, along with the decline of factions acting 'on behalf of the princes' and the rise of those 'according to the cardinal-nephews', by the Venetian ambassador Paolo Tiepolo in 1576: one headed by Farnese and the other by Medici. 'In all matters they compete and vie with each other', Tiepolo was quick to point out.[50] Two years later, in addition to such figures as the heads of the French faction (Luigi d'Este), and the Spanish faction (Granvelle), another ambassador, Antonio Tiepolo, also mentioned the names of those who headed groups that had formed outside the sphere of the great political and curial wheeling and dealing: Ferdinando de' Medici, Farnese, Borromeo, Altemps and the cardinal-nephew Michele Bonelli.[51] 'There are three *qui dant lumen in Curia*: Farnese, Este et Medici' – so ran the 1584 *avvisi* – 'but because *hi tres unum non sunt*, the individuals patronized separately by each of them end up coming a cropper'.[52]

As Ferdinando's influence as a faction-leader grew, so did the number and importance of the 'practices' in which he took part. Not only did he continue, in the capacity of *mezzano* ('go-between', another characteristic term of his) to transmit requests and entreaties from Rome to Florence, but in the late 1570s and throughout the 1580s he also arranged the matrimonial strategies of his family and clients, once again thwarting the designs of Farnese. Thus it was that in 1576 he took the reins of the laborious 'kinship negotiation' between the nephew of Gregory XIII, Jacopo Boncompagni, and Costanza Sforza di Santa Fiora;[53] and of those between Eleonora, daughter of Francesco I de' Medici, and Vincenzo Gonzaga, and between Virginia (daughter of Cosimo I and Camilla Martelli) and Cesare d'Este.[54] From 1585 he conducted the

[49] Ibid. On Francesco's foreign policy, and his 'maniacal miserliness', cf. G. Spini, 'Il principato e il sistema degli stati europei del Cinquecento', in *Firenze e la Toscana dei Medici nell' Europa del '500*, Florence, 1983, vol. I, pp. 202–7.

[50] In Albéri, *Relazioni degli ambasciatori veneti*, s. II, vol. IV, p. 224.

[51] Report from 1578, ibid., p. 251.

[52] *Avviso* in Rome, 12 December 1584, cited by Pastor, *Storia dei Papi*, vol. IX, p. 160.

[53] Letter of 21 January 1576 and following letters, ASF, MP, 5089. Cf. Pastor, *Storia dei Papi*, vol. IX, pp. 158–60.

[54] On the Mantua 'practice', started in 1580 and concluded in 1584, and that of Ferrara, started in 1583 and concluded in 1585–6, cf. letters in ASF, MP, 5090 and 5091.

overtures that were to lead, in 1588, to the marriage between his own nephew Virginio Orsini, son of Isabella de' Medici, and Flavia Peretti, niece of Sixtus V, thereby ending the family feud that had sprung from the murder of another Peretti at the behest of Virginio's father Paolo Giordano Orsini, Duke of Bracciano.[55] His patronage was not confined to recommendations for offices and benefits. In the 1580s it also involved mediating between the pontiff and the feudal warlords who were clients of the Medici, such as Alfonso Piccolomini, the Orsini of Pitigliano and Prospero Colonna, who were running amok in papal lands at the head of 'gangs of crooks' and bandits.[56] 'Practices' of this ilk were arduous and unrewarding, so much so that the cardinal-prince threatened to cut off his 'protection of [their] affairs', a protection that was hardly consonant 'with my rank and the profession I undertake as a respectable man'.[57]

Increasingly, he was also occupied with more specifically cardinalatial 'negotiations': supervising promotions, constituting of nunciatures and assigning other ecclesiastical posts, as well as active participation, in 1572 and even more so – as we will see – in 1585, in the intrigues that determined the outcome of conclaves. But above all, his letters were becoming concerned with the great political affairs that were hatched in Rome. Within a brief time Ferdinando learned to be no less alert than were the ambassadors and Florentine envoys to shreds of information that filtered through, concerning the rigging of galleys against the Turks in Spain and elsewhere, or how goings-on in France were seen from Rome, or Roman attitudes and feelings towards Spain. He became versed in conveying 'notices', rumours and 'whisperings', which sometimes opened on to a world-wide horizon.

If we wished to single out a precise moment that marked his initiation into high-level politics, we might point to his meeting with Pius V, two and a half years after Ferdinando's arrival in Rome.[58] One pleasant evening, His Holiness, 'not worn out as a result of audiences or such things, but fully restored after dining and well disposed', received him to go over a letter sent by Philip II to Cosimo on the subject of the grand-ducal title, and the reply by Cosimo. There was overall agreement between the Medici and the pontiff, equally distrustful of the Spanish:

---

[55] Letter to Francesco, 7 May 1585, ibid., 5092.
[56] On Alfonso Piccolomini cf. letters of 1583, ibid., 5091. On Prospero Colonna cf. in particular the letters from Ferdinando to Pietro Usimbardi, and to Prospero himself enclosed with the letter to Francesco, 31 May 1584, ibid. On banditry in the papal state in those years cf. I. Polverini Fosi, *La società violenta. Il banditismo nello Stato pontificio nella seconda metà del Cinquecento*, Rome, 1985.
[57] Letter to Prospero Colonna, 31 May 1584, ASF, MP, 5091.
[58] Letter to Cosimo I, 21 April 1571, ASF, MP, 5085.

'His Holiness recognized the Spaniards' art in all the places where I noticed it ...'. Indulging in one of the few religious observations to grace his pages, Ferdinando describes Pius V's indignation at the passage of Philip II's letter where the king asserted, 'according to the style of Spain', that Charles V was 'in heaven'.[59] But he is particularly concerned to underscore that Pius V strongly disapproved of the king's manner of proceeding not only in the Tuscan question but more generally in Italy, and was thoroughly disgruntled at the 'deceitfulness' of the king's ambassadors and council, who outmanoeuvred the king and 'pulled him this way and that and got him wherever they wanted'. He recalls the pope's warning to Philip II to take care to preserve the 'fine states' he had in Italy, 'without occasioning any tide of change, which latter could only result in loss because, if you make a move, the princes of Italy and foreign powers would not be content merely to look on'. Then the conversation broadened to include the issues of political balance in Italy and the crucial themes of European and Mediterranean policy. During the months preceding Lepanto the league against the Turks was obviously at the forefront of the pontiff's thoughts. The pope complained of Spain's lack of 'prowess' and expressed his fear that the Venetians could not be relied on, for 'if hopes should happen to move at a slow pace and clues emerge that point to private interests', they might, the pope meditated, have no compunction about striking a deal with the Ottoman Empire by giving up Cyprus and Candia in the hope that 'the whole impetus would be directed against the King of Spain'. Talk then turned to matters concerning France. Faced with an interlocutor whose benevolence towards Catherine de' Medici he knew full well,[60] Pius V was at pains to restrain the asperity and rigour that were to characterize the well-known instruction he imparted to Monsignor Salviati, the special nuncio in France, in December of that same year.[61] He had previously had a 'bad opinion' of her, the pope owned, but now he 'regarded her as a good Catholic'. Ferdinando himself offered an impassioned defence of the queen. A foreigner in her own kingdom and burdened with small children, she had been compelled 'amid much domestic strife and conflicting interests' to come to agreements with both sides, distributing graces and favours with a far-sighted sense of

---

[59] The Archbishop of Toledo, Bartolomé de Carranza, had earlier been charged with heresy for having assured the dying Emperor he would go to Paradise.

[60] On relations between Ferdinando and Catherine de' Medici during the former's cardinalate cf. A. Desjardins (ed.), *Négotiations diplomatiques de la France avec la République de Florence*, vols. III–V, Paris, 1872, *passim*, and G. Baguenault de Puchesse (ed.), *Lettres de Catherine de Médicis*, vols. III–X, Paris, 1887–1905, *passim*.

[61] Pastor, *Storia dei Papi*, vol. VIII, Rome, 1924, pp. 359–60.

balance 'in order to maintain dignity and her own authority as well as that of others'. Therefore at times she might have seemed to be a Huguenot, but in actual fact, Ferdinando went on, using phrases and tones that prefigure those that would be used a decade later by Giovanni Botero,[62]

> this is what was required by ordinary reasons of state, and Her Majesty had a genuinely Catholic spirit, as His Holiness indeed pointed out, so it was fitting to show fondness for her with blandishments and seize any opportunity to display esteem for her, the king and all their affairs.

Pius V, unmoved by the 'ordinary reasons of state', preferred to praise the 'most Catholic spirit' of Charles IX, who, after the murder of several Huguenots, had 'shown by words a great desire for the rest to go the same way'. But Ferdinando, in his letter to his father, stressed above all that the pope had misgivings as to the trustworthiness of Philip II and felt his policies towards England were ambivalent, to the point that the pontiff 'feared some sort of divine judgment against the Catholic King'. Pius V was apparently not even scandalized by the French intention of turning the Turks into allies to crush the King of Spain. Determined to be – as he was to declare shortly thereafter – 'neither French nor Spanish',[63] Pius V appeared to Ferdinando to be exercising a fair degree of independent-mindedness in his reflections on world affairs and politics. No actual verdict on the pope is to be found in Ferdinando's letter. But in the softly worded conclusion one senses a note of admiration, almost of amazement, at the unfolding of such an unusually vast and wide-ranging canvas: 'Many things were touched on during the space of the almost two hours His Holiness kept me there.'

Despite his support – perhaps less decisive than Ferdinando claimed – for the election of Gregory XIII, despite the influence of his faction and the close link established with Jacopo Boncompagni, Ferdinando de' Medici did not, judging from the accounts given by his contemporaries, succeed in fully winning the trust of the new pontiff.[64] In fact, in the 1580s their relations became strained, due to the widespread belief that the grand-duke was protecting rebel feudal lords and bandits. Gradually, the filial respect that had characterized the cardinal-prince's attitude to Pius V gave way to a more dispassionate appraisal of papal policy, veined with dissent. During the 1575 Genoese crisis, Ferdinando displayed concern over the old pope's pronounced anti-Spanish stance, suggesting that the pontiff was affected by excessive 'jealousy... not only of Genoa's

---

[62] The treatise *Della ragion di stato* by Giovanni Botero appeared in 1589.

[63] Letter of 7 July 1571, ASF, MP, 5085.

[64] Cf. report by Orazio Scopa to the Duke of Mantua, 17 January 1574, in Pastor, *Storia dei Papi*, vol. IX, pp. 883–5.

freedom but of the peacefulness of Italy which in his mind is associated with that freedom'.[65] At a somewhat delicate moment for the fate of the grand-ducal title, what was needed was to convince the pope that the Catholic King had neither 'a tyrannical spirit nor one inclined to the havoc of Italy', and to restrain him from engaging in 'threats and acts of defiance'.[66] In 1580 Ferdinando, at that time no less fervently pro-Spain than Francesco, expressed satisfaction both at Gregory XIII's – albeit tepid – propensity to help the Catholic King and at the pope's condemnation of Henri III.[67] But just a few years later he once again became critical of Gregory XIII's balancing act between France and Spain. His Holiness gave the impression of being lost in his schemes to set up a league against the infidel and seemed dangerously inclined to allow France and Spain to fight each other, without 'explicitly siding with anyone, and especially never against the French'; for the latter were 'dragging [him] by the ears' and could 'get him where they wanted'.[68]

However, as we have seen, it was precisely under the pontificate of Gregory XIII that the cardinal-prince made a clear distinction between the grand-duke's stubborn defence of his entrenched position and Ferdinando's own idea of Rome as the centre of the world and the prime venue for 'practices'. And through such 'practices' and public dealings, conducted in the name of Francesco I and also of other princes, he was gradually passing through the stages in his political apprenticeship.

In certain respects, it could almost be described as a technical apprenticeship. For Ferdinando was learning the

> gentle and modest negotiating procedures of this ... court, which is very loath to respond to any other type of prompt ... and what you must be prepared to do here is tailor the length of your stay to your bargaining procedures and not your bargaining to haste or to excessive eagerness for a rapid resolution that will put everything in its place.[69]

Such was the approach he sought to convey, in 1581, to the vehement ambassadors of the Republic of Venice, inclined to 'challenge' the Pope in their jurisdictional dispute with the patriarch of Aquileja. This episode is of interest for the insight it affords into the significance and dignity Ferdinando attributed to the role of political negotiator. He had volunteered as a mediator for the Serenissima, but had then been replaced by Farnese. When the ambassadors told him he had been ousted, he endeavoured to conceal the blow to his pride. But by denying any sense

---

[65] Letter of 1 June 1575, ASF, MP, 5089. On the 1575 events in Genoa, cf. R. Savelli, *La repubblica oligarchica. Legislazione, istituzioni e ceti a Genova nel Cinquecento*, Milan, 1981.

[66] Letter of 8 July 1575, ASF, MP, 5089.   [67] Letter of 2 February 1580, ibid., 5090.

[68] Letter of 17 January 1583, ibid., 5091.   [69] Lettter of 8 June 1581, ibid., 5090.

of pique, he revealed the depth of the wound. It mattered nothing to him – those had been his very words, he declared to Francesco – that the negotiations and agreements would be concluded 'by a hand other than mine'. The only issue that was genuinely close to his heart was 'public service' and 'the common good'. He cherished no ambition to meddle in Venetian affairs. These negotiations were not the linchpin of 'the honour that I claim in this court', since that honour was already sufficiently assured by his relations with the major princes.[70] Yet for all that 'the common good' and the 'desire to meddle in other people's affairs' were formally in opposition, the two terms were inextricably intermeshed in his world view. Negotiation was at once a 'public service' and a source of personal honour for Ferdinando, and it set the seal on the prestige of his lineage.

The deep-seated conviction that 'practices' and 'negotiation' led to the acquisition of honour and authoritative political stature can be discerned even more clearly in another episode, which is of greater biographical import. This pertained to his relations with the 'Catholic King' and the Spanish court and his duties in his ecclesiastical capacity as protector of Spain.

Ever since 1580, through his brother Pietro and the Viceroy of Naples, Don Juan de Zúñiga, who were his contacts at the Spanish court, Ferdinando 'profusely offered himself' to the Catholic King. He undertook to uphold the king's interests in the question of the Portuguese succession, a matter that was causing no small concern in Rome and among the European states.[71] In exchange, he hoped to procure Spanish support against the ever-dreaded 'prosperity of Farnese'. In order to bring about a preferential agreement with Philip II he contemplated accepting a pension from the latter, provided that the sum was big enough, on a par at least with the 12,000 *scudi* already bestowed on Cardinal Carlo Borromeo and others: anything less, he felt, would not be consonant with his honour. To complete the list of his desires, His Majesty should grant Ferdinando this gift without expecting him to solicit it.[72] The money could not have been a matter of indifference to Ferdinando, constantly debt-ridden as he was. But honour was of the utmost importance, and its measure would be expressed by the actual amount. Even more important was the political value of the relationship thereby crystallized. Ferdinando would become one of the king's men, and the resulting bond of allegiance, by establishing a direct and close relationship of trust between him and

---

[70] Letter of 6 July 1582, ibid.
[71] Letter of 2 February 1580, ibid., and subsequent letters.
[72] Letter of 1 June 1580, ibid. On Spanish royal patronage cf. A. Spagnoletti, *Principi italiani e Spagna nell'età barocca*, Milan, 1996, pp. 32–50.

Philip II, would protect him 'against the possible adverse machinations of his ministers and other persons ill-disposed to our family'.[73]

When, in 1581, the ecclesiastical post of protector of Spain fell vacant, Piero Usimbardi wrote to the grand-duke that it was of interest to his master the cardinal-prince, once again 'for the expediency, but far more for the honour'.[74] Obtaining it proved difficult, on account of conflict within the Spanish court and between the cardinals and the King's ministers; eventually, in 1582, the 'honour' arrived, but without the 'expediency'. However, it is interesting to note that even without pensions the cardinal-prince tenaciously sought to forge a special relationship with Philip II, dealing directly with his negotiations. He successfully advocated the king's requests, first in relation to the Portuguese question; subsequently, during 1581, in connection with the renewal of the financial privileges of *excusado* and *cruzada*; and finally, in 1582 and 1583, with the concession of a subsidy for the galleys.[75] However, as had already occurred in Venice, Ferdinando was to learn how fierce, in the Rome of 'practices', was the competition among negotiators and go-betweens, and how hard it was to shine among them and reap due recognition. For it was not merely obtaining a grace that was of vital importance. It was crucial also to get the credit for it. This concern led Ferdinando, in November 1581, to dispatch a Tuscan courier in a wild chase (which in the event proved unsuccessful) after the papal courier, who bore a brief wherein Gregory XIII granted 'the graces of Spain' and also carried a letter from Gregory's nephew, Jacopo Boncompagni: being the first to inform the sovereign would highlight Ferdinando's own role.[76]

As the cardinal-protector of Spain, Ferdinando directly experienced the acrimony of conflicts among the factions at the Spanish court. Asperities and resentment had jeopardized, or at the very least delayed, his appointment to the post to which he aspired. In addition, his friendship with the Viceroy of Naples was considered 'by spiteful and resentful' persons as a veritable 'league', and in this guise it was presented in 1583 to the new ambassador in Rome, Count Olivares, an adversary of the viceroy. Hence the count's hostility towards Ferdinando de' Medici: Olivares was firmly resolved to limit the scope of the protection to that which Ferdinando held least dear, the appointment of ecclesiastics to

---

[73] Letter of 1 June 1580, ASF, MP, 5090.

[74] Letter from P. Usimbardi to Francesco, 6 May 1581, ibid.

[75] Letters of 12 July, 24 July 1581 and 28 October 1581, ibid. On the 'galley subsidy' cf. also letters of 3 March and 17 March 1582, ibid.

[76] Letter of 21 November 1581, ibid. On this question cf. also Pastor, *Storia dei Papi*, vol. IX, p. 262.

bishoprics and other benefices.[77] Increasingly, Ferdinando was coming to realize that it was well-nigh impossible for the cardinal-prince of a minor state to establish a balanced relationship with the King of Spain. In a letter dated August 1584 he wrote of his reconciliation with Olivares.[78] But when Gregory XIII died, Philip II failed to entrust Ferdinando with 'overseeing the conclave negotiations' which the latter thought were linked to his charge, the protection of Spain; instead, this task went to Cardinal Madruzzo. Even more serious was the news from the king that Spain would not be vetoing any potential candidate. Ferdinando was profoundly aggrieved by this decision, reading it as a tacit intent to work against the Medici by favouring their eternal rival, Alessandro Farnese.[79]

At the end of the nineteenth century Alexander Hübner made a detailed reconstruction of the hurried preliminary transactions of the conclave that led to the election of Sixtus V (21–24 April 1585).[80] His pages afford a glimpse into the strategies and alliances forged by Ferdinando, by now a mature manipulator, which secured the exclusion of Farnese and the candidate closest to Farnese, Giacomo Savelli, and subsequently orchestrated and directed – in agreement with Luigi d'Este and Marco d'Altemps – the election of Felice Peretti, Cardinal of Montalto. We will not review in detail the letters Ferdinando wrote in this circumstance, which have already been partially utilized and published by Hübner together with other diplomatic sources. But it is germane to point out that he seized the opportunity of the conclave to urge the grand-duke again to resort to financial subsidies in order to increase the number of 'friends'. 'With eight or ten thousand *scudi* used well and wisely', he wrote, it would be possible to ensure the exclusion of the unwelcome candidates and 'do something our way'.[81] Francesco continued to regard 'stooping to bribery with money' as repugnant: small sums, he asserted, would be quite futile as compared to the amounts offered by Farnese, and as for large sums, 'it is not our wish to commit them with such a guilty conscience'.[82] Proudly, Ferdinando replied that the fruit he was about to pick had come to maturity after prolonged and careful cultivation, through work carried out 'for the service of Yourself and the satisfaction of friends':[83] i.e. with the 'tokens of benevolence' that had been distributed or through his ability to combine 'blandishments' with 'dissimulation'

[77] Letter of 19 February 1583, ASF, MP, 5091.   [78] Letter of 12 July 1584, ibid.
[79] Letter of 12 April 1585, ASF, MP, 5092.
[80] A. Hübner, *Sisto Quinto dietro la scorta delle corrispondenze inedite tratte dagli archivi di stato del Vaticano, di Simancas, di Venezia, di Parigi, di Vienna e di Firenze*, Rome, 1887, vol. I, pp. 101–96.
[81] Letter to Francesco, 12 April 1585, ASF, MP, 5092.
[82] Letter from Francesco to Ferdinando, 18 April 1585, ibid., 5110.
[83] Letter from Ferdinando to Francesco, 19 April 1585, ibid., 5092.

and through his unflagging efforts in his 'pratices', both public and private. A marriage – between Virginia, daughter of Cosimo I, and Cesare d'Este – had restored closer relations with Cardinal Luigi, head of the French party and Ferdinando's fervent ally during the conclave. Another marriage had drawn Jacopo Boncompagni into a close tie with him, so that the latter was now ready to intervene on Ferdinando's behalf by exerting pressure on Gregory XIII's undecided cardinals, who were weakly directed by two cardinal-nephews, San Sisto and Guastavillani. Ferdinando's privately accumulated credits now constituted a winning hand that could be played to achieve a triumphant design, inspired by the interests of the dynasty and the state.

Yet he obtained no great personal advantages from his role in the conclave. On the contrary, the election of Sixtus V marked the beginning of a period of retrenchment. Certainly, many continued to 'look to' Ferdinando. But the grand-duke, perhaps troubled by his brother's prestige and increasingly espousing the haughty aloofness his brother chided him for, exhorted Ferdinando not to overburden the pope 'with continual requests for friends', to limit himself to making 'appeals to His Holiness for our own particular affairs and those of our house'.[84] Ferdinando, whose relations with his brother were souring, remained dutifully obedient, 'restricting attention to our own and more substantial affairs'.[85] Nothing could have given the pope greater pleasure, for the latter knew that 'for what I've done I am in a position to make higher claims than others' but praised Ferdinando because 'I bother him considerably less than he himself might even want'.[86] The growing detachment would gradually be compounded by frictions of various kinds.

Moreover, despite the formal correctness of relations, Ferdinando's wariness and resentment towards Spain did not abate. 'With respect to the Count of Olivares I dissimulate', he wrote to Francesco, 'but I shouldn't have to grovel to pacify him or them.' Nor did he relish the fact that the Spaniards were aiming to 'secure the pope as an associate in their interests' and that the pontiff appeared prepared to support the 'English enterprise' by providing soldiers and horses, ostensibly intended for Flanders.[87]

Now and then in his letters to his brother, the younger son of the Medici still depicted a broad sweep of European political affairs. But between 1585 and 1587 his letters grew drier and shorter, as if the body of information to be conveyed were smaller, the questions to be discussed of lesser import, and the desire to communicate diminished. The

---

[84] Letter from Francesco to Ferdinando, 18 April 1585, ibid., 5110.
[85] Letter of 25 May 1585, ibid., 5092.
[86] Letter from Ferdinando to Francesco, 17 May 1585, ibid.
[87] Letter from Ferdinando to Francesco, 26 July 1585, ibid.

long-drawn-out Roman experience was soon to end, and he was perhaps aware of this. Nevertheless, he had by now acquired a well-established store of *savoir-faire*.

When, in October 1587, he ascended the grand-ducal throne, Ferdinando was still in possession of the cardinal's hat and the attendant benefits and revenues, which he did not surrender until six months later, shortly before marrying Christine de Lorraine. These were not the only rewards he brought back from the See of Rome. The network of 'friends' he had made in the college and at court would prove to be much longer-lasting, eventually enabling him to influence the conclaves that took place in rapid succession after the death of Sixtus V (1590) and to favour the election of candidates congenial to him. Similarly, the political alliances he had formed in Rome – first and foremost with the Este and the Gonzaga – would turn out to be solid and enduring. They would provide the nucleus around which the new grand-duke would construct that momentous 'Italian' policy which, after his death, would earn him the eminent praise of the Venetian ambassador Francesco Badoer:

> He declared himself to be a most worthy Italian prince and to have ex-
> cellent knowledge of how necessary it was, on the occasion of any distur-
> bances in this province, to leave aside all other concerns and allegiances
> and kinship relationships, and do his utmost to preserve the peace and
> freedom of the aforesaid province.[88]

From Rome Ferdinando also brought back cultural and institutional models. It is scarcely credible that the idea of the court, to which he would give a strong impetus, an appropriate residence and pomp, rules and ceremonial, did not stem at least in part from his experiences in Rome.[89] For the college and the papal court, surrounded by the constellation of the cardinals' courts, had appeared to him as the centre of the centre, not only as the representation and emblem of the power of the sovereign pontiff, but as the locus of 'friendships' and crossroads of political interaction.

But the most abiding elements of his long period in Rome were, first and foremost, the 'discipline' he had learned: the ability to build up interpersonal relations and conduct 'practices' and bargaining procedures. In a virtually unknown eulogistic *Vita*, written shortly after his death in the tones of the baroque panegyric,[90] Ferdinando's experience during his years as a cardinal occupies a prominent position. The anonymous

---

[88] In A. Segarizzi (ed.), *Relazioni degli ambasciatori veneti al Senato*, vol. III, Bari, 1916, p. 156.

[89] Fantoni, *La corte del granduca*, p. 24.

[90] *Di Ferdinando I granduca di Toscana* (c. 1610), BNF, Manuscrits italiens 189, cc. 45–86.

author links it with certain characteristics of the government of the third grand-duke. The 'immense stature', 'infinite good repute' and 'incredible benevolence of that court' are portrayed as the premise for the activity of the 'Prince blessed with good fortune, at peace in his state, beloved of his subjects, well liked by his neighbours, admired by his noble peers and esteemed by all the most supreme Princes'. In addition to his zeal for the faith of the apostles, his devotion to the popes and his friendly disposition towards the cardinals, the grand-duke is applauded for his 'strength' and skill in 'government', but above all for 'the intelligence and negotiations that rendered him venerable in the minds and eyes of those who looked upon him'. It was these talents that enabled him to fashion an intricate pattern of relations, transcending the confines of Tuscany to enter into the European dimension.

It is conceivable that Rome may also have been the source of his vision – which was far more dynamic than that of Francesco – of the balance among European powers, together with his evaluation of the opportunities for independent action by Italian states that could arise in the wake of conflicts among the great powers. This was the context in which he had acquired a certain mastery in making overtures and looking towards broader perspectives, an approach that was to guide him in the early period of his reign (for as long as the international conditions permitted) in his moves between France and Spain, whereby he sought in the former a counterweight to the latter.

Thus, with the support of his 'friends' and in concert with other authoritative negotiators, it was once again in Rome, after his accession to the grand-ducal throne, that Ferdinando I was to conduct, between 1593 and 1595, what would be his most important and sensitive 'practice', which was designed to secure papal absolution for Henry IV following his conversion. It was a 'practice' of crucial significance within the overall scheme Ferdinando was pursuing. It was a difficult 'practice', for the objections to absolution were both political and religious. In order to bring it to completion, Clement VIII's resistance had to be sapped. But in committing himself to such a task the former cardinal may have been sustained by the memory of other pontiffs, no less averse than he himself now was towards immoderate allegiance to Spain; pontiffs who had preferred not to take sides, seeking instead to broaden Rome's scope for action on the European political chess board. In turning to Rome he found confirmation of the centrality he had experienced personally and had so vehemently reproached his brother for failing to recognize.

THE 'WORLD'S THEATRE': THE COURT OF ROME AND POLITICS IN THE FIRST HALF OF THE SEVENTEENTH CENTURY

MARIO ROSA

THE 'WORLD'S THEATRE'

No less than the honour and advantage accruing to this Holy See and Catholic CHURCH and to good letters will be the glory afforded Your Highness and the house of Bavaria by the perpetual preservation of such precious spoils and so noble a trophy in this, the world's theatre.[1]

With these words Ludovico Ludovisi, cardinal-nephew of Gregory XV, thanked Duke Maximilian of Bavaria for donating the valuable Palatine Library of Heidelberg to the Vatican (a gesture which in this early phase of the Thirty Years' War was certainly not made without an eye to political advantage). And Rome in this period certainly deserved the title of the 'world's theatre', especially in the years between the tenures of Gregory XIII and Sixtus V, a period culminating in the variously magnificent papacy of Clement VIII, following as it did the abjuration of Henry IV and the end of the Religious Wars in France and coinciding with the renewed importance of the militant Counter-Reformation church, alongside France and Spain, on the international scene.[2] Rome was a 'theatre' above all in the 'political' sense, a place in which tensions and conflicts rife in Europe came to head, but where it was also possible to mediate and form alliances. It was a theatre in which individual bravura in dealing with the succession of events and 'turns' of fortune was indispensable and where the actors' ability to hold the stage was of vital

---

[1] A. Theiner, *Schenkung der Heidelberger Bibliothek durch Maximilian I. Herzog und Churfürsten von Bayern an Papst Gregor XV. und ihre Versendung nach Rom*, Munich, 1844, esp. pp. 57–63. On the political significance of Rome as the 'world's theatre' see M. Seidler, *Il teatro del mondo. Diplomatische und journalistische Relationen vom römischen Hof aus dem 17. Jahrhundert*, Frankfurt am Main, 1996.

[2] K. Jaitner, *Instructiones Pontificum Romanorum: Die Hauptinstruktionen Clemens' VIII. für die Nuntien und Legaten an den europäischen Fürstenhöfen,1592–1605*, 2 vols., Tübingen, 1984; G. Lutz (ed.), *Das Papsttum, die Christenheit und die Staaten Europas 1592–1605. Forschungen zu den Hauptinstruktionen Clemens' VIII*, Tübingen, 1994.

importance. For while the 'arcana imperii' were shaped behind the scenes, the ecclesiastical class pursued its transactions in full view, 'with the aim of becoming adept in the art of public affairs', as Cardinal Bentivoglio writes in his *Memorie*, a work emblematic of a whole age.[3] The rules of political activity in Rome were harsh and coloured by moral and religious concerns involving a strong sense of fatality. Indeed, politics was nothing less than a Machiavellian struggle between vice and virtue, 'two fighters', as Bentivoglio remarks, 'continually engaged in combat on this worthy stage and who make every effort now to raise and now to lower this or that person'. Yet aside from the papal court, Rome was also distinguished by those of the cardinals, as well as by the presence of ambassadors from the various European states, the Generalates of the religious orders and numerous other meeting places, including the residences of princes and nobles and a variety of academies. To quote Bentivoglio again, 'through the coming together there of so many nations and through the keen intelligence of those in power' Rome combined 'many theatres into one great, extremely challenging stage'.[4]

The 'world's theatre' had certainly suffered a setback under Paul V. The city's renewed importance on the international political scene, as well as the policy of universalism systematically pursued under Clement VIII, had been checked by the Interdict against Venice, and in the middle and long term this gave rise to a 'reason of Church' entailing not just a less flexible attitude towards questions of doctrine and discipline within the Church, but also a less receptive one towards current political, religious and cultural developments in Europe. However, this situation did not lessen the appeal which Rome traditionally held for men of letters, both lay and religious. For these were able to find posts as legal experts or as cardinals' secretaries in the offices of the curia, or in that great fund of benefices and pensions which, despite post-Tridentine reforms, that institution still represented in the early decades of the seventeenth century. Equally persistent was the city's appeal for the younger sons of urban patrician families or more ancient aristocratic houses. (Indeed, this had if anything increased with the general aristocratization of Italian and European society.) Rome offered these sons secure prospects of employment within the bureaucratic organs of the papal states, or still more frequently in the now firmly established nunciatures, among which those in Spain and France and at the imperial court especially enjoyed increasing renown as schools of court etiquette and training grounds for future 'advance' to the position of cardinal, or even to the threshold of the See

---

[3] G. Bentivoglio, *Memorie e lettere*, ed. C. Panigada, Bari, 1934, p. 92, but also pp. 398ff.
[4] Ibid., pp. 94, 46.

of Peter itself.[5] Nor, again, had the importance of Rome as a centre of business in any way diminished. For bankers and men of finance too, Rome was the 'world's theatre' in that it offered a marketplace that was both secure and neutral, thanks to the perfecting of the mechanics for the taxation of benefices, to a stable exchange and to the trust inspired by its public debt and the inflationary crises affecting the whole of the Mediterranean region in this period.[6]

Rome thus represented a goal for many, and for many different reasons. The city also commanded a broad view of the wider world, especially through the medium of its delegations and of its religious and political relations. This much is clear from the instructions issued by Cardinal Ludovisi in 1621 to Giovan Francesco Guidi di Bagno, about to take office as nuncio at Brussels, one of the nerve centres of European (and extra-European) politics, where, as the instructions state,

> most of Europe pursues its religious and state interests, while others come from Asia and Africa and from the West and East Indies too. For these peoples' great vessels leave no part of the world, however distant, without securing its connection with their own countries through trade.[7]

Under the stimulus of the universalist Counter-Reformation Church, this view of things led to the creation in Rome the following year of the Congregazione di Propaganda Fide.

It is significant therefore that in the war-stricken Europe of the early 1620s, and in the wake of the triumph of the Habsburg-led German Catholics, the 'world's theatre' seems to have recovered (and in certain respects even surpassed) the level reached under Clement VIII. This great dream of restoration and conquest is the context necessary for understanding the short Ludovisi papacy (1621–23), which followed the long period

---

[5] For the more recent literature see two important surveys: M. Pellegrini, 'Corte di Roma e aristocrazie italiane in età moderna. Per una lettura storico-sociale della curia romana', *Rivista di Storia e Letteratura Religiosa*, 30 (1994), pp. 543–602; and M. A. Visceglia, 'Burocrazia, mobilità sociale e *patronage* alla corte di Roma tra Cinque e Seicento. Alcuni aspetti del recente dibattito storiografico e prospettive di ricerca', *Roma moderna e contemporanea*, 3 (1995), pp. 11–55.

[6] G. Felloni, *Gli investimenti finanziari genovesi in Europa tra il Seicento e la Restaurazione*, Milan, 1971; E. Stumpo, *Il capitale finanziario a Roma fra Cinque e Seicento. Contributo alla storia della fiscalità pontificia in età moderna (1570–1660)*, Milan, 1985. But see also A. Gardi, 'La fiscalità pontificia tra medioevo ed età moderna', *Società e storia*, 9 (1986), pp. 509–57; M. Rosa, 'La "scarsella di Nostro Signore": aspetti della fiscalità spirituale pontificia nell'età moderna', *Società e storia*, 10 (1987), pp. 817–45.

[7] L. Cnockaert, *Giovanni-Francesco Guidi di Bagno nuntius te Brussel (1621–1627): enige aspecten van zijn opdracht en van zijn personlijkheid*, Brussels and Rome, 1956, p. 23, n. 1. For a more general account see K. Jaitner, *Die Hauptinstruktionen Gregors XV. für die Nuntien und Gesandten an den europäischen Fürstenhöfen (1621–1623)*, Tübingen, 1997.

of office of Paul V (1605–21) and preceded the even longer tenure of Urban VIII. The papacy of Gregory XV did not constitute a parenthesis but pursued a policy whose climax came in 1621–2, with the sending of a new group of nuncios to the imperial court, Madrid, Paris and Brussels (as already mentioned), as well as to an outpost of Catholic diplomacy recently created in Switzerland, at Lucerne. Moreover, these were the years in which Rome successfully mediated between France and Spain over the question of Valtellina and engaged in widespread diplomatic support of Maximilian of Bavaria's claim to the defeated Palatine Elector's title. Finally, the year 1622 saw an event of marked practical and symbolic significance, the triumphant group canonization of some of the principal figures of the Church of the previous century, founders or reformers of the various religious orders and missionaries such as Ignatius of Loyola, Philip Neri, Teresa of Avila, Francis Xavier and Peter of Alcántara.[8]

'REASON OF STATE' AND THE SCRIPTURES

In this brief period, then, religion and politics were closely intertwined. Yet, while the broad pattern of Roman politics is familiar enough, less is known about the questions which those who performed leading or minor roles in this political scenario actually discussed in the city's societies and academies, or elsewhere, in this period. Equally little is known about the political and religious views which underlay the discussion and which guided individual members of this ruling elite, or whole groups in power, through the tumultuous course of contemporary events and conflicts. A case in point is that of the Accademia dei Virtuosi, which met in the Palazzo Quirinale on Monte Cavallo in warm Roman summers between 1621 and 1623 and was presided over by the pope's cardinal-nephew Ludovisi.[9] This academy had its own place on the contemporary Roman political and cultural scene, which, in addition to the Accademia degli Umoristi (from 1603 a forum for literary and scholarly debate, and covertly a centre of libertine thought), comprised a shifting galaxy of other academies, led by a series of cardinals then at their apogee. There was the Accademia di cose dello stato, for example, which met every week in the house of Cardinal Cinzio Aldobrandini, nephew of Clement VIII, and before which in 1594 Monsignor Goffredo Lomellini severely criticized

---

[8] L. von Pastor, *Storia dei Papi*, vol. XIII, Rome, 1931, pp. 27–226; but also esp. D. Albrecht, *Die Politik Papst Gregors XV. Die Einwirkung der päpstlichen Diplomatie auf die Politik der Häuser Habsburg und Wittelsbach 1621–1623*, Munich, 1956.

[9] The proceedings of the Accademia dei Virtuosi are reported in the *Avvisi* for the years 1621, 1622 and 1623: BAV, Urb. Lat., 1090, 1092, 1093. For a more detailed account of these reports see below in the main text.

Botero's *Ragion di Stato*, published five years earlier. Or again there was the academy headed by the learned Cardinal Scipione Cobelluzzi, one of whose most active members was the cardinal's own secretary, Vincenzo Gramigna, author not only of a dialogue entitled *Il Segretario* (1620), a generic portrait of the figure of the cardinal's secretary, but also of *Del Governo regio e tirannico* (1615), a Neoplatonically inspired treatise on the figure of the prince, which aimed to overcome the divide between human and divine wisdom by promoting the idea of a Christian prince who conversed with philosophers and whose soul, 'if he is not to err, should always look heavenwards in contemplation'.[10] This was a theme debated at various meetings of the Accademia dei Virtuosi at the Palazzo Quirinale, as well as by the Accademia dei Desiosi, which met a few years later under Cardinal Maurizio of Savoy, and before which Agostino Mascardi discussed the subject in terms similar to those employed by Gramigna, but in a more passionately libertarian and anti-tyrannical manner.[11]

Aside from such patent differences, however, the various cardinals' academies active in Rome between the end of the sixteenth and the early decades of the seventeenth century shared not only a common cultural and political milieu (permitting a certain degree of interaction), but also other traits and aims. Since those who spoke at or attended their meetings included members of the curia, these academies ultimately constituted a sort of training ground where men at the start of their career might exercise themselves under the stimulus and guidance of others more expert than themselves. Moreover, in certain periods the academies promoted by the most important members of the sacred college permitted the transmission of messages whose political significance, though not overtly expressed, could not fail to be understood by an audience skilled in grasping the most obscurely worded allusions – nor to have wider repercussions on public opinion.

This dual role was performed throughout its brief existence by the Accademia dei Virtuosi, about which it would be desirable to possess

[10] For further information on the Accademia degli Umoristi see L. Alemanno, 'L'Accademia degli Umoristi', *Roma moderna e contemporanea*, 3 (1995), pp. 97–120; for the academy of Cardinal Cobelluzzi and the figure of Gramigna see S. Jucci, 'La trattatistica sul segretario tra la fine del Cinquecento e il primo ventennio del Seicento', ibid., pp. 81–96, esp. p. 93, n. 42 and p. 95, n. 50; and for the academy of Cardinal Cinzio Aldobrandini, see A. Personeni, *Notizie genealogiche, storiche, critiche e letterarie del cardinale Cinzio Personeni da Ca' Passero Aldobrandini*, Bergamo, 1786. Lastly, a useful overview, if somewhat outdated, may be found in R. De Mattei, 'Dispute filosofico-politiche nelle Accademie romane del Seicento', *Studi romani*, 9 (1961), pp. 148–67.

[11] For further information on the Accademia dei Desiosi and on the work of Agostino Mascardi, see R. Merolla, 'L'Accademia dei Desiosi', *Roma moderna e contemporanea*, 3 (1995), pp. 121–55.

more than the scant information currently available from the Roman *Avvisi*. It is not yet known, for instance, whether the original idea for the Accademia was Cardinal Ludovisi's own or was suggested by the Bolognese prelate Giambattista Agucchi, trusted counsellor of the Ludovisi and correspondent of Galileo between 1611 and 1613, who welcomed the stimulus represented by the new science and whose interest in art has earned him a place in the history of art criticism.[12] It is clear, however, that the Accademia dei Virtuosi had political and moral aims concerned with the foundation of a 'Christian' political system: aims different from those pursued in Cobelluzzi's academy, or again from the interests cultivated later under Cardinal Maurizio of Savoy. For with the demise of the Platonic outlook typical of Humanism, but still implicit in the addresses of Gramigna and Mascardi mentioned earlier, the members of the Accademia dei Virtuosi placed great weight on religious values inspired by the Holy Scriptures, in accordance with a tendency current throughout Europe in this phase of the Counter-Reformation. Devoid of its Platonic overtones, Gramigna's exhortation that the sovereign 'should always look heavenwards in contemplation' now translated itself into a form of political practice or 'reason of state' firmly grounded in the Bible, particularly in the Old Testament. And though the academicians continued to address the daily problems of political activity and life at court, which as is well known was far from tranquil, they now became more interested in those sudden shocks and 'turns of fortune' among the highest political echelons which seem to become more frequent in the first and second decades of the seventeenth century. These changes were in part provoked by groups or factions capable of disgracing ministers and favourites in the eyes of the sovereign, with frequently drastic consequences both for the individuals in question and for their extended network of associates and dependents. Another fundamental, if not the sole determining, factor was the question of the sovereign's 'absolute' will: it seemed more than ever important to consider ways of ensuring that this did not degenerate into dangerous willfulness or blatant tyranny.[13]

---

[12] For further information on Agucchi see the article on him by R. Zapperi and I. Toesca in *DBI*, vol. I, pp. 504–6; see also M. Bucciantini, 'Teologia e Nuova Filosofia. Galileo, Federico Cesi, Giovambattista Agucchi e la discussione sulla fluidità e corruttibilità del cielo', in *Sciences et religions de Copernic à Galilée (1540–1610). Actes du colloque international organisé par l'Ecole française de Rome..., Rome 12–14 décembre 1996*, Rome, 1999, pp. 411–42.

[13] For a general survey of the political background to these discussions see R. Bireley, *The Counter-Reformation Prince. Antimachiavellianism or Catholic Statecraft in Early Modern Europe*, Chapel Hill, NC, 1990. For an account of the Spanish political situation in particular see F. Benigno, *L'ombra del re. Ministri e lotta politica nella Spagna del Seicento*,

How else is one to interpret the session of 7 July 1621, the first of the meetings held at the Palazzo Quirinale, in which no less than twelve cardinals intervened, and in which Monsignor De Pretis, a member of the curia and of the Ludovisi circle, and at this time also an Abbreviator, 'gave a learned and useful address, based on the Testament of King David [1 Kings 2:1–9], on the question of whether and in what way vengeance might be permitted a prince'? Behind this address there certainly lay recent events in France and Spain (the fall of the celebrated Marshal of Ancre, Concino Concini, and his condemnation to death by Louis XIII in 1617, and the fall of the Duke of Lerma two years later). Yet it is still more likely to have been triggered by the very recent fall of the Duke of Ossuna, which had occurred on 7 April of that same year, when legal proceedings against him had commenced. The topic was a highly controversial one and was discussed at length after De Pretis' address by Girolamo Aleandro the younger, then secretary to Cardinal Bandini, an intimate of Ludovisi's, and two disputants, 'il Pollino' (possibly the Florentine man of letters Alessandro Pollini, who in 1644 was a member of the Congregazione dell'Indice) and the better-known Francesco Ingoli, who the following year became secretary to the newly instituted Congregazione di Propaganda Fide, who condemned hatred and revenge, 'although', as the *Avvisi* point out, '[vengeance] is allowed a prince as a means of avoiding still greater scandals, as in David's case for the sake of justice and universal peace'.[14]

This justification of vengeance is frequently found in treatises arguing the 'legitimacy' of the principle of 'reason of state', a principle, however, which might here seem all too transparent an expression of support for monarchic absolutism, or for Spain, in accordance with a general tendency under the Ludovisi papacy. Understandably enough, this position did not receive unanimous support in the highly diversified political context of Rome, as is shown by the fact that not long afterwards the Accademia dei Virtuosi was (perhaps rather too openly) attacked by Mascardi. In a second address, entitled 'How a Courtier Should not be Pained to See the Ignorant Fare Better at Court than the Learned, or the Plebeian than the Noble', given before the Accademia dei Desiosi (headed by Cardinal Maurizio of Savoy, who was moreover currently the co-protector of the French crown), Mascardi was especially critical of those who employed 'the vainest of conceits' to express 'paradoxes representing a danger to morals'. He particularly mentions a person who

Venice, 1992; A. Feros, 'Twin Souls: Monarchs and Favourites in Early Seventeenth-Century Spain', in R. L. Kagan and G. Parker (eds.), *Spain, Europe and the Atlantic World. Essays in Honour of John H. Elliott*, Cambridge, 1995, pp. 27–47.
[14] See the entry for 7 July in *Avvisi dell'anno 1621*, f. 12v.

had 'made every effort to convince those attending an esteemed public assembly that vengeance was necessary to a prince, citing as his authority the Testament of David – a wicked piece of foolery, this, than which the present age has witnessed nothing more despicable and devoid of sense'.[15]

Despite the dangers implicit in such topics, however, the sessions at the Palazzo Quirinale were evidently not always so turbulent. For on the following 4 August the erudite Venetian Monsignor Bianchi gave a learned oration on a verse from Ecclesiasticus 7:5, 'Noli velle videri sapiens coram Principe' (read 'penes Regem'), which was also fraught with implications regarding relations between the sovereign and the men of letters at his court. Among those who spoke after Bianchi was a gentleman from the court of the cardinal-nephew, the reasonably well-known Marinian poet Girolamo Preti who 'authoritatively satisfied both sides in the question' by considering both good and evil monarchs.[16]

These subjects were taken up again and (so to speak) 'modulated' in meetings held the following year. On 8 June 1622, for instance, Monsignor Muzio De Rosis, later Bishop of Teano, revived the classic theme of adulation, while on 13 July a certain Monsignor Figgino considered that of curiosity. Lastly, on 7 September the better-known Jesuit Famiano Strada, author of a book on the war in Flanders, focused the discussion on the biblical story of David and Goliath, one much performed in the theatre of the Company of Jesus. This permitted Strada, in addressing the question as to whether the young biblical hero had acted through prudence or arrogant ambition, to exalt the cardinal virtue of the Counter-Reformation, Prudence, 'arguing from Scripture'.[17] Only Monsignor Montevecchio, in an address on the verse 'Cor regis in manu Domini' (Proverbs 21:1) held on 27 July, seems explicitly to have addressed the political and religious subject of a sovereign's power and responsibilities. This topic was again discussed the following year, 1623, in meetings held on 14 and 28 June, not long before the death of Gregory XV on 8 July. In both these meetings the speakers attempted to define the virtues requisite in a sovereign, such as beneficence, of which Monsignor De Rosis found an example in the life of Solomon, and magnanimity, illustrated by the Jesuit Tarquinio Gallucci before a large group of Cardinals, which according to the *Avvisi* included Maurizio of Savoy.[18]

---

[15] For Mascardi's position see his *Prose vulgari*, Venice, 1630, pp. 14–31, esp. p. 24.

[16] See *Avvisi dell'anno 1621*, ff. 76v–77r (4 August), and for the later meetings ff. 146r (1 September) and 288r (20 October).

[17] *Avvisi dell'anno 1622*, vol. I, f. 435r (8 June); vol. II, f. 43v (13 July); f. 201v (7 September).

[18] Ibid., vol. I, f. 81v (27 July); and *Avvisi dell'anno 1623*, f. 445v (14 June) and f. 492v (28 June).

On close examination, it is clear that in the course of its various meetings the Accademia dei Virtuosi may be said to have sketched out or even carefully outlined the various chapters of a short but substantial treatise on the figure of the prince and the court. This included subjects such as princely revenge (treated negatively), relations between the prince and his courtiers and counsellors, the obedience binding the 'king's heart' to the divine will, and lastly the virtues required in a monarch, identified as beneficence and magnanimity. Interspersed with such discussions were reflections on court life, discussed indirectly through reference to the *topoi* of good and ill fortune, adulation, curiosity and prudence. This series of discussions was moreover based on the authority of Scripture, a tendency widely echoed in contemporary political and religious tracts, especially where the power of the sovereign was concerned. This was only to be expected in Reformed Europe, reference to Scripture having been one of the fundamental features of the political theology of Calvin and Luther, as it was later an essential factor in defining the political aims of the Huguenots during the religious wars in France as well as in the political and confessional struggles between Protestants and Catholics in the sixteenth and seventeenth centuries. Yet it was also the case in certain far-from-marginal areas of Catholic politics,[19] where reference to Scripture expressed the wish to sever all ties with the classic matrix of Renaissance politics, and especially to deny all Machiavellianism and the theory of 'reason of state'.[20]

In 1589, the year which also saw the publication of Botero's *Ragion di Stato*, the eminent scholar and exegete Benito Arias Montano, librarian of the Escorial and editor of the Antwerp Bible under the auspices of Philip II, had produced a powerful instance of this kind of tract in his *De optimo imperio, sive in lib. Josuae commentarium*. This was followed in 1592 by *De varia republica, sive commentaria in librum Judicum* by the same author. Finally, in 1615 a less well-known political author, François Regeau, had published *Leges politicae ex Sacrae Scripturae libris collectae*, a sort of anthology of verses from the Bible either explicitly 'political' in meaning or susceptible of a political interpretation.[21] In the same year Paolo Giuseppe Meroni, a Milanese cleric resident in Rome, dedicated a commentary on Psalm 145 'ad aulicos et principes', later supplementing it with a series of 'exercitationes' on the subject of the ideal prince, identified, through

---

[19] See the essays in G. Bedouelle and B. Roussel (eds.), *Le Temps des Réformes et la Bible*, Paris, 1989, and J.-R. Armogathe (ed.), *Le Grand Siècle et la Bible*, Paris, 1989.

[20] See note 13 above, but also R. De Mattei, *Il pensiero politico italiano nell'età della Controriforma*, vols. I–II, Milan and Naples, 1982–4.

[21] On Montano see esp. B. Rekers, *Benito Arias Montano (1527–1598)*, London and Leiden, 1972.

a reading of Psalm 100, with the figure of David. When this commentary appeared in 1637 it caught the attention of Gabriel Naudé, then in Italy as the secretary, librarian and trusted counsellor of Cardinal Giovan Francesco Guidi di Bagno – a fact that shows how, in addition to countering the debate on 'reason of state', this kind of discussion also had links with the sceptical and libertine trends of which Naudé was an exponent.[22] Indeed, in the Guidi, Barberini or Chigi libraries tracts on 'reason of state' by Botero, Naudé or Scipione Chiaramonti might easily be found alongside the works of politico-biblical exegesis just mentioned, or others such as *Hieropoliticon, sive institutionis politicae a Sacris Scripturis depromptae libri tres* (1625), by the Jesuit Giovanni Stefano Menochio, who held several important posts in the Company, or *Regnum Dei seu Dissertationes in libros Regum* (1650), by another, perhaps more famous Jesuit, Father Nicolas Caussin, confessor to Louis XIII.[23] Nor is this trend limited to the political and religious climate of the 1620s and 1630s: it continues up to the end of the century and in Catholicism leads not only to the development of the scripturally based political theology of the Jansenists, as in Nicole's *Essais de morale* and Duguet's *Traité de l'éducation d'un prince*, but also to an opposed and (so to speak) orthodox celebration of monarchic absolutism, as in Bossuet's *Politique tirée des propres paroles de l'Ecriture sainte.*[24]

This is the context in which the tracts written in these years return, with still greater urgency, to the subject of the court, perceived no longer – or not only – as the 'stage' for individual and collective forms of behaviour or courtly rituals and hierarchies, but also as a political motor or 'theatre'. As with the figure of the monarch, an effort is made to define the image of a 'Christian' court, on lines derived from the Scriptures. The question

---

[22] On Paolo Giuseppe Meroni and his works (*Ad Aulicos et Principes Commentarii in Psalmum CXLV*, Lyon, Sumptibus Horatij Cardon, 1615, and *Ad Aulam Davidicam in Psalmo Centesimo descriptam Exercitationes sive de optimo principe liber unus*, Rome, Stephanus Paulinus excudebat, 1637) see T. Bozza, *Scrittori politici italiani dal 1550 al 1650*, Rome, 1949, pp. 125–6, 180. On the interest in Naudé aroused by Meroni's second book, see P. Wolfe (ed.), *Lettres de Gabriel Naudé à Jacques Dupuy (1632–1652)*, Lealta, Canada, 1982, p. 37 (letter written at Rieti, 10 October 1637).

[23] For further information on Giovanni Stefano Menochio see C. Sommervogel, *Bibliothèque de la Compagnie de Jésus*, vol. v, Brussels and Paris, 1894, cols. 948–55. Menochio was also the author of *Institutiones Oeconomicae ex Sacris litteris depromptae libri duo*, Lyon, Ex officina Rovilliana, 1627, which was dedicated to Cardinal Ludovisi. On Caussin, in addition to Sommervogel, *Bibliothèque*, vol. II, Brussels and Paris, 1891, cols. 902–27, see M. Fumaroli, *L'âge de l'éloquence. Rhétorique et 'res literaria' de la Renaissance au seuil de l'époque classique*, Geneva, 1980, esp. pp. 279–98.

[24] On the use of the Bible by Nicole and Duguet see M. Rosa, 'Il "cuore del re": l' "Institution d'un prince" del giansenista Duguet', in A. Contini and M. G. Parri (eds.), *Il Granducato di Toscana e i Lorena nel secolo XVIII. Incontro di studio 22–24 settembre 1994*, Florence, 1999, pp. 385–416. On the biblical inspiration of Bossuet's *Politique* see the critical edition by J. Le Brun, Geneva, 1967, esp. pp. xxv–xxvi.

was addressed in 1630 by a well-known 'political' Jesuit, Adam Contzen, confessor to Maximilian I of Bavaria, in his *Daniel, sive de statu, vita, virtute Aulicorum atque Magnatum*.[25] Contzen, however, was anticipated by another Jesuit, that same Father Caussin mentioned earlier, whose *La Cour sainte ou l'Institution chrestienne des grands*, first published in 1624, became a kind of best-seller, going through no less than thirteen editions by 1638. Caussin's target was not 'reason of state' itself, but an opponent which at that time and for long afterwards was considered a still greater peril, because of the insidious manner in which it had penetrated the citadel of faith and Christian morality: Christian Stoicism, whose main champion in Europe was Justus Lipsius and which had met such widespread sympathy in French political and philosophical circles in the early decades of the seventeenth century.[26] It was not so much a question of providing rules of behaviour as of finding a means of 'controlling the passions'. For if the anti-Stoical polemic, in which Caussin and other Jesuits were now front-line combatants, aimed at defeating libertinism, it also aimed at suppressing a more radical underlying tendency towards atheism. After a temporary lapse, owing to fierce opposition from this vehement group of apologists, Stoicism, of a more or less rigorous kind, revived in the 1660s, when it was attacked less by the Jesuits than by Augustinians such as Malebranche and Jansenists such as Nicole. Nor is it a coincidence (to return to the specific context of Rome) that Monsignor Giuseppe Maria Suares devoted the solemn opening session of Christina of Sweden's Royal Academy, founded at Palazzo Riario in 1674, to 'moral philosophy', or that the two disputants who also spoke on that occasion, Fathers Nicolò Pallavicino and Antonio Cottone, debated the question 'which of the two philosophical sects, the Stoic or the Epicurean', had been 'a greater opponent of true philosophy'; or again that both reached the same conclusions, namely that, of the two, Stoicism was in greater conflict with the truth of Christianity.[27]

Whereas the Royal Academy founded by Christina at the close of the seventeenth century belongs to another phase of European and Roman culture, the Accademia dei Virtuosi at the Palazzo Quirinale represents an

[25] See Sommervogel, *Bibliothèque*, vol. II, cols. 1399–403.

[26] See esp. Julien-Eymard d'Angers, OFM Cap., 'Sénèque et le stoïcisme dans la "Cour sainte" du jésuite Nicolas Caussin (1583–1651)', *Revue des Sciences Religieuses*, 28 (1954), pp. 258–85; V. Kapp, 'La théologie des réalités terrestres dans la Cour sainte de N. Caussin', in *Les jésuites parmi les hommes au XVIIe et XVIIIe siècle*, Clermont-Ferrand, 1987, pp. 141–51. For a more general account see G. Oestreich, *Neostoicism and the Early Modern State*, Cambridge, 1982.

[27] See R. Stephan, 'A Note on Christina and her Academies', in M. von Platen (ed.), *Queen Christina of Sweden. Documents and Studies*, Stockholm, 1966, pp. 365–71; and also the essays in *Cristina di Svezia. Scienza ed alchimia nella Roma barocca*, Bari, 1990.

interesting transition from debates concerning the figure of the prince and the court, tied to late sixteenth-century political and cultural concerns with the 'conservation' of the state and the definition of a problematic court etiquette, to a climate of opinion reflecting the most drastic political events and manifold cultural needs of the early seventeenth century in Europe. Alongside positions such as those of the Accademia dei Virtuosi, clearly inspired by the Bible in their search for moral and religious guarantees essential to enlighten the actions of the sovereign and to mitigate, if not to prevent, the harshness of political practice, other positions, such as those not long afterwards expressed by Naudé in his *Considérations politiques sur les coups d'état*, follow in the wake of the debate on 'reason of state', in an attempt to establish the origin and meaning of such *coups d'état*, or daring and extraordinarily effective assaults on common rites which sovereigns were obliged to perform for the public good.

Conflicting interpretations of the *Considérations*, according to which it either carries Machiavelli's ideas to extreme conclusions, or else aims to outline a necessary morality of political action, only confirm the text's complexity.[28] It is important to point out here that, though published in Rome in 1639, the book arose out of discussions that took place nearly ten years earlier between the author and his patron, Cardinal Guidi di Bagno, during the journey that brought Guidi back to Italy at the end of his term as nuncio in Paris. It should furthermore be stressed that while the later phases of these discussions, and the reasons for the delay in publication of the *Considérations*, remain somewhat obscure, the text is the product of the same situation that fostered the debates of the Accademia dei Virtuosi at the Palazzo Quirinale. For though the conclusions reached in the *Considérations*, and the routes by which they are arrived at, are different, what the book has in common with the academicians who gathered under Cardinal Ludovisi is the background against which the effective political action of the sovereign was considered, a background characterized by conspiracies by various factions and assaults on the power of the monarch; or by the general effort which those in power had made or were making to construct a political reality. For earlier sovereigns had made wise choices at the right time: choices some of which had entailed violence, such as the execution of Concini by order of Louis XIII, whereas others had been more peaceful, such as Clovis' conversion to Christianity, an event foreshadowing Henri IV's more recent conversion.

---

[28] See the remarks by G. Lutz, *Kardinal Giovanni Francesco Guidi di Bagno. Politik und Religion im Zeitalter Richelieus und Urbans VIII*, Tübingen, 1971, pp. 538–49. On Naudé see L. Bianchi, *Rinascimento e libertinismo. Studi su Gabriel Naudé*, Naples, 1996; and on the *Considérations* in particular see L. Marin's introductory essay 'Pour une théorie baroque de l'action politique' in his recent edition, Paris, 1988.

Thus the political reflections of the Virtuosi as well as those of Naudé reveal the shadows of recent events. In the former instance the events in question were probably those accompanying the fall of the *validos* in Spain between the reigns of Philip III and Philip IV. In the latter a greater role was probably played by events in France, namely those *coups d'état* with which both Naudé and Guidi were familiar, and which had increased the absolute power of the monarch between the death of Henri IV and the end of the regency of Marie de Médicis, partly owing to the growing influence of Richelieu, initially over the young king and his mother, and later over the king and his ministers. Indeed, the *coup* which had attempted to overthrow the powerful Cardinal and minister, but which a change of heart on the part of the king on the *journée des dupes* of 1630 had transformed into a triumph for Richelieu, was probably the episode which prompted Naudé to write the *Considérations*.[29]

However, with regard both to the reflections of the Virtuosi in the Palazzo Quirinale and also to Naudé's *Considérations*, one important thing needs to be borne in mind. Both are closely tied to an oligarchic conception of politics and power, a system driven by the motive power of the sovereign and comprising the reality of the court and the dynamics governing the groups of nobles and factions, as well as clashes between elites within the government. It was thus not solely for reasons of chronology that neither were abreast of the great changes already occurring in European culture and politics at the start of the 1620s, changes that would become still more pronounced in the 1640s. These changes find early expression in Grotius' irenic doctrine of natural law, as put forward in his *De jure belli ac pacis* (1625), and subsequently in that of Pufendorf, as well of course as in Hobbes, all three of whom were inspired by a general vision of the relations among states and by an organic conception of the origin of society, in the wake of the Thirty Years' War and later of the 'revolutions' in Spain, France and England. In other words, the meetings at the Palazzo Quirinale and Naudé's *Considérations* represent a last great wave, which closes an era but does not open a new one, though it continues to find a place in the literature of 'political aphorisms', in the consummate diplomatic skills of the curial 'transactions', and in the interest which

---

[29] Of the numerous studies on these questions, see esp. the following: on Spain, J. Elliott, *The Count-Duke of Olivares: the Statesman in an Age of Decline*, New Haven, 1986; R. A. Stradling, *Philip IV and the Government of Spain 1621–1665*, Cambridge, 1988; Benigno, *L'ombra del re*; on France, in addition to Elliott, *The Count-Duke of Olivares*, see also K. Malettke, 'The Crown, Ministeriat and Nobility at the Court of Louis XIII', in R. G. Asch and A. M. Birke (eds.), *Princes, Patronage and Nobility*, Oxford, 1991, pp. 415–39.

Rome continued to show in this political phase throughout the rest of the century.[30]

TO 'KEEP FUTURE TURNS OF FORTUNE WELL IN MIND...'

Meanwhile, between discussions at the Palazzo Quirinale and Naudé's *Considérations*, it was the harsh conditions at the 'holy' court of Rome which preoccupied those who made up its higher ranks. As much as any other court, it was a theatre in which political enthusiasms might conflict and thus need to be 'controlled'. It was the focus of a system where certain peculiar forms of compensation, namely agreements and exchanges between its higher members over the question of ecclesiastical benefices (a possibility not open to secular courts) attenuated, if they did not entirely do away with, those traumatic falls from grace which were so common at European courts. On the other hand, the principles of celibacy and mobility, deriving from the elective nature of papal monarchy, meant that positions were less stable than under other absolute monarchs in Europe and that posts were more frequently redistributed and structures of patronage continually dismantled and rebuilt.[31]

This situation must soon have occupied the thoughts of the cardinal-nephew Ludovisi under the protective papacy of Gregory XV, which, though marked by political success and intense activity, was not expected to last long owing to the pope's poor health. Ludovico had immediately collected a large number of posts and wealthy ecclesiastical benefices, such as the archbishopric of Bologna, formerly belonging to his uncle Gregory XV; that of *camerlengo*, formerly held by Cardinal Pietro Aldobrandini, the Chancellor and Prefect of Papal Briefs; and various abbacies and priories, which together soon brought in over 100,000 *scudi* per year, a sum further added to by income from temporal sources. At the same time, the rise of the Ludovisi among the papal families had rapidly been consolidated by the purchase in 1621 of the duchy of Fiano, for which they paid the Sforza 200,000 *scudi*, and in 1622 that of Zagarolo, for which the Colonna received 860,000 *scudi*. After the purchase of Villa

---

[30] For an account of the political and religious situation at the end of the seventeenth century see B. Neveu, 'Culture religieuse et aspirations réformistes à la cour d'Innocent XI', now in his *Erudition et Religion aux XVIIe et XVIIIe siècles*, Paris, 1994, pp. 235–76. See also B. Pellegrino (ed.), *Riforme, religione e politica durante il pontificato di Innocenzo XII (1691–1700). Atti del convegno di studio (Lecce 11–13 dicembre 1991)*, Galatina, 1994.

[31] See Visceglia, 'Burocrazia, mobilità sociale e *patronage*', esp. pp. 43ff., where numerous studies are discussed, among which the most pertinent in the present context is W. Reinhard, *Freunde und Kreaturen. 'Verflechtung' als Konzept zur Erforschung historischer Führungsgruppen. Römische Oligarchie um 1600*, Munich, 1979.

Altemps at Frascati, the Ludovisi built their villa near the Pincian Gate
in Rome, where they began to pursue those activities of collecting and
patronage (to the benefit of artists such as Domenichino and Guercino,
and writers such as Marino and Tassoni) which distinguish the Ludovisi
era in between those dominated by the Borghese and the Barberini.[32]

Ludovico nevertheless had to do more, and soon, in order to render
his already prestigious personal position more secure, given the imminent
inevitability of a turn of fortune that closely concerned him. The examples to follow among the cardinal-nephews or papal families under previous popes were numerous. The diplomatic skills of Cardinal
Pietro Aldobrandini, for example, had culminated in the marriage
of Margherita, great-niece of Clement VIII, to the Duke of Parma,
Ranuccio Farnese. The different outlook of Paul V, on the other hand,
had secured the Borghese the rank of 'great and wealthy private gentlemen', capable of 'rivalling and even surpassing the Colonna and
the Orsini'.[33] The easiest and most practical of the paths open to
the Ludovisi was offered by family ties, within Rome and the Curia,
which would in time transform themselves into political alliances and
entourages. It was vital above all to secure the support of the still-
influential Aldobrandini. This was obtained first through the marriage
of Ippolita, daughter of Gregory XV's brother, to Giovan Giorgio
Aldobrandini, nephew of Clement VIII. Then, in June 1623, just before the death of Gregory XV, Ludovico ceded the post of *camerlengo*,
formerly held by Pietro Aldobrandini, to Ippolito, another Aldobrandini
cardinal, on extremely advantageous (indeed, as the *Avvisi* point out,
'familial') terms, following Ludovico's inheritance, thanks to his uncle the pope, of a rather meagre benefice from the recently deceased Cardinal of Montalto, nephew of Sixtus V.[34] For Ludovico
such marriage ties and 'exchanging' of benefices might translate into

---

[32] On the family politics of the Ludovisi see Pastor, *Storia dei papi*, vol. XIII, esp. pp. 45–52.
On the Ludovisi as collectors and patrons of the arts see A. A. Amadio, 'La villa Ludovisi
e la collezione di sculture', in A. Giuliano (ed.), *La collezione Boncompagni Ludovisi.
Algardi, Bernini e la fortuna dell'antico*, Venice, 1992, pp. 9–17. For information, in addition to that supplied by Pastor, on the benefices held by Ludovico as cardinal-nephew
and redistributed after his death, see W. Reinhard, 'Nepotismus. Der Funktionswandel
einer papstgeschichtlichen Konstanten', *Zeitschrift für Kirchengeschichte*, 86 (1975),
pp. 145–85, esp. p. 173.

[33] W. Reinhard, *Papstfinanz und Nepotismus unter Paul V. (1605–1621). Studien und Quellen
zur Struktur und zu quantitativen Aspekten des päpstlichen Herrschaftssystems*, Stuttgart,
1974, p. 157n.

[34] On the marriage alliance between the Ludovisi and the Aldobrandini see Pastor,
Storia dei papi, vol. XIII, pp. 53–55. For another marriage, between Prince Ludovisi,
Ludovico's brother, and the Princess of Venosa, of the Neapolitan family of the
Gesualdo, arranged through Cardinal Antonio Caetani, a creature of Gregory XV,

the solid political coin of the support of the cardinals appointed by Clement VIII in the coming conclave, which was full of uncertainties, owing to the reform of the electoral procedures following the bull expressly issued on the subject by Gregory XV immediately after his election.

This atmosphere of expectancy produced a short but remarkable political text, entitled *Ricordi dati da Gregorio XV al cardinale Lodovisio suo nipote* (Memoir Addressed by Gregory XV to his Nephew Cardinal Lodovisio), which aroused considerable interest in this period, as is shown by the numerous manuscript copies held in libraries both in Italy and abroad. The *Ricordi* are unusual in that, while a large number of tracts exist dealing with the best way of embarking on a career in the curia, texts instructing how best to act in view of the frequent 'turns of fortune' occurring in the theatre of Rome, were, as far as we can tell today, much less common.[35] One text that might perhaps be compared to Gregory XV's *Ricordi* is the letter sent by Cardinal Pietro Aldobrandini from Ravenna on 22 August 1607 to his sister Olimpia, though this is a private letter and so not destined for general circulation.[36] Moreover, in this particular instance the 'turn of fortune' in question was not anticipated but had already taken place, for the purpose of the letter was to console Olimpia during an illness, attributed to a bout of 'melancholy', occurring two years after the death of Clement VIII, when Pietro had already left Rome for his diocesan see in Ravenna. Closer to the *Ricordi*, in both composition and aim, is the memoir addressed by the Farnese pope Paul III to his cardinal-nephew Alessandro. This may be dated between 1546 and 1549, and was probably quite widely circulated after the pope's death. This Farnese memoir has various things in common with the *Ricordi*, such as their shared origin in conversations between the respective pope and nephew; the emphasis placed in both cases on the bond uniting the two; the insistence on the necessity that the

---

see A. M. Visceglia, '"La Giusta statera de' porporati". Sulla composizione e rappresentazione del Sacro Collegio nella prima metà del Seicento', *Roma moderna e contemporanea*, 4 (1996), pp. 167–211, esp. p. 177. For Ludovico's ceding of the post of *camerlengo* to Cardinal Ippolito Aldobrandini see *Avvisi di Roma dell'anno 1623*, f. 451r (n.d.).

35 Numerous manuscripts are mentioned in Pastor, *Storia dei papi*, vol. XIII, p. 59n. Quotations are taken from the copy in BAV, Barb. Lat. 4632. The text has received no close study since Pastor (pp. 59–67). On tracts concerning court careers in Rome, see the survey by Pellegrini and Visceglia, mentioned above, and also the recent edition by C. Mozzarelli of G. F. Commendone, *Discorso sopra la corte di Roma*, Rome, 1996.

36 ASV, Fondo Borghese, s. IV, n. 293, fasc. 2, *Lettera del cardinale Pietro Aldobrandini a sua sorella Donna Olimpia scritta da Ravenna li 22 agosto 1607*. I wish to thank Giampiero Brunelli for telling me of this letter.

nephew should dedicate himself with renewed vigour to the service of
the Church after the death of the pope; the cardinal-nephew's behaviour
towards other cardinals, both those appointed by his uncle and those appointed by his predecessors; and a common concern for the future of the
family.[37]

Whatever the model adopted, Pastor argued on the basis of internal
evidence that the text of the *Ricordi* originated in conversations actually
held in April 1622 between Gregory XV, already in poor health, and
his nephew, and that it acquired its final form a year later, when a further decline in the pope's health increased the urgency of the situation.
The person responsible may have been the above-mentioned Monsignor
Agucchi, although the text is written in the first person, and reads as
though Ludovico himself were recounting his memories of his uncle as
he recalled them.[38] However, various aspects of the text itself and its
overall tone rather suggest that the *Ricordi* were composed, and above
all circulated, not in anticipation of the conclave following the death
of Gregory XV, but immediately after the election of Urban VIII. This
would make them less an attempt on the part of the cardinal-nephew to
influence a situation which he felt unable fully to control, than a declaration *post-eventum* (though expressed in the not uncommon form of
premonitory pieces of 'advice') of good intentions and willingness to be
of service, not only to the new pope and nephew, but also to the new
entourage of counsellors, and more generally to that complex network of
allies and dependents which the turns of fortune in the upper ranks of the
curia were rapidly reconstructing on new foundations. Ludovisi was thus
undoubtedly aiming at defending himself from the danger of a resounding
fall by seeking a discreet form of alliance with an adverse reality. In the
Ricordi this position is marked not only by scriptural arguments such
as were systematically employed at the meetings of the Accademia dei
Virtuosi, but also by an insistent invocation of Christian Stoicism, and
sometimes even by references to the most impartial, though here duly
Christianized, arguments of 'reason of state', in order to 'keep future
turns of fortune well in mind'. Its singular reworking of all these elements
suggests that the aims of the *Ricordi* were not simply of an immediately
practical nature with respect to a transitional phase between two papacies,
but also those of a more intimate and intense meditation on individual

[37] The text of Paul III's memoir is reproduced in C. Robertson, *"Il gran cardinale"
Alessandro Farnese: Patron of the Arts*, New Haven and London, 1992, pp. 292–3. On
the family politics of the Farnese see G. Fragnito, 'Il nepotismo farnesiano tra ragioni
di Stato e ragioni di Chiesa', in *Continuità e discontinuità nella storia politica, economica e
religiosa. Studi in onore di Aldo Stella*, Vicenza, 1993, pp. 117–25.

[38] See Pastor, *Storia dei papi*, vol. XIII, p. 59.

destiny and the drama of power in a moment of turning fortune – which is the secret of the text's subsequent popularity as a concise handbook of political and moral conduct.

In the first part of the *Ricordi* there is evident insistence on the reform of the conclave, with regard to which the pope counters all insidious but still obvious attempts at nullification by stating that he has placed his duty to God before all family interest (limitations on the effective sphere of influence of the most important cardinals also meant limitations on the cardinal-nephew's power to interpose between parties). Yet still more significant, in this first part of the text, is its careful consideration of the difficult situation in which the cardinal-nephew would find himself should the new pope show him 'little love'. The abundant advice given on the subject may be summarized under the dual recommendations of 'honest dissimulation', guided by a 'moderate and prudentially governed temperament', and the invitation to leave Rome for his diocese of Bologna, a 'holy resolution' which would enable him to not only to perform a duty, but also to leave 'little room for envy and ill-fortune'.[39] The section which follows, devoted to Ludovico's relations with the other cardinals, is still more important. Here 'dissimulation' seems to become an absolute rule, above all if the cardinals appointed by Gregory XV should prove forgetful of the benefices they have received – since, as the text comments, and not without irony, 'such is the character of this heaven, so friendly towards current interests and so opposed to the gratitude of the past, that it would be a wonder if they behaved differently'.[40] This cruel analysis of the situation broadens to include political considerations when the text deals with the relations binding the cardinal-nephew and various sovereigns, once the former's power has been drastically reduced by the death of his uncle. 'Delicate services' would then compensate for the loss of authority, thus allowing Ludovico to continue to take part in diplomatic negotiations – for which he had shown such skill under Gregory XV – but without hampering the political and diplomatic relations of the new papacy, and without showing 'partiality' towards the 'loyalty' or (already well-defined) 'multiple loyalties' towards certain sovereigns whether for the sake of service, duty or interest.[41]

Little distance separates the public and private realms in this work. The latter emerges in passages dealing with concern for the family, especially for the cardinal's younger brother, and for his servants. Important light

---

[39] BAV, Barb. Lat. 4632, *Ricordi dati da Gregorio XV al cardinale Lodovisio suo nipote*, ff. 37r–38r.

[40] Ibid., ff. 38v–39r.

[41] Ibid., f. 39r. On the 'politics of multiple loyalties', see A. Spagnoletti, *Stato, aristocrazie e Ordine di Malta*, Rome and Bari, 1988, p. 4.

is shed on the role played by powerful ministers and favourites in the dynamics of political power and at court in this period by what the *Ricordi* have to say about the presence of a favourite in the cardinal's 'family'. This must absolutely be avoided, as shown by

> the examples offered by Sejanus and freed men in ancient times, without considering the many modern examples before our eyes, because even if it brought no other harm, the court would still consider you a man who allowed himself to be ruled by his own and who was incapable of self-government, and people would approach your favourite rather than you.

This leads in the final pages of the *Ricordi* to a portrait of the ideal 'political' cardinal or prelate of the Counter-Reformation, in whom respect and love are in harmony with one another and pomp and splendour are not dissociated from generous concern for the poor, and in whom 'pleasing affability' is accompanied by 'grave modesty', and this in turn by 'grave courtesy', qualities destined to emerge in 'conversations' with learned and virtuous persons, and which seem to constitute an ideal link between the *Ricordi* and the meetings of the Accademia dei Virtuosi at the Palazzo Quirinale.[42]

Despite all his precautions, however, Ludovico seemed a doomed man once he ceased to be a cardinal-nephew. With the election of Urban VIII he lost control of the situation. Here was a relatively young pope and a new and aggressively ambitious entourage, with the prospect of a long papacy ahead of it. Perhaps the splendid banquets held in Ludovico's villa near the Pincian Gate on 30 August 1623 for Cardinals Capponi, Ubaldini and Ridolfi, and on 4 October for the same company together with Cardinals Dietrichstein and Medici, or again the 'noble cortège' which accompanied him on his way to a papal audience on 30 September (carefully recorded in the *Avvisi*) were intended to conceal the first checks which the cardinal-nephew began to suffer immediately after the election of Urban VIII. Don Camillo Colonna, for instance, soon seized the opportunity to revenge himself at last for the sale to the Ludovisi of the Duchy of Zagarolo, an offence for which Don Camillo's expulsion from Rome, following Ludovico's angry protestations to the pope, was little compensation. Or again, Cardinal Torres, a creature of Gregory XV, acted the turncoat and abandoned the Ludovisi for the Barberini 'faction', to avail himself, as the *Avvisi* point out, of more than he had managed to obtain under the previous pope.[43]

---

[42] *Ricordi*, ff. 40r and 41r–v.

[43] See *Avvisi dell'anno 1623*, ff. 652r (30 August) and 763v (4 October). For the opposition of Cardinals Ubaldini, Capponi and Medici to the candidacy of Maffeo Barberini during the conclave, see Visceglia, '"La Giusta statera de' porporati"', pp. 192–3. For

This is obviously not the place to consider the final decade of Ludovico's life, during which he either remained at Rome or moved between Rome and his villa at Frascati, in disregard of Gregory XV, who had urged him to move to his bishop's see in Bologna, where he eventually went in 1632 by order of Urban VIII, and where, already failing in health, he died soon afterwards. What is important here is to emphasize that a new era opened in Rome in this period, one in which the centrality of politics, though without entailing any diminution of informative and diplomatic channels, seemed to find different forms of expression from those found in the debates of the early seventeenth century. Scientific interests on the one hand, such as the physical and mathematical pursuits of the Academy of Monsignor Ciampini at the end of the century, and artistic and literary interests on the other, such as those informing a constellation of cardinals' courts and academies linked to, but also independent from, the world of the curia, gradually seem to assume importance in a complex historical period which goes from the age of the Barberini to the 'difficult' decades following the Treaty of Westphalia. Christina of Sweden's Academy constitutes something of an exception in the last three decades of the seventeenth century in Rome. The peculiar tone of Roman culture in the late baroque is set rather by the literary, theatrical and musical meetings organized by Cardinal Giulio Rospigliosi (later Clement IX), or the perhaps still more splendid meetings convened by Cardinal Pietro Ottoboni, nephew of Alexander VIII, as well as by the formation of collections of art-works, especially of antiquities, by cardinals and eminent members of the curia.[44] Against this background the image of the 'world's theatre' fades almost to vanishing-point. It is no coincidence that in a letter written at the start of the 1660s and addressed to Gian Luca Durazzo, formerly Genoese ambassador to France and England, Cardinal Pietro Sforza Pallavicino employs a different image:

> Yet remember that Genoa is not your only fatherland. You are like the rivers, whose fatherland is the bed in which they first spring up. But their universal fatherland is the sea, which is the kingdom of all the waters. Your own fatherland is Genoa, where you were born, but your universal fatherland is Rome, which is the kingdom of all the virtues. The simile is

the offence dealt Ludovico by Don Camillo Colonna and his 'betrayal' by Cardinal Torres, see *Avvisi dell'anno 1623*, ff. 694r–v (n.d.).

44 Stephan, 'A Note on Christina and her Academies'. On the world of art and antiquities in Rome at the end of the seventeenth century see D. Gallo, 'Rome, mythe et réalité pour le citoyen de la République des Lettres', in H. Bots and F. Waquet (eds.), *Commercium litterarium. La communication dans la république des lettres 1600–1750*, Amsterdam and Maarssen, 1994, pp. 191–205.

defective in one thing only: rivers lose their names when they flow into
the sea, whereas in Rome virtue achieves, or else grows in, renown.[45]

It is significant that in the Jesuit's eloquent prose, the dynamic image of
the 'world's theatre', full of dramatic connotations, which the Ludovisi
had appropriated for the purposes of their ambitious political plans in the
militant phase of the Counter-Reformation is replaced by the tranquil
and inviting metaphor of the sea. There is no doubt that this too reflects
a continuing, indeed unbroken, interest in universalism, but the choice
of the one image rather than the other cannot be an arbitrary one. And
behind the substitution of one by the other it is not hard to make out
quite another story.

[45] P. S. Pallavicino, *Lettere . . . Edizione corretta e accresciuta sopra i mss. casanatensi*, Rome,
1848, p. 147 (letter to Marchese Gianluca Durazzo dated 7 June 1662). On the
idea of Rome as a 'common fatherland' see Visceglia, 'Burocrazia, mobilità sociale
e *patronage*', p. 43. For a more general account of the image of Rome, see E. and
J. Garms, 'Mito e realtà di Roma nella cultura europea. Viaggio e idea, immagine e
immaginazione', in C. De Seta (ed.), *Storia d'Italia*, Annali 5, *Il paesaggio*, Turin, 1982,
pp. 561–662; G. Labrot, *L'image de Rome. Une arme pour la Contre-Réforme 1534–1677*,
Seyssel, 1987.

FACTIONS IN THE SACRED COLLEGE IN THE SIXTEENTH AND SEVENTEENTH CENTURIES

MARIA ANTONIETTA VISCEGLIA

For decades, social anthropologists have examined local political conflicts, both in European and more especially in non-European contexts, on a micro-analytical scale in terms of 'factions'. A faction is defined as a non-corporate political group which gathers friends and supporters around an important person, a leader, and enters into conflict with other similar groups in order to control resources and power.[1] More recently, modern historians too have rediscovered the importance of factionalism in the study of political conflict, as part of a general review of the objectives and methods of a political history which favours centrifugal forces, tenacious particularisms and pervasive personal and informal ties, as opposed to the formal use of the modern state paradigm.

Indeed, it can be said that the 'revision' of the traditional concept of the modern state,[2] and the reconsideration of the role of factions, lie at the core of all the basic features unifying the contemporary historiographical debate in Europe; these latter are not seen as archaic forms of socio-political organization, but as political configurations that emerge from the mesh of horizontal and vertical relations, patronage systems and family ties.

The study of factions has recently become an important key to understanding the operation of local power in the early modern age

---

[1] See R. A. Nicholas, 'Faction: A Comparative Analysis', in S. W. Schmidt, L. Guasti, C. H. Landé and J. C. Scott (eds.), *Friends, Followers and Factions. A Reader in Political Clientelism*, Berkeley, Los Angeles and London, 1977, pp. 55–73.

[2] For Italian studies on the 'nature' and evolution of political systems during the early modern age, see E. Fasano Guarini, 'Centro e periferia, accentramento e particolarismi: dicotomia o sostanza degli Stati in Età Moderna?' in G. Chittolini, A. Molho and P. Schiera (eds.), *Origini dello Stato. Processi di formazione statale in Italia fra Medioevo ed Età Moderna*, Bologna, 1994, pp. 147–76, esp. p. 166, translated as 'Center and Periphery' in J. Kirchner (ed.), *The Origins of the State in Italy, 14th–16th Centuries*, Chicago and London, 1995; eadem, '"Etat moderne" et anciens états italiens. Eléments d'histoire comparée', *Revue d'Histoire Moderne et Contemporaine*, 45 (1998) pp. 59–84.

(in feudal contexts, communities and cities and, more generally, in the conflictual relationship between centre and periphery),[3] and has at the same time been used as an interpretative grid for the study of courts.

English-speaking historians have undoubtedly played a major role in orientating debate in this direction.

From J. E. Neale's investigation into competition at the Elizabethan court[4] to more recent studies which have emerged from the revisionist tendency of English historical writing as a whole, the presence of factions has been recognized as a fundamental condition for the working of a political system that, notwithstanding the turmoil caused by the English Civil War, maintained one of its most vital centres in the court both before and after the conflict.[5] We may add that in many ways a

---

[3] On the use of the concept of 'faction' in studies on local power in Italy and more generally in the Mediterranean area, see D. Andreozzi, *Nascita di un disordine. Una famiglia signorile e una valle piacentina tra XV e XVI Secolo*, Milan, 1993, and D. Andreozzi, 'Valli, fazioni, comunità e Stato', *Società e Storia*, 67 (1995) pp. 129–40; G. Delille, 'Storia politica e antropologia: gruppi di potere locale nel Mediterraneo occidentale dal XV al XVII secolo', in M. Minicuci (ed.), 'Riunirsi, riconoscersi, rappresentarsi', *L'Uomo*, 7 (1994), pp. 131–5 and idem, 'Marriage, Faction and Conflict in Sixteenth-Century Italy: An Example and a Few Questions', in T. Dean and K. Lowe (eds.), *Marriage in Italy, 1300–1650*, Cambridge, 1998, pp. 155–73; C. Bitossi, 'Famiglia e fazioni a Genova 1576–1657', *Miscellanea storica ligure*, 2 (1980), pp. 57–135; W. Kaiser, *Marseille au temps des Troubles. 1559–1596. Morphologie sociale et luttes des factions*, Paris, 1992; O. Raggio, *Faide e parentele. Lo Stato genovese visto dalla Fontanabuona*, Turin, 1990; idem, 'Parentele, fazioni e banditi, la Val Fontanabuona tra Cinque e Seicento', in G. Ortalli (ed.), *Bande armate, banditi, banditismo e repressione di giustizia negli Stati europei di Antico Regime*, Rome, 1986; idem, 'Visto dalla periferia. Formazioni politiche di Antico Regime e Stato moderno', in M. Aymard (ed.), *Storia d'Europa*, vol. IV, *L'Età moderna. Secoli XVII–XVIII*, Turin, 1995, pp. 483–527; A. Torre, 'Faide, fazioni e partiti, ovvero la ridefinizione della politica nei feudi imperiali delle Langhe tra Sei e Settecento', *Quaderni storici*, 63 (1986), pp. 775–810.

[4] J. E. Neale, *The Elizabethan Political Scene*, Oxford, 1948.

[5] The essential reference works are: S. Adams, 'Favourites and Factions at the Elizabethan Court', in R. G. Asch and A. M. Birke (eds.), *Princes, Patronage and the Nobility. The Court at the Beginning of the Modern Age*, Oxford, 1991, pp. 265–87; J. Guy (ed.), *The Reign of Elizabeth I. Court and Culture in the Last Decade (1585–1603)*, Cambridge, 1995, especially J. Guy, 'The 1590s: The Second Reign of Elizabeth I', pp. 1–19; S. Adams, 'The Patronage of the Crown in Elizabethan Politics: The 1590s in Perspective', pp. 20–45; P. E. J. Hammer, 'Patronage at Court: The Faction of the Earl of Essex', pp. 65–86; D. Hirst, *Authority and Conflict. England 1603–1658*, London, 1986; L. Levy Peck, 'Court Patronage and Government Policy: The Jacobean Dilemma', in G. Lytle and S. Orgel (eds.), *Patronage in the Renaissance*, Princeton, 1981; eadem, *Court Patronage and Corruption in Early Stuart England*, London, 1991; eadem, *The Mental World of the Jacobean Court*, Cambridge, 1991; R. Shepard, 'Court Factions in Early Modern England', *The Journal of Modern History*, 64 (1992) pp. 721–45; D. Loades, *The Tudor Court*, London, 1986; K. Sharpe (ed.), *Faction and Parliament. Essays on Early Stuart History*, Oxford, 1978; D. Starkey, 'Court, Council, and Nobility in Tudor England', in Asch and Birke (eds.), *Princes, Patronage and the*

similar tendency characterizes Spanish historiography. Re-elaborating the category of 'composite monarchy',[6] Spanish historians have progressed beyond the traditional, formal method used to study the institutions of the *Monarquía* and have investigated the systems of network and patronage which were used to consolidate factions at court both in the *consejos* and in other peripheral bodies.[7] A similar evolution characterized the English and Spanish courts in the sixteenth and seventeenth centuries. There was a transition from a political system in which the sovereign personally balanced the various factions to that of the age of Philip III and James I, in which the sovereign's entourage, and especially his 'favourite', as well as the dominant faction in court, accumulated greater power.[8]

In contrast to this abundance is the present dearth of studies on the Roman court.[9] There are constant references to factional conflict in

Nobility, pp. 175–203; idem (ed.), *The English Court from the Wars of the Roses to the Civil War*, London and New York, 1987.

[6] J. H. Elliott, 'A Europe of Composite Monarchies', *Past and Present*, 137 (1992), pp. 48–71.

[7] An important work dealing with this issue was produced by a group coordinated by J. Martínez Millán, *Instituciones y élites de poder en la Monarquía Hispana durante el siglo XVI*, Madrid, 1992; idem (ed.), *La corte de Felipe II*, Madrid, 1994; idem (ed.), *Felipe II (1527–1598). Europa y la Monarquía Católica de Felipe II*, Madrid, 1998, vols. I–IV. For the age of Philip II, see also E. Belenguer Cebrià (ed.), *Felipe II y el Mediterráneo*, Madrid, 1999, in particular vol. II, *La nobleza y la corte*, pp. 17–138; vol. III, *La corte y su entorno político*, pp. 15–193; J. M. Boyden, *The Courtier and the King: Ruy Gómez de Silva, Philip II and the Court of Spain*, Berkeley, Los Angeles and London, 1995; H. Kamen, *Spain 1469–1714. A Society of Conflict*, London and New York, 1991; M. Rivero Rodríguez, *Felipe II y el gobierno de Italia*, Madrid, 1998. Regarding the earlier phase, significant references to the relations between factions in the courts of Madrid and Italy can be found in C. J. Hernando Sánchez, *Castilla y Nápoles en el siglo XVI. El virrey Pedro de Toledo. Linaje, estado y cultura (1532–1553)*, Salamanca, 1994; M. J. Rodríguez-Salgado, 'The Court of Philip II of Spain', in Asch and Birke (eds.), *Princes, Patronage and the Nobility*, pp. 205–44.

[8] For the Spanish court following the death of Philip II, see F. Benigno, *L'ombra del re. Ministri e lotta politica nella Spagna del Seicento*, Venice, 1992, pp. 16–17; for the English court after the death of Elizabeth, besides the works by Levy Peck mentioned above, see S. Adams, 'Foreign Policy and the Parliaments of 1621 and 1624', in Sharpe (ed.), *Faction and Parliament*, pp. 139–74; R. G. Asch, 'The Revival of Monopolies: Court and Patronage during the Personal Rule of Charles I, 1629–40', in Asch and Birke (eds.), *Princes, Patronage and Nobility*, pp. 357–92; N. Cuddy, 'The Revival of Entourage: the Bedchamber of James I, 1603–1625', in Starkey (ed.), *The English Court*, pp. 173–225; D. Hirst, 'Court, Country and Politics before 1629', in Sharpe (ed.), *Faction and Parliament*, pp. 105–37; K. Sharpe, 'The Image of Virtue: The Court and the Household of Charles I, 1625–1642', in Starkey (ed.), *The English Court*, pp. 226–60.

[9] For an approach to the social history of the Roman court that also addresses the patronage system and the mechanisms through which groups and individuals aggregated see W. Reinhard, *Freunde und Kreaturen: 'Verflechtung' als Konzept zur Erforschung historischer Führungsgruppen. Römische Oligarchie um 1600*, Munich, 1979; idem, 'Papal Power

nineteenth-century political and diplomatic historiography, both in the work of Ranke (who is still the obligatory point of departure for any study of the Roman court from a political point of view) and in the writings of papal historians with a strong ecclesiastical or confessional inspiration, especially Ludwig von Pastor in his *Geschichte der Päpste*.[10] The representatives of the European powers in Rome and the papal families were the principal centres of factional aggregation, and the preparations for the election of a new pope represented the most acute period of political conflict. Conclaves were battles which had consequences for Rome, Italy, Catholic Europe and beyond. Political and diplomatic historians have devoted attention and space to the Roman factions, but their moralistic judgments of factional conflict, which they perceived as base political in-fighting, led them to describe factions as a static reality, closed circles featuring only a few players whose family, social and patronal ties with the external world were therefore often undervalued. According to this view, the history of Roman factions proved that only the characters, not the roles, changed, and, as these were all curial dynasties even the names often remained identical.[11]

My aim is to reconsider this issue over a given time period and to portray the vision that contemporaries had of Roman factions and the way in which they were represented, as well as to investigate the type of political culture that developed out of them. Moreover, it is interesting to analyse the institutional and regulatory steps that were taken in order to regulate conflicts among factions over papal elections during the process of renewal of the Roman church in the sixteenth and seventeenth centuries.

Thus I shall demonstrate that factions were neither a static reality nor a source of perennial political instability, but rather dynamic aggregations whose political value must be defined in relation to a set of variables: the influence and ability of external powers to shape alliances within the

and Family Strategy in the Sixteenth and Seventeenth Centuries', in Asch and Birke (eds.), *Princes, Patronage and Nobility*, pp. 329–56; R. Ago, *Carriere e clientele nella Roma barocca*, Rome and Bari, 1990; I. Fosi, *All'ombra dei Barberini. Fedeltà e servizio nella Roma barocca*, Rome, 1997.

[10] L. Ranke, *The Ecclesiastical and Political History of the Popes of Rome during the Sixteenth and Seventeenth Centuries*, London, 1840 (original edn *Die römischen Päpste, ihre Kirche und ihr Staat im 16. und 17. Jahrhundert*, Leipzig, 1836); L. von Pastor, *Storia dei papi*, vols. I–XL (original edn *Geschichte der Päpste seit dem Ausgang des Mittelalters*, Freiburg im Breisgau, 1899–1907).

[11] Petruccelli della Gattina pointed out that 'Dans les conclaves, les personnages changent, mais il n'y a de changé que cela, car les astuces, les intrigues, les passions en mouvement peuvent former des groupes et des figures diverses mais elles sont toujours identiques. Les noms même des acteurs ne varient pas: le nom est un moule'. F. Petruccelli della Gattina, *Histoire diplomatique des conclaves*, vol. I, Paris, 1864, p. 5. (Francesco Petruccelli della Gattina was a member of the Italian Parliament.)

court, and the ability of papal families to form matrimonial alliances and devise patronage systems that would allow them to bypass the political chasm caused by each pope's death, as well as the amount of resources and the ever-changing means which were used to obtain them.

THE SPECIFICITY OF THE ROMAN COURT

If factions were the basic form of political aggregation through which power was controlled at all European courts, how should we interpret the dynamics of such factions in the Roman context? Furthermore, and more importantly, what were the characteristics of the Roman court as opposed to other courts?

In Rome, obviously, unlike England and France during the wars of religion, factions did not divide themselves into religious confessions, although internal curial conflicts could be very bitter precisely on account of religious and doctrinal issues.[12] In Rome, factions were groups that systematically occupied the most important offices in order to elect a sovereign to their liking. Therefore the Roman court witnessed many transitional phases. Every conclave represented a divide that tested factions, either reinforcing or dissolving them, but in any case modifying them.

Contemporaries understood this extremely clearly. Factional reality was portrayed as being coherent with the social system of a city in which

> foreigners hurry in such great numbers as though to a common Fatherland, where little difference is made between person and person, between nation and nation, and where each year in a brief space of time they are recognized as citizens, without serious difficulties ... where each one can, perhaps more than anywhere else ... aspire with his fortune and virtues to the highest offices in the court and the church.[13]

In this specific urban reality, factions not only involved restricted segments of the curial elite, but also characterized political groups that were endorsed and financed by their international connections. 'The pope',

---

[12] By studying the Holy Office as a 'centre of power removed from the institutions of ordinary government and secreted', Adriano Prosperi has recently emphasized how during the sixteenth century 'the new police of the Faith' altered the physiognomy of the papacy and transformed the history of conclaves by eliminating all candidates unacceptable to the Inquisition: A. Prosperi, *Tribunali della coscienza. Inquisitori, confessori, missionari*, Turin, 1996, pp. 135–41.

[13] BL, Additional (Add.) 8474, *Relatione di Roma e di tutto lo stato temporale e spirituale del Papa*, f. 217. The same idea underlies the *Discours politique de l'estat de Rome au Roy Treschrestien*, Paris, 1626, p. 17 and the famous *Discorso del Cardinale Commendone sopra la Corte di Roma*, ed. C. Mozzarelli, Rome, 1996; see Mozzarelli's introduction.

as we read in one of the many manuscript versions of the report on Rome by the Fleming Ameyden (1641), 'cannot really trust the Roman people any more than a myriad of [other] nations, nor the nobility [which is] distracted by the many factions. The people of Rome are constantly divided into Spanish and French factions. Shopkeepers and lowly people belong to the French, gentlemen and citizens to the Spanish.'[14]

But the centrality of factions in the life of the city and the court is also generally attributed to a form of government based on continual transformations.

The composite urban reality of Rome, and its complex and unique political system, were at the basis of Italian instability: 'things in Italy change often, especially with new popes, changes in the College of Cardinals, and in the entire court, which is often renewed with the new principate; these innovations give rise to the mutations and universal alterations of Italy and all of Christendom'.[15] This is a recurrent *topos* in sixteenth- and seventeenth-century political literature,[16] one which overturns the notion, cherished by nineteenth-century diplomatic historians, that the Roman factions were always re-enacting the same conflict, and favours the concept of a faction as an ever-changing political configuration.

I should like to emphasize this point. If the study of factions is viewed in a spatial context, it must also, in the same Roman scenario, be carefully dated. Moreover, between the first and second halves of the seventeenth century, even contemporaries developed different attitudes to court factions and the various ways in which they were formed.

The material that I have analysed for this study includes the sources on cardinals' factions and on conclaves contained in the archives of the Biblioteca Apostolica Vaticana, the major European libraries and the archives of the Foreign Ministries of Madrid and Paris for the early seventeenth century. In brief, it covers the period between the conversion

---

[14] BNF, ms. it. 1700, f. 198v.

[15] This excerpt is attributed to the Cardinal of Burgos: *Discorso al Re Filippo sopra le cose d'Italia* (BL, Egerton 534, f. 86v). The Cardinal of Burgos was Francisco Pacheco Ossorio, who was related through his mother to the Toledo–Alba clan, an important axis of Spanish politics in Italy. He was one of Pius IV's cardinals in 1561, and became Archbishop of Burgos in 1567. Regarding the Sacred College during this period, see J. Lestocquoy and L. Duval-Arnould, 'Le Cardinal Santa Croce et le Sacré Collège en 1565', *Archivum Historiae Pontificiae*, 18 (1980), pp. 263–96; on the role of the cardinal in Rome, see M. Rivero Rodríguez, 'El servicio a dos cortes: Marco Antonio Colonna Almirante pontificio y vasallo de la Monarquía', in Martínez Millán (ed.), *La Corte de Felipe II*, pp. 333–4.

[16] The idea that the roots of the transformation of European politics must be looked for in Rome is expressed various times in Richelieu's *Testament politique*, Amsterdam, 1688 (particularly chap. VII).

of Henri IV, which brought about a renewed influence of French politics on the Roman court, and the pontificate of Innocent X Pamphili, upon whose death a new faction known as the 'squadrone volante' was formed.[17] These were fifty years of turmoil, an international scenario of war characterized by five pontificates of varying length. Some were very brief – only a few weeks in the cases of Leo XI Medici – while some were very long, as in the cases of Paul V Borghese, who reigned for sixteen years, and Urban VIII Barberini, who reigned for twenty-one.

A very important institutional change took place in this fifty-year period. This transformation was brought about by Gregory XV's bull *Aeterni patris filius* promulgated on 15 November 1621 and, the following year, the bull *Decet Romanum pontificem* of 12 March. The former regulated the general procedure for the election of a pope, while the latter concerned the ceremonial aspects of the conclave.[18] In early seventeenth-century sources, Gregory XV's bull is often presented as the outcome of a long and difficult institutional and religious process that started at the beginning of the modern age with the constitution *Cum tam divino* of Julius II Della Rovere (24 January 1505) and which had been increasingly complicated, throughout the century, by the growing interference of Spain. It is difficult fully to accept the hypothesis of a coherent continuity between Gregory XV's bull and prior legislative measures. Certainly, however, the many conclaves that were held over this short period of time at the end of the sixteenth century, the political significance that conclaves had acquired for the Spain of Philip II, the frequency with which the *adoratio*[19] system of election was used and the doubts that it raised (it did not permit the number of votes received by a given candidate to be verified) were all factors that induced Gregory XV to issue the bull. It was the result, after all, of the

---

[17] See the study by G. Signorotto in the same volume.

[18] *Bullarium Romanum*, vol. XII, Turin, 1867, pp. 619–27 (*Aeterni patris filius*) and 662–73 (*Decet Romanum pontificem*). On the procedures for papal elections, see L. Lector (J. Güthlin), *Le Conclave. Origines, histoire, organisation, législation ancienne et moderne*, Paris, 1894; G. Lunadoro, *Della elezione, coronazione e possesso de' Romani Pontefici, trattato accresciuto e illustrato da Fr. Antonio Zaccaria*, Rome, n. d.; A. Molien, 'Conclave', in *Dictionnaire de Droit Canonique*, vol. III, Paris, 1942, pp. 1319–42; G. Moroni, *Dizionario di erudizione storico-ecclesiastica*, vol. XV, Venice 1842, pp. 238–315: G. Meuschen, *Caerimonialia Electionis et Coronationis Pontificis Romani*, Frankfurt, 1732; and the unpublished works by G. Ghetti, *Trattato dell'Eletione del Sommo Pontefice*, BA, Ms. 294; BAV, Vat. Lat. 12175, *Relatione del modo che nelli conclavi si usa di eleggere il papa*, ff. 29-32v; Barb. Lat. 5682, *Istruzione del modo e regola con il quale si viene all'elettione del Sommo Pontefice*, ff. 177–216.

[19] 'Adoratio can take place in the following manner: various faction heads lead a cardinal into the chapel, during the day or the night, and when they achieve enough votes, they elect and revere him', BAV, Vat. Lat., 12175/3, ff. 29r–32v.

profound conviction and zealous operation of a few members of the curia, especially Cardinals Bellarmino and Borromeo – who convinced the cardinal-nephew Ludovisi to put an end to 'the inconveniences caused by the way the pontiff is elected by *adoratio*'.[20] The regulations passed by Gregory XV imposed a rigid formal procedure which made the rules for seclusion during the conclave even stricter and clearly listed all the procedures that were to be followed during the voting. These included the guarantee of voting secrecy by means of carefully prepared and sealed ballot papers; the presence of elected scrutators; and the minimum requirement, for a valid election, of a two-thirds majority. Gregory XV's reform made the election of a pontiff by acclamation (which favoured the power of a single faction-leader) much more difficult. It was therefore disliked by princes, aroused the opposition of the Spanish ambassador and cardinals, and irritated Cardinal Borghese who, together with a powerful faction of Paul V's creations (*creature*), potentially controlled the College of Cardinals.[21]

In a most interesting document in the Magalotti Archives we read that

> Many people thought that the new bull was intended to deprive, in the future, the cardinals who headed factions of their power and authority in conclaves, while the strengthening of secret-suffrage elections removed from the *creature* the danger of being accused of ingratitude ... But the shrewder men who could see into things understood that, although some of them could in this way vote differently from how they had promised, they would not in fact do so if they did not dislike their leader ... Secondly, because if someone did not vote for his leader, it would have been very hard for this not be known ... as there are so many interests and so much is heard of the needs, nature and customs of all, that with minimal observation by the others it would be almost impossible not to notice their deeds.[22]

Like many other sources, this demonstrates that contemporaries clearly perceived the fact that the new bull would not put an end to lobbying during papal elections, as it was in the 'interest of every creation' to make the most of his leader's directives and especially because the new constitution did not forbid declaring one's voting intention, as had long been customary in the conclave. Nonetheless, the new electoral system did complicate the factions' manoeuvres. It renewed the principle of freedom of choice in papal elections and in practice, it required far more

---

[20] BAV, Barb. Lat., 4660, f. 1 (Letter of Card. Ludovisi to S. Card. Borromeo regarding the new procedure for electing the pontiff).

[21] ASF, MP, 3893, f. 149v.   [22] ASF, Fondo Magalotti, 91.

prudent negotiations, as they had to take place without disobeying the new papal rules.[23]

The new atmosphere that developed during the early decades of the seventeenth century was embodied by this papal bull, but there was a further element that oriented the formation of opposite factions in the Sacred College: the *jus exclusivae*. In the sixteenth and seventeenth century sources, the term 'granting exclusion' simply meant that a certain group of electors would not vote for a given papal candidate.[24] The *jus exclusivae*, however, acquired a far different and harsher meaning when the 'exclusion' was formulated at the suggestion of one of the great powers. The King of Spain, as the heir to the imperial tradition of the *Advocatus Ecclesiae Romae* which Charles V had claimed, made use of this practice throughout the sixteenth century, transforming it into a kind of right of veto at papal elections.[25]

In the last years of Philip II's reign, however, the custom whereby the Spanish ambassador excluded the names of those cardinals who were not *confidenti* of Spain became the object of an institutional and moral debate. In 1594, the Duke of Sessa, at that time Spanish ambassador in Rome, appointed a committee of theologians, comprising Juan Vicente, Procurator and Vicar-General of the Dominicans, the Jesuit José de Acosta and the auditor of the *Rota* Francisco Peña, to study this delicate matter from a religious, rather than a political, point of view. The three 'doctors' met on 12 February in the Dominican convent of Santa Maria sopra Minerva in Rome. A long memorandum contains the general conclusions reached by the committee.[26] It is a very interesting document for understanding

---

[23] *Discorso Sopra la Nuova Bolla del Conclave*, in BAV, Vat. Lat., 12178/7, ff. 39–41; *Commento alla Bolla in Cui si Mostrano i Modi di Fraudarla*, Vat. Lat., 12175, ff. 67–78v.

[24] Lector, *Le Conclave*, p. 469.

[25] An essential reference work is L. Wahrmund, *Das Ausschliessungsrecht (Jus Exclusivae) katholischen Staaten Österreich, Frankreich und Spanien bei den Papstwahlen*, Vienna, 1888. I owe this reference to Prof. C. Weber, to whom I renew my thanks.

[26] AGS, Estado, Roma, legajo 1870. The Dominican friar Juan Vicente was the confessor of Cardinal Archduke Albert (AGS, Estado, Milán y Saboya, legajo 1277/54); on Acosta's mission to Rome from 2 December 1592 to 9 March 1594 in order to oppose the policies of the Jesuit General Acquaviva, see M. de la Pinta Llorente, *Actividades diplomáticas del P. José de Acosta. Entorno a una política y a un sentimiento religioso*, Madrid, 1952. Regarding Peña, an important jurist, reviser of the *Directorium inquisitorum* by Nicolas Eymerich for the 1578 Roman edition and councillor of the Congregation of the Index, see A. Borromeo, 'A proposito del "Directorium Inquisitorum" di Nicolas Eymerich e delle sue edizioni cinquecentesche', *Critica storica*, 20 (1983) pp. 499–547; V. Frajese, 'Regno ecclesiastico e Stato moderno. La polemica fra Francesco Peña e Roberto Bellarmino nell'esenzione dei chierici', *Annali dell'Istituto Storico Italo-Germanico in Trento*, 14 (1988), pp. 273–339; Prosperi, *Tribunali della coscienza*, pp. 196–7, 204–6; G. Fragnito, *La Bibbia al rogo. La censura ecclesiastica e i volgarizzamenti della Scrittura (1471–1605)*, Bologna, 1997,

all of the implications surrounding the political battles that were waged around the election of a pope, and it develops five main issues that were essential in order that the Duke of Sessa's doubts might be resolved. In the first place the committee considers the universal character of the papacy, which affects all Christian princes, and the twofold reality of papal sovereignty which implied the sacred and ecclesiastical nature of the election, but also the temporal nature of the dominion. The document then moves on to more 'contextual' motives: the pervasive qualities of the Roman factions, that divided not only the Sacred College, but even the court and city – on which the ambassador could not abstain from taking a stance for the reputation of his king – and the recurrent practice of electing a pontiff not by secret scrutiny but by means of 'negotiations'. Given these premises, the document indicates the general cases in which 'exclusion' could be considered legitimate. It could be formulated when it contained a proposal, not an obligation, and when, in harmony with the Spanish mission to defend the faith, it was used as a tool with which to elect a pope who would rigorously accept this role in harmony with the Spanish king. It was licit, therefore, to exclude a cardinal who could be considered pernicious to the church and detrimental to Spain, although not by means of fraud or other unworthy measures. Thus, the memorandum continues, it is best to refrain from generously handing out pensions during a vacancy of the Holy See, as this would look like 'mental simony', and to restrict oneself to presenting gifts to the vassals and friends of the Spanish king only during the pontiff's lifetime, and 'without pacts or explicit negotiations'.[27]

These principles were confirmed on 5 and 10 June 1598 by the commission convened in Madrid and comprising the Jesuit Father Acosta, the Franciscan friar Diego de Yepes and the Dominican Gaspar de Córdoba (these latter being, respectively, the confessors of the King and the Crown prince).[28] These tenets were subsequently reiterated at the beginning of the seventeenth century in the *Junta de Pontificado* of August 1601[29] and again in 1604, when – among other things – the restoration of a

---

pp. 143–5. Regarding the role of clerics, and in particular of confessors, in influencing political action during the age of Philip II, see C. J. de Carlos Morales, 'La partecipación en el gobierno a través de la conciencia regia. Fray Diego de Chaves, O. P. confesor de Felipe II', in F. Rurale (ed.), *I religiosi a corte. Teologia, politica e diplomazia in Antico regime*, Rome, 1998, pp. 131–57 and more amply in Rurale's introduction, pp. 9–50.

[27] *Dum modo nulla praecedat aut interveniat pactio aut obligatio, et cardinales reliquantur in plenissima libertate ut conscientiis suis possint satisfacere*, AGS, Estado, Roma, legajo 1870.

[28] Ibid.

[29] The 1601 junta was formed by Gaspar de Córdoba, Don Juan de Idiáquez, the Count of Miranda and the Cardinal of Seville who were in charge of analytically specifying

powerful French faction in the curia and the renewed claims of the King of France to an analogous right of 'exclusion' (on account of an imperial tradition that the King of France had inherited from Charlemagne)[30] seemed seriously to endanger the Spanish supremacy at the court of Rome.

During the first decades of the century these principles were turned into general directives for the Spanish ambassadors in Rome, although the idea of reducing the Roman politics of the *Monarquía* to the application of these tenets was absolutely inconceivable. The complexity of Spanish politics in Rome must be held to account for the attempt to adjust their strategies to the changes in the political situation and to use different political tactics: that of diplomacy, but also that of force. An example of this occurred in 1605 in the clash with Cardinal Baronio, and upon the death of Urban VIII, with the veto on the candidature of Cardinal Sacchetti, both of which were 'exclusions' that seemed to be an open breach of the guidelines that had been so cleverly designed by the court theologians.

REPRESENTATION AND THEORY OF THE FACTIONS: A FEW EXPONENTS

Outside the court: ambassadors and agents of the European powers

In 1631, Don Diego Saavedra Fajardo,[31] the learned and shrewd Spanish agent in Rome, charged with settling a number of issues for the Marquis of Castel Rodrigo (who had been appointed ambassador[32] at the *Consejo de Estado* of 21 May 1630), explained that 'I have always refused to write the

'cosa / el Rey / podría hacer con seguridad de su conciencia en tiempo de sede vacante', AMAE, Estado, legajo 54, ff. 2–7.

[30] *Discours Politique de l'Estat de Rome au Roy Treschrestien*, p. 84.

[31] D. Diego Saavedra Fajardo, 'letrado de Cámara' for Cardinal Borgia, was the secretary of the Spanish embassy in Rome; the ambassador was the Count of Monterey (1628–31), secretary in 1631 of the *Junta de Reforma de abusos en Roma* and plenipotentiary for the Congress of Münster. See M. Fraga Iribarne, *Don Diego de Saavedra y Fajardo y la diplomacia de su época*, Madrid, 1955; F. Murillo Ferrol, *Saavedra Fayardo y la política del Barroco*, Madrid, 1989, 1st edn 1957; J. Sánchez Moreno, *Formación cultural de Saavedra Fajardo*, Murcia, 1959; J. M. Jover Zamora and M. V. López-Cordón Cortezo, 'La imagen de Europa y el pensamiento político internacional', in *El siglo del Quijote (1580–1680). Religión. Filosofía. Ciencia*, Madrid, 1996, pp. 467–691; Q. Aldea Vaquero, *España y Europa en el siglo XVII. Correspondencia de Saavedra Fajardo*, vol. 1, *1631–33*, Madrid, 1986.

[32] On the Spanish ambassadors to Rome during the seventeenth century, see J. Lefèvre, 'L'ambassade d'Espagne auprès du Saint Siège au XVIIe siècle', *Bulletin de l'Institut*

instructions for the ambassadors in Rome, as they are fencing lessons that are immediately forgotten; documents and guidelines are rarely adhered to, if they are not followed with prudence due to the accidents that alter and change the substance of things'.[33]

Saavedra Fajardo, who rejected the prevailing notion that an ambassador in Rome had necessarily to be deceitful, insisted on prudence as a practical rule for political behaviour, and on the ability to adapt general directives to suit particular situations. Nonetheless, he listed a number of 'maximas fixas de la negociación' to be used in Rome: peace, the attainment of the pontiff's good graces and an active role in the Sacred College in view of the subsequent papal election. An ambassador had to work towards these objectives and be aware of the fact that in the 'great court' of Rome 'there is neither bond nor faction between friends or foes that will not dissolve'.[34]

These maxims can be found in the document drawn up by Saavedra Fajardo for the Marquis of Castel Rodrigo and, more generally, in all the official instructions given by the Spanish monarchs to their ambassadors to Rome throughout the seventeenth century.

Although it was outside the *Monarquía*'s direct dominion, Rome was regarded in these instructions as part of an integrated Italian system. Consequently, the king's representatives had to work in concert with all the other Spanish ministers in order to defend his jurisdictional prerogatives in Naples, Sicily and Milan, to assist the negotiations at the Holy Office and to gain the friendship of cardinals, Roman princes and barons.[35]

Historique Belge de Rome, 17 (1936), pp. 1–56; T. Dandelet, 'Spanish Conquest and Colonization at the Center of the Old World: The Spanish Nation in Rome 1555–1625', *The Journal of Modern History*, 69 (1997), pp. 479–511.

[33] *Noticias de la Negociación de Roma*. The document is published in Q. Aldea Vaquero (ed.), 'España, el Papado y el Imperio durante la Guerra de los Treinta Años. Instrucciones a los embajadores de España en Roma (1631–1643)', *Miscelánea Comillas*, 29 (1958), p. 305.

[34] Ibid.

[35] The instructions for the Marquis of Aytona can be found in AMAE, Estado, legajo 54, ff. 272–6. G. de Moncada, Marquis of Aytona and Viceroy of Sardinia, was appointed ambassador in Rome from 1606 to 1609, and then Viceroy of Aragon. Regarding Philip II's instructions to the Duke of Albuquerque, see AMAE, Estado, legajo 57/37 (*Original instrucción del S. Rey Philippe Tercero al Duque de Albuquerque su Ambaxador en Roma*). Francisco Fernández de la Cueva, Duke of Albuquerque, was the ambassador in Rome from 1619 to 1623, after which he joined the *Consejo de Estado*. On the instructions of Cardinal Borgia (Madrid, 19 December 1631), see Quintín Aldea (ed.), 'España, el Papado y el Imperio', pp. 341–4. On the relationship between the 'system of the ancient Italian states' and Spain, and the relations between 'peripheral' and 'central' administrative spheres, see A. Musi (ed.), *Nel sistema imperiale. L'Italia spagnola*, Naples, 1994; A. Musi, 'El Reino de Nápoles

Let us compare the instructions of the King of Spain to his ambassador to Rome with those which the King of France sent to the French ambassador.[36] In the first place, the structure, rhetoric and discursive approach of these instructions express the same objectives. The first task of the French ambassador is to gather precise information on all the cardinals and curial officials, especially all those among them who can be considered servants of the king in order to form a French faction. However, unlike the instructions of the Spanish king, those of the French king did not include a list of the benefices and rewards bestowed upon the families of the Roman nobility, nor lists of pensions paid to loyal cardinals. In 1624, when the councillor of state Monsieur de Béthune was sent to Rome as ambassador, his instructions informed him that 'Cardinal Bevilacqua is the only cardinal with a pension that the king has at this moment in the Sacred College.'[37] The French court was aware of the difficulty of competing on this level with Spain, a country that had a well-organized territorial power-base in Italy and could rely on the reserves of the estates and bishoprics of the Kingdom of Naples. Thus, in order to 'improve the fortunes of the French party', rather than relying on the nobility the French aimed directly at the Sacred College, where they could count not only on the cardinal-protector and the French-born cardinals, but also on experienced pro-French politicians such as Cardinal Bentivoglio, Cardinal Spada and, later, Cardinal Bichi, who came to be considered a French 'minister'.[38]

A parallel reading of the French and Spanish instructions reveals two clearly diverging political strategies lurking behind the ideological

y el sistema imperial español', in Martínez Millán, *Europa y la Monarquía*, vol. 1/2, pp. 555–65; P. Pissavino and G. Signorotto (eds.), *Lombardia Borromaica. Lombardia Spagnola 1554–1659*, Roma 1995; Rivero Rodríguez, *Felipe II y el gobierno de Italia*, in particular pp. 37–56; A. Spagnoletti, *Principi italiani e Spagna nell'età barocca*, Milan, 1996; idem, 'La visione dell'Italia e degli Stati italiani nell'età di Filippo II,' in *Europa y la Monarquía*, pp. 893–903.

[36] See AMAE, Mémoires et Documents, Rome, vol. xv (*Instructions à Divers Ambassadeurs de France 1568–1611*); Correspondance politique, Rome, vol. xxx, which includes *L'Instruction Donnée au Bailly de Sillery envoyé par le Roi Ambassadeur à Rome* (18 March 1622), and the correspondence between the Cardinal of Savoy and Cardinal Bentivoglio. A copy of these *Istruzioni* dated between 1624 and 1655 is in BL, Add. 5459.

[37] *Instruction au S. de Bethune allant Ambassadeur à Rome*, 13 April 1624 (ibid., f. 16).

[38] *Instruction à Mr. de Brassac allant Ambassadeur à Rome du 13 Fevrier 1630*, ibid., f. 329; *Instruction que le Roy a Commandée estre donnée à Mr. Le Marquis de Fontenay du 21 Juin 1641*, ibid., f. 370r; *L'Instruction au Marquis de Chamond*, ibid., f. 407. On Guido Bentivoglio see A. Merola in *DBI*, VIII, pp. 634–8; M. Rosa, 'Nobiltà e carriera nelle "Memorie" di due cardinali della Controriforma: Scipione Gonzaga e Guido Bentivoglio', in M. A. Visceglia (ed.), *Signori, patrizi, cavalieri nell'Età Moderna*, Bari, 1992, pp. 231–55. On Alessandro Bichi see G. de Caro in *DBI*, x, pp. 334–40.

emphasis on key words such as the 'paz' and 'quietud' of Italy in the Spanish documents and 'liberté du Saint Siège' and 'au salut de l'Italie' in the French ones. It would have been impossible to create a Spanish faction in Rome during the early seventeenth century without the help of the great Roman families and the resources that the imperial system was capable of exploiting and redistributing. On the other hand, the creation of circumstances favourable to France did not depend on the effective strength of the French faction so much as on the ability to coagulate dissatisfaction and anti-Spanish sentiments or, to use the words from our sources, 'independent spirits'.[39]

We will return to the variations that these political strategies underwent in practice in the following pages, but at this point let us examine some other ways in which the clash between factions was represented by those who directed it from outside the court.

In order to understand the theoretical basis for the actions of the agents of the European powers, who were ordered to form a faction favourable to their king's interests, what is perhaps more helpful than the official Instructions is a kind of parallel documentation, the work of political informers who developed the idea that anyone who was to operate in the Roman court had above all to become acquainted with the character and customs of the men who moved in curial circles.

A very interesting example of this is the *Discurso para el Embaxador Conde de Castro del modo como se ha de governar en la Embaxada de Roma* (Discourse for the Ambassador Conde de Castro on how the Roman Embassy ought to be governed) (1609),[40] which had an extraordinarily wide circulation and served as a model for many other similar documents. It describes the Roman court as a melting-pot of nationalities, each of which is characterized by a particular temperament. The French are described as chivalrous men who, whether lay or clerical, 'do not like to see their native liberty reduced at the court of Rome, where they seldom appear'. Among the Italians, it lists the docile and Spanish-loving Lombards; the arrogant and ceremonious Neapolitans, who pretend to love the Spaniards; the mercantile Genoese, some of whom have a penchant for the French, others for the Spaniards; and the Florentines and Venetians, who side with the French.

---

[39] *Discours Politique sur l'Estat de Rome*, p. 93.

[40] The *Discurso* is in BNM, ms. 8755. Slightly different Italian versions can be found in BAV, Barb. Lat., 4650 and in the Archivio della Chiesa di Santa Maria di Monserrato, Rome, ms. 49, ff. 35–46. Here I refer to the latter version. On the other hand, there are substantial differences in the *Instruttione all'Ambasciatore del Re Cattolico D. Francisco de Castro circa il modo come deve governare a Roma*, in BNF, ms. it. 629. See also BA, ms. 1657, in which the same *Istruzione* is dedicated to the Count of Oñate; Bodleian Library Oxford, ms. e Mus. 109, pp. 1–19 (dedicated to the Duke of Terranova).

The idea that every nation had a particular inclination was deeply rooted in the culture of the early modern age,[41] as was the belief that political behaviour had to conform to the 'humours' and follow the 'genius' of a nation. Thus, the opposition between the French and Spanish factions is represented by means of a recomposition into greater aggregations of all the countries present in Rome, with inclinations and affinities that had to be understood and satisfied.

The other fundamental rule for the constitution of a faction for the King of Spain was based on the ability to negotiate differently with curial officials on the basis of their offices, and with cardinals depending on their attitude with regard to the king.

According to the *Istruzioni* given to Francisco de Castro, cardinals were divided into three basic types: devoted vassals of the king, enemies, and neutral cardinals. Each category had to be addressed with a different modulation when communicating political information. Vassals, if they were Spanish, had to be addressed with 'great familiarity and friendship, and should be informed about most dealings'. If they were Neapolitan or Milanese, a 'good correspondence' could be kept up, but only matters of little importance should be disclosed to them 'because, in the end, they are vassals who can be bought, creations of the pope, rather than of His Majesty'. Relations with outright enemies should entail 'little intimacy', but courtesy and kind words. One should not accept services, but occasionally provide them in order to create a mechanism of reciprocity. The 'neutral' cardinals were considered the most dangerous and arrogant type, though it was useful to keep on good terms with them in view of the papal elections, although not to trust them.

Thus, behaviour had to be differentiated according to the functions of the various prelates, intertwining the consideration of passions with the satisfaction of interests. According to the writer of this memorandum, it was also important to analyse to what extent the cardinals were bound by the obligations of reciprocity which they had contracted with the king by means of benefices and pensions.

This basic issue, which does not appear to have been addressed in official instructions, is one of the points that were developed in the long *Relación de la cosas que hay dignas de saberse de Roma* (Report on the things that should be known about Rome), perhaps the work of Cardinal Gaspar Borgia, written during the last years of Paul V's pontificate. One of the rules that the king had to impose on his ambassador and dependent cardinals was the reciprocity of the pensions and other benefices that

---

[41] M. A. Visceglia, 'Gli "humori" delle nazioni. La rappresentazione della Spagna nella Francia del primo Seicento (1590–1635)', in G. di Febo (ed.), 'Spagna: immagine e autorappresentazione', *Dimensioni e problemi della ricerca storica*, vol. II (1995), pp. 39–68.

he dealt out, as 'many of those who receive them treat them as goods (*mercadurías*) without feeling obliged in the least'.[42] The awareness of double loyalties within the same families (examples are provided by the Orsini and Frangipane especially), and the numerous ties that the Roman nobility had not only with the two great monarchies, but also with princes and other Italian powers, made it clear that all bonds were weak and transient 'since affections and blood are made up of interests and so are only as secure and lasting as the interests [themselves]'.[43] The idea that emerges from these political writings, including French ones from the same period, is that although it was necessary to bestow appointments and benefices in times both of war and peace on the relatives of cardinals, the system was still not sufficiently binding if the faction heads were not secured, especially the pope's nephews. The cardinal-nephew – referred to by the Spaniards as 'valido de su tío'[44] and as by the French as 'le prince de la fortune'[45] on account of the immediate accumulation of power and wealth that this position allowed – was the true intermediary for negotiating with the pope. The lasting favours of the cardinal-nephew, whose power was continuously increasing, were necessary in order to control the factions within the Sacred College, especially as the appointment of new cardinals depended almost entirely on his decisions.

How much could pensions and gifts sway the cardinal-nephew, who, behind a façade of neutrality, had 'obligations' to every prince? And how did the cardinal-nephew gather men and build his own faction? In opposition to the European powers or with their help?

Inside the court: the cardinal-nephew,
the papabili *and the conclavists*

From the point of view of a cardinal-nephew, the creation of a faction followed different rules. A brief *Istruzione al cardinal Padrone circa il modo come si deve procurare una fazione di cardinali con tutti i requisiti che deve avere per lo stabilimento della sua grandezza* (Instructions to the chief cardinal on how to create a faction of cardinals with all the requisites for the establishment of his grandeur), in the archive of the Spaniards' church of Santa Maria di Monserrato in Rome, lists the criteria that the cardinal-nephew should follow in order to recruit cardinals and consolidate his power even after the pontiff's death.[46]

---

[42] BNM, ms. 3062, f. 15 (*Relación de las cosas que hay dignas de saberse de Roma. Para quien trata del servicio del Rey de España*).

[43] Ibid., f. 15v.   [44] Ibid., f. 17r.

[45] *Discours Politique de l'Estat de Rome*, p. 79.

[46] Archivio della Chiesa di Santa Maria di Monserrato, Rome, *Avvisi, Istruzioni, Relazioni*, 403ff., 27r–36v. It can also be found, with a few variations and

The first rule is 'to promote many cardinals, for which the only requisite is a long life for the pope your uncle'. The second is to avoid the promotion of cardinals solely on account of 'interest', but rather to help individuals who were 'eminent and meritorious'. Moreover, these cardinals should not 'depend on any other families than the pontiff's'. The third rule is to pay attention to the nationality of the future cardinals. The most trustworthy individuals for the cardinal-nephew are subjects of the papal state, as they have no allegiance to other countries or laws and are consequently independent. Aside from these, the best choices are found among citizens of the Republics as, apart from jurisdictional conflicts with the Apostolic See, they rarely have other disagreements with the cardinal-nephew. The worst choices are the subjects of kings, who are not free to make their own decisions and are obliged to obey their natural princes.

With regard to the social status of the prelates, 'as gratitude is a sentiment of noble souls', it is a good rule to prefer those of gentle birth. However, the author of these instructions specifies that he means 'by the word *gentilhuomini*, those of middle rank and fortune'.[47] In fact, individuals from these social groups still require patronage; hence it will be easier to ensure their fidelity to the cardinal-nephew, while higher prelates and nobility should be avoided altogether as they are too haughty and arrogant.

It is also good practice for the cardinal-nephew not to overdo the nomination of cardinals from venal offices, 'as those who become cardinals through purchased offices then claim to be completely free and make their own choices'.[48]

Finally, the original conditions through which bonds are developed are essential to safeguard their solidity, but it is also necessary to reinforce these ties through generous and supportive practices. The cardinal-nephew must regard his cardinals as comrades and friends, rather than as dependent clients.

Promoting many cardinals, favouring the small and middle nobility, creating personal ties that did not exclude individual merits: these criteria were indicative of that blend of 'friendship, merit and dependence' that was essential in appointing a cardinal and indeed for the entire recruitment system of the Roman court.[49]

entitled *Considerationi che convengono ad un Cardinal Nepote di Papa nel promuovere altri al Cardinalato*, in BAV, Barb. Lat, 4650/II. Here I shall refer to the former text.

[47] Ibid., p. 32.   [48] Ibid., p. 35.

[49] See C. Weber, *Senatus Divinus. Verbogene Strukturen im Kardinalskollegium der Frühen Neuzeit (1500–1800)*, Frankfurt, 1996, and, spanning a shorter period, M. A. Visceglia, ' "La Giusta Statera dei Porporati". Sulla composizione e rappresentazione del Sacro Collegio nella prima metà del Seicento', *Roma moderna e contemporanea*, 4 (1996), pp. 167–211.

Above all, the concept of friendship[50] was central. It was the hinge that held dependence and fidelity together, as well as the principle that organized individuals on a hierarchical ladder. In order to form a solid faction that would resist the power vacuums caused by the death of a pontiff, the cardinal-nephew had to be certain, by means of the rules we have just examined, that he had the friendship of the future cardinals. In turn, the elected cardinals had to be 'grateful, *officioso* (obliging), beneficent'. They had to learn to display virtues that would add both amiability and severity to their official role in order to please both those above and those below them in the court hierarchy. According to the *Discorso della corte di Roma su come si debba governare un cardinale* (Discourse of the Court of Rome on how a cardinal should behave),[51] being *officioso* meant, above all, requesting favours for others at court. Reputation and following were acquired through an individual's ability to promote and advance friends and followers. Thus, in order to be able to help friends, a truly *officioso* cardinal had to be a member of many Congregations, especially those which were often held in the pope's presence – the Holy Office, the Congregation of *Propaganda Fide* and the *Segnatura di Grazia* – in order to have the opportunity of speaking directly to the pope.[52]

'Friendship' was therefore a principle based on favours, as opposed to an exercise of generosity. It was a reciprocal relationship, a mutual exchange of credits and debts.

In these terms, friendship was the main bond that held factions together, as well as a political objective for 'papable' cardinals that had to be pursued at length by means of well-established criteria. These included a prudent attitude so as to avoid offending even the 'lowest' members of the court; making sure not to appear 'too partial' towards the leader of a prince or king's faction (unless one owed them one's cardinalate) and not appearing too friendly with a widely despised or disliked curial minister.[53]

The procedures for interpersonal relations defined a *papabile* cardinal's arena of political action. Positive values certainly included gratitude towards one's master and the ability to obtain appointments and favours

---

[50] M. Aymard, 'Amitié et convivialité', in P. Ariès and R. Chartier (eds.), *Histoire de la vie privée*, vol. III, *De la Renaissance aux Lumières*, Paris, 1986, pp. 455–99.

[51] BAV, Fondo Boncompagni, cod. C 20 (the ms. is dated 1626).

[52] Ibid., f. 363.

[53] Biblioteca Corsiniana, Rome, 875–33. D. 26, *Raccolta di scritture diverse politiche e apologetiche (Osservationi da praticarsi dall'aspirante Cardinale al Papato tanto dentro, come fuori dal Conclave)*, pp. 123–7. Another copy of this document is in BAV, Vat. Lat., 12175.

for relatives and clients, but above all, prudence: keeping away from questionable characters or individuals with too much power and the ability to obtain the assent of kings and princes without being, or appearing to be, their favourites. Although this political game may seem to be conducted in a state of constant precariousness, subject to the court's uncertainties and to the risks of international political situations, it had to be carefully and skilfully studied and prepared.

The conclavist,[54] a cardinal's ecclesiastical or lay minister and advisor in the complex and intricate events that surrounded papal elections, was the master of this difficult art. Conclavists, typical characters of the Roman court, enjoyed many benefits. They had the right of citizenship in any city of the papal state, and besides the sum in *scudi* they received from the pope, they also received 10,000 *scudi* from the Apostolic Chamber.[55] Some conclavists made for themselves important careers. One such was Francesco Adriano Ceva,[56] a cardinal under Urban VIII, who despite his noble birth had served a long apprenticeship at the Roman court as a *familiaris* of Cardinal Maffeo Barberini's secretary. In 1623, Ceva became Cardinal Barberini's conclavist and then, with the assent of Cardinal Borghese, masterminded the ascent of Cardinal Barberini to the papal throne. Similarly, Decio Azzolini, Panciroli's conclavist, became one of Innocent X's cardinals in 1654.[57]

A few conclavists were the authors of works that have remained largely unpublished, but that are extremely enlightening for an understanding of the rules that governed the conflicts between factions. At the end of the sixteenth century, two important personalities of the Roman court wrote such documents: Giovanni Francesco Lottini di Volterra,[58] special secretary to Cosimo de' Medici, author of the famous *Discorso sopra l'attioni del Conclave*,[59] and another Tuscan, Felice Gualtiero.[60] A 'dispute' arose between Gualtiero and the older and powerful Lottini, a courtier and friend of many influential personalities, regarding the theoretical basis of

[54] See A. Molien, 'Conclaviste', in *Dictionnaire*, vol. III, pp. 1342–8; Moroni, *Dizionario*, vol. XVI, pp. 1–25.

[55] Lunadoro, *Dell'Elezione*, pp. 21–2.   [56] G. de Caro in *DBI*, vol. XXIV, pp. 310–14.

[57] R. Nielsen in *DBI*, vol. III, pp. 768–71; Azzolini (attributed) BAV, Vat. Lat., 12178/18 (*Il Conclavista Moderno della Penna d'Oro*).

[58] For biographical sketch of Lottini see T. Bozza, *Scrittori politici italiani dal 1550 al 1650*, Rome, 1949, pp. 46–8. Also see A. Prosperi, 'I cristiani e la guerra: una controversia fra '500 e '700', *Rivista di Storia e Letteratura Religiosa*, 30 (1994), pp. 73–4.

[59] The *Discorso* was published in *La prima parte del Thesoro politico in cui si contengono relationi, instruttioni, trattati e varij discorsi pertinenti alla perfetta intelligenza della Ragion di Stato*, Milan, 1600, pp. 482–502. The mss. of Lottini on the conclave are in BAV, Barb. Lat., 4648, 4756, 4699.

[60] F. Gualtiero, *Il Conclavista*, in BAV, Vat. Lat., 12175 and Barb. Lat., 4756 (ff. 24–41), 4680, 4699, 5121.

the *Discorso sul Conclave*.[61] In this work, Lottini insisted on the inspired nature of papal elections, which allowed cardinals to vote as if they were possessed by an uncontrollable impulse guiding them against their own will 'without force or reason'. Gualtiero believed that Lottini's conclave theory was unsatisfactory, as it avoided the central issue: by what means and instruments is a pope elected?

Although he admitted that the means by which the Holy Spirit influenced the Sacred College during a pontiff's election were mysterious,[62] and therefore restricted the role of 'civil activity' ('industria civile'), Gualtiero believed that not only conclavists, but even the king's ministers, the *papabili* cardinals and the heads of factions should operate in an Aristotelian manner, with clarity and intelligence, 'as in every other council that has to elect a magistrate'.[63]

This is not the place to proffer an analysis of the many aspects of a controversy dealing with a crucial problem concerning the role of politics in papal elections and in the court in general. However, based on the works of Gualtiero and Lottini (who notwithstanding their dispute agreed on many other issues) and others, it is worth trying to reach a better comprehension of that 'civil prudence' that had to be practised by cardinals and conclavists. According to these documents, how were factions organized? How was a conclave directed?

A frequently used metaphor, similar to the well-known one of Rome as the theatre of the world, was that of the conclave as a scene requiring constant action.[64] Another metaphor represents the conclave as a labyrinth, a closed space, but one nonetheless related to the outside world where the 'true practice' took place and where friends were made for one's faction before the pope's death.[65] Operating on the boundary between 'inside' and 'outside', the conclavist had to be as adaptable as a chameleon

---

[61] This controversy is analytically narrated in BNM, ms. 412/XI (*Giuditio sopra le scritture passate fra M. Giovanni Francesco Lottino et M. Felice Gualtiero circa l'attione de' Conclavi con la replica*).

[62] Gualtiero wrote: 'We who are men must address these things as men.' He wanted to write a treatise that, without addressing the theological issue of papal elections, would be the work of a 'courtier for courtiers' (*Il Conclavista*, BAV, Vat. Lat., 12175, f. 143v).

[63] Ibid., f. 218. As well as elsewhere: '[The conclavist] ought, to bear in mind Aristotle's rules in his *Politics*, which concern all the qualities of governments, and to regulate his conclave according to the one that was closest to it [in Aristotle's books]', ibid., f. 201.

[64] 'The Roman Court, which for a long time was accustomed to perpetual variations, still requires cardinals and conclavists who know how to and are capable of opportunely changing and adapting the many different scenes to different theatres' (ASF, MP, 3983, f. 82, *Della diversità delle fazioni che hoggi si possono notare nel Collegio Apostolico*, 1623).

[65] Lottini, *Discorso*, p. 490. See also *Teorica del Conclave*, in BAV, Barb. Lat., 4873, f. 118.

to the changing events and moods of individuals.[66] He had to observe inclinations, examine past and present relations of the cardinals' families with friends and allies,[67] and take note of pensions, benefices and other advantages that the members of the Sacred College received from princes. Above all, however, he had to discover the intentions of others by means of clever conversation.[68] It was only possible to attain a profound knowledge of the men who belonged to other factions if the conclavist was a careful student of ancient and modern history, an expert on past conclaves, a good politician and a talented 'merchant' who, by analysing the composition of the Sacred College, was capable of imagining aggregations and elaborating strategies for possible alliances.[69]

What was the relation between the function of a conclavist and a *papabile* cardinal? The policies of the faction leader were based on the investigative survey carried out by the conclavist. A faction leader had to be careful not to disappoint any of his followers' aspirations, never to put his main candidate in the foreground and always to be ready for confrontation with other faction leaders. In the conflicts among factions, the heads of the different groups of cardinals had not only to be certain of an undoubted number of votes, but also to know how to gain enough additional votes to constitute a safe majority. Thus faction leaders had to conduct negotiations on many fronts, with different methods and without ever neglecting the desires and orientations of a group that was potentially available for a 'free' vote, the so-called neutral cardinals.[70]

In this process of aggregation and recomposition of groups, friendship and enmity were often confused. Relative exclusion (*esclusione relativa*), a sort of non-absolute veto that had to be used with moderation, was practised against adversaries, but also as a 'great warning' against friends whose candidature appeared too strong and problematic for the faction leader.

---

[66] The comparison to a chameleon can be found in Gualtieri: 'I wish my conclavist would transform himself, if it were possible, into the nature of a chameleon, as this animal takes on the quality of the colours of all things which he comes near to and so, speaking and dealing with humans, he would be able to satisfy everyone's nature' (BAV, Vat. Lat., 12175, f. 161r).

[67] '[The conclavist] should also take note of all the squabbles that take place among cardinals or among their relatives and friends' (*Brevi Ricordi di quanto s'appartenga d'operare ad un Gentilhuomo eletto per Conclavista in servizio al Card.le suo Signore*, 1644, BAV, Barb. Lat., 4702, f. 23).

[68] *Trattato del Conclave*, BAV, Barb. Lat., 4699, f. 58; see also *Teorica intorno al Conclave*, ibid., 4673, f. 125v; the same precept can be found in *Brevi Ricordi*, f. 24.

[69] The first task of the conclavist is to collect and carefully to study all the documents concerning prior conclaves and *papabili* cardinals; see *Brevi Ricordi*, f. 22v; Gualtieri, BAV, Vat. Lat., 12175, f. 160r and Lottini, Barb. Lat., 4699, f. 59r, but also *Il Conclavista Moderno*, Vat. Lat., 12178/18, f. 194.

[70] Gualtieri, f. 150v; Lottini, BAV, Barb. Lat., 4699, f. 79.

In such an intricate game of vetoes, counter-vetoes and changing alliances, it was sometimes better for a faction head to elect the candidate of another faction, if he possessed good human qualities, rather than a friend who could threaten his leadership.

Thus the issue of friendship surfaces once again in these pamphlets, and its connotation grows even clearer. This faction theory shows how, in the Roman court, friendship was dependent on interests rather than the other way round, since mutual interests can make one love those who are different by nature and inclination. Friendship, however, dictated rules for conflicts and excluded slander and flattery even during the harshest phases of confrontation.[71]

An analytic distinction between 'instrumental friendship' and 'emotional friendship' comes across as abstract in the context of the complex notion of friendship that we have theorized.[72] It certainly has the aspects of an individual sentiment based on a social value – *familiaritas* – but it is also a category of exclusion/inclusion belonging to the sphere of 'reason of state'.

Let us draw a first conclusion. The theory of factions, as it emerges from the documents produced by the informative and diplomatic apparatus of kings and princes and from the treatises that members of the Sacred College put into circulation within the court, cannot be traced solely to the language of dissimulation as an exclusive key to baroque politics. The theory of factions also refers to other political categories. It is based, in fact, on the absolute importance of information in the management of decision-making processes, on the idea that negotiation – a central concept in all seventeenth-century political literature – could sway decisions that, although made after a realistic consideration of a variety of interests, were also based on an understanding of the inclinations, nature and affections of individuals. The 'art of the faction' penetrated the character of the men who had to use courtesy, persuasion and humanity in order to govern their factions.[73] In this political grammar, friendship bows to interests, but bestows upon them a kinder, gentler language. Thus, the bonds that held factions together were not only a political mortar, but also a stimulus of honour and an obligation of gratitude.

---

[71] Ibid., f. 160v and 163r; *Teorica intorno al Conclave*, f. 117.

[72] J. Boissevain, *Friends of Friends. Networks, Manipulators and Coalitions*, Oxford, 1974; E. R. Wolf, 'Kinship, Friendship and Patron–Client Relations in Complex Societies', in Schmidt, Guasti, Landé and Scott (eds.), *Friends, Followers and Factions*, pp. 167–77.

[73] This idea of Rome as a school of 'courtesy' often emerges from documents: see *Discurso para el Sir Don Iuan de Austria sobre su Yda à Italia*, BNM, ms. 8755, f. 41v; *Discurso de Mons. Varela para el Card. Borja*, ibid., f. 106; Lottini, *Discorso sopra le Attioni del Conclave*, p. 493.

These precepts on the procedures for forming factions in the Roman court reached their greatest application during conclaves, but how close to reality are these representations? How did these general rules apply to the constantly changing political situation? Were the conflicts dominated by chance or circumstance, or did they adhere to rules, deep trends or implicit mechanisms?

THE PRACTICE OF FACTIONS

In conclusion, without attempting an analysis of the five conclaves held between 1605 and 1644, let us compare the principles of the theory of factions, as elaborated in Rome in the sixteenth and seventeenth centuries, with the outcome of the factional conflicts in relation to three main points: (a) the true power of the cardinal-nephew in determining the outcome of the papal election following the death of his pontiff-uncle; (b) the procedures governing interactions between the faction of the cardinal-nephew and those of the international powers; (c) the transformation of this interaction over a given period.

Let us begin with an observation: the number of cardinals appointed is directly proportionate to the length of a papacy. In the period under examination, Paul V Borghese created sixty cardinals, Gregory XV Ludovisi ten, and Urban VIII Barberini seventy-four. In theory, therefore, the number of cardinals appointed and the demographic rate of transformation of the Sacred College determined the size of every cardinal-nephew's faction. In practice, however, the vicissitudes of factions were related to factors that are difficult to quantify, such as the fidelity of the *creature*, the ability of a cardinal-nephew to form alliances with other faction heads and establish wider fronts and, above all, the quality of the relationship between the cardinal-nephew and the European powers that could use the *jus exclusivae* against papal candidates.

An analysis of the results of these conclaves appears to show a pattern: generally, the cardinal-nephew's candidate was not successful, although the victor was often one of the deceased pope's *creature*.

Cardinal Pietro Aldobrandini,[74] the nephew of Pope Clement VIII, did not succeed in controlling the two 1605 conclaves as he would have wished. In the first, which elected Leo XI Medici, the cardinal-nephew Aldobrandini – who endorsed the election of Cardinal Zacchia – could count on twenty-two to twenty-eight votes out of the sixty-nine members of the Sacred College, and on the backing of the French, the Venetians and the Florentines against the coalition of Cardinals Montalto

---

[74] For the life of Pietro Aldobrandini, see E. Fasano Guarini in *DBI*, vol. II, pp. 107–12.

and Farnese with the Spaniards. The latter upheld Tolomeo Gallio against the candidature of Cardinal Baronio,[75] who, despite the opposition's counteractions, was very nearly elected on 30 March 1605. In the ensuing stalemate, the successful diplomatic manoeuvres of the French Cardinal Joyeuse isolated the Spanish faction, gained the backing of Cardinal Montalto, political heir of Pope Sixtus V, and forced Cardinal Aldobrandini to abandon his initial candidate.[76] In May 1605, following Alessandro de' Medici's brief reign as Leo XI, the coalitions remained practically unaltered, but the allies had grown farther apart and distrust had set in. The first Spanish candidate, Sauli, was vetoed by Cardinal Aldobrandini; Pierbendetti's candidature, proposed by Montalto, was rejected by the Spanish faction; Aldobrandini's Cardinal Tosco was blocked by the 'spiritual' cardinals, who continued to endorse Baronio. As a result of this conflict between Baronio and Tosco, Cardinal Borghese, a *creatura* of Clement VIII, was elected *per adoratione*. Spain assented to this election because Camillo Borghese had been nuncio extraordinary to Phillip II (1593). On the death of Paul V, in 1621, the powerful cardinal-nephew Scipione Borghese, who headed forty-two of his uncle's *creature*, took for granted the election of Cardinal Pietro Campora, administrator of the Borghese family and personal secretary and major-domo to the cardinal-nephew.[77] However, the cardinal-nephew had undervalued the Aldobrandini opposition and had privileged relations with only a few of the cardinal-princes. The initiative of Cardinal Orsini, a personal 'enemy' of the Borghese, who was related to the Bishop of Béziers, the Florentine Giambattista Bonsi (who was very close to Marie de Médicis) rested upon the French exclusion of Campora.[78] The election of Cardinal Ludovisi was the outcome of negotiations carried out by the two opposing fronts. Although Ludovisi had been promoted by Paul V, he was not the cardinal-nephew's choice, but rather the *creatura* of that pope and preferred by the coalition between the French and Aldobrandini. In 1623 (the first elections after Gregory XV's bull), the election dynamics seem to have remained the same, although contemporaries believed that the foreign ambassadors appeared to have less influence.[79] The Borghese faction, given the

---

[75] For the life of Cesare Baronio, see A. Pincherle in *DBI*, vol. VI, pp. 470–8.

[76] *Conclave dove fu creato Papa il Cardinale Alessandro de' Medici*, in Archivio dell'Ufficio delle Celebrazioni Liturgiche del Sommo Pontefice, vol. 214, f. 160.

[77] A. Tassoni, 'Relazione sopra il Conclave in cui fu eletto Papa Gregorio XV' (1621), in P. Puliatti (ed.), *Annali e scritti storici e politici*, Modena, 1990, vol. I, p. 267. On Cardinal Campora see E. Becker in *DBI*, XVII, pp. 602–4.

[78] *Les Differents Arrivez a Rome Entre les Ambassadeurs de France et l'Espagne à la nouvelle élection du Pape*, Paris, 1621.

[79] *Le relazioni degli Stati europei lette al Senato*, Series I, *Spagna*, vol. I, Venice, 1858, pp. 688–9.

short duration of the next papacy, was still numerous and, according to a Florentine document compiled during the pope's illness in 1622, could still count on twenty-two or twenty-three definite votes.[80] These votes were once again, but with greater discretion, reserved for Cardinal Campora, while the cardinal Borghese subordinately indicated Cardinals Veralli, Cennino and Millino as possible candidates. The cardinal-nephew chose Cardinal Bandini,[81] a candidature which immediately encountered the firm opposition of the Grand Duke – a hostility that dated back to Florentine factional conflicts during the age of Cosimo I – as well as Aldobrandini's diffidence. A solution was finally reached, thanks to Cardinal Caetani's mediation, with the candidature of Cardinal Barberini, a Tuscan who, though not a confidant of the Grand-Duke, was not as disliked as Bandini. Maffeo Barberini had become a cardinal under Paul V, but was not considered a *creatura* strictly bound to the Borghese faction, as he had earned his fame in the court as the nuncio to France during the pontificate of Clement VIII Aldobrandini.[82]

During the troubled conclave of 1644, a Barberini *creatura*, Pamphili, was elected after a full-fledged clash that had not left any space for mediation with the anti-Barberini bloc.

Thus, while acknowledging the unique nature of every conclave, it seems possible to hypothesize that the key role in negotiations was generally played by the previous pope's cardinal-nephew, or by the most important personalities of the old college if the cardinal-nephew was not present.

The opposition between older and younger cardinals, which is clear in the sources, was not a conflict between two opposing blocs. However, it is certainly indicative of the profound difference between the election of a 'young' and an 'old' pontiff. Naturally, a young pontiff implied a long papacy and the chance to reinforce a given family and faction by means of a systematic policy of office appointments. In reality, however, the old and new colleges did not represent two clear-cut sides. At the crucial moment of a papal election, the solution always depended on negotiations between segments of the old and the new colleges.

Wolfgang Reinhard has recently proposed an interpretation of the relationship between the Roman factional coalitions: 'In conclave as in everyday policy the ruling family tended to form a coalition with their

---

[80] ASF, MP, 3983, f. 101, *Ristretto della Relazione sopra il Conclave*, dated 12 April 1622.

[81] On Ottavio Bandini see A. Merola in *DBI*, vol. v, pp. 712–18.

[82] BAV, Barb. Lat., 9927, ff. 1–97 (*Conclave dell'anno 1623 nel quale fu messa la prima volta in uso la Bolla dell'elettione di Gregorio XV*); Vat. Lat., 12175/7, ff. 79–83 (*Discorso sopra l'elettione del futuro Pontefice*); BL, Royal 14 A xviii, ff. 125r–175v (*Conclave della Sede Vacante di Papa Gregorio XV*); Bodleian Library, ms. e Museo 105, ff. 1–33 (*Conclave nel quale è stato creato Papa Urbano VIII*).

predecessors once removed, whereas the immediate predecessors usually joined those twice removed in opposition, waiting for the successors of the present lords of Rome'.[83]

Although this scheme cannot be taken as a general rule for explaining the Roman political system, which must be studied through to precise historical phases, it does adequately describe certain aspects of the evolution of relations among papal families in the first half of the seventeenth century.

During the reign of Pope Gregory XV Ludovisi a formidable alliance was created. This alliance between the families of the reigning pope and the Aldobrandini (the ruling papal family before the time of Paul V Borghese, who, in turn, had preceded Gregory XV Ludovisi) is one of the keys to understanding the factional system of the early seventeenth century. It went back a long way. The career of Gregory XV Ludovisi had been furthered by Clement VIII Aldobrandini, who as a cardinal had facilitated his nomination as 'Referendary of the Signature of Justice'. This bond was reinforced after the election of Gregory XV through the selection of the pope's closest collaborators. After the death of Cardinal Pietro Aldobrandini on 10 February 1621, his major-domo Monsignor Giovan Battista Agucchi became papal secretary. Moreover, Gregory XV created Pietro's nephew, Ippolito Aldobrandini, cardinal on 19 April, and on 25 April celebrated the marriage between his own niece Ippolita Ludovisi and Giovanni Giorgio Aldobrandini, the brother of Cardinal Ippolito, who became the pope's nephew. From this moment onwards, the Aldobrandini and the Ludovisi were one faction.

Marriages between the families of popes and cardinals played a major role in the forging of factions.[84] After the Aldobrandini–Ludovisi wedding, another very important strategic matrimonial union was celebrated for political reasons. The marriage between Olimpia, daughter of Giovanni Giorgio and Ippolita Ludovisi, and Paolo Borghese was agreed on 4 September 1638, as it had been imposed by Cardinal Aldobrandini's testament.[85] The Barberini waged a long battle against

---

[83] Reinhard, *Papal Power*, p. 351.

[84] The conferment of the cardinalship often took place at the same time as the matrimonial alliance between a cardinal's sister and the family of the reigning pope. (Weber, *Senatus Divinus*, pp. 92–101.) On the importance of weddings for conclave alliances, see I. Fosi and M. A. Visceglia, 'Marriage and Politics at the Papal Court in the Sixteenth and Seventeenth Centuries', in *Marriage in Italy*, pp. 197–224, note 84. On the relations between the families of cardinals, see the documented genealogical reconstruction by C. Weber, *Genealogien zur Papstgeschichte*, vol. II, Stuttgart, 1999.

[85] The testament of Cardinal Ippolito is in BAV, Barb. Lat., 5822, ff. 13–18. Cardinale Aldobrandini died in July 1638. The matrimonial agreement between the sixteen-year-old Olimpia and Paolo Borghese, the son of Marco Antonio Borghese and Camilla Orsini, was signed on 4 September 1638.

this union, which they perceived as the consolidation of a vast hostile bloc.[86]

In the phase immediately preceding conclaves, and even during them, negotiations for papal elections were very closely related to matrimonial negotiations.

L'avviso per li ministri del re Cattolico (Admonition for the ministers of the Catholic King [King of Spain]), a document compiled in 1644 during the complex phase following the death of Urban VIII, vehemently insisted that every means should be used to hinder a possible matrimonial alliance between the Barberini and the Pamfili (since the latter was a possible candidate), and to isolate the former. Moreover, it stated that the alliance between the Pamphili and the Ludovisi should be encouraged in order to consolidate the Aldobrandini/Ludovisi/Borghese coalition that had formed over the previous decades against the Barberini.[87]

The election of a Pamphili to the papal throne was in fact confirmed by means of a matrimonial alliance when on 21 December 1644 Costanza Pamphili became the third wife of Prince Nicolò Ludovisi. Years later, a 'peace' between the Pamphili and Barberini would be concluded as a result of the marriage between Olimpia Giustiniani, the pope's niece, and Maffeo Barberini, heir to the Barberini estates and the title of Prince of Palestrina.

Marriages – results of the interaction between the curial elite, former cardinal-nephews, and international factions – were a powerful dynamic factor in the greater process of transformation of factional fronts.

Let us now return to the conflicts between France and Spain during the early seventeenth century.

Early in 1605, the troubled year which witnessed two successive conclaves and the elections of Leo XI Medici and Paul V Borghese, the Duke of Sessa wrote to the Duke of Lerma alarmed about the agitation caused by the arrival of Cardinal Joyeuse, the protector of France, who had been sent to Rome to reorganize the French faction at the Roman court.[88] The Duke of Escalona, who was nominated during the same year to replace the Duke of Sessa, confirmed the troublesome news in his dispatches: the king of France had sent 20,000 *scudi* from Lyon to Rome, by means of bills of exchange lodged with Florentine merchants.

---

[86] See AGS, Estados Pequeños, legajo 3841 on the 'great aversion of the pope', who had his own designs regarding Olimpia's wedding.

[87] 'I must use every means to make sure that no matrimony or matrimonial agreement is made between the future pontiff and the Barberini': BAV, Barb. Lat., 5324, f. 10v; also BNM, ms. 978.

[88] AGS, Estado, Roma, legajo 1870. The ambassador ended: 'In conclusion, I believe that the nephews of popes who display an inclination to serve His Majesty should be embraced, but be sure not to lose old friends and act in a way that will keep the faction together.'

Cardinal Aldobrandini had become the pivot of a bloc that united the French, Venetians and Florentines.[89]

During the second half of the sixteenth century, in the absence of French initiative due to the wars of religion, traditional Spanish policy in Rome consisted in attracting papal families into the orbit of Spain through the concession of Neapolitan estates. This proved to be an extremely successful ploy with the Boncompagni, who became Dukes of Sora, and the Peretti, who became Princes of Venafro. After that, however, the game became far more complex and competitive. Not only did the Spanish faction need to be consolidated, as did the great and small Roman nobility (the Colonna, the Boncompagni, the Caetani, the Savelli, the Conti, the Capranica, the Mattei, the Caffarelli, the Capizucchi) who were divided by profound rivalries based on titles, *encomiendas*, knightly customs and pensions,[90] but the Spanish also needed to allure the powerful former cardinal-nephew Aldobrandini to their side and re-inforce the 'confidence' of the reigning pope. The complete transition of the Aldobrandini family to the Spanish side took place, once again, through the bestowal of land.[91] In 1612, the Rossano estate was sold for 85,000 ducats to Giovan Giorgio, the nephew of Cardinal Pietro. In the 1620s, the alliance between the Aldobrandini and the Ludovisi was consolidated. In 1621, when cardinal-nephew Ludovisi requested that the Spanish court allow his brother Nicolò Ludovisi to marry Isabella Gesualdo, heiress to the Principality of Venosa in the Kingdom of Naples, he did this not only – as Cardinal Borgia noted – in the pope's name, but also in that of the two families: 'Cardinal Ludovisio, who wishes to maintain and increase the prestige of his Family, will always be bound to the service of Your Majesty in person and with his faction, which will be increasingly powerful as it has been united with that of Cardinal Aldobrandini, after the new relationship with the Prince of Rossano.'[92]

The Barberini followed an even more tortuous political route after gaining the papal throne. Paris rejoiced at the crowning of Maffeo Barberini, as the French court knew the 'great inclination' that the new pope had for France, 'as his fortune had been greatly helped by the late King Henri IV'.[93] However, until the 1630s, the bond between Paris and Rome, which was also cemented by a great fervour of intellectual exchange, did not obstruct the traditional Spanish policy of 'extending

---

[89] AGS, Estado, Roma, legajo 980, 23 August 1605 and ibid., 23 July 1605.

[90] See AMAE, Estado, legajo 54, ff. 441–3 (*Pensionarios y Feudatarios del Rey Phelippe Tercero en el Reyno de Napoles siendo Ambaxador de S. Mag. a Roma el Marqués de Aytona*).

[91] R. Lefevre, 'Il patrimonio romano degli Aldobrandini nel Seicento', *Archivio della Società Romana di Storia patria*, 82 (1959), 18ff.

[92] AGS, Estado, Roma, legajo 1868 (*Lettera del Cardinale Borgia al Re*, dated 18 June 1621). On the ascent of the Ludovisi, see also Mario Rosa's contribution in this volume.

[93] *Advis donné au Roy sur l'estat present des affaires de Rome sous Urbain VIII* (n. d.), p. 3.

their arms to the popes' nephews' ('abrazar los sobrinos'). The special instructions to the Marquis of Castel Rodrigo stated that 'A pension of 10,000 ducats was offered to the Barberino cardinal when he came here (Madrid) as a legate *a latere* … but the cardinal refused the money and only accepted the protection of the Kingdoms of Aragon and Portugal.'[94]

Nonetheless, even before the period of open conflict (1635) between France and Spain, the fact that the pope had not condemned the alliance between Richelieu's France and the heretics widened the gap between the *Monarquía* and the reigning pontiff. This culminated in an open crisis with Madrid on 8 March 1632, when Cardinal Borgia, protector of Spain and ambassador of the Spanish king, protested in the consistory. This event may have concealed a real conspiracy.[95] During the 1630s, faced with a deep crisis in the Spanish faction in Rome,[96] Madrid's policy abruptly changed in style. While the French diplomats continued to work to keep the pope's family united, the Spanish strove to dismantle the group that had formed around the reigning pontiff: 'we will take the faction over by means of the disagreements between brothers.'[97]

Nonetheless, Ranke's authoritatively advanced *topos* of an entirely pro-French papacy must be reviewed. The internal rivalries of the papal family, Urban VIII's authoritarianism and the crisis sparked by the novelties introduced into court ceremonial[98] created repeated occasions for dissatisfaction even with the French ambassador. In 1641, the tone of the instructions to the Marquis of Fontenay turned harsh and peremptory:

> The Marquis must know that rumour has it that [Francesco Barberini] is a good ecclesiastic and is therefore said (*taxê*) not to love the grandeur of the Kings and the Princes of Christendom, following the inclinations of his uncle the pope who wants to lower [this respect] more than any of his predecessors; and if the cardinal has any affection for any prince, it is surely greater for Spain than for France.[99]

---

[94] Quintín Aldea (ed.), *España, el Papado y el Imperio*, p. 332 (the instructions are dated Madrid, 20 March 1631).

[95] Regarding this event, which has not been addressed by recent studies, see A. Leman, *Urbain VIII et la rivalité de la France et de la Maison d'Autriche de 1631 à 1635*, Lille and Paris, 1920, pp. 129–44.

[96] AGS, Estados Pequeños, legajo 3837 (*Consulta de Estado*, 11 August 1635).

[97] AGS, *Estado, Rome*, legajo 2996. Also see *Noticias de la Negociación de Roma* prepared by Saavedra Fajardo for the Count of Castel Rodrigo: Quintín Aldea (ed.), *España, el Papado y el Imperio*, p. 314.

[98] On the political operation to restore the office of prefect carried out during the Barberini papacy, see M. A. Visceglia, 'Il cerimoniale come linguaggio politico: su alcuni conflitti di precedenza alla corte di Roma tra Cinquecento e Seicento', in M. A. Visceglia and C. Brice (eds.), *Cérémonial et rituel à Rome (XVIe–XIXe siècle)*, Rome, 1997, pp. 117–76.

[99] BL, Add. 5459 (*Instruction que le Roy a commandé estre donnée a Mr. le Marquis de Fontanay s'allant resider son Ambassade ordinaire à Rome*, ff. 365–404).

During the conclave of 1644, when Antonio Barberini was cardinal protector of France, the crucial help of a segment of the Barberini faction, headed by Francesco, led to the election of Cardinal Pamfili.[100] After the pope's death, the shift towards the Spanish side was completed through the purchase of estates in Abruzzo and aggregation, in 1663, with the Neapolitan nobility of Seggio di Nido.

The comparison of these roughly outlined events certainly reveals the non-linear evolution and the intensity of the conflicts, but it also seems to warrant a complex picture, laden with *chiaroscuro*, of the relations existing between Spain and the Court of Rome. On the one hand, during the first half of the seventeenth century, notwithstanding pensions and awards, the outcome of conclaves was never certain and sometimes, as in the case of the first conclave of 1605, turned out to be a complete upset. The result depended on the outcome of negotiations in which the role of the anti-Spanish bloc was invariably significant. On the other hand, following a papal election, the attraction that the Spanish feudal system had for the papal families seemed to be irresistible and capable of prolonging itself, of vanquishing the idea of a precocious Spanish crisis after the Peace of Westphalia.

Furthermore, the families of cardinals and popes were never integrated into the patronage system of the European powers by means of direct negotiations. On the contrary, it was the result of a dynamic process administered by various intermediaries and especially the cardinal-princes.

During the period examined in this chapter, this role belonged to Cardinal Carlo de' Medici, who had been made a cardinal by Paul V in 1615. A document dated 12 April 1622, written during the illness of Gregory XV Ludovisi, suggested – despite the new situation brought about by the papal bull of 1621 – that the cardinal could become the principal mediator of the conclave as the leader of a transversal bloc spanning those of the French, of the Spanish and of the last two cardinal-nephews.[101] Thus, in the 1620s, the Medici cardinal was ready to act, not as the head of a Tuscan faction, but as the representative of a far more prestigious coalition of Italian cardinal-princes, who were ambiguously 'equidistant from France and Spain and, through the alliance with the Medici, had annexed important segments of the Roman aristocracy'.[102] The Medici faction had been consolidated during the pontificate of Urban VIII in order to counter the Barberini faction and favour the Spanish one. Its first test took place in 1637, during the

---

[100] BL, Harley 3585, f. 570v; Bodleian Library ms. Clarendon 135.
[101] ASF, MP, 3983, f. 90v.
[102] Ibid., 3883, f. 67 (letter in cypher dated August 24).

pope's serious illness, when Carlo de' Medici acted as if the Holy See were vacant and became the true protagonist of the 1644 conclave, the backbone of an alliance that embraced the noble Roman cardinals and Spain.[103]

Thus, both international patronage and that of the cardinal princes could strengthen, as well as weaken, the patronage of a cardinal-nephew. Following each conclave, there was a crucial period in which the most important appointments, those that changed after every papal election, had to be distributed. This was when the pope's electors formulated their requests. The correspondence of Cardinal Medici during the months following the election of Urban VIII allows us to look into the mechanism used to balance the power of factions: the distribution of curial offices. Cardinal Caetani demanded the nunciature in Spain for his nephew; Cardinal Maurizio of Savoy made numerous requests: the *Dataria* for Monsignor Verospi, the Governorship of Rome for Monsignor Vulpio. The Borghese cardinal recommended Curzio Caffarelli for the generalship in Avignon, Cardinal Cennini for the bishopric of Faenza and requested an extension on the deadline of the family *Monte*. There were various aspirants to the legations in Bologna and Ferrara as well as the nunciature in Florence.[104]

A significant element for the composition of factions was the way in which the pope and his family reacted to this great number of requests for reciprocity, which were often incompatible. In the case of the Barberini, one of the keys to understanding how it was that – with a Sacred College completely renewed after a pontificate of twenty years, without any competition from other cardinal-nephews (Ludovisi had died in 1632, Borghese in 1633 and Aldobrandini in 1638), and when a majority of the voting cardinals were *creature* of Urban VIII – the cardinal-nephew Francesco still did not manage to impose his candidate, Cardinal Giulio Sacchetti,[105] is an analysis of the way in which the pope his uncle had made appointments to the Sacred College.

---

[103] Cardinal Medici arrived in Rome after the death of the pope on 7 August. On 9 August, he wrote: 'Cardinal Albornoz has the following, but he cannot do anything without the counsel of his fellow nationals and us, the king's servants, and we will hold our ground in order to mortify the Barberini as much as possible' (ibid., 3889, letter dated 9 August).

[104] ASF, MP, 3883, f. 35 (letter dated 2 August 1623); f. 44 (letter dated 16 August 1623); ff. 118–19 (letter dated 2 September 1623); f. 256 (letter dated 15 September 1623); f. 255 (enclosure dated 13 October 1623); f. 192 (letter dated 29 September 1623).

[105] On the Medici opposition in the Barberini conclave, see ibid., 3889 (letter dated 30 August 1644). On the defeats of Cardinal Sacchetti in the two conclaves of 1644 and 1655, and the complex relations between the prelate, his family and the Medici, see Fosi, *All'ombra dei Barberini*, pp. 139–70.

The pope's attitude to appointments had changed profoundly during his long pontificate. During the first years, he had clearly acted according to the mechanisms of reciprocity, although it had never been the only criterion he used to make his choices. The rigid concentration of power in the pontiff's family, the choice of curial collaborators on the basis of their personal ties with the pope's relatives (but also on account of cultural and intellectual affinities) and the distribution of charges favouring the requests of kings and princes of the blood only when it was absolutely necessary to the mechanisms of papal policy, naturally caused the bloc of cardinal-princes, who had been of essential assistance in Urban VIII's election, profound disappointment.

On the other hand, the War of Castro upset the political *ratio* of Urban's papacy. From the 1640s onwards, the logic of a fiscal dictatorship forced the Barberini pope to accentuate his dependence on the Genoese.[106] The venal 'College of the Clerics of the Chamber' was revived in favour of Genoese prelates, who often prevailed in the important appointment to the treasury and in many nominations of cardinals.

Nonetheless, the strengthening of the venal appointments – as judged by the contemporary treatises on factions mentioned above – was wholly prejudicial to the guarantee of fidelity to the cardinal-nephew. As declared enemies of the Spaniards, who considered the Rome of the 1640s as a warfront, the scene of an armed conflict in which Castilians opposed Catalans and Portuguese, suspected by the French themselves and hated by the Roman nobility, the Barberini could certainly not depend on the fidelity of that milieux of business and finance which they had favoured almost exclusively for years.

At the heart of these factional problems lies the ambiguous issue of fidelity. Fidelity to the cardinal-nephew seems to have been weak in the case of cardinals who, although closely related to the papal family, were the subjects of foreign powers, and it was similarly uncertain with *creature* who recognized the dual sovereignty of the pope – and that was not only due to the ease with which patronage bonds were dissolved.[107]

During the period under examination, the theory of factions appears to vacillate as regards some of its very basic tenets. Following the election

---

[106] See C. Costantini, 'Corrispondenti genovesi dei Barberini', in *La storia dei Genovesi*, vol. VII, Genoa, 1987, p. 192.

[107] S. Kettering, 'The Historical Development of Political Clientelism', *The Journal of Interdisciplinary History*, 18 (1988), pp. 419–47. For a recent and well-researched analysis of the dissolution of the Barberini patronage system during the Castro War and the initial years of Innocent X's pontificate, see C. Costantini, 'Fazione urbana. Sbandamento e ricomposizione di una grande clientela a metà Seicento', in *Quaderni di storia e letteratura*, Genoa, 4 (1998), pp. 9–189.

of Innocent X, the *jus exclusivae* exercised by kings began to be criticized with renewed vigour and for new reasons. And a new issue came to the surface. It concerned the fidelity to the pope and the pope's family and the implications of friendship as a bond for factions.[108]

The collapse of the Barberini faction at the conclave of 1644 dramatically highlighted the issue of ingratitude,[109] which emerged from many documents circulating in the Sacred College. To the charge of ingratitude made in the *Istruttione per gli ambasciatori che assisteranno alla Corte di Roma per il re Christianissimo* (Instructions for the ambassadors to the Court of Rome for the most christian [French] King), attributed to Baly di Valenzé but possibly written by Capponi or Pallotta,[110] Cardinal Cesi replied:

> I am not ungrateful: the uncle of Barberini made me a cardinal and I cherish his memory and maintain the obligation that I have and which a Roman knight owes as a member of a family that in the space of only one hundred years has had the honour of the purple no fewer than four times, not counting my own appointment; moreover, having fulfilled the most important offices with praise, and purchased offices at the right prices, I feel free to choose and to do as I please.[111]

The contradiction sparked by the bull of 1621, between the freedom of a secret vote and factional logic, ambiguously began to bear its fruits, but this process became clearer and more dramatic in 1655 during the first conclave, which witnessed the birth of a new faction, 'the faction of God'.[112]

---

[108] The debate on the *jus esclusivae* took place, in fact, during the pontificate of Alexander VII. The most important document referring to the conclave of Innocent X is probably the *Discorso del Sig.r Card. Albizi col quale si prova che non possono le Corone nè altri Principi secolari escludere i Cardinali dal Pontificato* (BNM, ms. 1391, ff. 1–22). Moreover, the precepts regarding the tasks of the *papabile* cardinal are very different from those relating to the earlier part of the century that we have analysed here: 'Whoever is elected will not be obliged to thank anyone but God; he will not have to acknowledge the work of his friends; he will be free to do everything that is for the glory of God and useful to Holy Church, without remorse for ingratitude towards his benefactors who often have other interests' (Biblioteca Casanatense, Rome, ms. 2098, ff. 121r–131r, *Avvisi e Considerazioni da suggerire ad un Cardinale che fosse assegnato al Pontificato*).

[109] This point can be found in BNM, ms. 418, ff. 89r–126v (*Discorso a D. Luigi de Haro fatto da persone confidenti alla Corona di Spagna*).

[110] BAV, Vat. Lat., 8354.

[111] BAV, Barb. Lat., 5682, f. 331v, *Istruzione e regola per i Cardinali papabili*.

[112] See M.-L. Rodén, *Church Politics in Seventeenth-Century Rome. Cardinal Decio Azzolino Queen Christina of Sweden, and the* Squadrone Volante, Stockholm 2000, which was published during the compilation of the present work.

THE SECRETARIAT OF STATE AS THE POPE'S
SPECIAL MINISTRY*

ANTONIO MENNITI IPPOLITO

METHODOLOGICAL PROBLEMS

Scholars who have tried to work their way through the intricate web of relationships that characterized the Roman curia at different times in its history have often been faced with a complex situation because historians dealing with the several agencies that made up the curia have often tended to assess each agency independently from the rest, as though it were isolated from the general context. One example will suffice to illustrate this point. Madelaine Laurain-Portemer, in her work (which is of considerable importance) on the cardinal-nephew superintendent of the ecclesiastical state,[1] confines her attention to that office and thus ends by neglecting all the other curial offices (notably the Secretariat of State). It is remarkable how many studies on the Roman curia insist on the competition between the various offices and dwell on the overwhelming power of one over the rest rather than on the balance between them – as though this latter approach were out of the question, and the very life of government agencies were not normally (and, for obvious reasons, necessarily) based on some form of equilibrium.

This approach has produced a strong tendency toward the fragmentation of research and has influenced the latter in the way I have just described, focusing attention on one specific aspect while neglecting others, or promoting studies (some of them quite significant) on broader topics, but above all on individual pontificates.[2] Given the narrow chronological

---

* The English translation is by Professor Domenico Sella, who was especially generous in giving his time, offering an example of style and scholarship for which I am more than grateful and which I will not forget.
[1] M. Laurain-Portemer, 'Absolutisme et népotisme. La surintendance de l'Etat ecclésiastique', *Bibliothèque de l'Ecole des Chartes*, 131 (1973), pp. 487–568.
[2] The most significant research on the role of the Secretary of State has been by German scholars, under the auspices of the Istituto Storico Germanico in Rome. A. Kraus, 'Secretarius und Sekretariat. Der Ursprung der Institution des Staatssekretariats

parameters which successful research sometimes requires, it has often been impossible to appreciate the fact that in the original framework of the Roman curia what holds true of one pope almost invariably does not hold true of his successor.

The classic evolutionary pattern, which rests on the notion of a continuous, linear transformation of men and structures, is not, therefore, really applicable to the landscape we are dealing with here, a landscape in which it was hard for 'innovations' to become permanent parts of the system as they had to be reconfirmed again and again in each pontificate. Therefore, identifying short- or even medium-term politico-institutional 'models' is largely an illusory enterprise.

Lastly, it is not uncommon for scholars to keep different lines of investigation separate: diplomatic historians have not always been of assistance to 'political' historians (and vice versa), and both groups have allowed themselves to be conditioned by the false objective of identifying the *first* Secretary, the *first* traces of the Secretariat, each scholar being anxious to detect the 'most' *first* (or *last*) rather than inquiring into the role of an office and its incumbent within the overall structure of the Curia.[3] This tendency also accounts for (e.g.) the persistent confusion between the

und ihr Einfluss auf die Entwicklung moderner Regierungsformen in Europa', *Römische Quartalschrift*, 55 (1960), pp. 43–84; idem, *Das päpstliche Staatssekretariat unter Urban VIII. 1623–1644*, Rome, Freiburg and Vienna, 1964; J. Semmler, 'Beiträge zum Aufbau des päpstilichen Staatssekretariats unter Paul V (1605–1621)', *Römische Quartalschrift*, 54 (1959), pp. 40–80; idem, *Das päpstliche Staatssekretariat in den Pontificaten Pauls V. und Gregors XV. 1605–1623*, Rome, Freiburg and Vienna, 1969; L. Hammermayer, 'Grundlinien der Entwicklung des päpstlichen Staatssekretariats von Paul V. bis Innozenz X. (1605–1655)', ibid., pp. 157–202; K. Jaitner, *Instructiones Pontificum Romanorum: Die Hauptinstruktionen Clemens VIII für die Nuntien und Legaten an den europäischen Fürstenhofen (1592–1605)*, Tübingen, 1983. On this research period see G. Lutz, 'Le ricerche internazionali sulle nunziature e l'edizione delle istruzioni generali di Clemente VIII (1592–1605)', in P. Vian (ed.), *L'Archivio Segreto Vaticano e le ricerche storiche*, Rome, 1983, pp. 167–80. At the source of these studies, however, stands the fundamental essay by P. Richard, 'Origines et développement de la Secrétairerie d'Etat apostolique (1417–1623)', *Revue d'Histoire Ecclésiastique*, 11 (1910), pp. 56–72.

3 The search for the earliest Secretary authorized to sign official letters, or the earliest Secretary to whom such letters were addressed rather than to the cardinal-nephew, has yielded meagre results. The earliest may have been Giacomo Panciroli or Fabio Chigi, but this does not really matter, since in subsequent pontificates the situation changed and one finds the 'cardinal padrone' stealing the show. Equally misleading is the attempt to pin down the beginning of the series of Secretaries of State who were cardinals, as if wearing the cardinal's hat would of itself guarantee a special dignity to that office: at the source of this false, yet widely shared interpretation (shared also by Frenz and by Jedin) is a passage in Hammermayer, 'Grundlinien'. N. Del Re, *La Curia Romana*, Rome, 3rd edn 1970, dates the beginning of the series of the cardinal Secretaries of State from 1644 with Giacomo Panciroli. This point will be discussed later on.

cardinal-nephew and the Secretary of State, two distinct figures who rarely coincided in the same person, but who have often – indeed, habitually – been assimilated to each other.[4]

CARDINAL-NEPHEW AND SECRETARY OF STATE

The most obvious instance of curial offices that should not be approached in isolation from each other is that of the two figures just mentioned, the cardinal-nephew and the Secretary of State.

The role of the former, as a fundamental component in the life of the curia, took shape during the pontificate of Pius IV and gradually acquired more precise features through the actions of Pius V, Gregory XIV, Paul V, Gregory XV and Urban VIII. But while the cardinal-nephew was the pope's *alter ego* in an increasingly official form, under some circumstances it was the Secretary of State who filled that role and at times that of the nephew's *alter ego* as well.

For a long time the Secretary acted as a discreet assistant to the sovereign pontiff and to his closest kinsman. His role long remained behind the scenes: confined to the task (no mean task, to be sure) of ensuring the smooth operation of the papal Secretariat, the incumbent was occasionally entrusted with specific, temporary responsibilities. During the seventeenth century the office of Secretary gradually acquired more clearly defined features: the Secretary assumed ever greater responsibilities and eventually became, at first occasionally and then more regularly, a serious rival to the pope's nephew.

At the end of this evolution – which was by no means as linear as I have described it – the Secretary of State definitely replaced the cardinal-nephew, thus depriving the practice of nepotism of any institutional alibi and any functional justification. In doing so – and this is the most interesting aspect of the process – the Secretary, rather than expanding his traditional duties as head of the pope's private Secretariat, acquired all or nearly all, those of the cardinal-nephew. In a word, by the close of the seventeenth century, the Secretary of State had become a sort of 'cardinal-nephew' unrelated by blood to the pontiff.

In the following pages I shall reconstruct this process, dealing equally with the nephew and the Secretary, for, as I have already suggested more than once, it was the outcome of the 'competition' between the two

---

[4] See the catalogue of errors presented by C. Mozzarelli, 'Introduzione' to Giovanni Francesco Commendone, *Discorso sopra la Corte di Roma*, Rome, 1996, pp. 10ff.

figures that helped make nepotism indefensible, even from a practical and political standpoint.

The nephew and the pope's secretary

Before the Secretary of State became 'nepotized' – before, that is, he took up the role that had been the papal nephew's – it was the pope's kinsman who lorded it over the curia, coordinating its activities, interpreting the sovereign's will – and, at times, as our sources suggest, replacing it altogether.

The cardinal-nephew's role was essential in many respects, above all because, in the performance of his normal duties, he also had to assure his own future for the day when his uncle would pass away. He therefore had to strive to keep on good terms with the various factions, whether friendly or hostile, in the curia – and occasionally had to act as peacemaker in conflicts between them; besides, he must play the mediating role which the sovereign, secure in his office and whose authority needed no earthly justification, might despise.

The cardinal-nephew, in short, was valued above all because he must look after his uncle on the one hand and himself on the other: he must be concerned for his own future, which depended more on his own personal abilities than on the assets his uncle the pope could provide while still living (material assets in the form of a large endowment; political assets in the form of a faction of *creature* within the College of Cardinals who would always be ready to support the nephew). Caught between these commitments, the cardinal-nephew became the linchpin in a web of relationships that proved indispensable for the smooth operation of the curia. The pontiff's kinsman thus stood as the 'earthly' instrument of a supreme, unchallengeable, absolute authority that found its legitimacy only in the divine sphere. As such, he could contribute to moderating and humanizing that authority and making it less distant from the curial structure – and not only from that structure.[5]

Also significant, and at times totally overwhelming, was the influence the 'cardinal padrone' (literally 'cardinal-boss') exerted on the bureaucratic structure closest to the pope, namely his personal secretariat. It was an efficient agency, and a little mysterious as well. The Venetian ambassador Paolo Paruta, writing in 1595, disclosed that the pontiff never

---

[5] For a careful analysis of the dynamics and the equilibria inside the College of Cardinals see M. A. Visceglia, '"La Giusta Statera de' porporati". Sulla composizione e rappresentazione del Sacro Collegio nella prima metà del Seicento', *Roma moderna e contemporanea*, 4 (1996), pp. 167–212.

relied on the venal college of Apostolic Secretaries (which remained inactive), but rather on other unspecified secretaries to whom he entrusted all matters of importance.[6] Commendone is a more precise observer of these secretaries: he tells us that access to that office was not easy due to the sensitivity of the duties involved, and that practical talent and efficiency were preferred to intellectual gifts.[7] There is little doubt that service in the Secretariat gradually came to be held in greater esteem. In 1651 the ambassador Giovanni Giustiniani noted that one would have thought that at least twenty individuals would be employed in that agency dictating or drafting letters, but he was told that no more than three or four secretaries (obviously he could not verify this in person) were doing all the work and that they 'amply sufficed for the task'.[8]

At this point we may step back for a moment in order briefly to recall the origins of that agency. In the second half of the fifteenth century, under Innocent VIII, the pope's private Secretariat was thoroughly restructured. Innocent created the venal office of Apostolic Secretaries: a body of thirty scribes, *abbreviatores* and code experts whose job it was to draft confidential documents. At the head of the college was the pope's 'secretarius domesticus'. The college of Apostolic Secretaries was subsequently subdivided and rearranged, and during the sixteenth century was turned into the His Holiness's Secretariat also known as the Secret Secretariat, responsible for handling anything to do with secret briefs, briefs addressed to princes, diplomatic dispatches, confidential correspondence and so on.[9] The reorganization was completed sometime

---

[6] E. Alberi (ed.), *Le relazioni degli ambasciatori veneti al Senato*, ser. II, tome IV, vol. X, *Corte di Roma*, Florence, 1857, p. 372. In a *Stato degli Uffitii che si devono spedire alla Dataria con il prezzo corrente nel mese di giugno 1659*, BAV, Chigi, C.III.72, the price listed for each of the twenty-four positions of Apostolic Secretary is 16,500 *scudi*.

[7] The secretaries found 'l'entrata difficile' into their jobs 'per la confidenza che si richiede[va]' ('on account of the confidentiality that was expected'), and the lords preferred 'piuttosto servirsi di chi [avesse] buona mano che di chi [vantasse] un bell'ingegno' ('to avail themselves of someone who had good penmanship rather than of someone who boasted a brilliant mind'): Commendone, *Discorso sopra la Corte*, p. 84.

[8] N. Barozzi and G. Berchet, *Le relazioni della Corte di Roma lette al Senato dagli ambasciatori veneti nel secolo decimosettimo*, ser. III, *Italia, Relazioni di Roma*, vol. I, Venice, 1877; vol. II, Venice, 1879, vol. II, p. 96. The secretaries were so efficient that 'avanza[va] loro anche tempo per altro; così poco cura[va] il papa di diffondersi in negoziati per lettere' ('they had time left for other things; so that the pope wasted little time in handling negotiations by letter').

[9] Ibid., pp. 8off. Commendone, who wrote his *Discorso* in 1554, advised anyone who went to the curia in search of a *professional* career and happened to be 'poor' to seek 'l'utile' ahead of 'l'onore', 'il che però [era] cosa lunga e faticosa'. To succeed it was necessary 'far buona mano di scrivere ed avere almeno una tintura di lettere umane e con tali mezzi e con qualche favore proccurare d'aver luoco sotto i secretari maggiori, e principalmente di quelli del papa o di coloro ch'hanno in mano il governo, e quivi con

in the late sixteenth or early seventeenth century with the creation of the autonomous offices of Secretary of Briefs and Secretary of Briefs to Princes. In the same period the leadership of the Secretariat was redefined: the figure of 'secretarius domesticus' faded away, overshadowed by the encroaching figure of the cardinal-nephew, and the 'secretarius intimus' or major secretary of the pope assumed greater importance; the origin of the office of Secretary of State is generally traced back to the latter.[10]

The 'secretarius domesticus' thus made room for the cardinal-nephew, while the 'secretarius intimus' was called upon to cooperate sometimes with the pope himself, sometimes with the cardinal-nephew, to ensure the proper operation of the secretariat.

The evolution was slow and intermittent, which makes it all the more difficult to retrace and reconstruct its course; responsibilities assumed later by the Secretary of State are often wrongly thought to date back to the earlier period. Finding nothing significant in the figure of 'secretarius intimus', some scholars have confused him with the cardinal-nephew. This has sometimes made it especially hard to identify the actual incumbent of the office of Secretary of State. During the pontificate of Paul V, for instance, a series of individuals (Valenti, Margotti, Malacrida, Feliciani, Perugino, Agucchia) filled that office, and yet, often enough, only Scipione Borghese is referred to as the incumbent although he was never Secretary of State, at least in a formal sense. Moreover, under Urban VIII the pope's nephew, Cardinal Francesco Barberini, is

---

diligenza attendere ad imparare le cose di stato, onde nascono ordinariamente grandi occasioni' ('to have good penmanship and at least a smattering of humanities and with such qualifications and some recommendations to try to find work under the higher secretaries, especially the pope's or those who control the government, and there with diligence concentrate on learning about affairs of state, from which great opportunities often arise'). Commendone's words reveal several interesting aspects: in the first place, that this career was considered especially hard and demanding, so much so that it was recommended to prospective curial candidates of limited resources and, as such, more highly motivated and willing to make sacrifices.

[10] A. Serafini, *Le origini della Pontificia Segreteria di Stato e la "Sapienti Consilio" del B. Pio X*, Città del Vaticano, 1952; T. Frenz, *I documenti pontifici nel medioevo e nell'età moderna*, ed. S. Pagano, Città del Vaticano, 1989, pp. 65ff.; L. Pásztor, 'L'histoire de la Curie Romaine, problème d'histoire de l'Eglise', *Revue d'Histoire Ecclésiastique*, 64 no. 2 (1969), pp. 353–366; L. Pásztor, 'Archivio Segreto Vaticano', in *Guida delle fonti per l'America Latina negli archivi della Santa Sede e negli archivi ecclesiastici d'Italia*, Città del Vaticano, 1970, pp. 73ff.; idem, 'La riforma della Segreteria di Stato di Gregorio XVI. Contributo alla storia delle riforme nello Stato Pontificio', *Bibliofilia*, 55 (1958), pp. 285–305; idem, 'Per la storia della Segreteria di Stato nell'Ottocento. La riforma del 1816', in *Mélanges Eugène Tisserant*, vol. v, Città del Vaticano, 1964, pp. 209–72; P. Partner, *The Pope's Men. The Papal Civil Service in the Renaissance*, Oxford, 1990, pp. 26ff., 42ff., 70ff. and *passim*.

frequently referred to as the head of the Secretariat, although it is certain that other individuals officially succeeded one another in that position.[11]

The question of who held that office may look even more confusing during the ponticates of Clement X and Innocent XI. Over the correct sequence of Federico Borromeo, Francesco Nerli and Alderano Cybo as Secretaries of State another sequence is superimposed which improperly inserts into the list the name of Cardinal Paluzzi Altieri, and it has even been suggested that throughout this long period the only secretary was Decio Azzolini.[12]

The difficulty of finding one's way through this labyrinth is compounded by other 'disturbing' elements. From the later sixteenth century we at times come across impressive figures as Secretary of State, while at other times he appears as a shadowy figure or even a mere stand-in for other curial personages, primarily, of course, the cardinal-nephew. But even at a much later date, when papal nepotism had long been abolished and the Secretaries of State should have had no rivals in the curia, situations arose that seem to contradict all that we have already said. Indeed at the close of the eighteenth century pope Clement XIV's Secretary, Cardinal Pallavicini, was notoriously excluded from all decision making. Pius VI kept this uninfluential Pallavicini in office and at the latter's death went so far as to appoint Ignazio Boncompagni, who was subsequently

---

[11] Lorenzo Magalotti to 1628; Lorenzo Azzolini to 1632; Pietro Benessa in 1634; Francesco Ceva to 1643; Giovambattista Spada in 1644. P. Blet, 'La Congrégation des Affaires de France de 1640', in *Mélanges Eugène Tisserant*, vol. IV, Città del Vaticano, 1964, p. 59 and n. (pp. 59–105). Blet draws on the works of Hammermayer and Kraus cited above. However, G. Moroni in his *Dizionario d'erudizione storico-ecclesiastica*, vol. LXIII, Venice, 1853, p. 281, had already distinguished Francesco Barberini's role from that of the actual Secretaries of State who succeeded one another in that office during Urban VIII's pontificate. I. Fosi, *All'ombra dei Barberini. Fedeltà e servizio nella Roma barocca*, Roma, 1997, p. 66, has recently drawn attention to the existence of 'in proprio' correspondence between nuncios and Barberini, the Superintendent of the ecclesiastical state, as distinct from the correspondence between papal diplomats and the Secretariat of State (on p. 102 she speaks of a Secretariat 'guided' by Francesco Barberini after 1628, but a better word would be 'inspired'). Such instances of overlapping are entirely natural and unavoidable, and not only in government agencies under the *Ancien Régime*. Irrespective of the greater or lesser responsibilities assigned to the Secretary of State or to the nephew, what must be stressed here is that the two figures, and their respective roles, remained distinct.

[12] According to Moroni's *Dizionario*, Pope Altieri's Secretaries of State were Federico Borromeo until his death in 1673 and then Francesco Nerli; several entries in *DBI* report that Borromeo was directly succeeded by the pope's nephew Paluzzi Altieri, who for all practical purposes had already exercised that role, sidelining the proper incumbent (see the entry 'Borromeo, Federico' by G. Lutz). However, the entry 'Azzolini, Decio' by G. De Caro would seem to indicate that Azzolini exercised the office of Secretary of State uninterruptedly from Clement IX's pontificate to Innocent XI's, while others have correctly maintained that the office was held by Alderano Cybo.

forced to resign for reasons of 'indignity' – a case certainly unusual, and perhaps unique.[13] All this should serve, first of all, as a warning against reading the history of that office – and indeed of all curial offices – in terms of a purely mechanical evolution. It is no accident that the line between incumbents *de iure* and incumbents *de facto* is blurred, and Lajos Pásztor has rightly remarked that a Secretariat of State, as we understand it, is discernible only at the opening of the nineteenth century, when Cardinal Consalvi could declare that 'the Secretary of State is minister of the Interior and of Foreign Affairs and of all kinds of affairs'.[14] Thus there was a marked discontinuity of status and roles, between cardinal-nephew and Secretary; but following a path which, in the long run, turns out to be coherent and which I shall now try to retrace.[15]

SECRETARY OF STATE AND CARDINAL-NEPHEW

In contrast to the title of an earlier section and on the basis of the reflections offered so far, I have reversed the order in which the two offices are traditionally presented. If, as we have seen, many scholars have confused the two roles, almost invariably ascribing to the nephew the role of Secretary of State, this has occurred for factual reasons that are easy to understand. There was an absolute need for this extraordinary character in the curia – for a collaborator of the pope who could identify with him and act as his main tool in the management of every conceivable matter – all the more so within the new curial structure based on the congregations, a structure which, insofar as it marginalized the Consistory as the pope's senate, ended by enhancing the pope's absolute and centralized authority.

For a long time this 'special' role belonged to the pope's nephew, to whom everything – and not just the direction of the Secretariat – could be entrusted, and only later was that role handed over to another curial officer who was judged capable and trustworthy; that officer came to be identified as the Secretary of State. He was assigned responsibilities and functions that had slowly taken shape over time, and it was this 'normal' evolution of the office that ensured the Secretary's pre-eminence over the Curia. Thereafter it was no longer possible (for reasons I shall try to clarify in due course) to speak of a cardinal-nephew, and the Secretary assumed all of the latter's prerogatives and duties (thought not the revenues), while radically altering his own traditional responsibilities, also shaped by a long

---

[13] On Pallavicini and Boncompagni see the final volume of Pastor's monumental *Storia dei papi*.

[14] L. Pásztor, *La Segreteria di Stato e il suo Archivio 1814–1833*, vol. I, Stuttgart, 1984, p. 3.

[15] Hammermayer, 'Grundlinien', explores the logic of the balance between pope, nephew and Secretary in the first half of the seventeenth century.

evolution. Even Cardinal Spada, Innocent XII's Secretary of State and the first of the post-nepotist era, had little in common with his predecessors. His role was closer to that of the cardinal 'padroni' who had earlier operated in the pope's entourage.

Having stated and indeed reiterated this point, the time has come to reconstruct some aspects of the evolution, which I earlier described as 'normal', of a curial figure who, thanks to what events in the second half of the sixteenth and the seventeenth century, rose to a position of extraordinary importance in the curia. Everything began with Saint Carlo Borromeo.

Pius IV's nephew represented a striking exception among cardinal-nephews. At a very young age he made his mark at a very difficult juncture, for Paul IV had thrown the curia into a total disarray by prosecuting some of its most highly respected members and had led the papal states into a disastrous war which had threatened the very capital of the Catholic church. To make things even worse, his own nephews, including the cardinal-nephew, had sunk in the mud, having been charged with crimes and fallen victims to the very strong resentment most people felt toward their uncle.[16] Saddled with this heavy legacy, Borromeo, then little more than twenty years old, availed himself of the assistance of Tolomeo Gallio, a man of low birth from Como, when handling the affairs of the Secretariat.[17]

In 1563 the Venetian ambassador described his activity, reporting that every day the pope spent two or three hours with his nephew Carlo Borromeo and with Gallio in order to discuss all important matters, both 'public' and 'private'.[18] According to another Venetian envoy, the respect Gallio enjoyed caused a good deal of amazement at court. What people found especially surprising was the fact that the pope, in such difficult times and with a council in progress, relied almost exclusively on a young and inexperienced man.[19] Here was a genuine revolution and one which in such delicate circumstances looked all the more significant.

---

[16] On the four Carafa nephews (two of whom were executed in 1561 under Pius IV) see *DBI*, vol. xix: the entries 'Carafa, Antonio' by M. G. Cruciani Troncarelli, pp. 470–82; 'Carafa, Alfonso' and 'Carafa, Carlo' by A. Prosperi, pp. 473–76 and 497–509; and 'Carafa, Giovanni' by M. Raffaelli Cammarota, pp. 556–9.

[17] Carlo Borromeo had been put in charge of the pope's Secret Secretariat one month after the election of Pius IV, who had initially offered the position to Cardinal Morone, but the latter refused it (Pastor, *Storia dei papi*, vol. vii, pp. 77–8).

[18] Alberi (ed.), *Le relazioni degli ambasciatori veneti*, p. 77. It was Pastor who first called Tolomeo Gallio the 'first Secretary of State of the church' (*Storia dei papi*, vol. vii, p. 86 and especially vol. viii, p. 24); apparently it was Carlo Borromeo, eager in 1565 to go to the diocese of Milan and thus wishing to rid himself of all curial commitments, who urged Pius IV to delegate so many responsibilities to Gallio.

[19] 'Dagli altri pontefici, in tempo che le cose della Sede Apostolica passavano quietamente, [son] stati sempre tenuti quattro o sei segretari consumati nei negozi e letterati, e che . . .

In 1565, when the last batch of cardinals was appointed before Pius IV's death, Gallio was among them.[20] With the advent of Pius V, however, he was marginalized: the new pope chose Girolamo Rusticucci rather than Gallio as his intimate secretary, and for Secretary of State he chose to have the Gascon Cardinal Reuman at his side. Above all, Pius V, who at first did not want a cardinal–nephew, 'reserved . . . to himself the actual direction of government affairs'.[21] But after Reuman's death he summoned the cardinal–nephew Michele Bonelli and explicitly made him 'Superintendent of the ecclesiastical state', thus contributing decisively (at least up to a point, since, as far as we know, he always studiously avoided giving him any autonomy) to the institutionalization of the office reserved to his first kinsman.[22]

Tolomeo Gallio was restored to office by Gregory XIII, and this, given the pope's personality and ambitions, stands as a definitive confirmation of Gallio's qualities. In this instance, too, the comments of a Venetian shed much light. In 1576 Paolo Tiepolo explained to the Venetian Senate how the pontiff had entrusted the management of the affairs of the ecclesiastical state to his nephews, with the assistance of a Congregation of Cardinals. These matters of 'ecclesiastical state', said Tiepolo, introducing an interesting distinction, were far less important than those pertaining to the administration of the 'civil' state and to relations with foreign powers; for the latter the pontiff relied entirely on Gallio alone, who thus became the full-fledged 'dispositore delle cose di Stato'.[23] In 1578

ora che vi sono tanti travagli, con un Concilio aperto, non sia adoperato se non questo solo, giovane di 29 anni, con poche lettere e niuna cognizione delle cose del mondo' ('Other popes, in times past when the affairs of the Apostolic See ran quietly, have always kept three or four highly experienced and learned secretaries and . . . now that there are so many troubles, and that a Council is in session, there is but a single twenty-nine-year-old secretary of little learning and with no experience of worldly matters'), ibid., p. 95. The same news is repeated a second time: the diplomat is surprised as he observes that 'in matters of state' the pope 'avails himself . . . of no one but Monsignor Tolomeo, his secretary'. At meetings of the Vatican Academy established by Carlo Borromeo, Tolomeo Gallio's nickname was 'il Segreto' (see Pastor, *Storia dei papi*, vol. VII, p. 549).

[20] 'Nato . . . assai bassamente' ('very low born'). Elsewhere ambassador Tiepolo writes that he had been born 'in assai umile e povero stato' ('in very humble and poor state'). 'Tutti dicono che sarà fatto cardinale', wrote the Venetian envoy, 'ed è questo uno di quegli esempi che . . . invita gli uomini ad andar a correr la loro fortuna a Roma' ('everybody says that he will be made a cardinal, and this is one of those examples that . . . encourage people to try their luck in Rome').

[21] Pastor, *Storia dei papi*, vol. VIII, p. 52. Only after Cardinal Reuman's death did Pius V put a cardinal-nephew, Michele Bonelli, in charge of those vast traditional functions.

[22] Laurain-Portemer, 'Absolutisme et népotisme', p. 502. At any rate, the pontiff always treated his nephew rather brusquely in order to make plain that he was in no way under his influence when dealing with official business.

[23] Alberi (ed.), *Le relazioni degli ambasciatori veneti*, pp. 215–17.

another Venetian ambassador, who also drew a distinction between the
governance of the *ecclesiastical* state and that of 'the State', speaks of Gallio
as 'Secretary of affairs of State'[24] and, so far as I can tell (but in this area
that my hypothesis is admittedly risky), this is one of the earliest mentions
of the office. (The earliest documented official use of the term refers to
Erminio Valenti, who is called Secretary of State in a 1605 papal roll.)[25]
Owing to his authority, the same ambassador goes on to say, Gallio was
viewed with hostility by the pope's nephews. This information, apparently based on gossip, must be kept in mind, for some historians have
assimilated the figure of 'secretarius intimus' with that of the nephew,
whereas what we often in fact find is a more direct bond of obedience
to the pontiff, and a relationship of competition, rather than subordi-
nation, with the nephews. At any rate it must be stressed that Gregory
XIII's cardinal-nephew, Filippo Boncompagni (who had been appointed
only after persistent requests from influential members of the College of
Cardinals), was, according to Pastor, 'a gentle, insignificant, and inexperienced nephew'.[26] The primacy of the Secretary of State was much helped
by this circumstance. It is also worth recalling that the pope personally
attended, directly and indirectly, to all government matters, systematically
encroaching on Gallio's patch.[27]

At any rate, the importance of Gallio's role is confirmed by the *Informatione del Secretario et secreteria di nostro Signore* . . . compiled by Giovanni
Carga in 1574.[28] Its author describes the Secretary's role as 'very important for the good government of Holy Church' and explains that it was
a key step towards a career in the curia. The office, writes Carga, stems
from that of household secretary created by Innocent VIII. The pope
required a close collaborator 'cui liceat nostra et Romanae Ecclesiae sec-
reta nostrum et eiusdem Ecclesiae aut orthodoxae fidei statum concernentia, quomodocumque fuerit a nobis iussus legitime expedire'. To the
Secretary, writes Carga, are reserved the affairs 'Pontificum et Ecclesiae
ac orthodoxae fidei statum concernentia'. In the current pontificate, he

---

[24] Ibid., p. 267. The man in question is Antonio Tiepolo.

[25] Kraus, *Das päpstliche Staatssekretariat unter Urban VIII.*

[26] Pastor, *Storia dei papi*, vol. IX, p. 25.

[27] Ibid., p. 43n: 'Gallio's determination was not as forceful, his vision not always as sharp
as his Lord's . . . at times Gallio also lacked the necessary sagacity', ibid. Ad indicem
for numerous references to interventions of the cardinal and Secretary of State in all
sorts of issues. Laurain-Portemer, 'Absolutisme et népotisme', p. 502, agrees that the
nephew's ineptitude greatly contributed to the rise of the Secretary of State.

[28] 'Informatione del Secretario et secreteria di nostro Signore et di tutti li offitii che da
quella dependono del sgr. Giovanni Carga. 1574', in H. Laemmer (ed.), *Monumenta
Vaticana Historiam Ecclesiasticam Saeculi XVI illustrantia*, Freiburg-im-Breisgau, 1861,
pp. 457ff.

continues, Tolomeo Gallio supervises all business, drafts confidential letters, and acts as intimate secretary to the pope. For each of these duties he receives monetary compensation. ('In this pontificate [Tolomeo Gallio], as is well known, has the superintendence of affairs and the signature of secret letters and, moreover, he represents the person of, and acts in lieu of, the intimate secretary, and enjoys all the prerogatives and perquisites of both offices.')

Ultimately, writes Carga, confirming and indeed adding new meanings to the Venetian ambassadors' reports quoted earlier, Gallio was able to concentrate in his own person powers that would normally belong to more than one man: to the power normally reserved to the pope's nephew he added that of the pope's private secretary, and consequently that of the head of the papal Secretariat. The author of the *Informatione* also noted that the functions of the Secretariat and the qualities of its incumbent were not matched by adequate structures. The staff was small, if not insufficient, and the agency had no office of its own in the Palace. Carga, in short, exposed a degree of precariousness in the Secretariat, and the immediate future would fully bear out his misgivings.[29]

While with Tolomeo Gallio the office had witnessed a moment of unprecedented splendour, after Gregory XIII's death it was not until Innocent X's pontificate that the Secretariat again had a head, Giacomo Panciroli, nearly as influential as Gallio.[30] Of course, we are referring here to a Secretary of State who was not at the same time cardinal-nephew, for under Clement VIII (though this was exceptional) all the various roles were concentrated in the persons of Pietro and Cinzio Aldobrandini, who moreover, were appointed even though they could boast neither

---

[29] P. Pecchiai, *Roma nel Cinquecento*, Bologna, 1948, taking up the subject of the Secretariat of State (p. 184), does so in nine lines which open with the observation that 'there is not much to say' on the subject. Inevitably, he then identifies the Secretary of State with the cardinal-nephew (pp. 171–3).

[30] Sixtus V appointed Girolamo Rusticucci, whose role (Pastor, *Storia dei papi*, vol. x, p. 48) was purely nominal, because the energetic pope attended to all matters in person. As his private secretary the pope appointed Decio Azzolini, a native of the Marches, whom he later made a cardinal. From then on, members of the Azzolini family were nearly always present in the papal Secretariat. Gregory XIV appointed the cardinal-nephew Paolo Emilio Sfondrati who, owing to the pope's poor health, wielded broad authority. He took so much advantage of the situation during the little more than ten months of his uncle's pontificate that discontent seemed likely to erupt into mob violence (ibid., pp. 538ff.). Innocent IX was pope for just two months, raised his grand-nephew Antonio Facchinetti to the cardinalate, and managed to launch one of the most important reforms of the Secretariat of State: he split it into three sections (for the affairs of France and Poland, Italy and Spain, and Germany) putting at the head of each individuals selected for their experience (ibid., p. 585).

the cardinalate nor ordination to any ecclesiastical rank.[31] The ground-work for the nephews' ascent to power and for the Secretary's descent into obscurity had been laid by an innovation introduced by Gregory XIV (Niccolò Sfondrati) at the start of his very brief pontificate (December 1590–September 1591). Soon after his election, the new pontiff inaugurated the practice of creating cardinal-nephews whose nomination coincided *de facto* with their formal appointment and was kept separate from the ordinary procedure used for other cardinals:[32] a 'strong' legitimation of the new role. And there is no doubt that further, significant innovations checked only by the pope's premature death: the power of cardinal-nephew Sfondrati had reached such heights that the heads of the orders of cardinals and Cardinal Camerino, feeling ill-at-ease in the unusual, unexpected situation, managed to wrest from the new pontiff a brief (dated 12 October 1591) which gave them the right to be kept informed of current affairs along with the nephew.[33]

Under Paul V the curia was taken over by the pope's nephew Scipione, who laid hands on every available office and amassed a huge fortune in the process, while at his side not one, but a whole succession of Secretaries of State passed the baton.[34] In a brief issued on 11 September 1605 Paul V extended to his nephew the same authority Clement VIII had bestowed on Pietro Aldobrandini; a *motu proprio* of 30 April 1618 finally spelled out the prerogatives, responsibilities and revenues of the

---

[31] Clement VIII entrusted the Secretariat to his two nephews, Pietro and Cinzio Aldobrandini, and tried in vain – as the two soon quarrelled – to separate with precision their respective responsibilities (Pietro was supposed to attend to the affairs of France, Spain and Savoy; Cinzio to those of Poland, Germany and Italy). This unusual form of joint management of the Secretariat of State has been discussed by Jaitner, *Instructiones Pontificum Romanorum*, pp. xcviff. See also Pastor, *Storia dei papi*, vol. xi, pp. 35ff. The two nephews, who were not only quarrelsome but also inept, were assisted by others in the business of the Secretariat. Among them was Erminio Valenti, a native of Umbria, who served as Pietro's secretary, and Lanfranco Margotti, who assisted Cinzio. Under Paul V both were to hold the office in their own right. As can be seen, long careers within the Secretariat were becoming more and more common:, officials were managing to remain in office for more than one pontificate (in addition to the two cases I have just mentioned, I referred earlier to Tolomeo Gallio and the elder Decio Azzolini). Leo XI's pontificate was so short that he did not have time to raise to the cardinalate his nephew, Roberto Ubaldini, who, however, was so raised by Paul V.

[32] Laurain-Portemer, 'Absolutisme et népotisme', p. 502.

[33] Pastor, *Storia dei papi*, vol. ix.

[34] These secretaries, some of whom were replaced as they died in office while others voluntarily resigned, have been studied by Semmler, 'Beiträge zum Aufbau des päpstlichen Staatssekretariats'. The author distinguishes three stages of the Secretariat during the Borghese pontificate: the initial stage, the stage of reconstruction of the office on the basis of the division and regrouping of functions, and a final stage when Porfirio Feliciani (from 1613 to 1621) was in charge and the office experienced a new stability, but certainly did not achieve any autonomy vis-à-vis the cardinal-nephew.

cardinal-nephew/Superintendent-General of the State: Scipione was now more than ever the 'cardinal padrone', the official *alter ego* of his uncle the pope. Thus began what Laurain-Portemer calls 'l'age classique' of nepotism.[35] The institutionalization of the personage was now complete and the climax was reached under Gregory XV with the appointment of his nephew Ludovico Ludovisi, who lorded it over the curia – and over his sovereign uncle as well – and in just the two years of his uncle's pontificate amassed an extraordinary fortune.[36]

So much for the nephew's status. As for the Secretary, it is worth recalling the description of his office in an *Istruzione* of the 1620s drafted by Cristoforo Caetani for Monsignor Lorenzo Magalotti, Urban VIII's new Secretary of State.[37] The 'Secretary of State and of Letters to Princes' meets daily with the pontiff and reports to him on the contents of the nuncios' letters; he himself opens those letters even if they are addressed to the nephew. To this end the Secretary, once he has received those letters, divides them among the four or five secretaries who assist him and requests concise summaries, which he then submits to the pope. Having analysed them with the sovereign, the Secretary passes them on to the agencies competent to deal with the issues raised in them. Once they have completed their own analysis of the material, the agencies report their findings to the Secretariat. Here a reply is drafted, signed by the cardinal-nephew and sent to its destination. The Secretary himself writes rough drafts of letters addressed to heads of state or letters dealing with highly sensitive matters, and he also coordinates the work of the Secretary of the Cipher and of the Latin Secretary, both of whom are his trusted collaborators. He may also be sent by the pope to communicate his views to the congregations. Other responsibilities (concludes our source) include supervising his own agency and subordinate agencies so as to ensure the required efficiency and discretion.

The *Istruzione* to Magalotti portrays the Secretary as the pope's confidant; he has hardly any contact with the nephew, and it is no accident that a near-contemporaneous text on the cardinal-nephew,[38] dedicated

---

[35] Laurain-Portemer, 'Absolutisme et népotisme', p. 502.

[36] Ludovico Ludovisi became a cardinal the day after his uncle's election to the papacy. As Secretary of State he performed adequately (Pastor, *Storia dei papi*, vol. XIII, pp. 43ff.); as cardinal-nephew, 'in him the usual flaws were not lacking'. With Gregory XV and Cardinal Ludovisi 'the sad spectacle Rome had already witnessed under Clement VIII and Paul V repeated itself'. Ludovisi was 'showered to excess with honours, titles, lucrative offices and ecclesiastical benefices'.

[37] See text in A. Kraus, 'Das päpstliche Staatssekretariat im Jahre 1623. Eine Denkschrift des ausscheidenden Sostituto an den neuernannten Staatssekretar', *Römische Quartalschrift*, 52 (1957), pp. 93–122.

[38] See BAV, Barb. Lat., 5672, 'Cardinale nipote di papa'.

to Cardinal Francesco Barberini, describes the latter's role as superintendent of the 'affairs of state' without paying the slightest attention to the
Secretary. It is on the nephew, says this text, that everything depends:
he deals with all interchanges between the Apostolic See and foreign
rulers and is also responsible for all major matters pertaining to the good
administration of the temporal state. To assist him in carrying out his
duties he has numerous ministers. In particular, for matters pertaining to
relations with foreign rulers he has 'several secretaries' (not the plural)
who are known as the 'domestic secretaries of the pope'. For the most
important 'transactions', however, he relies on a personal 'agent or secretary of embassies and memoranda' who has more or less the same duties
which, according to our previous text (the *Istruzione* to Magalotti), the
Secretary of State performed for the pope. The 'Embassy Secretary' was
expected to be 'a mature and skilful man who shall maintain relationships, report on the contents of memoranda, and pass them on to the
appropriate officials according to the cardinal's instructions'. But should
the nephew wish neither the Embassy Secretary nor his majordomo to
handle his private correspondence, he might appoint a private secretary
who could take over as one of the Secretaries of State whenever a post
became vacant.

From this and other writings that deal with the Secretary it is clear that
cardinal-nephew and Secretary of State were two distinct (I hesitate to say
rival) offices: their respective authority was certainly not comparable, for
the authority of the former was overwhelming, but their authoritativeness
was (or could be) comparable, if the pope wanted it to be so. The Secretary
of State was the only man outside the pope's immediate family to be
entrusted with the most serious and sensitive business and, linked as he
was to the sovereign by a close and exclusive rapport of trust, he could
offset the nephew's enormous power. Some scholars have gone so far as
to portray the Secretary of State as a mentor placed by the pope at the
side of the inexperienced cardinal-nephew, but this seems farfetched and
cannot be proved.[39]

But let us return to Magalotti (who, by the way, was the brother-
in-law of Urban VIII's brother and who, after being made a cardinal,
was sometimes referred to as 'cardinal-uncle'). His work as Secretary of

[39] Serafini, *Le origini della Pontificia Segreteria di Stato*, pp. 37ff.; Del Re, *La Curia Romana*,
p. 63 (chapter on the Secretariat of State, pp. 63–76). The hypothesis rests on the
assumption that the Secretary of State was often a man of great experience, whereas
the nephews, as a rule, had none. Theoretically – if such an argument is permissible –
these elements would rather show the Secretary not as the nephew's tutor, but as a
possible counterweight to the latter's great and not always controllable power. As an
experienced and highly qualified man personally chosen by the pope, the Secretary
could act as a check on initiatives by the nephew that were too invasive or reckless.

State was described by the Venetian envoy Pietro Contarini in 1627. He has great influence over the pope, wrote the ambassador, but studiously tries to conceal the fact and is careful to keep out of the limelight. In public he handles only such matters as have been directly assigned to him and makes every effort not to stir up jealousy by revealing an excessive closeness to the pontiff; above all he is careful not to compete with the cardinal-nephew.[40] This view of Magalotti's position is confirmed by another Venetian envoy, Giovanni Nani, who, writing in 1640 about a later Secretary, Francesco Ceva, says that he 'is little loved, yet highly respected by the nephews on account of the affection His Holiness feels for him'.[41] In short, sources of this kind, for all their diversity, often reveal the cardinal-nephew's uneasiness vis-à-vis an authoritative Secretary of State – never (I am tempted to say 'obviously') the other way around.

With Innocent X the balance shifts decisively in favour of the Secretary of State, now Giacomo Panciroli, considered by one scholar as the first full-fledged holder of that office.[42]

In fact the situation within the papal court at the time was nearly unique. In 1650 a cardinal-nephew, Camillo Pamphili, whom his uncle had ostentatiously sidelined and who had ended by resigning from the clergy and getting married (the fact that he was destined for an ecclesiastical career had generated much surprise, since he was the only male in the Pamphili family who could ensure the continuation of the lineage),[43]

---

[40] 'Solo tratta di negozi, ch'espressamente li sono incaricati, e procura evitar l'odio che per l'ordinario suole cadere sopra quelli che si veggono piu vicini o partecipano dell'autorità o grazia del Prencipe; e lo fa maggiormente per non ingelosire il cardinal Barberini' ('he only deals with matters that have been explicitly entrusted to him, and seeks to avoid the hatred which is normally directed against those who are perceived as being closer to the Prince or who share his authority and discretionary power; and he does so especially in order not to make cardinal Barberini jealous'): Barozzi and Berchet, *Le relazioni della Corte di Roma*, vol. I, p. 214. Eventually, however, his activity did make the Barberini nephews very jealous, so much so that the pontiff removed him from his office and put him in charge of the diocese of Ferrara 'in order to leave the field wide open to his nephews' meddling in government affairs'. The removal from office greatly saddened him (Fosi, *All'ombra dei Barberini*, pp. 100, 102).

[41] Barozzi and Berchet, *Le relazioni della Corte di Roma*, vol. II, p. 26. On this prelate see G. De Caro, 'Ceva, Francesco Adriano', *DBI*, vol. XXIV, pp. 310–14. Ceva was in Barberini's service as early as 1604 and only in 1632, when he was the pope's 'maestro di camera', did he get his first autonomous appointment, namely the very important position of nuncio extraordinary to France. He returned to the curia in 1634 and the pope made him Secretary of State. In 1643 he was made a cardinal. He died in 1655. His biography, in short, reveals an unusually close relationship with the pope.

[42] See e.g. M. L. Rodén, 'Cardinal Decio Azzolino and the Problem of Papal Nepotism', *Archivium Historiae Pontificiae*, 34 (1996), p. 131 (pp. 127–57).

[43] Pastor, *Storia dei papi*, vol. XIV/1, pp. 30–1. Camillo had been General of Holy Roman Church, commander of the papal navy, commander of the guard and Governor of

was replaced, after a few years during which the office was left vacant, by a mediocre adopted nephew, Camillo Astalli Pamphili.[44] The curia was dominated for a long time by Innocent's sister-in-law, Lady Olimpia, on whom (the Venetian ambassadors insinuated) Panciroli's authority was totally dependent. And Panciroli, like Gallio before him, was of 'low and plebeian birth'.[45] Actually the broad role assigned to him was viewed by the papal court as a major innovation.[46] Panciroli, too, wrote Contarini, made a point of refusing to handle matters not explicitly assigned to him by the pope,[47] which caused no little inconvenience to foreign ambassadors, as on many issues they had no choice but to deal directly, and not without difficulty, with Innocent X himself. To a pope one could not speak as freely as to a nephew, and with the latter it was also much easier to reiterate one's requests and be persistent.[48] The outcome, according

the Borgo; he then took holy orders and became cardinal-nephew. He had talent, but since the pope kept him in the dark about everything, he soon lost all zeal. When he decided to give up that kind of life and to get married, he ran into opposition both from his uncle and from Lady Olimpia (neither of whom attended his wedding).

[44] Ibid., pp. 32–3. Actually Olimpia's position began to weaken at that very time, from 1649 to 1650. The scandalous situation that had developed led the pope to bar her from setting foot in the Vatican. But in the final years of the pontificate she managed to regain her former position.

[45] According to Giovanni Giustiniani it was Olimpia who urged the pope to support Panciroli and put an end to Cardinal Camillo Pamphili's aspirations. See ibid., p. 71, for the information on Panciroli's low birth. The fact that the figures of Gallio and Panciroli are comparable, both in terms of the unusually high respect they enjoyed as Secretaries of State and in terms of their humble social extraction, is a fact deserving our attention. From their *creature*, i.e. from individuals who had been raised from nowhere to high honours and positions of great responsibility, the pontiffs could expect more certain, if not total, dependability and loyalty. On some of the more obscure aspects of the career of Panciroli, who had been Lorenzo Magalotti's secretary and thus had some experience in that area, see Fosi, *All'ombra dei Barberini*, p. 76.

[46] Barozzi and Berchet, *Le relazioni della Corte di Roma*, vol. II, pp. 93ff.

[47] Ibid., pp. 71ff., report of 1648.

[48] Contarini wrote: 'trovai hora nel presente pontificato un insolito e strano accidente et è la privatione di nepote che eserciti la sopraintendenza generale dello Stato Ecclesiastico. Onde conviene a' ministri dei prencipi far parola d'ogni affare con S. Santità e reiterar seco l'istanze, poiché il cardinale Panzirolo, benché sopraintendente alla Segreteria di Stato, ricusa di negoziare quando peró non sia materia individualmente incaricatagli da S. Beatitudine' ('I have now found in the current pontificate an unusual and strange occurrence, and it is the absence of a nephew in charge of the general superintendence of the Ecclesiastical State. Hence the princes' envoys have no choice but to discuss every matter with His Holiness and submit their requests to him, because Cardinal Panzirolo, superintendent of the Secretariat though he is, declines to negotiate unless it is a matter specifically entrusted to him by His Beatitude'). The pope, wrote the ambassador, was torn, for, on the one hand, he could not resign himself to the fact that his nephew Camillo was bound to count for so little at court and, on the other, he was faced with his sister-in-law and with Panciroli both of whom 'acerrime' (strenuously) opposed his nephew.

to Gregorio Leti, was that Innocent X made any negotiation in the curia practically impossible.[49]

In such a situation, the role of the Secretary of State could certainly be more clearly drawn, but would not thereby grow automatically in prestige; nor, as we have seen, could it be perceived as especially effective, nor could it be appreciated by those who, like the Venetian ambassador, must deal with him on a daily basis in an official capacity.[50]

There are, however, numerous indications that the reputation of the office, and indeed of all offices in the Secretariat, was growing. In 1643 (to mention but one instance), Jacopo Altoviti, in a letter to Fabio Chigi, who was then nuncio in Cologne, noted that the office of Secretary of Briefs (one of the main positions in the Secretariat, for which the Sienese prelate was being considered) was one of the key offices, as only a few candidates could aspire to it, given the qualifications needed for the job, and it was the only curial office that gave to its holder the status of a learned man.[51] The observation is very significant and shows why the consolidation of the various offices connected with the Secretariat – into an agency employing some of the most talented individuals in the entire curial structure – might occasionally slow down, but would never stop.

After Panciroli's death in 1651, toward the end of Innocent X's pontificate, Fabio Chigi himself[52] replaced the late Secretary. Cardinal-nephew Camillo Astalli Pamphili had been under serious consideration for the

---

[49] Leti, *Il Nipotismo di Roma [. . .]*, vol. I/II, n.p., 1667, p. 98: 'Innocentio Decimo haveva ridotto la Corte in uno stato tanto imbrigliato che alcuno non sapeva di dove cominciare a trattare' ('Innocent X had brought the Court to such state of paralysis that no one knew where to start doing business').

[50] L. von Ranke (*Storia dei papi*, vol. II, Florence, 1965, p. 842), credits Innocent X with substantially undermining the cardinal-nephew's power and definitively strengthening the Congregation of State established by Urban VIII, placing it under Cardinal Panciroli's leadership. But Ranke is quite wrong to present the pontiff as a sovereign with autonomous power only in matters ecclesiastical: 'In all temporal affairs, by contrast – if he wanted to go to war, sign peace, alienate a territory, or introduce a new tax – he must seek the cardinals' advice.' H. Jedin ('La controriforma europea e gli inizi della controriforma nell'Europa centrale', in H. Jedin, ed., *Storia della Chiesa*, vol. VI, *Riforma e Controriforma, XVI e XVII secoli*, Milan, 1975, p. 771) endorses Ranke's opinion: 'Under Innocent X a change occurred at the summit of political power, the effects of which are still felt even today: the cardinal-nephew lost his position as leading minister to the Secretary of State.'

[51] The office was 'stimatissima, perché rari son quelli che vi possono aspirar et e l'unica in questa Corte che canonizzi chi la sostiene per soggetto dotto' ('highly esteemed, because rare are those who can aspire to it and is the only one at this court that bestows on the incumbent the title of learned man'): BAV, Chigi A.III.54, 'Lettere di cinque persone scritte a N.S. prima della sua assuntione', c. 285.

[52] Chigi cooperated closely with Decio Azzolini, who had been considered for the Secretariat during the 1651 vacancy.

position, but was judged to be totally unfit for the task, and Pastor tells us that the pope even regretted having raised him to the cardinalate.

THE TIDE TURNS IN THE SECRETARY'S FAVOUR

It is Chigi who must be credited for imparting, directly and indirectly, a new course to the Secretariat of State. Elected pope a few years later and at first reluctant to bring to Rome his relations from Siena, he appointed Giulio Rospigliosi to succeed him in the Secretariat; Clement IX, that is to say Rospigliosi himself, appointed Decio Azzolini, who had long served in the Secretariat and had been, among other things, Panciroli's secretary. In this crucial period, then, during three pontificates the office was held by men of high calibre who were linked by a common thread, and Azzolini continued to play a key role in the curia in later years, as leader of a group of cardinals who shared above all a common approach to foreign policy and a common, very conservative, view of the structure of curial power.

It was primarily, if not exclusively, due to the quality of the men who were called upon to fill the office that the Secretariat of State acquired new prestige in those years, as can be demonstrated from a concrete example: the letters Giulio Rospigliosi, the future Clement IX, wrote to his brother Camillo on the occasion of his own appointment to that position.

At the beginning of 1655,[53] when the Consistory made him Governor of Rome (the appointment was out of the ordinary, for the assembly of cardinals were intervening – albeit *sede vacante* – in a matter that was strictly reserved to the pope), Rospigliosi was convinced that he had reached the best of all possible goals: the office, he wrote, was 'the highest there is in Italy'.[54] A few months later his satisfaction over his appointment to the Secretariat was much less intense. In the letter which he wrote on 17 April 1655 to his brother Camillo, reporting the news, Rospigliosi

---

[53] In a letter written in 1632 this prelate, who had built up an important career thanks to his family's large financial outlays, had drawn a distinction between the congregations that provided a good return, those that ensured high respect, and those that handled a multiplicity of matters being and offered opportunities for direct contact with the bosses: BAV, Vat. Lat., 13362, *Lettere di Clemente IX essendo nella Corte di Urbano VIII dal 1630 al 1637. Lettere famigliari*, cc. 14–15.

[54] Ibid., *Lettere di Clemente IX nel governo di Roma e doppo fatto cardinale dal 1655 al 1667. Par. III*, c. 63r–v. The appointment, he joyfully reported, would exempt him from excise taxes as well as from paying for letters (ibid., c. 65). Rospigliosi's description of the office may be a little exaggerated: there is no doubt, however, that the office of governor gave the incumbent a broad jurisdiction and placed a substantial militia at his disposal.

declared that he was best pleased with the show of benevolence he had received from Alexander VII: the pope had passed on to him the office he himself had just held; but the newly appointed Secretary made no mention of the functions and responsibilities attached to his new role. He merely reported that he had received from Chigi the key to a secret door which enabled him to go, 'unseen by all', from his new quarters to the pope's.

Replying, his brother Camillo urged him to think twice, for it was far from certain that it was wise for him to accept the appointment. Was Giulio sure that his career in the curia would not suffer? Would the office enable him to secure positions or revenues for his two nephews in the future? The newly elected Secretary reassured Camillo on this score, but significantly told him that he (Giulio) could no longer hope for any future promotion for himself:[55] careers in the curia – he went on to lament – were always hazardous; it did not take much for a man to lose all he had laboured so hard to conquer. This remark seems to be born of a feeling of dissatisfaction, which again seems rather odd in the light of what we know about the office: what further promotion would be possible for a Secretary of State? Perhaps Giulio Rospigliosi was thinking of the cardinalate. It is very unlikely that he was referring to the pontificate.[56]

This episode may be marginal, despite the rank of its protagonists; and yet it may well provide an insight into the role of Secretary of State in a time of transition. We might venture to say it bears witness to the aura of uncertainty which surrounded such curial offices as were more directly tied to the transient presence of a pontiff. At the time of his appointment, in other words, Rospigliosi must have realized that his role might be more or less significant depending on circumstances. An active cardinal-nephew could have pared down his authority to almost nothing; the pontiff himself could have crushed him. The experience of Fabio Chigi, who had moved up from that office to the pontificate – an experience which Rospigliosi was destined to repeat – had been too short and too recent to set a significant precedent. For a champion in the curial race for promotions, such as Rospigliosi, such misgivings were not insignificant.

His uncertainty was all the more serious in that it was not tainted with the errors historians have often committed. For instance, it is grossly

---

[55] Rospigliosi wrote: 'nelle cose della Corte non si camina mai con certezza di quello che habbia da essere nascendo bene spesso mille accidenti impensati ('in the affairs of the court one is never sure what may happen next, for a thousand accidents often come up unexpectedly').

[56] Ibid., cc. 79, 83, 90v.

inaccurate to say that the series of Secretaries of State begins with Fabio Chigi.[57] Careers were not all alike. Chigi's predecessor Panciroli was a cardinal, but the future pontiff, when he was appointed Secretary, was not, and had to wait a year before joining the Sacred College. Similarly in 1655 Rospigliosi was not yet a cardinal, and one of his successors, Francesco Nerli, waited for more than two years before being made one. Moroni goes so far as to place 'the honourable and important office of Secretary of State permanently among the cardinals' at the start of the eighteenth century: following de Luca,[58] he informs us that previously whenever the office was bestowed on a cardinal the appointment had been considered temporary and the incumbent was accordingly called, at least up to 1683, 'acting Secretary of State'.[59]

What really seems to have happened, starting with Chigi, is a decisive strengthening of the office in the sense that it became far more than in the past, a key point of reference in the curia. Chigi's diplomatic skills are well known, and it is also evident that until Innocent X's death he was able to work in the absence of nephews. This circumstance guaranteed him an autonomy which none of his predecessors had enjoyed, but it is highly significant that, as aforesaid, over nearly twenty years the position was filled successively by three men – Chigi, Rospigliosi and Azzolini – who had much in common and were thus able to consolidate the new trend and bring coherence to the innovations. (Incidentally, it was Alexander VII himself who ordered a very timely archival preservation of the diplomatic papers of the Holy See).[60] Rospigliosi as Secretary of State played an active role under Alexander VII, even in the presence of the cardinal-nephew, who used to keep quiet when the two men met to discuss serious issues.[61] In 1664, according once again to the testimony of a Venetian ambassador, Rospigliosi proved so efficient and authoritative

[57] As suggested by Frenz, *I documenti pontifici*, p. 66, and Jedin, 'La Controriforma europea', p. 771.

[58] See G. B. de Luca, *Il cardinale della S.R. Chiesa pratico*, Rome, 1680.

[59] G. Moroni, *Dizionario d'erudizione storico-ecclesiastica*, vol. LXIII, Venice, 1853, p. 282.

[60] But see L. Pásztor, 'Per la storia dell'Archivio Segreto Vaticano nei secoli XVII–XVIII (Eredità Passionei, Carte Favoriti-Casoni, Archivio dei cardinali Bernardino e Fabrizio Spada)', *Archivio della Società Romana di Storia Patria*, 1968, pp. 157–249, for a memorandum in which Garampi complains that anybody could tap into the archives of the Secretariat: he himself has bought back many papers from Roman 'pizzicaroli' (grocers).

[61] In 1661 Niccolò Sagredo wrote that the pope met every evening with Rospigliosi, who read to him a list of current affairs, pausing after each item. Alexander VII lingered over the matters which interested him, but if he had nothing to say he kept quiet, and Rospigliosi then resumed reading with the usual, peculiar rhythm. Cardinal Flavio Chigi was always present but never opened his mouth (Barozzi and Berchet, *Le relazioni della Corte di Roma*, vol. II, p. 234). Flavio's role was always very marginal.

that he became insufferable to the pope: he seemed destined to succeed him, and to Alexander VII it looked as if 'with an envious eye he was shortening his [the pope's] life day by day'.[62] During the pontificate of Clement IX Decio Azzolini, too, was able to work very effectively in spite of the cardinal-nephew.

From that time on, the reports of Venetian ambassadors begin to devote a good deal of attention to the Secretary of State,[63] and this seems relevant, although (as I have already pointed out) it is wrong to force rigid evolutionary patterns on the development of curial offices; I have already argued that in this context the greater or lesser energy of the pope, as well as the character and the ambitions of the cardinal-nephew and of the Secretary of State himself, could have a decisive impact. After Clement IX the common thread linking the experience of the last three Secretaries of State was broken. Clement X's nephew, Paluzzi Altieri, *de facto* nullified the Secretary and assumed his role, arrogating the whole authority to himself.[64] Innocent XI dispensed with a nephew, preferring either to decide all matters himself[65] or to delegate them to other assistants rather than increase the prerogatives of Alderano

---

[62] Ibid., p. 269.

[63] See ibid., p. 350, Antonio Grimani's 1671 report: the role is described as very difficult, 'perché l'altezza del posto rende sempre azzardoso il passeggiarlo' ('because the height of the place makes it always hazardous to walk on it'). Note that by now the reports always have something to say about the datary and the maestro di camera, thus redrawing the contours of the pope's restricted household.

[64] See A. Stella, 'Altieri (Paluzzi degli Albertoni), Paluzzo', *DBI*, vol. ii, pp. 661–64. After demonstrating his personal qualities over a long career in the curia, Paluzzo Paluzzi degli Albertoni was 'adopted' by Emilio Altieri during the conclave in which the latter was elected pope as Clement X. Appointed cardinal-nephew, Paluzzi was very active in every field, so much so that he was accused of megalomania and a propensity for grabbing offices and revenues. The latter were estimated at 100,000 *scudi*. The ageing pope could no longer keep up with current affairs and Paluzzi Altieri's diplomatic inexperience caused problems for the Holy See, especially vis-à-vis France and the Venetian Republic. It was said in Rome that the pope was responsible for 'benedire e santificare' and the nephew for 'reggere e governare'.

[65] Pope Odescalchi's centralizing policy baffled people in the curia, excluded as they were from the decision-making process and yet threatened by the pope's plans for moral reform. See BAV, Boncompagni, E.119, *Baglioni. Lettere dell'anno 1682 fino all'anno 1700*, cc. 65ff., news of a meeting of the Consistory on 13 October 1688: 'Nel Concistoro S.B. nulla disse su queste materie [di politica estera riguardanti anzitutto il problema francese], anzi da molti si crede che non sia per tenerne discorso coi cardinali forse dentro di sé meditando coi lumi dello Spirito Santo ciò che possa convenire all'autorità e alla prudenza sua' ('In the Consistory His Beatitude said nothing about these matters [of foreign policy regarding above all the French problem], indeed many believe that he is not about to discuss them with the cardinals, possibly because he ponders in his own mind, in the light of the Holy Spirit, that which may accord with his own authority and prudence').

Cybo, his Secretary of State, who was also – incredibly – a pensioner of the king of France[66] and, as such, potentially beholden to two masters. The last nepotist pope, Alexander VIII, behaved in another quite different way, so different in fact that his case looks very peculiar: he had a cardinal-nephew, Pietro Jr, and also a Secretary of State, Giovanni Battista Rubini. Finally, Innocent XII put an end to nepotism[67] and ushered the office of Secretary of State into the final phase of its evolution. That all things would fall within the Secretary's purview became clear immediately after the election of that innovating pope. According to Domenico Contarini, 'what people were most anxious to know was who was going to be appointed Secretary of State, [an appointment] that came only after several days' and fell to Cardinal Spada, who had been nuncio to France.[68]

Having retraced, albeit rather briefly, the uneven evolution of the relationship between the cardinal-nephew and the Secretary of State, we must inevitably mention Giovan Battista de Luca, the reforming jurist and author of the best reconstruction ever made of the organization of the Roman curia. It is richly textured and meticulous, and always aims at suggesting improvements to the practices and offices described: as such, it is very helpful in showing how the analysis of any politico-institutional body must deal with realities that are constantly evolving rather than being static and fossilized.

In his description of the Roman curia, de Luca presents the cardinal-nephew and the Secretary of State as the first- and second-ranking officers at the papal court. What is important in de Luca's treatise is that, while still distinguishing between the functions of the pope's kinsman and those of the Secretary of State, he tends basically to assimilate them to each other and consider them as somehow interchangeable. The nephew, he writes, is the first minister of the papal state and performs the duties of an overall superintendent: he has jurisdiction over the temporal state and interacts

---

[66] Pastor, *Storia dei papi*, vol. XIV/2, pp. 15ff. Cybo, who is remembered today more for his magnificent tomb in Santa Maria del Popolo than for anything else, was Secretary of State in name only, while the office itself was *de facto* managed by his deputies, Agostino Favoriti (who died in 1682) and, subsequently, Lorenzo Casoni.

[67] On this point I take the liberty of referring the reader to my essay 'Nepotisti e antinepotisti: i "conservatori" di Curia e i pontefici Odescalchi e Pignatelli', in B. Pellegrino (ed.), *Riforme, religione e politica durante il pontificato di Innocenzo XII (1691–1700)*, Lecce, 1994, pp. 233–48, especially pp. 242–4.

[68] Barozzi and Berchet, *Le relazioni della Corte di Roma*, vol. II, p. 436. Spada's appointment as Secretary of State did not end the evolution of the office, but rather (as stated earlier) represented its beginning. Innocent XII, like his homonymous predecessor, acted 'with great independence, and thus Spada had nothing else to do but carry out his orders' (Pastor, *Storia dei papi*, vol. XIV/2, p. 243).

with the pontiff, but also with all the other agencies and congregations.[69] He also (albeit rarely) deals with issues that pertain to the ecclesiastical state, especially political issues that concern foreign powers. The Secretary of State is responsible for all matters relating to sovereigns and rulers, and coordinates and controls nuncios and legates. He can, however, also look into issues of internal policy insofar as they affect the civil and ecclesiastical administration.[70]

The responsibilities of the nephew and the Secretary of State may thus overlap, and indeed one may substitute for the other. Neither appears to occupy a formal position in the official hierarchy of the curia: they are outside it and are indeed above it,[71] for they represent the main tools – sometimes cooperating, sometimes in competition – of papal power inside the organization. But it is pointless, de Luca suggests, to force the matter into a straitjacket: ultimately it depends on the pope's discretionary power, since he is free to bestow greater or lesser authority on whomever he likes.[72]

The concept is clear, and indeed it is difficult to imagine the opposite: suffice it to say that the current *Annuario pontificio* explains in a footnote that even today the pope has full executive, legislative and judicial powers in all matters pertaining to the papal state. No power, no statute can by itself condition him.[73] It remains for us to define (or try to, in order to supplement what we have learned from de Luca) the nature of the responsibilities that were assigned to the Secretary of State as time went by, so as to grasp with greater clarity how he could overturn an institutional

---

[69] The Prefettura delle Congregazioni della Consulta e del Buon Governo, an office (almost) invariably held by the cardinal-nephew, is the focus of P. J. A.-N. Rietbergen, 'Problems of Government. Some Observations upon a Sixteenth-Century "Istruttione per li Governatori delle città e luoghi dello Stato Ecclesiastico"', *Mededelingen van Ret Nederlands Institut te Rome*, 41 (1979), pp. 173–201; idem, 'Pausen, Prelaten, Bureaucraten. Aspecten van des Geschiedenis van het Pausschap en de Pauselijke Staat in de 17e Euw' dissertation, University of Nijmegen, 1983. The list of Secretaries of State provided by Rietbergen is not accurate, however.

[70] See P. Prodi, *Il sovrano pontefice. Un corpo e due anime: la monarchia papale nella prima età moderna*, Bologna, 1982, pp. 195ff.

[71] G. B. de Luca, *Theatrum veritatis et iustitiae*, vols. I–XVI, Rome, 1669–73: vol. XV, pp. 242ff. The pontifical yearbooks made no mention of the Secretariat of State: see C. Weber, *Die altesten päpstlichen Staats-Handbucher. Elenchus Congregationum, Tribunalium et Collegiorum Urbis. 1629–1714*, Rome, Freiburg and Vienna, 1991.

[72] 'Non è [infatti] cosa capace di regola certa, mentre il tutto dipende dallo stile o genio del papa nel dare a' ministri maggiore o minore autorità' ('It is not a matter subject to a firm rule, as everything depends on the style or discretion of the pope in granting greater or lesser authority to his ministers'): G. B. De Luca, *Il cardinale della S. R. Chiesa pratico*, Rome, 1680, p. 383.

[73] *Annuario pontificio per l'anno 1995*, Città del Vaticano, 1995, p. 1789: see the paragraph in the section 'Notizie storiche' dealing with the *Governatorato*.

equilibrium based on the nephew's role. At this point (and I apologize in advance for the somewhat farfetched terminology I shall be using) we must resist the inevitable temptation of seeing the Secretary of State as an official responsible for, or, worse still, a minister of, foreign affairs. This has been done many times for reasons of convenience, especially when the Secretary has been identified with the cardinal-nephew. Not only was the Secretary of State no foreign minister, but no other minister for foreign affairs (even had there been, in any government of that time, an individual or agency exclusively responsible for foreign relations) would have had the same functions as the Secretary of State. Beyond the normal conduct of diplomatic relations, the Secretary of State kept an eye on the widely scattered community of clerics as well as on the vast endowments of the church; he collected all the indispensable information the Consistory, or rather the pope, needed for handing out benefices, selecting personnel, and exercising temporal as well as spiritual authority. The Secretary daily received and sifted through an impressive mass of reports, petitions, complaints and denunciations, which represent a phenomenal store of evidence for today's scholars, constantly arousing their amazement and making them wonder, as they explore those archival holdings, how all that material could have been used and digested by a single office.

The Secretary of State did coordinate the activity of nuncios and legates, but that activity – as de Luca pointed out – undeniably had significant repercussions on domestic policy. The Secretary's responsibilities were thus quite broad and he was an essential tool was for the pontiff when formulating such decisions as would be useful to the exercise of his temporal and spiritual power.

As I have already said, the Secretary's actual authority was less broad, and his autonomy was not unequivocally defined, at least not in the first half of the seventeenth century. Since he was informed about every item of business even before the pope and the nephew (if there was a nephew), it seems possible that the Secretary of State, even as early as the opening of the seventeenth century, did have the powers which Francescantonio Zaccaria chose to describe in the 1774 revised edition of Girolamo Lunadoro's handbook to the curia: the Secretary, writes Zaccaria, receives letters sent by legates, provincial governors, nuncios and so on, and then distributes them among such agencies as may have a reason for wanting the information, or be entitled to express an opinion on it.[74]

---

[74] 'Le distribuisce allorché sia duopo alle rispettive Congregazioni onde vengano consultate maturamente, il che tutto però ei medesimo preventivamente espone a Sua Santità' ('When necessary, he forwards them to the respective congregations so that that they may be carefully considered, the whole of which, however, he himself first submits to His Holiness'): G. Lunadoro, *Relazione della Corte di Roma* (revised by F. A. Zaccaria),

The Secretary of State's participation in the work of the congregations had already been described in the *Istruzione* to Magalotti referred to earlier: this role of the Secretary of State, as at least 'assistant stage-manager' of curial activity, may represent more than a hypothesis and a clue deserving of further inquiry. From a functional standpoint, this particular coordinating function, which was facilitated by a familiarity with curial procedures few cardinal-nephews could claim at the time of their appointment, represented the extra asset the new strong man of the curia brought to his office when, at the close of the seventeenth century, he assumed, once and for all, the responsibilities and the role that had long been the nephew's.

Rome, 1774, p. 214. In all the numerous previous editions of Lunadoro's treatise on the curia (originally written in 1611) the pope's secretary is identified as the cardinal-nephew, who writes and signs the correspondence addressed to heads of state, nuncios, and others ... Among the higher officers of the Court, on the other hand, are the Secretaries of State, who wear purple and depend on the cardinal-nephew, who gives them orders and whose letters he countersigns. 'Questi segretarii hanno distribuite fra loro le Nunziature e Provincie, essendovi anche fra questi un Segretario della Cifra.' ('The Nunciatures and the Provinces are allocated among these secretaries, and one of them is Secretary of the Cipher'). The secretaries live in the Palace with an annual salary of 1,500 *scudi* plus perquisites.

THE CARDINAL-PROTECTORS OF THE CROWNS IN THE ROMAN CURIA DURING THE FIRST HALF OF THE SEVENTEENTH CENTURY: THE CASE OF FRANCE[*]

Of all the forms of representation available for use by rulers and their subjects in their relations with the pope and the Roman curia during the early modern period, that of the cardinal protectors of the crowns is the most novel and the least known. Studies devoted to the institution have been few and published almost exclusively by German-speaking authors. In the most comprehensive synthesis of the subject to date, published in 1938, the Austrian historian Josef Wodka focused essentially on the origins of the institution, from the 1420s to the early sixteenth century.[1] In the seventeenth century, when authors of treatises on the Roman curia or on the rank of cardinal mentioned the protectorships granted to cardinals, which some of them, like Giovanni Battista de Luca, described as *posti cardinalizi*,[2] they usually divided their account into two or three parts, dealing in turn with the protectorships of religious orders, that of Roman religious establishments and bodies, and finally that of the European states.[3]

It was in the thirteenth century that the first protectorships were given to cardinals with a view to safeguarding the interests of religious orders.[4]

---

[*] I would like to thank Professor Joseph Bergin for translating this essay.

[1] J Wodka, *Zur Geschichte der nationalen Protektorate der Kardinäle an der römischen Kurie*, Innsbruck and Leipzig, 1938. It contains an extremely interesting and useful list of the cardinal-protectors of countries during the sixteenth and seventeenth centuries (pp. 46–130). Wodka's work was continued for the following centuries, but only for the 'German nation', by R. Blaas, 'Das Kardinalprotektorat der deutschen und der österreichischen Nation im 18. und 19. Jahrhundert', *Mitteilungen des österreichischen Staatsarchivs*, 10 (1957), pp. 148–85.

[2] G. B. de Luca, *Il cardinale della S. R. Chiesa pratico*, Rome, 1680, p. 166.

[3] J. Cohelli, *Notitia cardinalatus in qua nedum de S. R. E. cardinalium origine, dignitate, preeminentia et privilegiis, sed de praecipuis Romanae Aulae officialibus uberrime pertractatur*, Rome, 1653, pp. 326–8; De Luca, *Il cardinale*, pp. 165–71; G. Piatti, *De cardinalis dignitate et oficio tractatus*, 4th edn, Rome, 1746, pp. 422–37.

[4] Groups of Waldensians and *poveri catholici* who had returned to the church were placed under the protectorship of cardinals around 1208 (W. Maleczek,

The *regula bullata* which organized the Order of St Francis of Assisi in 1223 defined, among other things, the role assigned to Cardinal Ugolino, Bishop of Ostia and the future Pope Gregory IX (1227–41). It may be regarded as the real origin of the institution of protector,[5] as St Francis requested his brethren 'to take steps to ensure they always had close to the sovereign pontiff a cardinal-protector and corrector'.[6]

This text may seem condensed to the point of obscurity, but it does enable us to identify certain constant features of the function of protector, which was to be extended to other religious orders during the thirteenth century, although the Dominicans waited until the second half of the fourteenth century before imitating the Franciscans. In the seventeenth century, the function was still reserved to a cardinal and was exercised in Rome. Though each order had its own procurator, who defended its interests in the curia and pressed its case on particular matters involving the papal administration, the function of corrector mentioned in 1223 was reserved for the cardinal-protector. That function varied from order to order, and according to the personality of the protector, as de Luca was at pains to point out;[7] but it often included the prerogative of convening and presiding over the general chapters and congregations of the orders when they met in Rome, defending the order's interests at meetings of congregations of cardinals or with the pope himself, and even defending individual members of the order who felt they had been mistreated by their superior or general. In no case, however, did the protectorship entail jurisdiction over the order, and the cardinal-protectors were never in a position (for example) to select a general or superior. In sum, the role was honorary, and its holder was a kind of superior advocate whose only means of action were his own resourcefulness and standing in the curia: two aspects which we shall encounter again among the cardinal-protectors of the crowns.

The initiative in designating a protector could lie with the religious orders, especially when there were personal links between the cardinal

'Ein Kardinalprotektor im Kreuzherrenorden um 1213/1214?', *Zeitschrift der Savigny-Stiftung für Rechtsgeschichte*, 91, kan. Abt. LX (1974), pp. 365–74, p. 365) but they were merely religious groups, not fully constituted orders. As for the alleged cardinal-protector of the order of Templars under Innocent III, Maleczek concludes that he did not exist (ibid., p. 374).

5 This is, at least, how writers on the subject during the early modern period viewed the matter. Piatti, *De cardinalis dignitate*, p. 423: 'semper apud Pontificem curarent aliquem habere cardinalem protectorem et correctorem'.

6 On Ugolino and his relations with the Franciscans, see K. V. Selge, 'Franz von Assisi und Hugolino von Ostia', in Accademia Tudertina (ed.), *San Francesco nella ricerca storica degli ultimi ottanta anni*, Todi, 1971, pp. 157–222, and idem, 'Franz von Assisi und die römische Kurie', *Zeitschrift für Theologie und Kirche,* 67 (1970), pp. 129–61.

7 De Luca, *Il cardinale*, pp. 166–7.

and the order whose interests were confided to him, as with Cardinal Ugolino; but papal influence could also be decisive, as was shown by the choice of Cardinal Pio di Carpi as protector of the Jesuits in 1545.[8] More revealing is the well-publicized determination of popes like Paul V or Urban VIII to appoint their cardinal-nephews as protectors of numerous religious orders and congregations. The pope's approval was in any case always required, and only he could authorize individual cardinals to hold several protectorships at once.[9] During the early modern period, protectors were appointed by means of a papal brief officially conferring the position on a cardinal, who usually kept it until his death.[10] In the seventeenth century the protectorship of monastic orders was universal,[11] while secular and military orders were distinctive by their lack of a protector.[12] For example, the Jesuits ensured that Pio de Carpi had no successor as protector after his death in 1564.[13]

If the protectorship of orders precluded the conferral of jurisdiction, the same was not true of the second type of protectorship, involving churches, monasteries or religious foundations, usually situated in Rome, and placed under the protectorship of cardinals. Examples of this would be the Pauline and Sistine chapels, the basilica of Santa Maria Maggiore, or the Companies of the Annunziata, the Gonfalone and the Trinità dei Pellegrini.[14] The most important and most representative protectorship of all, in terms of the jurisdiction and the numbers of people subject to it, was that of the Holy House of Loreto, where the cardinal-protector played a decisive role throughout the sixteenth and seventeenth centuries,

---

[8] J. Wicki, 'Rodolfo Pio da Carpi, erster und einziger Kardinalprotektor der Gesellschaft Jesu', in *Saggi storici intorno al papato dei Professori della Facoltà di Storia ecclesiastica*, Rome, 1959, pp. 243–67. See also P. M. Sevesi, 'Carlo Borromeo cardinal protettore dell'ordine dei frati minori (1564–1572)', *Archivum Franciscanum Historicum*, 31 (1938), pp. 73–126, 387–439.

[9] De Luca, *Il cardinale*, p. 166: 'al arbitrio del papa'. See e.g. S. Forte, 'I domenicani nel carteggio del card. Scipione Borghese protettore dell'ordine (1606–1633)', *Archivum Fratrum Praedicatorum*, 30 (1960), pp. 351–416.

[10] See e.g. ASV, Segreteria dei Brevi, 948, 479r–479v, brief appointing Antonio Barberini as protector of the Dominican order, Rome, 3 October 1633.

[11] I have found no evidence for a decision by Paul V to ensure that every order had a protector, as asserted by Girolamo Piatti (*De cardinalis dignitate*, p. 423).

[12] De Luca, *Il cardinale*, p. 166.

[13] Wicki, 'Rodolfo Pio da Carpi', pp. 264–7.

[14] M. Völkel, *Römische Kardinalhaushalte des 17. Jahrhunderts: Borghese, Barberini, Chigi*, Tübingen, 1993, pp. 414–15. For the protection of Mount Sinai at the end of the seventeenth century see G. Hofmann, 'Lettere pontificie edite ed inedite intorno ai monasteri del Monte Sinai', *Orientalia Christiana Periodica*, 17 (1951), pp. 283–303, especially 292–3.

and where the term 'corrector' was understood in the widest possible sense.[15]

The first explicit mention of protectorship in relation to states or persons dates back to 1425, when Martin V forbade cardinals to 'assume the protection of any king, prince or commune ruled by a tyrant or any other secular person whatsoever'; cardinals who were protectors of orders were to receive no remuneration for their work.[16] While we can assume that the practice had existed for some time before steps were taken to suppress it, it remains difficult to date its first appearance with any accuracy. However, the number of papal decrees expressing the intention either to tolerate or to suppress it suggests that it was not until the fifteenth century, and probably the final phase of the Great Schism, that it began to take shape. The reasons for the suppression issued by Martin V were simple enough: the pope wanted to secure the complete devotion of the cardinals of the Sacred College, who were forbidden to declare themselves openly for any particular power, or to represent their interests before him. This demand for neutrality and the rendering of unpaid services was renewed at the Council of Basle, but no clear condemnation of protection as an institution figured in the conclusions of the council; at most, it was stipulated that a cardinal should not show himself to be a partisan of his country of origin. In reality, the function of the cardinal-protector of a state or a nation – the expression dates from 1464[17] – had become an established fact, a custom and practice that the reform proposals drafted under Pius II and Alexander VI failed to suppress. It was during the second of these pontificates that the first actual names of cardinal-protectors appear, and it is clear that they had a virtual monopoly on presentations in the Consistory for all bishoprics in the countries which they 'protected'.[18] That being so, the papacy had to come to terms with a reality whose basis it could no longer challenge. It therefore tried to define its remit, which was the point of the decrees of the Fifth Lateran Council.

The decree of 1515 implicitly abandoned the division of work among the cardinals according to their ecclesiastical rank (deacon, priest, bishop),[19] and laid down the framework within which the protectors

---

[15] De Luca, *Il cardinale*, pp. 168–9; F. Da Morrovale, *L'Archivio storico della Santa Casa di Loreto, inventario*, Città del Vaticano, 1965, pp. XIII, LXX, 15.

[16] Wodka, *Zur Geschichte*, p. 34: 'statuit et ordinavit, quod de cetero nullus dominorum cardinalium protectionem alicuius regis, principis aut communitatis tyranni aut alterius saecularis personae sibi vendicare praesumat'.

[17] Ibid., p. 6.   [18] Ibid., p. 31.

[19] According to the council of Basel (article 118, *etsi quamlibet*), cardinal-bishops were to deal with questions of heresy, cardinal-priests with observance and ecclesiastical discipline, and cardinal-deacons with conflicts with the states, whereas the Lateran council

could exercise their functions:

> statuimus, ne partialitatem suscipiant aliquam, neque principum aut com-
> munitatum, vel quorumcumque aliorum contra quemquam, nisi quantum
> justitia et aequitas postulat, eorumque dignitas et conditio requirit, promo-
> tores aut defensores fiant, sed a privata omni passione sejuncti sedandis et
> componendis inter quoscumque litibus, omni diligentia vacent incum-
> bantque: principum et quorumcumque aliorum, ac praesertim pauperum
> et religiosorum justa negotia pio promoveant affectu.[20]

The fact that the term 'protection' was not used made no difference: the nuance between the words 'promotor' and 'protector' fooled nobody and, despite the reservations of principle surrounding it, it was the protectorship of individual countries that was acknowledged in the final decree of the council.

Moreover, the reform project submitted to Hadrian VI a few years later, in 1522–3, openly admitted the existence of the protectorship. It made provision for the protector to be assisted by a vice-protector in case of absence. It was further suggested that the protectorship should become a 'dignity' above that of patriarch, and even that the holder of the position should assume responsibility for ecclesiastical affairs, the cure of souls, and the monitoring of religious orthodoxy in the kingdom assigned to him.[21] But we should not misread this proposal, since its ultimate objective was to encourage residence by cardinals near to the pope, and thus to make the position of a cardinal resident in Rome as attractive as possible. However, the reform remained no more than a set of reflections: the protectorship of the different countries was already a well-established institution, the success of which did not depend on decisions made in Rome. The originating phase of the institution came to an end during the first third of the sixteenth century with the establishment of the permanent protectorships. The papacy therefore recognized the legitimacy of the particular attachment of a cardinal to the interests of a prince, on condition that it did not undermine the principal role of those elevated to the rank of cardinal – that of counsellor to the sovereign pontiff.

The problem of what to call this type of cardinal-protectorship was never discussed during the early modern period. We have seen that in the fifteenth century people spoke indiscriminately of protectors of kings, princes, communes, countries, provinces, nations. In the seventeenth century, these terms were used in the same way, without any

---

acknowledged the right of every cardinal, without distinction, to act as counsellor to the pope on all these issues (art. 26, *quoniam*). Ibid, pp. 36–7.

[20] Ibid., p. 36   [21] Ibid., pp. 37–8.

greater differentiation between them, and it would seem that too much importance should not be attached to references in the documents emanating from the papal administration, such as the registers of the papal Consistory. One expression, which contemporaries did not apparently use, would seem to fit best – 'cardinal-protector of the crowns of Europe'. One need only glance at the list of countries which officially appointed a cardinal-protector: the Empire, the hereditary lands of the House of Austria, France, Castile and the West Indies, Aragon, Sicily, Naples, Flanders, Portugal, Savoy, Poland. The common feature among these political entities is their subjection to the authority of a prince.[22] Thus, the Republic of Venice, though it enjoyed close state-to-state relations with the Holy See via its permanent ambassador, did not have a cardinal-protector. Moreover, according to its ambassador, Alvise Contarini, it did not seek to obtain one because it wished to retain the goodwill of the entire College of Cardinals – a rather feeble excuse, and one which no doubt hid more decisive reasons for this state of affairs.[23] The first consequence of this division was the unequal treatment of different powers. While the King of Spain could in theory count on five or six cardinal-protectors – it was only from 1664 to 1666 that all of the Spanish protectorships were united under Cardinal Federico Sforza[24] – the king of France only had one. In practice, this was not of great importance, since the protector to whom the King of Spain most frequently turned in order to defend his interests as ruler was the protector of Castile; likewise the protector of the Empire was often the same person as the protector of the Austrian hereditary lands. Moreover, France, which was mainly concerned to smooth over possible jealousies and to acquire new allies, did develop, during the

[22] In the case of England, Scotland and Ireland, it was the pope who chose their protectors, so we should be careful not to confuse them with the other protectorships. The cardinal was imposed from above rather than chosen, and does not appear to have had any direct relationship with the governments of these countries. Wodka (ibid., pp. 117–24) provides a list of the cardinals chosen by the pope to keep an eye on the interests of the Catholics there. Switzerland should also be added to the list. See, for example, the brief nominating Francesco Barberini as protector of Switzerland: ASV, Segreteria dei Brevi, 940, ff. 221r–222r, Rome, 26 February 1626. For the protectors of England before the Reformation, see W. E. Wilkie, *The Cardinal Protectors of England. Rome and the Tudors before the Reformation*, Cambridge, 1974.

[23] ASVe, Dispacci degli ambasciatori, Roma 108, 326v–330v, Alvise Contarini to the Senate, Rome, 10 December 1633. Contarini pointed out that for the referral in Consistory of the bishoprics situated in its territories, Venice resorted to cardinals like Guido Bentivoglio 'come di casa connumerata tra li nobili nostre'.

[24] In fact, Cardinal Sforza was only protector of Naples (1664–76) (Wodka, *Zur Geschichte*, p. 95). He was substitute protector of Castile from 1664 to 1667 (ibid., p. 81), Aragon and Sicily from 1664 to 1666 (ibid., p. 89) and Flanders, also from 1664 to 1666 (ibid., p. 98). Moreover, he was also substitute protector of the Empire and the hereditary lands of the house of Habsburg in the same period 1664 to 1666 (ibid., pp. 58 and 68).

first half of the seventeenth century, the use of a co-protector alongside the vice-protectors who were only substitute-protectors during the absences of the protector. The co-protector was a sort of 'twin' protector whose role did *not* cease with the protector's return to the curia.

The choice of a protector or co-protector of France involved a certain number of power centres from which, unlike the procedures for the choice of the protectors of the religious orders, the pope was excluded. It gave rise to an elaborate set of manoeuvres in which the king, the secretary of state for foreign affairs, the French ambassador in Rome and certain influential figures (the first minister, the royal favourite, French ecclesiastics resident in Rome, a francophile Roman such as Mazarin) all played a part. It is not always easy to disentangle the role of each of these players. In some cases it was clearly the king's decision (Cardinal Joyeuse); in others this was much less evident (Orsini, appointed during a period of regency). But one point may be emphasized: these dealings were conducted in absolute secrecy and with complete discretion in a milieu in which rumours were wont to circulate quickly. Let us take the case of Cardinal Guido Bentivoglio, nuncio to France from 1616 to 1621, who was nominated co-protector after the defection of Cardinal Alessandro Orsini in late 1620. His appointment had been considered even before his elevation to the cardinalate on 11 January 1621, when his mission as nuncio was just about to end. When Orsini's departure was announced, Guido's brother Enzio, Marquis of Bentivoglio, paid a visit to the French ambassador, the Marquis de Cœuvres, and presented his brother as a man wholly suited for the post of co-protector. At the same time, if Bentivoglio himself is to be believed, the king and the Duc de Luynes, his favourite at the time and head of the government, offered the co-protection via Père Arnoux, the king's confessor, 'in extraordinary secrecy'. How could it have been otherwise, given that the cardinal was still officially the diplomatic representative of Paul V? The combination of these sources of support enabled Bentivoglio to triumph relatively easily over his adversaries, such as Cœuvres himself, and over his competitors among the francophile cardinals in Rome.[25]

The king's approval was always necessary, and was expressed in the act which formally conferred the position of protector of France. If we take only the late sixteenth and the first two-thirds of the seventeenth century, the act in question was not uniform. In 1570, Luigi d'Este received special treatment in the form of *lettres de sceau plaqué* commissioning and deputing him as 'procureur, vicaire et coadjuteur' of his uncle, the

---

[25] L. Scarabelli (ed.), *Lettere diplomatiche di Guido Bentivoglio*, 2 vols., Turin, 1852–3, vol. II, pp. 410–15, Guido Bentivoglio to Scipione Borghese, [Paris], 31 January 1621.

cardinal-protector Ippolito d'Este.[26] His successor, François de Joyeuse, for his part, obtained so-called 'little' letters patent, identical to those given to governors on their appointment.[27] The protectorship cannot be classified as a royal office since no royal edict had ever created such an office, and offices were filled by letters of provision. Nor can it be regarded as a commission, revocable at will, since the appropriate term 'commit' is conspicuous by its absence from the document. Rather like provincial governorships in France, it seems that the protectorship of France in the Roman curia does not belong to either of those two familiar categories of royal agents during the early modern period, the commission and the office. Despite this, the protector was without question a 'minister' – in the older sense of a servant – of the king. Henri III 'established' Joyeuse as 'protector general and special in the said court of Rome of our affairs and those of our kingdoms, country and subjects', and his function was defined as an 'estate, charge and office' about whose responsibilities the *brevet* remained silent. Over time, the formulae would become simpler but the terminology would remain the same, as is shown by the 1645 *brevet* to Cardinal Rinaldo d'Este, in which the king 'granted' him the post of 'protector of his affairs at the court of Rome'.[28] As for the vice-protectorship, it possessed no such official character, since it was left to the cardinal-protector himself to designate the person who would act as his replacement. Thus Cardinal Joyeuse, on the point of returning to France in summer 1599, unsuccessfully offered the vice-protectorship to Cardinals Aquaviva and Giustiniani, before it finally went to the French Cardinal Arnaud d'Ossat.[29]

With the exception of François de Joyeuse (d. 1615), Alessandro Bichi (d. 1657) and Rinaldo d'Este (d. 1672), it was rare for the protectorship to remain in the hands of a cardinal until his death. The others vacated the post, as Orsini did in 1620, or were simply removed from it. In the latter case, the King of France and his ministers used either the velvet glove or more peremptory means. When it was decided, in 1633, to confer the co-protectorship on Antonio Barberini, the French ambassador, the Comte de Noailles, prepared the ground by approaching the ageing Cardinal Bentivoglio, who had always served France well, but whose resignation would offer an excellent opportunity to attach Urban VIII's nephew more firmly to France.[30] The same Antonio Barberini was in turn sacked

---

[26] ASMo, Casa e Stato, filza 409, Monceaux, 11 January [1570].

[27] BNF, Dupuy 589, ff. 17r–17v, Paris, 16 February 1587 (Sixteenth-century copy).

[28] ASMo, Casa e Stato, filza 431, Paris, 13 December 1645.

[29] *Lettres du cardinal d'Ossat*, 5 vols., Amsterdam, 1714, vol. III, pp. 474–82, letter CXCII, Arnaud d'Ossat to Nicolas de Neufville, Rome, 25 August 1599.

[30] ASVe, Dispacci degli ambasciatori, Roma 108, ff. 326r–330v, Alvise Contarini to the Senate, Rome, 10 December 1633.

(virtually in public) in 1644 by Mazarin who, furious at being duped by Barberini who had voted in the conclave for his enemy Cardinal Pamphili (whom Mazarin had put a veto on), ordered the French ambassador to summon the cardinal to return his *brevet* and remove the arms of France from the gates of his palace. It was one of several ways of humiliating someone who had betrayed the confidence placed in him by France.[31]

The protectorship of France was a prestigious post, but one subject to the fluctuations of French diplomacy; its scope for action varied according to the personality of the protectors and the freedom of action allowed by other representatives of France in Rome.

But how did the cardinal-protector of French affairs differ from those other cardinals, whether French or francophile – not to mention the French faction or the French party, the existence of which seems questionable except in the run-up to papal conclaves?[32] If he enjoyed a pension, like the other cardinals whose support the King of France had secured, that pension was bigger by far than that of a mere cardinal, French or Italian, especially when the protector was from a princely family or was a relative of the pope. To give just a few examples: Maurice of Savoy was rewarded with a pension of 24,000 *livres* from the archbishopric of Auch, not to mention other benefits;[33] Antonio Barberini was promised two pensions of 18,000 *livres* in 1633,[34] while Rinaldo d'Este received a single pension worth 36,000 *livres*.[35] And this does not include the church benefices held by such men within France and in the king's gift. From an external point of view, the cardinal-protector figures among

---

[31] H. Coville, *Étude sur Mazarin et ses démêlés avec le pape Innocent X (1644–1648)*, Paris, 1914, pp. 37–40.

[32] This is a subject which extends far beyond the scope of the present chapter and deserves study over a longer timescale, from the mid-sixteenth to the mid-seventeenth century – and even down to the early twentieth century. It would require a clear definition of the terms 'faction' and 'party', which should not be confused with interest-based groups, and should include for the early modern period a critical reading of the reports by Venetian ambassadors, who were all too prompt to assign the cardinals of the Sacred College to clearly defined camps. Finally, the perspective of such a study should not be exclusively Roman, but should pay substantial attention to the objectives of the different powers.

[33] ASV, Archivio concistoriale, Processus 18, ff. 48v–49r, Louis XIII to Urban VIII, Compiègne, 29 April 1624, letter appointing Dominique de Vic as coadjutor to the Archbishop of Auch. ASVe, Dispacci degli ambasciatori, Roma 83, ff. 499r–499v, Girolamo Soranzo to the Senate, Rome, 22 February 1621: 'È giunta al signore cardinale di Savoia la protettione di Francia con promesse di grosse provisioni et ricche ricompense.'

[34] BAV, Archivio Barberini, Indice I, 215, royal *brevets*, issued at Nancy, 30 September 1633.

[35] Archivio di Stato di Modena, Casa e Stato, filza 431, royal *brevet*, Paris, 13 December 1645.

those cardinals who openly advertised their support of France, whose arms figured prominently at the entrance to their palaces. Rome was therefore a permanent stage where the façades themselves could display either favour or disgrace, as we saw in the case of Antonio Barberini. Romans discovered from the news circulating at daybreak which family had embraced which cause, since this kind of behaviour was not confined to princes of the church. Nevertheless, what really distinguished the protector was his functions in the formal process of appointment to a major benefice ('expédition'), and the eminent position which he enjoyed within the French system of representation in the Roman curia.

The first and most visible function of the cardinal-protector lay in the 'referring' and proposal of candidates to bishoprics and abbeys in Consistory. When the king decided to nominate a new bishop or, more rarely, a new abbot, a royal letter was sent to the protector, and this letter was accompanied by various papers: the inquiry into the nominee's life and morals, his profession of faith, a procuration from the previous incumbent in a case of resignation. Once he had the full file in his possession, the cardinal 'referred' the new nominee – that is he announced his intention to present his report on the case to the next Consistory. The pope then gave permission for the 'proposal' that would follow. In order to do this, the protector had his auditor examine the documents provided and, if everything was in order, the protector signified his approval at the end of the record. This approval then went to the cardinals known as the 'heads of order', who in turn added their approval. Lastly the auditor drafted the memoranda to be submitted to the pope and the cardinals on the day before the Consistory at which the proposal was to take place. This procedure was not a pure formality, and the cardinal-protector could prove himself to be more than a mere go-between, for example when a dossier was defective in some formal sense. So, for example, Cardinal Delfino, the vice-protector, himself conducted supplementary inquiries on candidates when those done in France were judged to be inadequate.[36] The referring of candidates in Consistory, a function clearly inseparable from the protectorship, was also a source of income, since every referring cardinal was entitled to collect the 'offering' (*propina*), which amounted to 15% of the final tax on the benefice in question, the returns from which were extremely variable in the first half of the seventeenth century.[37]

[36] See e.g. the inquiry *de vita et statu* for the Archbishop of Toulouse, conducted in Rome 26–31 July 1613 (ASV, Archivio concistoriale, Processus 13, ff. 35r–42v), or that *de statu* for the coadjutorship of Vienne of 16 June 1613 (ibid., ff. 238r–240v).

[37] A memorandum of 1624 estimated the returns from this tax at between 27,000 and 30,000 *livres* under Henri IV, but only 2,400 *livres* in 1621 and 3,900 in 1622: BNF, Morel de Thoisy 19, ff. 110r–111r, *Mémoire sur le droit de propine* (1624).

But his activity as an ambassador with highly variable duties did far more to make the protector a figure of significance, and one who was genuinely exceptional in relations between the Holy See and the kingdom of France. Ultimately, he had only a few things in common with the king's ambassador. A minister of the king, he engaged in continuous correspondence with the king, but especially with the secretary of state responsible for relations with Rome, and eventually with the first minister.[38] The first and most significant difference between them was that while the ambassador personified the king in Rome and represented his interests and those of the kingdom, the protector was entrusted merely with the defence of those interests.[39] Moreover, in order to give his mission an official stamp, the ambassador possessed one or more instructions defining his range of activity, as well as letters of credence for presentation to the pope. As for the cardinal-protector, all he had was his *brevet* appointing him as protector. It could happen that the protector received special instructions, but this was very rare.[40] Most of the time, it was through his own correspondence or via the ambassador himself that he was apprised of the king's intentions. Finally, as we have seen, the protector's services were remunerated by various forms of 'recompense', e.g. pensions, church benefices, gifts, but never by anything resembling the emoluments of an ambassador.[41]

The control of French diplomacy in Rome rested with the ambassador, and no protector ever objected to that. The protector's role was a function of the personality of the ambassador, the existence (or not) of a co-protector or a vice-protector, and the presence in the curia of French cardinals. As the latter tended to decline in numbers during Louis

---

[38] See, for example, the correspondence between Brulart de Puisieux and Cardinal Bentivoglio between 1621 and 1624 (ASV, Fondo Pio 88, register of 93 folios, seventeenth-century copy).

[39] A Wicquefort, *L'ambassadeur et ses fonctions*, 2 vols., The Hague, 1680–1, vol. I, p. 10: 'L'ambassadeur représente la personne du prince son maistre'. Wicquefort (ibid., p. 9) outlines the reasons why the protector should not be called a 'public minister': 'Il ne seroit peut-estre pas hors de propos de demander icy si les cardinaux protecteurs sont aussi ministres publics. Je n'oserois me déclarer pour l'affirmative, tant parce que parmy ceux qui ont escrit du droit public pas un ne les met au nombre des ministres que parce que leurs fonctions sont bien différentes. Le protecteur n'est pas un ambassadeur, parce qu'il n'a pas le caractère représentant et il ne peut pas estre ministre du second ordre parce que cette qualité est infiniment au-dessous de la dignité de cardinal. L'ambassadeur jouit de la protection du droit des gens et de toutes les prérogatives qui en dépendent mais le cardinal protecteur ne peut réclamer que l'autorité ou plutost l'intercession de la Couronne dont il protège les intérests et ne se peut exempter de la jurisdiction du pape.'

[40] See also BNF, MS français 17840, ff. 259r–263v, n.p., n.d., minute of instruction to Cardinal Francesco Gonzaga as he was leaving for Rome, April 1612.

[41] Wicquefort, *L'ambassadeur*, vol. I, p. 9.

XIII's reign and, above all, generally no longer resided for extended periods in Rome, the role of the protector grew correspondingly, so that
he did genuinely act as France's official representative in those parts of
the curia to which the ambassador did not have access, and where approaching the pope or the cardinal-nephew was either easier or more
frequent, such as the Consistory or the congregations of cardinals. It was
here that the protector could lobby (to use an anachronistic term) in
defence of the king's interests and the privileges of the kingdom and of
its clergy. A memorandum drafted by Cardinal d'Este's secretary around
1670 reviewed the extent of his responsibilities. The protector, he wrote,
was a genuine diplomat where all issues of a disciplinary and ecclesiastical
order were concerned, ensuring respect for the clauses of the Concordat
of Bologna (which he had to be familiar with), the proper conduct of
the 'expeditionary' bankers who dealt with the documentation of appointments to benefices, and good relations among the French religious
residents in Rome.[42] One of the permanent concerns of the secretary of
state was to ensure full coordination of the activities of the ambassador
and the protector. He could use one of them without the other – for
example, when the ambassador was no longer able to obtain the desired
results because he was out of favour, as happened several times to Annibal
d'Estrées, Marquis de Cœuvres – or when the attachment of the protector
to French interests suffered prolonged lapses, as with Maurice of Savoy
after 1630. It was a particularly important feature of the protectorship
that its incumbent should preserve, even in periods of open crisis, a sort
of semi-official contact with the pope which might bring about a return
to normal relations between the two powers – as Cardinal d'Este did in
1645–7, when the Roman embassy was vacant and the stand-in was a
man of inferior rank. The protector could not be dismissed, as a way
of signalling the breakdown of diplomatic relations, because he was not
officially accredited and it was, after all, his vocation, given his rank of
cardinal, to act as a counsellor to the pope.

   One task which the protector shared with the ambassador was the construction – or reconstruction – of a 'francophile' party with papal conclaves in mind, as the memorandum for Cardinal d'Este clearly states.[43] In
the first half of the seventeenth century, a great deal of diplomatic energy

---

[42] *Mémoires de monsieur le cardinal Reynaud d'Este, protecteur et directeur des affaires de France
en cour de Rome*, 2 vols., Cologne, 1677, vol. II, pp. 314–18.

[43] Ibid., p. 8: '8. Qu'il observe les cardinaux autant qu'il luy est possible de connoître
et pénétrer dans leur intérieur, et surtout des cardinaux papables pour pouvoir en
informer Sa Majesté ou directement ou par le moyen de l'ambassadeur et faire sçavoir
sur qui on peut faire plus de fonds à l'occasion d'un conclave, en se dépouillant de
toutes ses passions ou inclinations particulières. 9. Qu'il fasse sous main des brigues
pour lier des partis avantageux et rompre avec adresse ceux qui se forment au préjudice

was swallowed up in a welter of scheming, intrigue, secret meetings, pressure and promises, often implicit and often not honoured – not to mention the holes they left in the royal treasury. While the cardinal-protector was not automatically the leader of a party, especially if there was a French cardinal resident in Rome,[44] his role in the doings of the Roman curia was a constant problem throughout this period.

We saw that the papacy accepted the protectorship of the crowns rather unwillingly. Though the pope was not consulted in the process of designating a protector, his tacit agreement was necessary if the protectorship was to work effectively. This did not mean what we might call 'acceptance' of the kind to which papal nuncios in Paris were subjected, but rather an *a posteriori* scrutiny of the qualifications of the new holder of the post. News of a new protectorship circulated in oblique ways, but by the time the news reached the pope's ears the deed was already done. Not every protector was as tactful as Bentivoglio who, in a long letter to his cardinal-patron of the time, the papal nephew Scipione Borghese, outlined the proposals made to him for the co-protectorship of France in Rome once he had left Paris, and the scruples he would have about accepting the post, were it not for its value in promoting good relations between France and Rome.[45] Of course, Bentivoglio's position as a serving diplomat might be thought to require him to inform his superiors. For the most part, the papacy noted these appointments without any negative reaction, since the inclinations of the cardinals with ambitions to become protectors were well known. We might also add that France did not query the choices made by other rulers. Everything should have worked perfectly, with each state having its own protector and the pope tolerating a group of protectors at his court. However, one obstacle barred the way to a harmonious development of the institution: the cardinal-nephew.

There were a few cases of cardinal-nephews acting as protectors or vice-protectors in the sixteenth century, such as Saint Charles Borromeo, protector of Flanders, or Filippo Boncompagni, nephew of Gregory XIII and vice-protector of France, but the phenomenon was limited and still nowhere near the expansion it was to experience in the first half of the

---

du roy, en quoy sa prudence luy doit fournir de règle et les conjonctures de moyen propre pour y réussir.'

[44] Wicquefort, *L'ambassadeur*, vol. I, p. 9: 'Il est vray que la protection des deux premières couronnes [= France and Spain] donne une grande autorité aux cardinaux, particulièrement dans un conclave, où ils sont chefs de party.' ASV, Fondo Pio 88, ff. 22r–23v, Pierre Brulart to Guido Bentivoglio, camp before Montauban, 24 August 1621: 'La nécessité et l'usage nous obligent de luy [= the Cardinal of Sourdis] commettre les affaires d'Estat comme au cardinal national pendant qu'il n'y aura point d'ambassadeur.'

[45] Scarabelli (ed.), *Lettere diplomatiche*, vol. II, pp. 410–15, Guido Bentivoglio to Scipione Borghese, [Paris], 31 January 1621.

seventeenth century. The path taken by papal nepotism under Clement VIII, and the gradual emergence of the superintendance of the papal states, probably account for the violent Franco-Spanish clashes over the protectorships which the cardinal-nephews assumed. By concentrating an unprecedented number of offices and honours in the hands of their nephews, the popes themselves involuntarily encouraged the overstepping of the earlier limitations, as is evident from the huge accumulation of protectorships of orders and religious institutions by the brother and nephews of Urban VIII. When Cardinal Pietro Aldobrandini accepted the protectorship of Savoy in 1599, Cardinal Arnaud d'Ossat did not regard this as serious enough to provoke a crisis in relations between Clement VIII and Henri IV, even though he was uneasy about the rapprochement between Aldobrandini and the interests of Savoy which would inevitably ensue.[46] Only the protectorships of France and Spain were capable of seriously affecting the views of diplomats and their masters.

The pontificate of Paul V saw the first skirmish between the French and the Spaniards. The King of Spain offered Cardinal Scipione Borghese, who was already protector of Flanders and Germany, the protectorship of Spain, which Cardinal Borgia, who was due to reside in Naples, was about to vacate. The rumour provoked great excitement among the French diplomats, who made it known to the pope that their sovereign would regard Borghese's acceptance of the offer as an affront and as an act of defiance towards the French crown.[47] The papal nuncio, Bentivoglio, who relayed the responses elicited in Paris by the news, said that the king used the word *parzializzare* to describe the plan involving the nephew of Paul V.[48] This first attempt was a failure because the pope and his nephew, faced with the persistent recriminations of the French, judged it best not

---

[46] *Lettres du cardinal d'Ossat*, vol. III, pp. 319–40, letter CLXXII, Arnaud d'Ossat to Nicolas de Neufville, Rome, 17 February 1599.

[47] BNF, MS français 18014, 106, Jean de Bonsi to Pierre Brulart, Rome, 3 March 1620: '[L'ambassadeur] a bien faict de représenter à Sa Saincteté et aud. s[r] cardinal Borghese les raisons qui les doivent divertir de ceste nouveauté jamais praticquée par les nepveux des papes entre la France et l'Espagne, bien qu'ils ayent eu la protection de quelque autre province ou royaume de non pareille conséquence. C'est vrayment une grande démonstration de partialité car encore que la seule protection concernant simplement la proposition de bénéfices consistoriaux puisse être exercée par des cardinaux qui n'ayent la maxime des affaires publicques et d'Estat, néantmoins cela peut tirer à pensions et à s'obliger à choses plus grandes et préjudiciables aux affaires d'autres princes envers lesquels pendant ce pontificat mond. s[r] le cardinal Borghese se pourroit maintenir neutre et arbitre sans soy priver de la confiance que les uns et les autres pourroient avoir en luy.'

[48] *Lettere diplomatiche*, vol. II, Guido Bentivoglio to Scipione Borghese, pp. 311–13, [Paris], 8 April 1620.

to further aggravate the already tense relations with France. Of course, as far as the Borghese were concerned, to decline the Spanish offer was to alienate the court of Madrid. Fortunately for them, Borgia was slow to leave Rome for Naples, and that allowed them to prevaricate without hurting the feelings of the different parties. It took the death of Paul V in January 1621 to finally quell the agitation surrounding his nephew, who suddenly became much less attractive.

During the pontificate of Urban VIII the crisis arising out of the protectorship of France and Spain and the pope's nephews reached its peak. Early on, in 1626, Francesco Barberini received the protectorships of Aragon, Sicily and Portugal – to the great satisfaction of Urban VIII who, in his effusive letter of thanks to the King of Spain, regarded it purely as an expression of flattery and deference towards his family, failing to measure the true significance of the move.[49] The French secretary of state for foreign affairs complained vigorously to the nuncio about this,[50] and ordered the French ambassador in Rome, Philippe de Béthune, to communicate the king's discontent to the pope. Béthune did so vigorously but, reassured by the pope and his nephew, he was obliged to conclude that his fears were unfounded. In the early 1630s, the Franco-Spanish confrontation in Europe moved by stages towards open war. This (1633) was the moment France chose to offer the co-protectorship to Antonio Barberini. There were several reasons which led to this decision. First, the unfriendly relations between France and the house of Savoy made relations with the incumbent protector, Cardinal Maurice of Savoy, extremely tense. Secondly, there was the desire of Antonio Barberini to enjoy a position of eminence in the Roman curia alongside his elder brother, who had hitherto been the major beneficiary of pontifical favour. Nor should we underestimate the wish of the existing co-protector, Cardinal Bentivoglio, to vacate the post under honourable conditions so as to regain a degree of neutrality and thereby present himself as a candidate acceptable to the different parties in the event of a conclave. Finally, the daring manoeuvres of certain individuals, such as the Duc de Créqui, France's extraordinary ambassador in Rome, and undoubtedly Guilio Mazzarini, a client of Antonio Barberini, did much to speed up the conclusion of the negotiations.

The affair is very revealing of the intense manoeuvres engaged in by the French and Spaniards in order to consolidate their power in Rome. It began in September 1633 with the despatch of the *brevet* of co-protector,

[49] ASV, Epistulae ad principes 41, ff. 195v–196, Urban VIII to Philip IV, Rome, 30 January 1627.
[50] BNF, Dupuy 463, ff. 27r–29v, 'Mémoire de ce qui a esté traicté par Monsieur de Herbault avec le cardinal Spada, du samedi vi^e febvrier 1627'.

but the crisis only blew up in the spring of 1634. Alerted by stories emanating from the Barberinis' entourage or the French embassy, the Spaniards did not wait for the *brevet*, which was dated 30 September 1633,[51] before making strong complaints to Urban VIII 'gagliardissime' ('very energetically').[52] But it took several more weeks before news of this quarrel reached other European courts; the Venetian ambassador in Paris had not yet got wind of it in early November.[53] Moreover, the pope did not react, or did not wish to react, especially as the French had not yet officially announced the co-protectorship. It was understood that Bentivoglio would retain his post until the arrival of the new ambassador, Noailles, which was scheduled for April 1634. This delaying tactic, officially for reasons of protocol, at least helped to reduce the tension somewhat. But it did not prevent the Spaniards from remaining on their guard and in aggressive mood during the interviews accorded by the pope to the representatives of the Catholic King during the autumn and winter. Urban VIII, for his part, was only apprised of the news during the audience he granted Noailles just after his arrival, on Holy Saturday, 15 April 1634. At that point, the pope ordered Antonio to resign his post, which he was in fact preparing to do when Créqui reminded him that it was not done to offend the Most Christian King when he made such a gift. Not wishing to be left on the sidelines, the Spaniards ordered Francesco not to resign his protectorships. An impasse had been reached and the situation was one of extreme tension, with all eyes turned to the sovereign pontiff, waiting to see what his reaction would be in a conflict which, in the words of the Venetian ambassador, 'upstaged all the curiosities of Rome'.[54] Urban VIII finally understood the real meaning of the protectorships: they were far more than honours, they signified an open declaration of party allegiance between the two Catholic powers, both of which were seeking every pretext to promote what was still a covert war between them.

On 25 April, the pope summoned his two nephews and ordered them immediately to terminate their activities, which were seriously endangering his policy of mediating between the two crowns. He explained clearly that neutrality was one of the pillars of the proper operation of papal nepotism: if they wished to retain their offices – and here he was

---

[51] Cf. note 34.
[52] ASVe, Dispacci degli ambasciatori, Roma 108, ff. 69r–72v, Alvise Contarini to the Senate, Rome, 24 September 1633.
[53] ASVe, Dispacci degli ambasciatori, Francia 85, ff. 127r–130r, Giovanni Soranzo to the Senate, Paris, 1 November 1633.
[54] ASVe, Dispacci degli ambasciatori, Roma 109, ff. 137r–147v, Michiel Morosini to the Senate, Rome, 22 April 1634.

thinking mainly of Francesco, who was head of international relations –
then they must keep the confidence of all the princes and not give them
any occasion for doubting their good faith! Indeed, the memorandum
drafted by a Roman cleric on the subject towards the end of April laid
out the four reasons why the pope should do his best to maintain a
neutral position: (1) French policy was not at that moment oriented
towards Italy, but if it were to focus on Flanders or Navarre, the pope
could offer his good offices if he appeared as a 'common father'. (2) The
French claimed they wished to protect the church, in which case the
pope should encourage them and not declare himself to be their enemy.
(3) There was no sense in weakening the Holy See at a time when the
forces of evil were being unleashed. (4) Given that the Franco-Spanish
negotiations were going badly, finding an agreement between the two
states was becoming difficult, so that ignoring the absolute need for papal
neutrality was tantamount to condemning the negotiations to failure.[55]

Francesco Barberini drew the obvious conclusion from this warning, and resigned the protectorships the Spaniards had given him. But
Antonio, who was far less directly responsible for papal foreign policy
and was being heavily leaned on by French agents, refused to back down
in any way. Urban VIII failed to persuade his nephew to resign the co-
protectorship of France, and abandoned the intention that he had briefly
formed to reconfirm the old decree of Martin V banning cardinals from
taking up protectorships.[56] But France was unable to prevent the pope
from acting as he saw fit in Consistory, as he made a point of doing when
he himself referred the bishopric of Nîmes on 24 July 1634.[57] For its
part, France wanted the pope to allow his nephew to refer just one or
two sees, which would have enabled the matter to stand in such a way
that each side seemed to have carried its argument.

Though the situation became less tense, it nevertheless continued to
be intractable in the absence of concessions from the parties involved.
Cardinal Maurice of Savoy's return to Rome in 1635 made it possible to
process bulls for bishoprics and a number of abbeys that were then vacant
because no proposal had yet been made; but it also postponed the final
resolution of this tricky question.[58] Moreover, war broke out between
France and Spain, and the promotion of Antonio Barberini to the rank of

[55] BAV, Barb. Lat. 5316, ff. 49r–60r, 'Ragguaglio di quanto è seguito intorno alla com-
protettione di Francia data al signore cardinale Antonio Barberini in sin' alli 29 d'aprile
1634', n.p., n.d.
[56] BNF, Cinq-Cents Colbert 356, ff. 682r–687r, Etienne Gueffier to Léon Bouthillier,
[Rome], 18 July 1634.
[57] ASV, Archivio concistoriale, Acta camerarii 17, f. 74r, 24 July 1634.
[58] Ibid., f. 103v, 17 December 1635.

protector after the defection of the Cardinal of Savoy to the imperial cause in 1636, merely confirmed the existing situation. In response to France's persistence, Urban VIII confined himself to depriving his nephew of the most symbolic element of the protectorship – the right to refer French benefices in Consistory, something he did himself between 1636 until his death in 1644. The French pretended to regard this bizarre situation as a signal honour to their nation, whereas the real reason, as everyone knew, was the pope's own discontent, which they were prepared to put up with in relative equanimity.[59] However, for all his success in this face-saving exercise, Urban was obliged to yield to his nephew, who had chosen to play his own personal card rather than acting as an obedient cog in a pontifical and family policy which went against his self-interested devotion to the French crown.[60]

When Mazarin withdrew the *brevet* of protector from Antonio on 25 October 1644, he brought to an end the intrusion of papal nepotism into the system of protectorships. Indeed, from this point onwards, no papal nephew held the protectorship of a crown during his uncle's lifetime. France, for its part, chose individuals who were more reliable and less vulnerable to Spanish objections, even if it meant rediscovering ties with the house of Este that had been broken since the time of Clement VIII (as happened in 1645 when Rinaldo d'Este became protector), or reverting to a formula forgotten since the death of Joyeuse in 1615, as when the French cardinal, César d'Estrées, took up the post in 1676 and held

[59] M. Avenel (ed.), *Lettres, instructions diplomatiques et papiers d'Etat du cardinal de Richelieu*, 8 vols., Paris, 1853–77, vol. v, pp. 766–7, letter CDXXXII, Richelieu to Annibal d'Estrées, n.p., 8 April 1637: 'Son [= Louis XIII] désir a tousjours esté de contenter M. le cardinal Antoine. Il vous envoie le brevet de protecteur pour luy donner, si le pape trouve bon qu'il préconise, mais quand mesme il ne le voudra pas, Sa Majesté sera contente de Sa Sainteté si elle consent qu'il accepte ladicte protection, quoy qu'il ne l'exerce pas présentement. Enfin le roy vous envoie le brevet entre les mains, pour le donner audict s^r cardinal Antoine, sans l'obliger à autre chose qu'à ce que vous, qui estes sur les lieux, jugerés à propos, par l'advis de MM. Le cardinal de Bagny et Mazarin ... Si le pape ne veut pas que M. le cardinal Antoine fasse présentement les fonctions de protecteur, on peut choisir dès cette heure, par l'avis mesme dudict s^r cardinal, un comprotecteur ou vice-protecteur, selon qu'il l'aimera le mieux, lequel fera les fonctions de la charge durant la vie du pape.'

[60] N. Barozzi and G. Berchet (eds.), *Relazioni degli Stati europei lette al senato dagli ambasciatori veneti nel secolo XVII*, 10 vols., Venice, 1856–79, vol. II, pp. 2–42, report by Giovanni Nani, extraordinary ambassador in 1639–40, pp. 33–4: 'Il cardinale Antonio ... è affatto francese e perciò diffidentissimo della contraria fatione ha il titolo di protettor di quel regno ... Dall'ambasciatore francese tutto li veniva confidato.' For Antonio Barberini's place at the Roman court see O. Poncet, 'Antonio Barberini (1608–1671) et la papauté. Réflexions sur un destin individuel en cour de Rome au XVII_e siècle', *Mélanges de l'Ecole française de Rome. Italie et Méditerranée*, 108 (1996), pp. 407–42.

it along with that of ambassador after 1687.[61] During the pontificates of
Paul V and Urban VIII, the protectorship reached its limits. A representative activity defined by ruling sovereigns and tolerated since the sixteenth
century for members of the Sacred College, it could not be confused
with a papal office to be granted by the pope to members of his own
family. The popes had cherished the illusion – or more likely they had
tried to convince themselves – that it would not trouble their relations
with the Catholic powers. The discovery of the incompatibility between
an extreme form of protectorship, that exercised by cardinal-nephews,
and the public neutrality of the sovereign pontiff is an extremely revealing feature of the internal transformations which affected the papacy and
gradually sidelined it from international politics in Europe, amid which
the Roman curia was soon to become a theatre of shadows.

[61] Wodka, *Zur Geschichte*, p. 108.

THE *SQUADRONE VOLANTE*: 'INDEPENDENT' CARDINALS AND EUROPEAN POLITICS IN THE SECOND HALF OF THE SEVENTEENTH CENTURY

GIANVITTORIO SIGNOROTTO

Any observation concerning papal politics in the mid-seventeenth century which intends to relate the development of the conflict among European powers to the internal dynamics of the papal see must take into account the Innocentian Age during which the most significant and well-known changes occurred.[1] However, this does not mean that an inevitable progression of events led from the trauma of the 'iron century' to the dawn of the 'crisis of the European conscience'. It simply seems more correct and profitable to examine the latter from a mid-century viewpoint rather than taking a retrospective approach, as these aspects have already been looked upon as preliminary indications of the advances to be made during the Enlightenment.[2]

Therefore we must clarify whether during the traumatic middle years of the seventeenth century – which remain the most obscure period in early modern European history – any significant changes took place. The best way to do this is by examining the perceptions of contemporaries.

---

[1] The importance of the Innocentian Age was re-examined by B. Neveu, *Culture religieuse et aspirations réformistes à la cour d'Innocent XI*, Florence, 1979, now in idem, *Erudition et religion aux XVIIe et XVIIIe siècles*, Paris, 1994, pp. 235–76; C. Donati, 'La Chiesa di Roma tra antico regime e riforme settecentesche (1675–1760)', in G. Chittolini and G. Miccoli (eds.), *Storia d'Italia*, Annali 9, *La Chiesa e il potere politico*, Turin, 1986, pp. 721–66; B. Pellegrino (ed.), *Riforme, religione e politica durante il pontificato di Innocenzo XII (1691–1700)*, Galatina, 1994.

[2] On Hazard's widely accepted definition see J. de Viguerie, 'Quelques réflexions critiques à propos de l'ouvrage de Paul Hazard, *La crise de la conscience européenne*', in *Etudes d'histoire européenne. Mélanges offerts a René et Suzanne Pillorget*, Angers, 1990, pp. 37–54; P. Vernière, 'Peut-on parler d'une crise de la conscience européenne?', in *L'età dei lumi. Studi storici sul settecento in onore di Franco Venturi*, vol. I, Naples, 1985, pp. 57–78. These essays 'observe' the late seventeenth century from the point of view of the Enlightenment. According to T. K. Rabb's interpretation in *The Struggle for Stability in Early Modern Europe*, London and New York, 1976, the progress of the last quarter of the century must be related back to its most dramatic and forgotten decades (see in pp. 116–23).

According to the traditional perspective, the peace treaties of Westphalia and the Pyrenees marked the definitive demise of the Apostolic See as a protagonist on the international political scene. This does not require a historiographical review, but it should be emphasized that undervaluing the papacy has led to a simplified conception of political manoeuvres during the seventeenth century. (In fact, this is probably true of the entire modern age.) This is particularly evident if we evaluate this interpretation in terms of the immobility and subjection of the potentates in the Italian peninsula. A reconsideration of the ties which princely households boasted with Rome, and the fact that most members of the College of Cardinals were Italian, is sufficient to show that the potentates were always able to negotiate with the monarchies.[3] If we seek to understand the 'Spanish Age', we cannot begin by assuming that these princes were totally subject to the dominion of the Catholic Kings. On the contrary, they had a 'double loyalty'.

On the basis of this observation, which the political commentators of that age knew well, it is easier to comprehend how surveillance and other methods of conditioning the College of Cardinals and the papacy were continuously employed by those who wanted to influence the political choices of the *potentados*. As a matter of fact, the reverse is also documented: a stranglehold on the Italian princes was a sure way to influence the Holy See and its conclaves. Cateau-Cambrésis was not, for the states of the Italian peninsula, the beginning of passive subjection. The treaties of Westphalia and the Pyrenees did not deprive Rome of its 'central' position.

Although incidental to the object of this paper, it should be pointed out that the organization of the global policies of the European powers, beginning exactly at the end of the wars which characterized the first half of the century, reinstated the 'central' role of Rome by other means such as missions, and relations with the churches and societies of the colonies.

The stability that had been so arduously sought in Italy in the sixteenth century had never been stable enough for the counsellors of the Catholic sovereigns. After the Carafa papacy, the 'Age of the Barberini' rekindled Spain's intense distrust of Rome and raised rumours of 'treason' against

---

[3] On the growth in the number of Italian cardinals, see P. Prodi, *Il sovrano pontefice. Un corpo e due anime: la monarchia papale nella prima età moderna*, Bologna, 1982, pp. 174–7; P. Rietbergen, *Pausen, prelaten, bureaucraten. Aspecten van de geschiedenis van het pausschap en de pauselijke staat in de 17e eeuw*, Nijmegen, 1983, pp. 77–123; M. A. Visceglia, ' "La giusta statera de porporati". Sulla composizione del Sacro Collegio nella prima metà del seicento', *Roma moderna e contemporanea*, 1 (1996), pp. 197–200. See also B. McClung Hallman, *Italian Cardinals, Reform, and the Church as Property*, Berkeley, 1985, pp. 158–60, which analyses some aspects of the network of consanguinity and affinity that united the members of the Sacred College.

the most praiseworthy and pious monarch in Christendom.[4] The fact that the papacy was strong enough to conceive the ambitions of a great secular prince made the situation all the more alarming. In the 1640s, after the precedents set by the annexation of Ferrara (1598) and Urbino (1631), the desire to impose a direct dominion over Castro and Ronciglione, in order to hinder the Farnese, represented a serious threat to Italian equilibrium.[5]

The Habsburgs considered the reign of Urban VIII an 'accident' which fully confirmed the wide spread feeling of uneasiness. Shortly before the conclave which was to elect Barberini, a confidant of the crown had confirmed that it was in their interest to uphold a candidate 'of great age and little life expectancy', since such a man, lacking the time to consolidate his own family, would try to maintain 'good relations' with the King of Spain. Pontiffs who are certain of good health, the informer explained, are likely to become 'absolute lords of the government', and therefore 'despise dependence'. The Catholic ambassador to Rome, the Count of Monterey, believed that it was better to uphold a very old candidate 'of dubious loyalty' rather than a 'young and friendly' one.[6]

Notwithstanding the lessons of the past, great knowledge and unending caution, Roman policy remained to a certain extent unpredictable and this helped to make any hegemony over the peninsula uncertain. Thus, from a methodological point of view, when considering Italian and international policy it is absolutely necessary to start from the conflicts and balancing acts that took place at the summit of the Holy See. The 'universal' quality of Holy See politics cannot be appreciated without a far-reaching historical vision which can perceive the multiple thrusts and influences coming from the outside; at the same time, that universality was a basic component, the second nature of the 'Eternal City' and the papal court. The fact that awareness of, and interest in, the internal dynamics of the Roman court have grown significantly over the

---

[4] The special council which convened in Madrid in 1632 clearly enunciated the theory of indirect power on account of the pontiff's enmity towards Spain, giving rise to an approach defined by Q. Aldea Vaquero as 'la mentalidad científica de la segunda fase de la Contrarreforma' ('Iglesia y estado en la época barroca', in *Historia de España fundada por R. Menéndez Pidal*, vol. xxv, Madrid, 1982, p. 531).

[5] For an accurate reconstruction see Y.-M. Bercé, 'Rome et l'Italie au XVIIe siècle. Les dernières chances temporelles de l'Etat Ecclésiastique, 1641–1649', in *L'Europe, l'Alsace et la France, Etudes réunies en l'honneur du Doyen Georges Livet de l'université des sciences humaines de Strasbourg, Colmar*, n.d.. However, Bercé also resurrects the old idea that the Italian states were passive.

[6] BAV, Vat. Lat., 10408, 524–535v; ibid., 12178: *Parere dato dal conte di Monterey sovra l'elettione del sommo pontefice.*

past few years simplifies our task and allows us to verify the uniqueness of Rome as remarked on by many previous observers, who described it as a 'political laboratory' and the 'theatre of the world'.[7]

The internal vicissitudes of the Sacred College, and of the group of cardinals known as the *squadrone volante*, reveal the vitality and contradictions typical of a context which, as a subject of multiple converging and conflicting pressures, was characterized by particular instability and underwent continuous transformations.[8] Even the achievement of the *zelanti*, the protagonists of the Innocentian turn around, must be viewed in relation to political developments. However, as we shall see, this phase was quite exceptional. For the first time, in the dialectics of conservation and change, the emphasis was on the latter, giving rise to novel cultural openings and a new image of the papacy.[9] Verifying whether these results were part of the trends born in the mid-seventeenth century will allow us to review the chronology and effects of the other division which is traditionally seen as starting in the middle of the seventeenth century: the shift from 'Spanish hegemony' to the so-called 'French preponderance'.

THE BEGINNING

At a time when the outcome of the war between France and Spain was still uncertain, the *squadrone volante* made its first public appearance at the conclave that began in January after the death of Innocent X. These cardinals, who defined themselves as the 'faction of God', announced

[7] On the 'theatre of the world' metaphor and the distinction between the papal court and Apostolic See, see Rosa's chapter in this volume. See also R. Krautheimer, *The Rome of Alexander VII. 1655–1667*, Princeton, 1985, pp. 4–7; S. M. Seidler, *Il 'teatro del mondo'. Diplomatische und journalistische Relationen vom römischen Hof aus dem 17. Jahrhundert*, Frankfurt am Main, 1996, p. 15. Historiographical interpretations of the political role of Rome are discussed in M. Pellegrini, 'Corte di Roma e aristocrazie italiane in età moderna. Per una lettura storico-sociale della curia romana', *Rivista di storia e letteratura religiosa*, 30 (1994), pp. 543–602, and M. A. Visceglia, 'Burocrazia, mobilità sociale e patronage alla corte di Roma tra Cinque e Seicento. Alcuni aspetti del recente dibattito storiografico e prospettive di ricerca', *Roma moderna e contemporanea*, 1 (1995), pp. 11–55.

[8] For a good synopsis see W. Reinhard, 'Papal Power and Family Strategy in the Sixteenth and Seventeenth centuries', in R. G. Asch and A. M. Birke (eds.), *Princes, Patronage and the Nobility. The Court at the Beginning of the Modern Age, 1450–1650*, Oxford, 1991, pp. 329–56.

[9] L. von Pastor, *Storia dei papi*, vol. xv, Rome, 1943, pp. 7–8. In the balance that Pastor draws as a premise to his description of seventeenth-century events, there is an explicit relation between the disappointments and humiliations suffered by the pope and the 'moral renaissance' of the latter part of the century, which was manifested by the use of a 'new language'.

their objectives in a statement (written by Francesco Albizzi) in which they proclaimed that they were set on electing 'one of the most deserving' and were ready to die rather than forgo their objectives. They would only give their votes to a candidate who was 'prudent, learned and pious' and would never allow a prelate with such virtues to be excluded from the papacy because of a veto from a sovereign.[10]

In his *Vita di Alessandro VII*, Sforza Pallavicino lists the eleven 'confederate' cardinals: Giovanni Girolamo Lomellino and Lorenzo Imperiale from Genoa, Luigi Omodei and Giberto Borromeo from Milan, Benedetto Odescalchi from Como, Carlo Pio from Ferrara, Ottavio Acquaviva from Naples, Pietro Ottoboni from Venice, Francesco Albizzi from Cesena, Carlo Gualtieri from Orvieto and Decio Azzolini from Fermo. They were all *creature* of Pope Innocent X.[11]

The Chigi pope's biographer also provides an explanation for the group's name. At first, they were ironically referred to as the 'Canton degli Svizzeri' to indicate their isolation, but then the name 'squadrone volante' emerged, as it was more appropriate and more honourable. The Duke of Terranova coined this colourful name for the faction because it reminded him of special military units which were 'ready to go here or there to do things or provide aid'. What distinguished the *squadrone volante* was its *mobility*: freedom of movement, ability to act and, possibly, its unscrupulous nature. The fact that the eleven cardinals were also described as 'young cardinals' (some of them remained active into the 1680s and 1690s) means that we must also take the 'generation aspect' into consideration. The Spaniards knew that the advanced average age of their cardinals represented a disadvantage.

Another observation common to all commentators is that the *squadrone volante* cardinals (or at least the most representative of them) were the most talented members of the Sacred College.[12] That Pietro Ottoboni was an eminent personality was a commonly held opinion. The cardinal who was to become Pope Alexander VIII had a remarkable knowledge of canonical and juridical issues. He had been appointed auditor of the Rota by Urban VIII in 1643 and had continued his legal practice for over

---

[10] The 'manifiesto de los cardinales mozos' is included in the material dated 20 February 1655, sent by the Duke of Terranova (the Spanish ambassador to Rome) to the *Consejo de Estado*: AGS, Estado, Roma, legajo 3027. Another copy of this declaration is in BAV, Patetta, 2908, f. 219.

[11] Cristoforo Vidman, from Friuli, and Giovanni Stefano Dongo, from Genoa (the only cardinal appointed by Urban VIII), did not join until later. *Della vita di Alessandro VII libri cinque, Opera inedita del p. Sforza Pallavicino*, vol. I, Prato, 1839, p. 222.

[12] Leti believed that gifted men such as Ottoboni and Omodei would inevitably displease the monarchies, which strove to hire 'weak men, who could easily be ordered around'. G. Leti, *Il livello politico*, Castellana, 1678, vol. II, pp. 214–16.

a decade until, in 1652, he became a cardinal. When he presented himself to the conclave, he had just been appointed to the episcopal government of Brescia. There was a risk that his pastoral commitments would keep him away from the Roman court for long periods, but his participation in the *squadrone volante* allowed him to reinforce important friendships and open up new career prospects.[13]

Although younger, Decio Azzolini was already an expert in the intrigues of curial politics. He had followed Cardinal Panciroli to the Spanish nunciature and had then assisted him in the State Secretariat. Under the protection of Donna Olimpia, at the age of twenty-eight, he acted as head of the Secretariat until Fabio Chigi returned from Germany. Azzolini was made a cardinal by Pope Innocent X, in 1654, after he had denounced the secret agreement between Cardinal Astalli and the Spanish government.[14]

Francesco Albizzi was the third outstanding personality of the *squadrone volante*. For many years he was a counsellor of the Holy Office. Then, in 1654, he was made a cardinal as a reward for his intransigence when leading the anti-Jansenist front. As a 'cardinal judge' (*cardinale giudice*), he remained one of the most influential members of the Roman congregation. He had a very good relationship with the Jesuits, and since the condemnation of the *Augustinus* he had developed a close friendship and collaboration with Fabio Chigi and Giulio Rospigliosi, both of whom were to become pontiffs.[15]

Azzolini, Ottoboni and Albizzi, whom contemporary observers indicated as the leaders of the *squadrone volante*, belonged by birth and interests to the Italian context. They did not come from states subject to the direct authority of the Spanish court, nor were they connected with the French

[13] A. Petrucci, 'Alessandro VIII', in *DBI*, vol. II, pp. 215–19; G. Signorotto, *Inquisitori e mistici nel Seicento italiano. L'eresia di Santa Pelagia*, Bologna, 1989, pp. 146–9; A. Menniti Ippolito, *Politica e carriere ecclesiastiche nel secolo XVII. I vescovi veneti fra Roma e Venezia*, Bologna, 1993 (see index).

[14] As we shall see, Azzolini did not become the head of the State Secretariat until 1667, during the papacy of Clement IX. G. De Caro, 'Azzolini (Azzolino), Decio', in *DBI*, vol. IV, pp. 768–71; I. Ciampi, *Innocenzo X Pamfili e la sua corte. Storia di Roma dal 1644 al 1655 da nuovi documenti*, Imola, 1878, pp. 166–8. The following studies have given Azzolini the importance that he deserves: M.-L. Rodén, 'Cardinal Decio Azzolino, Queen Christina of Sweden and the Squadrone Volante. Political and Administrative Developments at the Roman Curia, 1644–1692', doctoral thesis, Princeton University, Ann Arbor, 1992, and 'Cardinal Decio Azzolino and the Problem of Papal Nepotism', *Archivum Historiae Pontificiae*, 34 (1996), pp. 127–57. See now Rodén, *Church Politics in Seventeenth-Century Rome. Cardinal Decio Azzolino, Queen Christina of Sweden, and the Squadrone Volante*, Stockholm 2000.

[15] L. Ceyssens, *Le cardinal François Albizzi (1593–1684). Un cas important dans l'histoire du jansénisme*, Rome, 1977; A. Legrand and L. Ceyssens, *La correspondance antijanséniste de Fabio Chigi, nonce à Cologne, plus tard pape Alexandre VII*, Brussels and Rome, 1957, pp. 5, 57ff.; A. Monticone, 'Albizzi, Francesco', in *DBI*, vol. II, pp. 23–6.

court. This explains, at least in part, the freedom of movement which the new faction demonstrated during the conclave.[16]

In Rome, the interests of the European powers were represented by the 'cardinal-protectors of the crowns', who were financed by pensions and ecclesiastical revenues and were active in conclaves and consistories. The pressure from the monarchies had become very strong by the final stages of the Thirty Years War, and not only in relation to papal elections. Every time a new cardinal was nominated, the monarchies raised violent arguments which pushed popes to make a far more frequent use of the *riserva in pectore* expedient.[17] The most striking aspect, however, remained the *esclusiva* against 'papable' cardinals. This was no longer a secret agreement; on the contrary, it had become an outright public announcement made by one of the cardinal-protectors. The problem of 'exclusion' had already been debated, but it became a crucial issue in the 1655 conclave.[18]

The consultations prior to the election of the Innocent X's successor began in January 1655 and continued for three months in a climate of great uncertainty. Among the most influential faction heads were the Dean of the Sacred College, Cardinal Carlo de' Medici, who had already established himself as the head of the Spanish party during the conclave of Pope Innocent X and who controlled a significant number of votes. Francesco Barberini could orient the votes of thirty-four conclavists, and although he did not openly present his preferred candidate, he was

---

[16] This statement remains true if we accept that the Genoese Cardinal Lorenzo Imperiali was responsible for the group's inception. See *Relazione della corte di Roma del marchese Francesco Nerli ambasciatore d'obbedienza del serenissimo signor duca Carlo II di Mantova alla Santità di N.S. Alessandro VII, 1655,* p. 307 (as it is quoted in its entirety in S. M. Seidler, *Il 'teatro del mondo',* pp. 284–334, I shall refer to the latter work). It was exactly during this period that the break between the Republic of Genoa and Spain developed. However, I shall address the behaviour of 'subject' or 'vassal' cardinals below.

[17] Concerning the 1647 promotions, which had angered Philip IV because his candidate, unlike the French one, had only obtained the *in pectore* appointment, Pedro Coloma (addressing the Secretary of State) said that cardinals should be appointed 'el mismo dia, y à la misma hora'; Biblioteca-Archivio storico comunali, Jesi, Arch. Azzolino, Corrispondenza 107, 20 January 1649. The situation was to become paradoxical during the papacy of Alexander VII, when the rival powers allied in order to force the pope to satisfy their requests (before the 1667 nominations) by threatening a schism: Pastor, *Storia dei papi,* vol. XIV/1, p. 406. A manuscript entitled *Nomina dei cardinali ad istanza delle corone,* BAV, Vat. Lat., 9712, ff. 9–21, summarizes the promotions made between the latter half of the seventeenth century and Benedict XIV's papacy and emphasizes the Pontiffs' efforts to satisfy the requests of the European powers.

[18] The practice – as Cardinal de Luca was to point out – could not be explained 'by justice, nor positive obligation', as there was no trace of it in the ancient canons or in the past councils. It could be traced back to the Council of Trent and had been motivated by the fact that, for far-distant countries, the pope could not have 'perfect news . . . to know which were the subjects welcome to people and princes': G. B. De Luca, *Il cardinale della S. R. Chiesa pratico,* Rome, 1680, p. 51.

resolute on promoting one of his *creature*. When the nephew of Urban VIII obstinately stuck to supporting the candidature of Giulio Sacchetti, he encountered firm opposition from Madrid, as it was well known that the Tuscan cardinal was bound to Mazarin.

Attitudes to the 'right of exclusion' imposed by the monarchies must be reconsidered under these new circumstances. The idea that the veto should be merely informative, and that the vote should remain free, was championed by those who wanted to force Spain to change its hostile attitude towards Cardinal Sacchetti. Even Fabio Chigi, who was proposed by Barberini with the agreement of the *squadrone volante*, was blocked by a French veto. In the end, however, his election was made possible when the French court decided to rescind this veto.[19]

It is not surprising that the Duke of Terranova, revealing the *squadrone volante*'s manoeuvres in favour of Sacchetti to the Consejo de Estado, acted in order to weaken it. Albizzi was considered an enemy by Madrid; Azzolini was seen as a schemer and 'traitor'. The formation of the *squadrone volante* and its actions were interpreted as an anti-Spanish conspiracy, all the more dangerous as it involved cardinals (the three Lombards and the Neapolitan) who should have been Spanish subjects. Even the behaviour of two Genoese cardinals was condemned, as the Spaniards considered they had a right to their loyalty.

Cardinal de Lugo and Don Gaspar de Sobremonte reported everything that had taken place during the conclave to the sovereign, but Philip IV's counsellors did not take any measures against those who had not adhered to their *obligación*. They knew that for a cardinal who was a vassal of a monarch, the only chance of obtaining a good number of votes was to show some resistance to demands from Madrid. Moreover, the fact that so many cardinals had been involved in this 'conspiracy' called for even greater caution.[20]

At the end of the conclave, however, the controversy over the use of the *jus exclusivae* was by no means finished. Albizzi even wrote a brief memorandum on the issue in which he described the idea that cardinals should not vote for candidates 'excluded' by the monarchies as 'heretical'. The election of a pontiff was free, by divine institution, and such vetoes exposed the church to the criticism of heretics, as they demonstrated that the election was not the work of the Holy Spirit, but of human interests.

[19] G. Gigli, *Diario romano (1608–1670)*, ed. G. Ricciotti, Rome, 1958, pp. 455, 459; I. Fosi, *All'ombra dei Barberini. Fedeltà e servizio nella Roma barocca*, Rome, 1997, pp. 141ff., where this episode is seen from Sacchetti's point of view. (Sacchetti wrote to Mazarin seeking to persuade him to withdraw the exclusion against the Chigi cardinal.)

[20] Sobremonte acted as ambassador until a new one was appointed. His letter (dated 20 July 1658) is very detailed.

Moreover, according to the author the veto even offended human justice, as it ruined the reputation of cardinals who, having participated in the conclave, were 'in competition' and would be accountable for their way of life, their doctrine and even the quality of their friends and relations. If a given candidate was quarrelsome and a fomenter of controversies, the princes were allowed to point out these dangers in a 'plea' to the cardinals in the conclave. However, if the cardinals were presented with an explicit 'exclusion', they were obliged to resist 'even if their life was endangered'.[21]

De Lugo, who together with the two Medici headed the Spanish imperial group, responded that conclavists should not vote for candidates who had received an 'exclusion' from one of the Catholic monarchs. Obviously, he intended to affirm that a sovereign as important and pious as the King of Spain had every right to see his demands executed.[22]

The position of those who, together with Albizzi, called for the church to be free from the interference of monarchs may seem closer to modern sensibility. However, we must also bear in mind that the Spanish arguments were not unfounded. They were the result of a serious debate. It would be superficial to think that they had not discussed *truths* which were held to be indisputable, such as the principle of the freedom of papal electors and the action of the Holy Spirit. These arguments were to be efficiently summarized a year later in a work probably written by an ecclesiastic at the request of a Spanish cardinal.[23]

The author of this work pointed out that, notwithstanding its importance, the issue was being ignored, and therefore it was necessary to make use 'de la invención propia, y del propio discurso'. He agreed that cardinals would be perpetrating a mortal sin if they did not take into account the Catholic King's 'right of exclusion'. The measures taken against Spain by Paul IV and Urban VIII amply proved that the clash with the monarchies brought about every kind of outrage, schism and calamity in the church. Why, then, ignore consequences that after repeated experiences were so easily predictable? Hostility against a monarch was a factor which made a cardinal unacceptable as a papal candidate; any choice that

---

[21] BNM, ms. 1391, ff. 1–18: *Discorso del signor cardinale Albizzi col quale si prova che non possono le corone, ne altri prencipi secolari escludere i cardinali dal pontificato. 1655.* Another copy in BAV, Vat. Lat., 12178, ff. 10–13.

[22] BAV, Urb. Lat., 1679, ff. 307–14: *Risposta al discorso del card. degl'Albici che le corone hanno jus d'escludere li cardinali dal Pontificato.* On Cardinal de Lugo and his order's support for the Chigi candidate (and their opposition to the candidature of the Dominican Vincenzo Maculano) see the *Relazione Nerli*, pp. 300–1.

[23] BL, Egmont 446, ff. 87r–107v: *Censura que se hizo a un sugeto mui docto de España: sobre si los cardenales pueden elegir Papa a un cardenal excluido por el Rey de España,* 15 April, 1662.

failed to take this into account flew in the face of prudence. The 'most deserving' man was the one who, besides personal virtues, brought benefits to the church. The author also specified that the 'right of exclusion' should not be based on threats, but on reason and equity, as when a doctor distinguishes what is bad from what is good. The 'right of exclusion' did not have the strength of a law or precept. It was to be viewed as an *información* and, since it provided useful facts, it ought to increase the conclave's freedom.

During the flurry of controversy raised by the exclusion of Cardinal Sacchetti, there were again those who pointed out that the resulting situation was quite paradoxical: those who raised their voices to defend the freedom of cardinals were the same electors who had, on many other occasions, worked to exclude candidates. Therefore, the personal interests of some cardinals clashed with the state councils and theological congregations that Spanish monarch used, along with his armies, to defend the Catholic faith. After all, if exclusions could be upheld by Cesena (Albizzi's birth place), it was absurd that they should not be sanctioned by Madrid.[24]

The idea that the *squadrone volante* had consistently attempted to fortify papal authority against interference from the monarchies is closely related to the image which the group portrayed of itself, which was amply aided by propaganda from France and her allies.[25] According to this view, Azzolini and his comrades were the tenacious advocates of a project destined to triumph. Although it is true that they sided with the French, this was only on account of 'practical circumstances', in order to split the Spanish bloc without sacrificing their own ideals.[26]

A few methodological observations can be made regarding this interpretation. If historical analysis focuses on the group, rather than its

---

[24] BAV, Barb. Lat., 4675, ff. 200–5: *Origine della lunghezza del conclave e pretentioni della fattione volante.*

[25] Sforza Pallavicino, who was the first to point out the autonomy of the *squadrone*, was in close contact with Albizzi, to whom he often submitted his work for copy-editing. See *Lettere del cardinal Sforza Pallavicino, ediz. corretta e accresciuta sopra i mss. casanatensi*, Rome, 1848, p. 77, letter dated 7 July 1663. Ranke was the first historian to emphasize the *squadrone's* 'freedom' in a historical and critical analysis (L. von Ranke, *History of the Popes*, trans. E. Fowler, rev. edn, 3 vols., New York, 1901, vol. 1, p. 839). This supported his hypothesis of a Roman transition towards an 'aristocratic constitution'. This was one of the weapons used by the powerful aristocracy of cardinals, which had grown stronger during the seventeenth century, against the papal monarchy (ibid., p. 845).

[26] Rodén, *Cardinal Decio Azzolino, Queen Christina*, p. 71. The repeated emergence of this problem over two centuries calls for caution over the idea that the *squadrone* deserved the credit for having freed Rome from interference by other states. L. Lector (J. Güthlin), *Le conclave et le "veto" des gouvernements*, Lyons, 1894, pp. 1–69.

individual members, a greater emphasis will be placed on principles rather than on opportunities and convenience. Furthermore, a great number of values and variables, and therefore uncertainties and ambiguities, remains obscure if only a single bond, such as that with France, is foregrounded (an approach which is favoured by the traditional interest in the relationship between Azzolini and Christina of Sweden).[27] Lastly, in order to depict the *squadrone volante* in a 'modern' key, it is necessary to portray the group in terms of a cohesion and duration which would allow us to suggest a continuity with the reforms of the *zelanti* during the Odescalchi papacy.[28] However, a study of the work accomplished by the survivors of the *squadrone volante* when faced with the Innocentian changes, and the overall significance of Alexander VIII's papacy, leads to a very different conclusion.

Let us therefore continue our examination of the central phase of the seventeenth century, taking into account both the success of the *squadrone volante* and the political dynamics of the Sacred College with regard to the Spanish monarchy.

THE YEARS OF UNCERTAINTY

The appeal against the monarchies' 'right of exclusion' arose from the general uncertainty regarding the outcome of the war between France and Spain during the years preceding the Treaty of the Pyrenees. The complexity and 'diversity' of the Roman scene call for a detailed analysis of this historical phase, going beyond a generic reference to the 'clash between the two monarchies', based on the schematic sequence of 'crisis of the Spanish monarchy – French hegemony', which has projected the shadow of Louis XIV's subsequent preponderance in Europe back on to the middle of the seventeenth century.

In the early 1650s, political actors and observers did not perceive this upsetting of the balance of power. They were preoccupied by the war and were far closer to it than we are. Even Cardinal de Retz, who was celebrating the actions of the *squadrone volante* (the front he had decided

---

[27] The ideas of C. Bildt (*Christine de Suède et le conclave de Clément X (1669–1670)*, Paris, 1906, vol. II, pp. 20–1) are also found in Rodén, *Cardinal Decio Azzolino, Queen Christina*, p. 21. On the limits of the 'Whig interpretation of history' applied to the study of Italian ecclesiastical and religious history, see S. Ditchfield, ' "In search of local knowledge": Rewriting Early Modern Italian Religious History', *Cristianesimo nella storia*, 19, 1998, pp. 255–96, quotation p. 257.

[28] When the debate was rekindled because of Emperor Leopold's veto against Cardinal Pignatelli, the defenders of 'exclusion' polemically defined the *zelanti* as the heirs of the *squadrone volante*: *L'esclusiva che danno i re a i cardinali*, Bibl. Casanatense, Rome, ms. 2315, ff. 157–202.

to join), credited it with the will to 'divide the Spaniards and weaken the French' and added that 'the advantage of being in such a situation is great, but rare. A similar series of circumstances would be necessary, but it might not recur for another ten thousand years.'[29]

The Spanish monarchy had not suffered irreparable damage. The disasters of the 1640s had been overcome and order had been restored in Naples and Barcelona. Mazarin had not managed to conquer Milan, notwithstanding repeated assaults, and the Fronde had forced him to withdraw his forces from the Italian front. The turning-point was the failure of the long siege of Cremona, which lasted from the winter of 1647 to the early months of 1648. Taking advantage of the serious internal problems then tormenting France, the Spaniards reacted spectacularly by occupying Casale and invading the Estense state. When the successor of Pope Innocent X was about to be elected in Rome, there was absolutely no reason to surmise that Spanish power in the Italian peninsula was on the verge of collapse.[30]

For the majority of the Italian potentates, the Spanish monarchy was the best source of rewards and honours; for the church, it continued to represent the greatest source of benefits and wealth, as well as the major power in the Italian peninsula which provided most of the cardinals.[31] Even later on, during the period of 'French preponderance', Gregorio Leti insisted that the popes should stay on good terms with the Catholic Kings, as most of Rome's riches came from their dominions.[32] Leti also pointed out that Spain's 'somnolent' attitude towards the frequent affronts it received from Rome was stupefying. We do know, however, that an 'ungrateful' (or even openly hostile) attitude from the pope was part of

---

[29] Cardinal de Retz, *Mémoires. Texte préfacé et annoté par Maurice Allem*, Paris, 1950, p. 822.

[30] For this succession of events see G. Signorotto, *Milano spagnola. Guerra, istituzioni, uomini di governo (1635–1660)*, Milan, 1996. Evaluating this historical phase, J. Black, 'Warfare, Crisis, and Absolutism', in E. Cameron (ed.), *Early Modern Europe*, Oxford, 1999, pp. 217–18, pointed out that historians have paid very little attention to the Spanish victories, as they do not fit in with the picture of an inevitable decline of Spain and rise of French power.

[31] This explains the optimism of the *Istruzione all'Ecc.mo sign. duca di Terranova*, BAV, Vat. Lat., 10446, ff. 40–52, n.d. (1654), which states that the Catholic king had no worries regarding the conclave, as anyone who had any ambition to become pope had to follow the Spanish court, 'which, today, is the only one to uphold this [the Roman] court' (f. 47). Terranova (Diego de Aragona y Tagliavia) was the ambassador to Rome from 1653 to 1657.

[32] Leti, *Il livello politico*, vol. II, 1678, p. 227. The attitude of the pro-French party is further proof of this. After the death of Pope Urban VIII, Taddeo Barberini reminded his cardinal brothers of the damage they would do to the household if they openly declared their support for France: 'we will lose large revenues from the abbeys in the states of the Spanish king'. P. Pecchiai, *I Barberini*, Rome, 1959, p. 180.

the game. Madrid accepted it, being well aware how volatile were the politics of the Holy See.[33]

Inevitably, the Spaniards were severely dejected by the many crises of the 1640s, and this included Spain's relations with Rome. One of these events was an incredible 'falta de paternal amor' towards Philip IV during the promotions to the cardinalship in October 1647, when Innocent X decided to reserve the position *in pectore* for Mazarin's brother and withhold it from Don Antonio de Aragón.[34] However, the tone and frequency of the contacts between the two courts was also determined by the belief that the 'Austrias' had the right to more favourable treatment than the other monarchies. This pretence was continually disputed, but the conditions that had brought it into being continued to exist. This explains why some of the lobbies which were very influential in Rome, such as the one headed by Francesco Barberini, sought formal recognition from the Catholic King despite his faction's traditionally pro-French inclination.[35]

The most critical event occurred in 1654 when Philip IV refused to meet Camillo de Massimi, the papal nuncio, who had come to replace Caetani, who had been barred from every office by the pope. As a result, the tribunal of the nunciature in Spain was shut down for eight months and the pope withheld his graces of *cruzada, subsidio* and *milliones* until the new nuncio was accepted.[36] However, in 1655, the papacy and the Habsburg court were drawn closer together by common anxieties: the alliance between Cromwell and the King of Sweden and the threat of a joint attack on Dunkirk. Peace with France was strongly desired, among other things, to save Catholicism from the menace of the English and their allies.[37]

---

[33] 'No hay Papa que después de serlo cumpla lo que ofreció', as the Marquis de la Fuente, the ambassador to Venice, wrote in a letter dated 20 March 1655: AHNM, Estado, libro 124, f. 52v.

[34] According to a letter sent by Pedro Coloma to the pontiff, from Madrid, on 20 January 1649: Biblioteca-Archivio storico comunali, Jesi, Arch. Azzolino, 107. Antonio de Aragón was not 'published' until March 1650; See V. Tornetta, 'La politica di Mazzarino verso il papato (1644–1646)', *Archivio storico italiano*, 3–4 (1942), p. 134.

[35] On 12 April 1655 the newly elected Pope Alexander VII asked the Milanese Cardinal Trivulzio to intercede with Philip IV to help the Barberini, as Cardinal Francesco had worked so hard to get him elected Pontiff; BL, Additional 26855, f. 104r, letter from Nuncio de Massimi, 11 September 1655. AGS, Estado, Roma, legajo 3026 and 3027, letters from Cardinal Trivulzio and the Duke of Terranova.

[36] G. Signorotto, 'Aristocrazie italiane e monarchia cattolica nel XVII secolo. Il "destino spagnolo" del duca di Sermoneta', *Annali di storia moderna e contemporanea*, 2 (1996), pp. 66–8. This incident was only resolved in 1658 with the appointment of Bonelli as nuncio, the grant of *milliones* and the promise of a cardinalship for Pascual de Aragón: AGS, Estado, Roma, legado 3030 and 3031.

[37] The nature of these anxieties is described by Nuncio de Massimi in a letter sent to Rome after a meeting with the imperial ambassador to Madrid, which described the

Thus it would be far too simplistic to affirm that the good fortune of the *squadrone volante* was the result of an irreversible 'crisis of the Spanish monarchy'. It is better to argue that Philip IV encountered persistent difficulties and that this situation provided his allies with an excuse to raise their demands, renegotiate old agreements and show an interest in French proposals. Even the cardinals who were, in various ways, bound to Spain were gaining greater freedom of movement and conducting unprecedented negotiations. Nonetheless, as their families, interests and riches still, depended, directly or indirectly, on the Spanish court and its representatives in Italy, they were certainly not about to become rebels. They were allies, who, at that moment, realized that they could obtain greater advantages in exchange for their friendship. The same is true of the Genoese. However, in their case, again, with the exception of the 1627 crisis, during which relations with the Spanish monarchy grew colder, the middle years of the seventeenth century witnessed the most important changes. The situation definitely worsened in 1654 due to the taxes which were levied on ships sailing through the port of Finale, as a result of which Genoese goods were confiscated throughout the dominions of the Spanish crown. The crisis was overcome not only because of the need for the financial contributions of the 'hombres de negocios' of the Genoese Republic, but also due to their presence, and especially that of their prelates and cardinals, on the Roman scene.

If the check on Italian cardinals of subject and allied families allowed the Spanish government to limit the risks caused by the physiological instability of the Holy See, the availability of the popes remained a decisive factor in preventing the potentates of the Italian peninsula, pushed by their ambitions, from becoming enemies of the monarchy.[38]

'COMPRAR LOS CARDINALES'

In the age we are examining, a cardinal free from any tie to the European powers would have been quite the exception. Gregorio Leti's description of how the members of the Sacred College 'from morning to evening study the book of the growth of their grandeur'[39] certainly does not strike the historian as hard fact. Nonetheless it cannot be completely ignored.

anti-Catholic projects of Oliver Cromwell: BL, Additional 26855 (Letters to Camillo de Massimi 1653–1658), f. 75r; from Madrid, 24 July 1655.

[38] On the 'primacy of Rome' over the other Italian states, see Prodi, *Il sovrano pontefice*, pp. 323–4. But see also the analysis by M. Rivero Rodríguez, 'Felipe II y los "potentados de Italia"', *Bulletin de l'Institut Historique Belge de Rome*, 63 (1993), pp. 337–70.

[39] G. Leti, *Il cardinalismo di santa Chiesa*, vol. II, n.p. (Geneva), 1668, p. 11.

Since the conclave of Alexander VII, the Catholic court had decided to take the insubordination of the *squadrone volante* into account when it came to distributing graces. In 1656 Cardinal Azzolini's agent, Francesco De Sanctis, wrote from Madrid that 'all the cardinals of the *squadrone volante*' were to be excluded from the allocation of rewards (pensions and other ecclesiastical revenues). In 1657, in retaliation, the group members proposed that Alexander VII suspend the court of Spain from his graces.[40]

In a letter written at the end of the year, agent De Sanctis told Azzolini that Madrid's attitude towards 'the *squadrone*'s dealings' was only apparently stern. In fact, a few members of the *Consejo de Estado* had confidentially hinted that things might be getting better. Although the Spanish ministers had censored the behaviour of the *squadrone volante*, they wanted to leave the door open for the group to 'honourably' change its mind. They need only wait for the right occasion. They had been stern in order to set a precedent, so that in future, cardinals would turn 'more willingly' to Spain to offer their services.[41]

The *Consejo de Estado* was more clearly aware than its ambassadors in Rome of the danger that could be posed by a weakening of the Habsburg group in the College of Cardinals. At the beginning of 1658, the *Consejo* was called to carefully evaluate the Italian and Roman situation. 'Great projects' were being put into action by Spain's enemies and it was absolutely essential to re-establish good relations with the Pontiff.[42]

Sobremonte prepared an accurate report on relations with Rome. There was concern that the group of Spanish cardinals might dwindle due to dissatisfaction with their rewards (they complained 'que se les ha ofrecido mucho, y cumplido nada'). Moreover, although they did not want to be subjected to the control of the Medici family cardinals, the possibility of placing a Spaniard at the head of the faction was hindered by the tradition of reserving the monarchies' cardinals *in pectore*. Thus the councils held on October 10 and 26 had to carefully consider how to satisfy the requests of individual cardinals, including some of the *squadrone volante* members. However, the talks also concerned other cardinals, such as Giulio Rospigliosi (the future pro-French pope who, 'atento a sus conbeniencias', kept in touch with the Spaniards through a secret informer).[43]

[40] Biblioteca-Archivio storico comunale, Jesi, Arch. Azzolino, Corrispondenza, 101, f. 1, from Madrid, 6 May 1656; AGS, Estado, Roma, legajo 3030.

[41] Biblioteca-Archivio storico comunale, Jesi, Arch. Azzolino, Corrispondenza, 101, f. 1, 12 December 1657.

[42] The situation as described by the Duke of San Lúcar is in a letter dated 12 February 1658; AGS, Estado, Roma, legajo 3031.

[43] Ibid.; the problem of Rospigliosi was raised by Sobremonte on 26 October 1658.

Naturally, the *Consejo* had initially considered the possibility of a reconciliation with the four vassal cardinals of Naples and Milan and had decided to tell the ambassador to Rome, Luis Ponce de León, to 'caminar templadamente', taking advantage of the fact that the cardinals had families and *haciendas* in the crown's dominions.[44]

Most of the group's members, besides being free, young and talented cardinals (as contemporary chronicles tell us), were also 'cardinali poveri' (poor cardinals) who were always ready to take advantage of favourable circumstances. This description was applied to Azzolini, who had very good reasons to follow Madrid's decisions in terms of graces and rewards, as well as to other important members of the *squadrone* such as Acquaviva, Borromeo, Imperiali, Ottoboni and Albizzi.[45] Albizzi, who had already received a pension and extra emoluments from Mazarin, soon began to receive money from Spain as well. It is interesting that both courts were aware of Albizzi's 'double payroll'.[46]

Every perception of loyalty or breakdown of relations had to be carefully evaluated. This applied all the more to the cardinals in the Spanish group, even if they belonged to rich and powerful families. In November 1654, Cardinal Omodei was passing through Milan, where a fierce dispute over precedence and jurisdiction was under way between the Spanish government and the Milanese curia. Omodei decided to hasten to the residence of the monarch's representative rather than calling on Archbishop Litta. This greatly irritated the archbishop, who interpreted it as fawning on Madrid.[47] Time, however, was on the side of the Catholic court. In 1657, a tragedy cast doubt on the future of the Omodei family: the Marquis of Almonacir died in his Spanish residence. His elder brother, the cardinal, was forced to plead for help for his brother's widow and three sons. In 1670 the Piedmontese ambassador firmly categorized Omodei as a 'devotee of the Spaniards', who, notwithstanding a few past events, had managed to keep his family 'well supplied with riches and related to the most important Spanish families'.[48]

---

[44] Ibid., council of 8 October 1658.

[45] Even Azzolini, in a secret letter to Lord Darlington (21 March 1667: see Petruccelli della Gattina, *Histoire diplomatique*, vol. III, p. 202), suggested that cash donations could easily lead to the election of a 'friendly' pope, thanks to the large number of 'cardinali poveri' present in the conclave. M. Rosa, 'Curia romana e pensioni ecclesiastiche. Fiscalità pontificia nel Mezzogiorno (secoli XVI–XVIII)', *Quaderni storici*, 42 (1979), p. 1028, describes the condition of a 'cardinale povero' in great and vivid detail.

[46] On the relations between Albizzi and Mazarin see Bildt, *Christine de Suède et le conclave*, pp. 42–3.

[47] BAV, Chigi, N III 78, ff. 249r–250v, letter dated 4 November 1654.

[48] ASV, Lettere di cardinali, 22, f. 38, from Pesaro, 23 February 1657; *Relatione della corte di Roma letta dal signor marchese Bigliore di Lucerna*, BAV, Urb. Lat., 12530, f. 112.

The documents that we have used also provide information on how cardinals were kept in check, as well as some insight into the moral and religious scruples of ministers. In October 1658, the *Consejo de Estado* convened to establish the pensions – including secret ones – to be paid to members of the Sacred College. Sobremonte states that Albizzi had hinted to him that he wanted to join the Spanish front, but would leave the question of the *merced* to His Majesty. The Cardinal of Cesena said that the money could be given directly to him or to his nephew, the canon of Santa Maria. The council decided to entrust the money to the nephew and also to abandon the idea of offering benefices – though that was the easiest method – because once the cardinals had 'pocketed a good amount' they tended to forget about their debt. Secret pensions were preferred, as the money could be punctually delivered by ambassadors once or twice a year. Any cardinal who requested greater emoluments was asked to publicly demonstrate his 'adherence' to the Spanish front.[49]

There seem to be no references to the future Pope Alexander VIII in Simancas's papers concerning graces, but who knows what the French ambassador meant when he said that Ottoboni 'loves France but still knows how to speak Spanish'? Nonetheless, the bottom line is that it could be very profitable to present oneself as a 'free and zealous' cardinal and thus raise the stakes and obtain greater favours from both monarchies.

For a comprehensive evaluation of the attitude of the Spanish court and the space that was available for mediation, it is also worth examining the different shades of language which were employed. Ambassadors were usually the most resolute defenders of the Spanish monarch's interests and rights. The Spanish cardinal, who collaborated with the ambassador to Rome, used a careful and articulate wording typical of the internal dynamics of the curia. Finally, on the basis of this and other information, the *Consejo de Estado* gave its judgment, often mitigating the ambassador's proposals. It is not surprising that at the Spanish court, where a thousand implications had to be weighed up, greater caution was employed in decision-making than in Rome.

The emphasis and tone of correspondence from Rome reflect, besides the personality and culture of the diplomats, the perception of an unstable equilibrium. One of the most scathing descriptions of the Roman court can be found in a letter ordering the Duke of Terranova to give cardinals 'the superficial honours they love to wallow in', but without forgetting the qualities of a good hunter: 'show the hawk the lure, but only give it a little at a time; thus, by keeping it in constant hope, you

---

[49] AGS, Estado, Roma, legajo 3031, report included in the council minutes dated 26 October 1658.

will obtain what you require'.[50] However, we must not conclude from such descriptions that ministers and ambassadors overlooked the spiritual aspects of a cardinal's role. Although this dimension did not appear in the instructions or in conclave reports, it remained an obvious fact and to ignore it was considered an unforgivable error.

In 1667, with the conclave looming closer, the Marquis of Astorga, a new Roman resident, wrote to his government requesting money 'porque quieren ser comprados los cardinales'.[51] These words were carefully considered by the *Consejo de Estado*. According to the Duke of San Lúcar, the ambassador had used unacceptable language. The money was not to 'buy' the cardinals, but to favour negotiations 'por los medios lícitos y dezentes', as had always been done. The Duke of Alba and Peñaranda agreed: no one could 'buy' cardinals. They could only hope that the best candidate would win and let the Holy Spirit make its choice. This, however, did not keep the council from approving the allocation of funds.[52]

The minutes of this session are a wonderful example of the peculiar mentality of the *Ancien Régime*, in which politics and religion, beliefs and interests, overlapped with a naturalness that modern sensibility views as contradictory or inadmissible.

THE CRISIS OF NEPOTISM

An anonymous document written during the reign of Clement X explains the difference between a 'faction' and a 'party'. The former united the *creature* who had been made cardinals by the same pontiff, while the latter included those cardinals who served a common sovereign or republic.[53] In accordance with this premise, many of the names that belonged to factions also appeared in parties. For example, Alfonso Litta, who belonged to the Chigi faction, was in the Spanish party. Federico Borromeo belonged to the same party, although he was a member of the Altieri faction. This issue concerned the *squadronisti* in particular, as they all were members of the Pamfili faction, but Ottoboni was in the Venetian party whereas Imperiali was in the Genoese party.

---

[50] BAV, Vat. Lat., 10446, *Istruzione all'Ecc.mo signor duca di Terranova*, n.d. (1654).

[51] Typical of the many negative descriptions of Astorga is Chaulnes's report that the Spanish ambassador was occupied by frivolities and liaisons: *Relatione della corte di Roma presentata dal Duca di Chaune al re suo signore tradotta dal franzese*, ASV, Carpegna, 38, f. 426v.

[52] Among other things, a thousand ducats were granted to all the 'declared' cardinals: AGS, Estado, Roma, legajo 3031.

[53] *Compendioso ragguaglio delle fattioni, nascita, età, costumi et inclinationi di tutti i cardinali viventi nel pontificato di Clemente X*: BAV, Barb. Lat., 4704.

Such precision is not often encountered. Contemporaries used both terms interchangeably, although 'faction' was the preferred term. This, of course, did not come about by chance. The Sacred College was mostly composed of Italian cardinals and their Roman duty (service to the pontiff and cardinal-nephew) was more important to them than their duty to foreign sovereigns. In any case, these comments on the ever-changing complexity of alliances and interests are worth making. The situation was only simplified during conclave voting. Defining the faction to which each man belonged was important in order to anticipate the number of votes which a given candidate would receive; but everyone knew that different inclinations and interests coexisted in each individual cardinal.

I have tried to define the originality of the *squadrone,* as opposed to the other Roman *parties,* by examining the choices the group made with regard to the European political scenario, the influence of the European powers in the Roman context and the political significance of the *jus exclusivae.* However, in order to understand the circumstances that had come about by 1655, as well as the developments that had taken place in the curia's policies, we must concentrate on events within the Roman court and appreciate the uniqueness of the *squadrone* as opposed to the other *factions.* As Sforza Pallavicino pointed out, the cardinals of this group were called the *squadrone volante* because 'they had no head'. They gathered around Ottoboni, Azzolini and Albizzi and did not obey Innocent X's nephew even though they were his *creature.* Thus the well-established tradition of loyalty to the nephew of the deceased pontiff had been broken. This was the result of the political vacuum left behind by the Pamfili pope, whose family intrigues are well known to historians.

Cardinal-nephews, from the Aldobrandini to Scipione Caffarelli-Borghese (under Paul V), Ludovico Ludovisi (under Gregory XV) and the Barberini, had discharged most important government functions.[54] During the reign of Innocent X, however, no prelate could be found with the qualities needed to fulfil the duties of both cardinal-secretary and superintendent of the papal state. This was the result of many different circumstances as well as the personality of the men who might have been entrusted with such a position. There is an eloquent judgment by the French ambassador regarding the adoptive Cardinal Pamfili: along with the biretta, the pope would have liked to give him a brain.[55]

The failure to find an adequate nephew for this role and the strengthening of the State Secretariat took place at the same time. The Secretariat,

---

[54] See W. Reinhard, 'Nepotismus: der Funktionswandel einer papstgeschichtlichen Konstanten', *Zeitschrift für Kirchengeschichte* (1975), pp. 145–85.
[55] *Descrizione di tutti i cardinali del Baly di Valenzé,* BAV, Vat. Lat., 8354, f. 249r.

formally inaugurated in 1644, began to appropriate the functions that had belonged to the cardinal-nephew. As Pastor points out, Camillo Astalli was no longer the *cardinal padrone*, but had become the 'cardinal in charge of major affairs'. Is it possible, on the basis of these facts, to identify this change as the beginning of the modernization of curial institutions?

The attempt to retrospectively apply a present-day model of bureaucracy to the very peculiar Roman politics of that age is questionable. Moreover, we do not have sufficient knowledge of the curia to make a judgment on the professionalization of its offices. Although during the sixteenth and seventeenth centuries there was a marked increase in the percentage of prelates who became cardinals by means of a bureaucratic career, this idea of service cannot be very effectively applied to a context in which impersonal management did not exist and personal loyalty to the pontiff and the cardinal-nephew remained fundamental values. It is far more worthwhile to evaluate the authority and true autonomy of the individual prelates who headed the State Secretariat, case by case.[56]

At the time of the dynastic crisis of the Pamfili papacy, the Secretariat was headed by Giovanni Giacomo Panciroli. This circumstance was to lead to the definitive consolidation of the Secretariat.[57] From this point onwards, the office was directed by experienced diplomats: Chigi (1651–5), Rospigliosi (1655–7) and Azzolini (1667–9). However, this shift seems related to the need to get a firmer grip on foreign affairs (in particular, to curb the growing aggressiveness of the European powers and their tendency to reform their national churches according to regal principles), rather than to a crisis of nepotism.

To consider the papal state as an early modern state often leads to undervaluing the position of the popes' nephews and attributing a merely dynastic role to them.[58] However, due to the elective nature of papacy and the short reigns of many of its incumbents, the pontiff needed a

---

[56] See G. F. Commendone, *Discorso sopra la corte di Roma*, ed. C. Mozzarelli, Roma, 1996, pp. 10–11. The editor asserts that curia bureaucracy must be viewed in its court context and in all its peculiarity. See also Visceglia, ' "La Giusta Statera" ', pp. 173–5. The patrimonial nature of Roman institutions was pointed out by P. Partner, 'Papal Financial Policy in the Renaissance and Counter Reformation', *Past and Present*, 88 (1980), pp. 17–62. Rodén, *Cardinal Decio Azzolino, Queen Christina*, believes that 'the end of nepotism as an institution was the logical extension of the *Curia*'s administrative professionalization' (p. 36).

[57] P. Richard, 'Origines et développement de la secretairie d'etat apostolique (1417–1923)', *Revue d'Histoire Ecclésiastique* (1910), pp. 56–72; M. Laurain-Portemer, 'Absolutisme et népotisme. La surintendance de l'Etat ecclésiastique', *Bibliothèque de l'Ecole des Chartes*, 131 (1973), pp. 487–568. See also A. Menniti Ippolito, *Il tramonto della curia nepotista. Papi, nipoti e burocrazia curiale tra XVI e XVII secolo*, Rome, 1999, and Menniti Ippolito's chapter in this volume.

[58] Rietbergen, *Pausen, prelaten, bureucraten*, p. 103ff., 419–21.

near relation to help him. That relation was his nephew, who ensured that the family's political weight was maintained. This was necessary, since those serving the pontiff knew that a change would occur before long and therefore oriented their decisions to favour those who, in turn, would favour them. Everyone agreed that 'the papacy seems to totter when it is deprived of the help of a close blood relation to the pontiff'.[59] Although it is true that the election of two successive pontiffs from the State Secretariat gave that office greater prestige, the particular constitution of the Roman court requires us to focus on the person and desires of the pontiff. The nature of the direct relationship with the 'sovereign' is far more important than a comparison between the cardinal-nephew and the Secretary of State. Their opposition was determined by the pope and the absence of a nephew did not necessarily imply a greater autonomy for the Secretary. No one could obtain, from St Peter's successors, the same authority that certain sovereigns allowed their *validos* or prime ministers.[60] Nonetheless, the cardinal-nephew appeared more important, closer to the Pontiff and irreplaceable because of the authority that legitimated him.

Panciroli had no room for manoeuvre and died almost immediately, in 1651.[61] He was succeeded by Fabio Chigi, who had not yet become a cardinal. He received the biretta two months later, in February 1651. Clearly, the fact that he had entered the office as a simple prelate, and only then become a cardinal, accentuated his dependence on the pontiff.[62] Similarly, in 1655, Alexander VII entrusted the Secretariat to Giulio Rospigliosi, reserving the right to promote him later (April 1657).[63] There is some evidence that as head of the Secretariat, Azzolini was very deferential to the cardinal-nephew, Rospigliosi, and that above all, state affairs were firmly controlled by Clement IX. Rospigliosi's manoeuvres might appear to have been 'harnessed and held back by the pope', but Azzolini does not seem to have had any more autonomy. The Duke of Chaulnes pointed out that Azzolini could conduct his business better 'if he were put in charge of it'. In reality, the pope 'likes...to do

---

[59] *Relatione alla Repubblica di Venezia delli suoi ambasciatori che mandò ad Alessandro VII nella sua assunzione al Pontificato*: BAV, Vat. Lat., 12179.

[60] Rumour had it that even Francesco Barberini could not undertake any action without the consent of Pope Urban VIII: A. Merola, 'Barberini, Francesco', in *DBI*, vol. VI, pp. 172–6.

[61] *Relatione di Roma fatta nell'anno 1647*, BV, Chigi N III 78 (Seidler, *Il teatro del mondo*, p. 32), f. 91v, with interesting notes on the curbs imposed on Panciroli, who – like Azzolini – was a *cardinale povero*.

[62] 'He is not free himself' is how Chigi is described in the *Descrizione di tutti i cardinali del Baly di Valenzé*, f. 258.

[63] L. Osbat, 'Clemente IX', in *DBI*, vol. XXVI, pp. 282–90.

everything his own way and doesn't easily accept counsel or the opinions of others'.[64]

These are the boundaries within which we may speak of 'professionalization', especially concerning an office which was in direct, daily contact with the pontiff. On the basis of the relationship with the sovereign and the configuration of the court, we must now evaluate the stance (which was far from innovative) taken by Azzolini and his comrades with regard to the issue of nepotism, from the survey of Alexander VII to the draft bull of Innocent XI.

APPROACHING FRANCE

The 'golden age' of Azzolini and the *squadrone* coincided with a historical phase which, unlike the period preceding the Treaty of the Pyrenees, was characterized by important innovations. The crucial episode was the sensational quarrel in 1662 between Louis XIV and Alexander VII. Following a clash between the Corsican soldiers of the papal guard and the guards of the French ambassador, the king made very harsh demands for reparation and even threatened to advance in arms against Rome.

At that time, much more than during the Westphalia negotiations, the political isolation of the Holy See emerged dramatically. Not so much because the pope had been dragged into this trial of strength with the King of France, but rather because, for the first time, the Spanish monarchy did not seem willing to defend the papacy. The Spanish nuncio, Monsignor Bonelli, had no room to manoeuvre. He was forced to ask the Catholic king to protect the Apostolic See, although Madrid had already given Louis XIV permission to march his troops through Spanish dominions up to the borders of the ecclesiastical state. The nuncio pointed out that the dispute with Alexander VII was really the pretext that the French had longed for in order to establish their supremacy in Italy, and that a tie between Rome and Spain would certainly gain the support of all the Italian princes. The nuncio even promised Philip IV precedence over the rival monarch – something which his predecessors had always coveted – together with all the privileges granted by the papacy to the Gallican church.

Naturally Monsignor Bonelli did not miss the opportunity to point out that unlike the French sovereigns, who were often willing to encourage

---

[64] The pope 'steadily continued his public meetings, attended Congregations twice a week from the window, met the ministers' ambassadors and attended services': Bibl. Queriniana, *Lettere dell'E.mo Sig.re cardinale Azzolini*; *Relatione della corte di Roma del Duca di Scione, stato ambasciatore Cristianissimo appresso la Santità di NS Clemente IX*, BAV, Patetta 964, ff. 329–58; see also ff. 337v–338. In ASV, see Carpegna, 38, 413–27. The Duke of Chaulnes had arrived in Rome in 1665 to replace Créqui.

heretics and infidels, the Austrian royal family had always upheld the church against heresies. By a kind of historical nemesis, the reasons were the same as had been used by Olivares to protest against Urban VIII's anti-Habsburg policy. This time, however, the relations between the parties were completely overturned.

Basically, the Holy See proposed a renewal and strengthening of the old anti-French alliance between the two branches of the Habsburg dynasty. Even Vienna would have profited from such an agreement, receiving aid in its struggle against the Turks. Madrid's answer was disarming. Spain delivered an apology for the conduct of the French kings (who apparently had always demonstrated an unquestionable Catholic faith) and, more importantly, the justifiable wrath of Louis XIV to whom Philip IV had wed his daughter, the infant Maria Teresa. Moreover, Paris had not demanded too much; it was the pope who had been wrong to risk the lives of so many people on account of his pride.[65]

This event had a far greater impact on the image of the papacy than the rhetorical arguments on liberty in the conclave and the *jus exclusivae* raised by the *squadrone* cardinals. Among other effects, it repositioned the papacy with respect to interference from the European monarchies. Many had to agree that the church should portray itself as 'innocent, pious and docile' when confronted with a powerful sovereign, if only because the Apostolic Chamber was empty and the population of the papal state was impoverished and discouraged. The most explicit witness to how the difficulties of the church of Rome were perceived is the *Memoria* that the aged and ailing Cardinal Sacchetti was to address 'with trembling hand' to Pope Alexander VII in June 1663.[66]

The document is especially important for its references to the internal circumstances of the papal state, but the denunciation of the pontiff's political decisions is also significant. It is impossible to place this document

---

[65] *Relatione di tutto ciò che passò tra il pontefice Alessandro VII e la maestà del re Christianissimo nell'anno 1662.* Leti, who affirmed that he had published this pamphlet for the first time in 1664, included it in *La dieta di diversi autori* (1669). This credit is in F. Barcia, *Bibliografia*, pp. 179ff. Also see G. Lutz, 'Bonelli, Carlo', in *DBI*, vol. XI, pp. 750–2. M. Rosa, *Alessandro VII*, in *DBI*, vol. II, p. 212, emphasizes the importance of these events because of their effect on the European equilibrium and the growth of French influence in Italy.

[66] The long letter dated June 1663, from which these passages have been extracted, can be found in Rietbergen, *Pausen, prelaten, bureucraten*, pp. 41–50. The problem of attribution has not been resolved; see Fosi, *All'ombra dei Barberini*, p. 166. The picture given in this work is very disheartening: the avidity of the ministers corrupted the papacy and its image. The shocking luxury of Rome contrasted with the poverty of many bishoprics, the abuse of power, the corruption of the supreme courts and the oppression caused by the many *gabelle* (taxes) levied on a population that was already starving.

in the right historical context without relating it to the abyss that had opened between Louis XIV and the pontiff. According to the author of the *Memoria*, the reason why the Apostolic See's dignity and authority had dropped so low was the pope's desire to 'be a secular prince' and pick a quarrel with powers 'that are the arms that support him'.

The incident was the perfect occasion for all those who still sided with France to consolidate a common front. The Chigi papacy was faced with an increasingly visible opposition which certainly included, besides the old cardinals of the French party such as Sacchetti, even Cardinal Antonio Barberini (who, in 1662, was sent to Paris to negotiate) and the Jesuit Gian Paolo Oliva, who promoted the settlement.[67]

The instructions sent from Paris to Créqui on 13 April 1662 proudly emphasized that the French party in the Sacred College had not been so strong for over a century. It would almost certainly overtake the Habsburg party, as the Milanese and Neapolitan cardinals did not seem very interested in obeying Spanish orders. Giulio Rospigliosi was among the 'papable' cardinals mentioned by the king. He had already proved his devotion and received pensions from the court. His chances of success in a conclave were deemed to be good, as he was not disliked by the Spaniards, having been nuncio in Madrid.[68]

Christina of Sweden played an important role in the election of Clement IX and in the policy of *rapprochement* with France that was taking hold in Rome. After her arrival (December 1655) and the beginning of her collaboration with Azzolini, the queen soon moved out of the Spanish orbit.[69] Her agreement with Mazarin became evident when she went to Paris between July and October 1656, in July 1657 and again in May 1658. The outcome of the last meeting was an agreement that if the Spaniards were defeated, she would become Queen of Naples.[70]

The 1667 conclave marked the fulfilment of Christina and Azzolini's labours. The *squadrone volante* was pleased to see the only openly pro-French pope elected during the latter half of the seventeenth century.

---

[67] Cardinal Barberini travelled to Paris as Grand Almoner of France and head of the Gallican clergy: Pecchiai, *I Barberini*, pp. 208–10. Oliva, who was to become general provost in 1664, had already collaborated with the Barberini and Albizzi in the first condemnation of Jansenism.

[68] *Recueil des instructions*, pp. 123–33.

[69] On the friendship and collaboration between the Queen and the Cardinal of Fermo, see C. Bildt, *Christine de Suède et le cardinal Azzolino. Lettres inédites (1666–1668)*, Paris, 1899.

[70] In Madrid, Christina was looked upon as a 'declared' French supporter and information about her was gathered from her secret correspondence with her confessor and chaplain: letter of Gaspar de Sobremonte, 3 June 1658; AGS, Estado, Roma, legado 3031.

Rospigliosi immediately allocated a generous pension to the queen; Azzolini received important benefits and in 1667 was made head of the State Secretariat. Azzolini's friend Ottoboni became head of the datary. The French ambassador was satisfied and hailed the downfall of the opposite party in the College of Cardinals: 'Today the Spaniards are as weak in Rome as they are in Madrid'.[71]

THE DISSOLUTION

The victory of Louis XIV played a significant role in the politics of the Holy See, but – as usual – the effects were controversial and conditioned by many different variables. We have already mentioned that just before the Treaty of the Pyrenees the papacy had moved closer to the Habsburgs for fear lest peace and a contemporaneous imperial election should favour the English and Swedish 'heretics'. During the reign of Clement IX, new reasons (including religious misgivings among the most intransigent individuals in the Sacred College) emerged for mistrusting the most powerful European sovereign.[72]

The events of the subsequent conclave, 1669–70, were described in great detail by Cristian Bildt. The election of the eighty-one-year-old Emilio Altieri as Clement X was a failure for Christina and the *squadrone volante*.[73] The only remaining members of the group were Azzolini, Ottoboni, Imperiali, Borromeo, Omodei and Gualtieri. The others, including Albizzi, no longer considered themselves 'confederated', although they still voted with the *squadrone*. The pro-French cardinals became the majority in the College and could rely on the 'external support' of the cardinal-nephew's faction as well as that of the Barberini. The tension between the papacy and the French agent in Rome reached a new height during the reign of Clement X.[74]

---

[71] *Relattione della corte di Roma presentata dal duca di Chaune*, f. 423. Ottoboni immediately took advantage of his role as datary, which allowed him to strengthen his power in the curia by manipulating the allocation of ecclesiastical benefits; see Menniti Ippolito, *Politica e carriere ecclesiastiche*, p. 217 and footnote.

[72] Albizzi and his friends in the Holy Office did not appreciate the treaty, supported by Louis XIV and the cardinal-nephew, Giacomo Rospigliosi, that was to ensure ten years of peace (1669–1679) for the church of France; see L. Ceyssens, 'Casanate, Girolamo', in *DBI*, vol. XXI, p. 144.

[73] On the other hand, this was a success for Barberino, who, along with Rospigliosi, had moved to help Spain; this is confirmed by Litta, 2 April 1670 (Biblioteca-Archivio storico comunali, Jesi, Arch. Azzolino, 107).

[74] *Relatione dello stato presente della corte di Roma fatta all'Ecc.mo signor principe di Ligné, governatore di Milano, dall'Ill.mo Federico Rozzoni*: BAV, Vat. Lat., 12539, ff. 74–94. The event that took place during the sitting of 21 May 1675 is recounted in the *Ristretto di quanto è passato intorno alla promotione per le corone*: ibid., 12184, ff. 286–9.

The internal organization of the papal state followed the tendencies that had emerged during the previous period. The pope, who had no relative suited to the role, declared that his 'adoptive nephew' would be Paluzzi (the future Cardinal Altieri) – who, however, did not acquire the vast powers of his predecessors. Although he was put in charge of the State Secretariat on account of his diplomatic experience as the papal nuncio in Spain, Federico Borromeo was not a cardinal. Clement X had maintained a consolidated tradition which he also applied to the datary. The Savoy ambassador noticed that, although the auditor and datary Mons. Carpegna (who had replaced Ottoboni in April 1670) was an able man, he was completely subordinated to Cardinal Altieri. In fact, as Carpegna hoped to become a cardinal, he blindly accepted the cardinal-nephew's choices of men to fill vacant benefices. In due time, Carpegna became a cardinal, but from then on showed unconditional obedience to the pontiff.[75]

In the 1676 conclave which elected Innocent XI, Azzolini, Ottoboni and Omodei once again made an agreement with Christina of Sweden. They had blocked Benedetto Odescalchi in the previous conclave, when he was vetoed by the French. However, now that Barberini, Chigi and Rospigliosi, with the consent of Paris, had agreed to support the candidature of the Lombard cardinal, the only thing that the survivors of the *squadrone* could do was vote for the *zelante* candidate.

From the 1670s, Ottoboni and Azzolini were looked upon as political operators who kept themselves completely independent of any faction or ideology. From the outset, some had seen them – notwithstanding the *squadrone's* proclamations – as unscrupulous manipulators. An anonymous detractor (certainly a cardinal from the opposite faction) has left us a manuscript with a short poem. The lines in the poem explain that the *squadrone* members were nothing but trouble-makers and stress their venality and ambiguous relationship with the Spanish court.[76]

Upon the death of Pope Clement IX, the *Colloquio delle volpi* ('Foxes' Dialogue') describes Ottoboni and Azzolini as the major protagonists on the Roman scene, but their image is very different from the one they had in the past: 'Morì fra due ladroni il Redentore / Spira Clemente in mezzo a due assassini / Ottobono e Azzolini' ('The Saviour died between two thieves / Clement dies between two assassins / Ottobono and

---

[75] *Relatione . . . fatta dal signor marchese Bigliore di Lucerna*, ff. 103v–104. Carpegna was made a cardinal by Clement X in December 1670 and was Datary until 1676: G. Romeo, 'Carpegna, Gaspare', in *DBI*, vol. xx, pp. 589–91.

[76] BAV, Patetta 2908, ff. 217–18: *Sopra il squadrone volante de cardinali*. The author is ironical about the cardinals' rebellion, which Spain neutralized by employing *ducatoni* as the 'medicine'.

Azzolini').[77] It is difficult to find cardinals who were not subjected to similar attacks. However, these rumours provide a certain continuity and give us a useful point of view. They remind us that the story of the *squadrone volante* unfolded in a very difficult context and that it can be reconstructed from many different points of view, some of which may still reserve surprises.

Azzolini's *Aforismi sul conclave* ('Aphorisms on the Conclave') can be consulted for information about the author.[78] If we compare them with the proclamations of independence from the European powers made at the conclave of Alexander VII, we will see that they scarcely refer to the *esclusiva*. On the other hand, they make constant generic references to various problems that can transform a possible candidate into a certain loser. No faction head should support a candidate who is in one of the following three situations:

(1) a candidate who has been excluded once will always be excluded, because the cardinals who blocked his candidature will continue to do so, especially as they know that their victim will not so easily forget what happened.

(2) a candidate who has had 'very close friendships' with the most influential cardinals of the previous papacy will be excluded, even more so if these prelates made enemies while they governed.

(3) a candidate who is too young, or who has not been a cardinal for long enough, will be excluded, as even his friends would be offended were such a brief 'service' to be immediately rewarded.

This brief treatise provides useful information both about the mentality of the *squadrone*'s foremost personality and about the logic which governed the behaviour of the conclavists. Azzolini was not interested in discussing the fairness of the exceptions. A pragmatist, he was only interested in defining the characteristics of a weak candidate. Virtues were not taken into account, since in the battle against the *jus exclusivae* they had been rhetorically acclaimed in the *squadrone*'s manifesto.

---

[77] On the *Colloquio delle volpi* see Menniti Ippolito, *Politica e carriere ecclesiastiche*, 217, note 112; Rodén, *Decio Azzolino, Queen Christina*, pp. 136–7. Text in by G. Leti, *L'ambasciata di Romolo a' romani*, Brussels, 1671, p. 138. According to Leti, the two main figures of the *squadrone* were two *sparvieri* (hawks), who controlled cardinal-nephew Girolamo as if they were *cardinali padroni*.

[78] The *Aforismi* were probably composed for the 1667 conclave and were widely circulated in manuscript form. They were published in 1668 as an appendix to Leti's *Il cardinalismo*, vol. III, pp. 366–91; for a list of the manuscript copies, see Bildt, *Christine de Suède et le conclave*, p. 21; Rodén, *Decio Azzolino, Queen Christina*, p. 148ff. See also Bibl. Casanatense, Rome, x VI 37 (2670); BAV, Patetta, 964, pp. 273–96; Archivio di Stato Modena, Cancelleria ducale, Ambasciatori Roma, p. 134.

The advice to endorse a 'silent individual with amiable manners and virtues, especially generosity' was entirely practical. It was a card to be played in extreme situations when such characteristics might well persuade the opposition to change their minds. Moreover, if the candidate was very old, the opposition would certainly be willing to vote for him as they would be sure 'of participating in a new conclave quite soon'. In the hierarchy of good qualities, the first place was assigned to gentleness, as it pacified electors; generosity was important because it could attract the interest of voters.

Azzolini also examines the case in which a faction head was 'macchiato di coscienza' (had a 'blemished' conscience). He suggested that a zealous prelate should never be appointed, as once he received the tiara he would turn into an enemy: the benefit received would soon be forgotten, as people's true 'nature never changes'. This passage casts some doubt on the idea of a continuity between the experience of the *squadrone volante* and that of Innocent XI's *zelanti*. Azzolini believed that a cardinal who demonstrated a particular moral integrity was no better than the others. As a matter of fact, such a cardinal would not adhere to the rules of political prudence, and would become unpredictable: feeling justified in acting with moral zeal, he might well prove ungrateful.[79] The Holy Spirit, which 'brings merits and not men', is only briefly mentioned by the author of the *Aforismi* as if it were a disturbing element, an unknown variable that clashed with his rational exposition.[80]

The *Aforismi* probably do not provide proof of an irreligious attitude or mentality. The brief treatise belongs to a well-established tradition. It is a 'Machiavellian' exercise concentrating on the political games which were enacted during conclaves. In any case, this short work confirms the image that Azzolini had earned as a shrewd and unscrupulous politician, certainly not a man interested in reforms or in moralizing. Men such as de Luca, Barbarigo and Colloredo, who emerged from a completely different context than that of the *squadrone* members, were to show new faith in reform and moral renewal.

---

[79] Azzolini points out that Paul IV had had no qualms about attacking Cardinal Morone, although the cardinal had upheld him, as he believed that it would save him from persecution by the Holy Office.

[80] This is not true of the *Discorso sopra l'attioni del conclave* by Giovanni Francesco Lottino, for which see *La prima parte del thesoro politico in cui si contengono relationi, instruttioni, trattati e varij discorsi pertinenti alla perfetta intelligenza della ragion di stato*, Milan, Girolamo Bordone, 1600, pp. 482–502. The preamble asserts that the election is the work of God: as a matter of fact – the author points out – the conclavists always elect a pontiff whom they do not want.

Under Innocent XI, some of the cardinals who had formed the *squadrone volante* were still active and influential thanks to the experience that they had accumulated in Roman offices and congregations (and also on account of their long lives). They were 'cardinali di curia' who, adamantly bound by tradition, might even unleash an attack on the pontiff in order to protect the church from reform.[81] One thing is certain: they certainly did not hand the key to modernity on to the *zelanti*. From this point of view, the debate on nepotism is exemplary.[82]

During the 1650s, the first germs of austerity and moral renewal had begun to spread. Alexander VII, who wanted to give a token of regeneration and dissociate his papacy from past scandals, decided to heed these signals and asked for the approval of the Sacred College before inviting his relatives to Rome. However, the context of Innocentian reform was far different. It marked the definitive end of nepotism. This and other reforms were passed during a period in which the economic conditions of the papal state appeared to be irredeemable. They were championed by a rigorous and literate pro-imperial party which strenuously defended papal authority against supporters of the policies of Louis XIV, including some Jesuits who were fighting against the Jansenists and Quietists.[83] At this point nepotism, which was still defended by Azzolini, was defeated thanks to the pontiff's efforts to reorganize Roman institutions and to the authority which he assigned to

---

[81] Azzolini's career was far more complex and contradictory than Albizzi's or Ottoboni's, partly owing to his relationship with Christina of Sweden. In his last years, Azzolini fell in line with the Odescalchi pope, moving away from the French party and towards the cultural and religious inclinations of the Pontiff's collaborators.

[82] Pastor, *Storia dei papi*, vol. xiv/2, p. 300ff., on Innocent XI's anti-nepotistic draft bull. For the opinions of the cardinals see BAV, Ottob. Lat., 792; Barb. Lat., 5662, ff. 105–10 (Azzolini's opinion). On the continuity with the *zelanti*, see Rodén, *Decio Azzolino, Queen Christina*, p. 100. For Azzolini's stance, see Rodén, 'Cardinal Decio Azzolino and the Problem of Papal Nepotism'. This is an in-depth analysis of the cardinal's role. While in Rodén's previous work the *squadronisti* are seen as reformers who had 'rebelled' against the system of nepotism (see p. 47), here a careful consideration of Azzolini's stance on nepotism leads to greater caution. For an assessment of the significance of the decline of nepotism see A. Lauro, *Il cardinale Giovan Battista de Luca. Diritto e riforme nello Stato della Chiesa (1676–1683)*, Naples, 1991, p. 457ff.; A. Menniti Ippolito, 'Nepotisti e antinepotisti: i "conservatori" di curia e i pontefici Odescalchi e Pignatelli', in *Riforme, religione e politica durante il pontificato di Innocenzo XII*, pp. 233–48.

[83] The disorder led Francesco D'Andrea to comment, in a colourful pun, that the Jesuits were no longer the *giannizzari* (Janissaries) of the pontiffs: D'Andrea, *Lettere a G.A. Doria. 1676–1683*, ed. I. Ascione, Naples, 1995, pp. 169, 207. E. Brambilla, 'Per una storia materiale delle istituzioni ecclesiastiche', *Società e storia*, 1984, n. 24, pp. 432–3, points out that new areas of politico-jurisdictional conflict had arisen which created new divisions 'even within the two parties'.

simple prelates, such as Giuseppe de Luca, to help them fight the elderly 'cardinali di curia'.

THE INNOCENTIAN REFORM

A new perception of the dignity and tasks of the episcopate is the most significant element of the reforms introduced by the Odescalchi pope and his collaborators.[84] There is a distinct feeling of a clear-cut separation with the past, notwithstanding the evident signs coming from the Council of Trent and the synodal revival, from Carlo Borromeo to Gregorio Barbarigo. Certainly, the tendency must be related to the increase in jurisdictional conflicts that took place following the seventeenth-century wars. The bishops' weakness vis-à-vis the Roman court was due to the cyclical granting of nepotistic favours and pressure from the more powerful cardinals, who claimed their rewards. This led, during Alexander VII's papacy, to a call to reform pensions in order to bring aid to the most needy episcopates. The problem emerged with even greater urgency when Clement IX appointed a special congregation to examine the proposal to modify the bull *In Coena Domini*, which constituted a serious impediment and open challenge to the authority of the Catholic European states. The congregation asked the cardinals to present reports on the 'sovereigns' complaints'.[85] The documentation that has been preserved shows that the greatest anxieties focused on the dominions of the Spanish monarchy, especially the Kingdom of Naples, in which the issue of local immunity had become an alarming problem. Even in Milan, the reactions of the lay authorities against the limitations imposed on royal power by the ecclesiastical authorities led to dramatic events.[86]

---

[84] This was emphasized by C. Donati, *Roma pontificia ed episcopati d'Italia nella seconda metà del XVII secolo: aspetti e problemi*, in L. Billanovich and P. Gios (eds.), *Gregorio Barbarigo patrizio veneto vescovo e cardinale nella tarda controriforma (1625–1697)*, Padua, 1999, pp. 107–27; see esp. p. 119.

[85] After the death of the Rospigliosi pope (1670), the congregation continued its work under Pope Clement X.

[86] On Naples following the Treaty of the Pyrenees, see G. Galasso, *Napoli spagnola dopo Masaniello. Politica, cultura, società*, Florence, 1982, vol. I, pp. 58–68; A. Lauro, *Il giurisdizionalismo pregiannoniano nel Regno di Napoli. Problema e storiografia (1563–1732)*, Rome, 1974, esp. pp. 125ff.; M. Rosa, 'La Chiesa meridionale nell'età della Controriforma', in *Storia d'Italia*, Annali 9, pp. 293–345; A. Musi, 'Fisco, religione e Stato nel Mezzogiorno d'Italia (secoli XVI–XVII)', in H. Kellenbenz and P. Prodi (eds.), *Fisco religione Stato nell'età confessionale*, Bologna, 1989, pp. 427–57. On Milan see A. Borromeo, 'La Chiesa milanese del seicento e la corte di Madrid', in A. De Maddalena (ed.), *"Millain the great." Milano nelle brume del seicento*, Milan, 1989, pp. 93–108; Signorotto, *Milano spagnola*, pp. 236ff.

The final phase in the long conflict between the Habsburgs and France had led to a heightened tension over jurisdictional conflicts, of which the effects on the bishoprics of the Italian peninsula must be evaluated from a comprehensive historical point of view. The Holy See had accentuated its defensive attitude following the break with Venice after that city had been interdicted by the pope. In 1626, the Barberini papacy had instituted the *Congregazione dell'immunità* as a reliable tool with which to control and coordinate so many different situations. However, during the subsequent decades, and as a result of the long war, relations with sovereigns *de facto* entered a new phase. Local ecclesiastical authorities were continuously under attack and Rome left them to fend for themselves and defend their own rights.

This emergency provided governments with an opportunity to defeat local resistance, to form alliances with classes that were active in the economic and social context and to fight ecclesiastical privileges and exemptions. The agents of the Catholic king – not without the backing of theological justifications provided by some of the clergy – energetically applied the principle that in an emergency all parties had a duty to participate in the defence of the state. The fact that these requests were justified by the defence of the faith, and that the advantages won by the state were viewed as graces received from the pontiff, did not in any way mitigate the erosion of ecclesiastical exemptions.[87]

The absolute limits set by the bull *In Coena Domini*, which had never been formally recognized by the states, now seemed in danger of total obliteration. Wherever there was a nunciature, as in Naples, it faced the difficult task of defending ecclesiastical rights while avoiding dangerous confrontations. However, the task of many bishops was even more complicated; in particular, of those who for historical and political reasons were not only responsible for pastoral government, but were also delegated by Rome to conduct diplomatic negotiations.

If we keep in mind the precise context of the relations between the papacy and the French and Spanish kings, as well as the unsuccessful results of the Congregation's work, it is difficult to interpret Clement IX's proposal as making concessions to the Catholic sovereign. The monarchy was in difficulties, and it looked as if the Holy See would be able to make some advantageous conquests. The minutes of the special Congregation's discussions prove that the prelates had already decided to 'hold their

---

[87] Although the reconstruction by D. Sella, *Italy in the Seventeenth Century*, London and New York, 1997, does not fully bring out these dynamics, the chapter on the relationship between church and state (pp. 161–87) is worth consulting for its balanced and detailed synthesis (it also deals with the situations in the Italian peninsula which are not addressed here).

ground' and not 'give in, unless they first obtained assurances regarding ecclesiastical immunity, liberty and jurisdiction'.[88] The two envoys chosen by Madrid (Senator Danese Casati, representing the government of Milan, and Don Antonio Gaeta, 'consigliero di Napoli') did not secure any significant concessions.[89]

Nonetheless, the issue of relations between local churches and Rome remained a foremost concern. In a *Discorso* published in 1671, Gaeta defended the bishops who had been 'disheartened by the Roman court'. The Archbishop of Milan, Alfonso Litta, joined in the debate and responded by complaining that the 'poor bishops' were not adequately backed by the Holy See. If princes did not abide by the law – the archbishop added – they were 'acting just as the pope' did as a secular sovereign.[90]

The ecclesiastical government had become the target of converging criticism, and the open challenge of Louis XIV had increased feelings of weakness and dissatisfaction. Up to the 1660s, jurisdictional conflicts had manifested themselves as intermittent quarrels, following precise rules, between the church and Catholic potentates. However, after the break between Alexander VII and the King of France, the shrewdest observers understood that it was time either to initiate far-reaching preventive measures or follow the only other available route: conciliation.

Besides the results that were obtained, this move by the Holy See at the end of the 1660s envisaged having to take a step backwards and spontaneously abandon positions that had now become indefensible owing to attacks by governments. The militant phase of the Counter-Reformation had come to an end, and a new willingness to negotiate with individual governments had replaced the *potestas indirecta in temporalibus*. It was

---

[88] *Atti della Congregazione particolare deputata dalla Santità di Clemente IX sopra le doglianze de Principi secolari contro l'osservanza della Bolla di Gregorio XIV in materia dell'immunità, libertà e giurisdizione ecclesiastica,* BAV, Carpegna, 98 (quotations on f. 30v). These are the minutes compiled by the Congregation secretary, Mons. Giacomo Altoviti, who was nuncio to Venice until 1666.

[89] The synopsis proposed by Pastor, *Storia dei papi,* vol. XIV/2, pp. 560–1, records this shift but, obviously, does not point out its contradictoriness. After the Congregation's first meetings, the problem no longer seemed to centre on 'abuses' related to church immunity, but rather on governments' 'usurpation' of the rights of the church. Besides the works mentioned above, see A. C. Jemolo, *Stato e Chiesa negli scrittori politici italiani del seicento e del settecento,* ed. F. Margiotta Broglio, 2nd edn, Naples, 1972, pp. 219–32.

[90] On Antonio Gaeta, see S. Mastellone, *Pensiero politico e vita culturale a Napoli nella seconda metà del seicento,* Messina and Florence, 1965, pp. 70ff. On the Milanese situation and Archbishop Alfonso Litta see my more detailed analysis in *Milano spagnola,* pp. 247–73.

time for far-reaching negotiations, rather than a stubborn defence of ecclesiastical exemption and immunity.[91]

Monsignor Giovan Battista de Luca, Innocent XI's most important advisor, faced the consequences of the two momentous issues: the urgent French problem and the confrontation over the revision of *In Coena Domini*. De Luca had an academic's experience of erudite confrontation and intellectual challenge, together with practical experience of the institutions of the papal state. His ability to realistically interpret the *de facto* situation was a result of the political, juridical and administrative debate that had been stimulated by events.[92]

With regard to the liberties of the French church, his attitude in the *Congregazione particolare della regalia* was interpreted as pro-Gallican. Experience pushed him to face the issue of the division of the pontiff's powers: his spiritual sovereignty had to be fully acknowledged, but his secular power could not remain limitless.[93] Only a few decades earlier, it would have been unthinkable for a pontiff's counsellor to make such a distinction or clarify the relation between state and church within the papal territory. In Rome, such theories were still looked upon as being pro-monarchist and opposed to *In Coena Domini* and ecclesiastical jurisdiction.

In order to rationalize papal government and legitimize the fiscal system imposed on ecclesiastics by the Apostolic Chamber, de Luca took advantage of the arguments already used by states against 'clerical abuses'. The attack on Holy Office *patentati* (laymen holding a patent that granted immunities and privileges such as carrying arms) was unleashed when governments' jurisdictional policies had already set curbs on the local tribunals of the Roman Inquisition.

However, de Luca's intervention in this delicate matter, which took the form of a radical attack on the Inquisition and its functions, was countered by the harsh reaction of the *cardinali di curia*.[94] At that time, the survivors of the *squadrone volante* – Azzolini, Ottoboni and Albizzi – were the eldest and most respected members of the Congregation. Once

[91] On this growing awareness, even outside Rome, see A. Zanotti, *Cultura giuridica del seicento e jus publicum ecclesiasticum nell'opera del cardinale Giovanni Battista de Luca*, Milan, 1983, pp. 18–20, 119–24.

[92] A. Mazzacane, 'De Luca, Giovan Battista', in *DBI*, vol. XXXVIII, pp. 340–7; Lauro, *Il cardinale Giovan Battista de Luca*, pp. 35–62.

[93] Lauro, *Il cardinale de Luca*, provides a comprehensive in-depth analysis of all de Luca's views. See also Zanotti, *Cultura giuridica del seicento*.

[94] See the reconstruction in Lauro, *Il cardinale de Luca*, pp. 532–82; on the *patentati* of the Holy Office, see also A. Prosperi, *Tribunali della coscienza. Inquisitori, confessori, missionari*, Turin, 1996, pp. 180–3.

again, Albizzi was the most vehement. He accused de Luca of striving to destroy the Inquisition and the Catholic religion, of encouraging the princes to continue their attacks on the church and of favouring heresy.[95] The style was the same as he had used twenty-five years earlier to fight Jansenism and Quietism in the all-out challenge which was now to be extended to Pope Innocent XI.

Albizzi died in early October 1684 and so was not able to witness the arrest of Molinos, the *maestro* of the *orazione di quiete* (1685); but Albizzi – and the Jesuits – had fought stubbornly for this result. It was Ottoboni who actually accomplished it. Azzolini, for his part, had a penchant for Quietism. This was certainly due to Queen Christina, who was in touch with Molinos, but also, I believe, to Azzolini's shift away from France and his decision to remain loyal to the pope. It was another sign that the days of the *squadrone volante* were over and that parties were forming according to different criteria. In particular, by this time, cultural and spiritual aspects had come to acquire a specific and decisive value.

Ottoboni maintained an inflexible hostility to the Quietists which allowed him to corner Innocent XI's reformist entourage. He was acting in accordance with the desires of the French court, as Louis XIV's most intransigent enemies in Rome had been jeopardized by the new spiritual ideas.[96] Certainly Ottoboni's attitude seems more likely to have been political in inspiration rather than theological or doctrinal. His tenacious hostility to Petrucci represented a challenge to the Odescalchi pope, which was not resolved until the beginning of 1687. After Innocent XI's decision to make Petrucci a cardinal (2 September 1686), although the Bishop of Jesi was close to Molinos and threatened by the Holy Office, the inquisitors decided to arrest a number of people in Rome instead of letting the situation calm down. This marked the end of the progressive phase of the Odescalchi papacy. After Innocent's death, the accession of Alexander VIII triggered a complete reversal in all fields. It is reported that the Ottoboni pope openly declared to the Duke of Chaulnes, Louis

---

[95] The fact that de Luca's writings circulated anonymously allowed Ottoboni and Albizzi to unleash a very vehement attack that led to disagreements within the Congregation itself (the dissension that arose with Carpegna). De Luca had anticipated his point of view six years earlier in *Il vescovo pratico*; and when the Pontiff made de Luca a cardinal (1681), Ottoboni opposed the promotion on the grounds that it would weaken the Holy Office and ecclesiastical jurisdiction: Lauro, *Il cardinale de Luca*, pp. 55, 557.

[96] G. Bandini, 'La lotta contro il quietismo in Italia', *Il diritto ecclesiastico*, I, 1947, pp. 26–50. This essay, which has been almost completely ignored by Italian historians, is very interesting and instructive regarding the decisions of the Holy Office, the extent of its autonomy from the church hierarchy and its interaction with the changes in European politics.

XIV's ambassador in Rome that 'we disapprove of everything done by Innocent XI and we will condemn it'.[97]

When Innocent XII gave new vitality to the reform movement, the men who had influenced the central decade of the century had all passed away. They were not involved in the changes of the 1670s, but were to blame for its initial, temporary failure. It might seem wrong to speak about progress and conservation in such a context; but it is also true that, as defenders of the existing curial structure, they had been reactionaries from the outset and against any move towards greater openness or reform.

In a way, their initiatives had sought to confirm the centrality of Rome. This explains their active involvement in the Holy Office, which dealt with the peculiar field of dogma and religious life. However, this attempt (which concerned principally discipline and censorship) was backward-looking and actually increased the sense of decline and isolation of the Holy See. The church's new position in the international context required a profound revision of its role. The *squadrone volante* had never got beyond a protagonism that boiled down to an obstinate defensive attitude. This is the most evident sign of that 'fall' of the papacy which they had striven so hard to prevent.

---

[97] These words were pronounced on 16 December 1689: E. Michaud, *Louis XIV et Innocent XI d'après les correspondances diplomatiques inédites*, Paris, 1882, p. 66. In the entire episode of the opposition to the Odescalchi pope, the French played a significant role; Ottoboni started moving towards France in March 1682 (ibid., p. 516).

ROMAN *AVVISI*: INFORMATION AND POLITICS IN THE SEVENTEENTH CENTURY

MARIO INFELISE

The hand-written newsletters – known in Europe by various names: *avvisi, reporti, gazzette, ragguagli, nouvelles, advis, corantos, courantes, zeitungen,* etc. – were the fastest and most efficient means by which military and political news could be circulated between 1500 and 1700. From the middle of the sixteenth century, the newsletter writers, variously called *menanti, reportisti* or, more generally, *gazzettieri* (gazetteers), depending on where they came from, set up regular news services, a regularity dictated by the postal service network which by then had spread to embrace the whole continent. These services could be used in different ways, at different (pre-set) costs, which varied in relation to the type and quality of service required.

In this period, these hand-written newsletters often served as the basis upon which European ambassadors would draw up and write the dispatches they sent back to their respective courts, each ambassador interpreting and dealing with the *avviso* according to specific diplomatic traditions: some would enclose them along with an account of the current political situation of the country, others would rewrite them or work them directly into the dispatch.

It did not take long for the newsletters to filter out from the chancelleries and spread throughout society. Indeed, they influenced the first stirrings of public opinion that began to appear during the course of the seventeenth century, if one can indeed use the term 'public opinion' in relation to this historical period.

The *avvisi* are seen as the forbears of printed gazettes, an evolution which, as will be seen, is not strictly accurate given the vast differences in their origins and functions. *Avvisi* were first developed in an Italian setting. They were generated by the political intrigues and debates which were a feature of Italian courts at the time: courts which were perennially preoccupied with projecting a specific image of their own activities and, equally, were committed to penetrating the political activities and secrets of other courts. Printed gazettes, however, first developed as reports on political activities involving the German states and the Flemish area, even though for a long time there was a link between these and the earlier hand-written, manuscript, Italian forms.[1]

The *avvisi* produced in Rome in the late sixteenth and early seventeenth century are very interesting for many reasons, in particular because they offered the rest of Europe a fairly well-developed, evolved model. Here we will only touch upon the way in which this material, this information, was produced in Rome. We will, however, look in depth at the impact, the reverberations, these *avvisi* were to have outside the borders of the papacy. Rome and Venice were the two cities where the newsletter reached its highest development. Perhaps, indeed, the sixteenth-century roots of the *avvisi* lie in Venice rather than in Rome, but by the middle of the century they were well established in both cities. The news arrived, was gathered, 'packaged' and broadcast.

It is not difficult to understand why these two cities, in particular, should have played a central role in the development of a 'news service'. The words of Vittorio Siri, explaining his reasons for choosing the place where he would work as a contemporary historian, offer one explanation. He says he needed 'a city like that which Plutarch sought for a historian, that is, where there was a great and powerful court, full of ambassadors and ministers', where 'more than in any other city in the world one could see a multitude of personages and soldiers who had been ambassadors at all the courts of Europe and where civil questions were managed by nobles, where people practised who possessed refined judicial abilities and were knowledgeable about the affairs of princes'.[2] Siri was referring to Venice, but the capital of the Roman Catholic church was no different. Indeed, only a few years earlier Maiolino Bisaccioni, one of the many adventurous historian-gazetteers of the period, had declared: 'Rome, as you know, [is] the place where all the news in the world is found'.[3]

---

[1] Little attention has so far been paid to the forms political information took in the early modern age in Italy. Knowledge of this world has mostly been drawn from two older articles that have been referred to in all subsequent publications: S. Bongi, 'Le prime gazzette in Italia', *Nuova antologia*, 11 (1869), pp. 311–46; R. Ancel, 'Etude critique sur quelques recueils d'Avvisi. Contribution à l'histoire du journalisme en Italie', *Mélanges d'Archéologie et d'Histoire*, 27 (1908), pp. 115–39. Interest has grown in recent years. For some articles on the Italian situation see H. Duranton and P. Rétat (eds.), *Gazettes et information politique sous l'Ancien Régime*, Saint-Etienne, 1999. The situation in Rome has been studied by B. Dooley, *The Social History of Scepticism. Experience and Doubt in Early Modern Culture*, Baltimore and London, 1999.
[2] V. Siri, *Il Mercurio overo storia de' tempi correnti*, vol. II, Casale, 1647.
[3] M. Bisaccioni, *L'albergo*, Venice, 1637, p. 531.

The pre-eminence of Rome and Venice does not mean that *avvisi* did not exist in other Italian cities. But information tended to be consumed there rather than produced, even though cities like Genoa, caught between France and Spain, and Milan and Naples, with their relations with Spain, were particularly important.

Initially *avvisi* were letters containing political, military and economic information and they were already in use before the sixteenth century. But, leaving aside their very early origins, by the mid-1500s the function and content of newsletters had changed enough to differentiate them from the usual, and occasional, letters containing information.

However, the first real attempt to 'discipline' this new art can be dated to 1570–1580. In 1570, Pope Pius V declared that he would proceed against the authors of defamatory broadsheets. That same year, in a famous case, Niccolò Franco, who was held responsible for such writings, and who was probably connected to the world of the copyists, was tried, condemned and hanged.[4] A few years later other repressive measures were taken: as well as being banned from writing in general, some writers were arrested and, as a paper dated 1571 tells us, the pope may have 'had them hanged, it is said on the grounds that they wrote things that did not bode well'.[5] On 22 March 1572, the pope issued a *Constitutio contra scribentes, exemplantes et dictantes monita vulgo dicta gli avvisi e ritorni* which hit out at defamatory, slanderous writings, at offensive sheets or at those which contained prognostications or predictions. Paolo Alessandro Maffei, the eighteenth-century biographer of Pius V, remembered that measure and described newsletter writers as a 'plague upon men', blaming them for the often ferocious disputes that not infrequently shook Rome. These authors, with their defamatory libels and 'secret *avvisi*', 'plotted' in order to 'blacken' the 'reputation and honour' of 'the most eminent citizens':

> on the one hand they always used the ploy of a vendetta and an uncontrolled vivacity of the spirit, on the other, greed and gain played their part: but in everything malice is involved, coupled with lies, neither saying nor reporting what is true, but just enough to spread scandal and to ruin others, so as to find more readers for those unworthy sheets of paper and to reap even greater profits from this iniquitous trade.[6]

The pope's successors renewed the bans but could not control the hand-written newsletters. Scribes were imprisoned and tortured and,

---

[4] A. Mercati, *I costituti di Niccolò Franco (1568–1570) dinanzi all'Inquisizione di Roma esistenti nell'Archivio Segreto Vaticano*, Città del Vaticano, 1955.

[5] Bongi, 'Le prime gazzette', p. 317.

[6] P. A. Maffei, *Vita di san Pio V*, Venezia, 1712, p. 303; Bongi, 'Le prime gazzette', p. 317.

in extreme cases, imprisoned for life or executed. In 1581, a writer, Luperzio, was given a life sentence, because the authorities feared that he might spread bad news about the health of Pope Gregory XIII;[7] in 1587, Annibale Cappello, 'head of a sect of gazetteers' was tortured and executed because he had leaked confidential information.[8] But while repression could force people to be more cautious and prudent, it could not silence them; indeed, everyone became aware that these sheets were becoming indispensable – everyone, even those who were trying to destroy them. Occasionally the Governor of Rome would arrest gazetteers and check on their writings, but if 'nothing unscrupulous' against the pope and his laws were found, no further sanctions would be imposed.[9] Thus the repression was anything but systematic: rather than, indiscriminately, hitting all production, it tended only to hit *avvisi* which contained scabrous material. However, there was an ongoing link between defamatory gazettes and libels.[10]

The gathering and editing of information had already developed into an established profession, not always honourable, but a full-time occupation for some people. In 1579 it was said that the number of writers in Rome was 'very large',[11] and it probably remained so for decades. In the late sixteenth and early seventeenth century similar professional figures emerged as a feature of all large urban centres. This was even reflected in the literature of the time: *Avvisi burleschi*, by Giulio Cesare Croce,[12] belongs to this period; so too does Traiano Boccalini's *Ragguagli di Parnaso*.

But *avvisi* were not simply literary inventions. Model newsletters, with advice either on criteria for editing or on rules for dealing with writers, are common in treatises and manuals on secretarial work, or in collections of letters of the period. In 1620, Panfilo Persico offered useful, detailed guidance to secretaries who had anything to do with editing newsletters.[13]

---

[7] BAV, Urb. Lat., 1049, f. 399v, 1581. I should like to thank Giampiero Brunelli for this reference.

[8] Bongi, 'Le prime gazzette', pp. 320–1.

[9] BAV, Urb. Lat., 1057, f. 539v, *Avvisi di Roma*, 13 September 1589.

[10] See, for example, the last provisions of 1601 concerning the copyists and authors of writings dealing with the case of Beatrice Cenci. On 28 December 1600, by order of Clement VIII, the governor, Ferrante Taverna, published an edict 'against those who detract from people's reputations' and those who 'without fear of God or of Justice, use their pestiferous tongues to produce newsletters (*avvisi*), filling the paper with lies and scandal … defaming and destroying the honour and reputations of others'. R. Bassani and F. Bellini, *Caravaggio assassino. La carriera di un 'valenthuomo' fazioso nella Roma della Controriforma*, Rome, 1994, p. 95.

[11] ASV, Inquisitori di Stato, b. 488, dispatch from the Venetian ambassador in Turin, Francesco Barbaro, 12 March 1579.

[12] G. C. Croce, *Avisi burleschi venuti da diverse parti del mondo, cose notabilissime e degne di essere intese*, Bologna, n.d.

[13] P. Persico, *Del segretario …*, Venice, 1620, pp. 186–95.

In other, political works such as *Il seminario de' governi di stato et di guerra* by Girolamo Frachetta, the question was raised whether, in wartime, it might be useful to influence the enemy's actions by releasing invented *avvisi*, falsifying the news.[14]

It soon became common practice, indeed a necessity, to adjust political behaviour to the reality of the fixed presence of writers and their information sheets, either to exploit them or to keep them at a distance, depending on the circumstances and the need. Cardinal Azzolini wisely suggested

> flattering *novellanti* [tale-tellers/informers] and men who serve and practise in the houses and waiting rooms of princes, because they will praise you, and it is important to be praised in public places; but because people like that are never much respected, you shouldn't get too close to them, just keep them friendly in order to reap the rewards.[15]

Such caution can also be found in treatises on the cardinal's courts. In 1598, among the prescriptions issued to the aide of a cardinal's secretary, Cesare Evitascandolo admonished him not to speak 'to anyone new' and not to 'associate with writers so as to avoid calling [your] loyalty into question' seeing that there were *novellanti* who could 'take the egg out of a chicken's body, let alone the secret out of a youth's mouth'.[16]

However, knowing how many writers were at work does not help assess the amount they each wrote. It is even more difficult to identify and reveal each of the myriad minor figures as a separate individual, even more so because they did not usually sign their work and, understandably, tended to keep out of the limelight. It should be remembered that the quality of the sheets circulating varied greatly. So-called 'public' *avvisi*, which limited themselves to publishing known facts, enjoyed no particular prestige. They were distributed and read at certain key points in the city. One such case is the 'Nuove di Banchi' (News from Banchi) sheets which circulated in the quarter of the same name, between Ponte Sant'Angelo and Via Giulia, which some also called 'Le scioccarie de' Banchi' (The Follies of Banchi).[17]

[14] G. Frachetta, *Il seminario de' governi di stato et di guerra*, 3rd edn, Venice, 1624 (1st edn 1617), p. 728.

[15] BMC, Codice Cicogna, 2576, *Afforismi et avvertimenti politici per signori che praticano la corte di Roma e quelle d'altri prencipi*, c. 308v.

[16] C. Evitascandalo, *Dialogo del maestro di casa, nel quale si contiene di quanto il maestro di casa deve essere instrutto*, Rome, 1598, pp. 11–12. For the cardinal's court and related dealings see G. Fragnito, '"Il vero ritratto d'una bellissima e ben governata corte"', *Annali dell' Istituto storico italo-germanico in Trento*, 17 (1991), pp. 135–85; idem, 'Le corti cardinalizie nella Roma del Cinquecento', *Rivista storica italiana*, 106 (1994), pp. 5–41. I thank Gigliola Fragnito for the reference to the treatise by Evitascandalo.

[17] Ancel, 'Etude critique', pp. 133–4.

The 'secret' *avvisi*, destined for a much more restricted readership, were far more sought after. In the middle of the sixteenth century, one such newsletter writer described the differences between these and ordinary *avvisi* very well when he admonished his correspondent and ordered him to send only 'quality' *avvisi*

> and not those the gazetteers write (because you well know that the governor only wants them to write trifles and lies that don't stir anything up) but rather those tales which gentlemen recount during the unobserved hours of the night, speaking in a language that cannot be understood by baboons, because as you know only too well, the streets of our quarters are frequented by spies sent by the palace and the governor, who go around catching simpletons.[18]

The compilers of these two types of hand-written newsletters were, however, often the same people, able to offer two versions, one public and one for a more restricted readership, to be sold with care. The Doge, Leonardo Donà, remembered an episode which had occurred while he was ambassador in Rome, concerning Roman writers' habit of 'doing two sheets of *avvisi*', one dealing with 'ordinary and rather unimportant things and the other with things of more import'. Once it happened that 'one of these [writers] by mistake gave the sheet with more important matters in it to the copyist; the sheet spoke critically of the pope's household. This fell into His Holiness's hands and gave the pope an opportunity to imprison and hang the offender.'[19]

This was not the only danger. At various times gazetteers became involved, voluntarily or involuntarily, in secret conflicts between courts, conflicts to which they sometimes fell victim.[20] But such risks could, at times, mean wealth. In 1693, people were scandalized when the pope issued a warrant for the arrest of a 'certain non-Roman of Casa Valle who was living like a lord in Rome and earning huge sums from his correspondents for whom he wrote satirically and with no regard for the pope, the cardinals or the princes'. He was not the only one: there are frequent allusions to the 'many' who 'live as vagabonds in Rome and

---

[18] ASV, Miscellanea atti diversi manoscritti, b. 65, *De gli avvisi di Roma della corrente estate del 1665. Posta prima Pasquino Romano al Gobbo di Rialto*.

[19] ASV, Collegio. Esposizioni principi, reg. 21, c. 112v, 20 November 1609.

[20] This refers not only to the sentences already mentioned, but also to the involvement of *avvisi* writers in complex spy operations for which they quite often reaped the worst possible rewards. Some such episodes are described in M. Infelise, 'La guerra, le nuove, i curiosi. I giornali militari negli anni della Lega contro il Turco (1683–1690)', in A. Bilotto, P. Del Negro and C. Mozzarelli (eds.), *I Farnese: corti, guerra e nobiltà in antico regime*, Rome, 1997, pp. 321–48.

who live very well on their writings without ever being questioned about their activities'.[21]

Naturally, the first places to be scoured for information were the seats of power, or places like embassies, where letters from abroad would arrive. Throughout the early modern age, faceless individuals, ready to intervene at any opportunity, always thronged the antechambers of the great and powerful. It is difficult, if not impossible, to distinguish between those who gathered information mainly for reasons of espionage, on commission from rival courts or princes, and those who were there in order to gather and then write up the news so as to offer it to a much wider public.[22] But perhaps it is futile even to attempt to make such a distinction. Political information was freed late, and then only with difficulty, from this type of ambiguity, and the concept of information as a public service was only really established, and freed from any negative connotations in the eighteenth century.

The news that was gathered often ended up in the studios of scribes, who would then make many copies and organize the sale and distribution of the sheets. In Venice, where there was no organized corporation, the scriptoria (scrittorie) were strategically placed between the Post Office and St Mark's Square. The directors of some of these scrittorie were true professionals in the field of information. They had a number of employees in their service and sometimes not only worked as gazetteers but also dealt with the sale of many kinds of manuscripts, often works of a political nature, but also tracts on magic and free thinking.[23] However, there was an organized body in Rome, a corporation of writers with its own statute. Even so, notwithstanding the corporation, an account dated 1629 speaks of a profession in crisis, 'almost desolate and extinct'.[24] However, it does not seem that the 'company of writers' regularly took part in compiling avvisi, though it was well known that both professional newsletter writers and copyists had their headquarters in Parione, near the statue of Pasquino.[25]

On the other hand, public places were little suited to the writing and editing of secret avvisi. Thus in Rome, those who were involved in gathering information were to be sought in the curia or the embassies.

---

[21] ASV, Inquisitori di Stato, b. 661, 1 March 1693.

[22] P. Preto, I servizi segreti di Venezia, Milan, 1994, pp. 87–94.

[23] M. Infelise, 'Professione reportista. Copisti e gazzettieri nella Venezia del '600', in S. Gasparri, G. Levi and P. Moro (eds.), Venezia. Itinerari per la storia della città, Bologna, 1997, pp. 183–209.

[24] ASR, Archivio camerale II, b. 35, fasc. 34, in which are printed the Statuta et ordinationes venerabilis societatis scribentium in urbe … aucta et confirmata de anno MDCLXII, Rome, Tip. rev. cam. ap., 1662.

[25] F. Martinelli, Roma ricercata nel suo sito, Venice, 1689, pp. 170, 172.

Weekly dispatches were sent from the papal nunciate to the Secretary of State, and these were often accompanied by copious sheets of news. Both the dispatches and the *avvisi* were destined to fall under the eyes of both interested and uninterested readers. In 1623 Cristoforo Caetani instructed the Secretary of State, Lorenzo Magalotti, to read, and very carefully follow up, the *avvisi* from Venice which had been sent by the papal representative in the Venetian Republic, for 'they are the best'. First they had to be given to the Pope and then passed, via the Secretary of State, to the Cardinal-nephew.[26] It not hard to see how easily information could leak out during all these interchanges, as not even the contents of official dispatches and coded letters remained confidential. Details that could arouse outside interest soon leaked out of the offices where they should have remained. Both in Rome and in Venice there was always someone ready to intercept the news at some stage or other as it was passed around, and then to pass this news on. During the years of war in Candia, there was no debate in the Venetian Senate, or message sent from Candia or Constantinople to the authorities, that could not be read in Rome within little more than a week. This 'publicity' could also lead to conflicts. Sensitive news regarding the relationship between Venice and Rome, or highly confidential discussions on questions still under negotiation, got out rapidly. No one could stop the leaks.

On 29 December 1657, the Venetian ambassador to the Roman court, Angelo Correr, described similar mechanisms very well and complained that

> the divulging of public matters . . . is so universal that you cannot say more of this than of that. I reckon that the root of the evil lies in what is said too freely, what you hear from some people in the senate who are perhaps unable to realize by themselves when they should shut up. The nuncio knows everything and tells everything: the details are written down by hearers who mix some truth in among the lies; the gazetteers have always recounted everything with scandalous indecency and talked in particular of the affairs of the Levant in such a way that a thousand prejudices have grown up.[27]

At that moment negotiations for peace were underway with the Sultan, but the terms were being drawn up in highly confidential discussions. One week later they came to the pope's attention and he, as the ambassador noted, read them with 'great curiosity'.[28] At the same time Correr,

---

[26] A. Kraus, 'Das päpstliche Staatssekretariat im Jahre 1623. Eine Denkschrift des ausscheidenden sostituto an den neuermahnten Staatssekretär', *Römische Quartalschrift*, 52 (1957), p. 117. I should like to thank Antonio Menniti Ippolito for this reference.

[27] ASV, Inquisitori di Stato, b. 473, 29 December 1657.

[28] Ibid., 19 January 1658.

arguing for greater controls over the flow of information, forwarded some
sheets that had come from Venice and that were circulating in Rome in
late January 1657:[29] a sheet from Venice, 12 January 1657, with news of
the Levant; a sheet from Prague, 26 December 1657, with news of central
northern Europe; a sheet from Cologne, 30 December 1657, with news
of northern Europe; and a sheet from London, 27 December 1657, with
English news of Jamaica and Brazil. The ambassador, Correr, was really
only worried about the sheet that had come from Venice, but it is clear
that many others, from all over Europe, used to arrive at the nunciate.

The title of this chapter uses the term *avvisi*, which was used in the
seventeenth century to denote information sheets that came from Rome.
The '*avvisi* of Rome' were those produced and edited in the city, but
which did not necessarily carry news of it. For example, one sheet which
is dated and headed 'Rome' contains news of events concerning the
whole of Europe. Thus, original news from the city was put together
with the 'foreign' news recopied from the *avvisi* that arrived in Rome. In
this way news bounced from one part of the continent to another, often
unchanged, but equally often with alterations, perhaps unintentional, as
may happen when a text is copied and recopied. The fact that *avvisi*
were copied and recopied makes it even harder to identify the original
writer of any particular sheet. Some idea of the incessant movement of
news can be gained from a dispatch sent to Venice in 1579 by Francesco
Barbaro, ambassador at the court of the Duke of Savoy. He had read in
'two separate reports', circulating in Turin, that confidential information
was being put about regarding debates in the Venetian Senate. One of
these, a public *avviso,* was fairly generic and had been shown to him
by a merchant from Nice who was travelling to Lyon. The other, the
classic 'secret' *avviso*, was particularly damaging to Venice, and had been
sent from Rome to the nuncio at the court of the Duke of Savoy. The
problem was particularly grave because the hand-written newsletters that
were sent from Rome to Turin were subsequently reproduced and sent
on into France. The ambassador investigated and discovered that the
nuncio received these *avvisi* from a Roman agent who bought them
freely and openly in the capital. Barbaro was even more surprised when he
discovered that in the same 'reports' he could read, almost word for word,
the opinions expressed by the cardinals in a top-secret meeting about
relations between Rome and Paris. 'From this,' commented Barbaro,
'one can understand the extent to which people who earn their daily
bread by this art are able to penetrate to the hearts of princes, given that
they think of nothing else but that.'[30]

[29] Ibid., 2 February 1658.   [30] Ibid., b. 488, 12 March 1579.

Thus the problem of identifying individual writers remains; however, it is not so difficult to understand the environment in which such writers developed. Roman *avvisi* are exceptionally vivacious, of a vivacity that is rarely found elsewhere. In the rest of Europe, the *avviso*'s sensitivity towards its readership was displayed by the selection and favourable adaptation of news items to the needs of its clientele. In Rome the procedure was often very different. The secret *avvisi* that circulated in the city were an integral part of the world of the curia. In this world newsletters were often written for specific political ends. Not infrequently they were written in a different form from those produced in other parts of Italy. The language was more refined and correct, and the style more attractive and readable. Sarcasm and irony were often used. Thus Roman *avvisi* of the period were often very lively documents which spoke of the political realities of the moment; they were not restricted to formal descriptions of exernal facts, but rather tried to illustrate intrigues and behind-the-scenes events in a spirited way.

A series of weekly gazettes (dated 1667) describes, very effectively, the crisis that hit the Chigi family when Alexander VII died and his successor, Clement IX (Giulio Rospigliosi), was elected.[31] The person who compiled these gazettes explicitly stated that he would ignore news that could be found in the public gazettes, by which he meant not only printed sheets but, more specifically, the hand-written newsletters which circulated freely in the city. Rather, he preferred to concentrate his efforts on the factions that had existed at the start of the conclave and on the relations between the cardinals and the European powers, in an attempt to give readers some idea of what choices were possible. The writer was not even attempting to offer an impartial account of the events, as he quite openly declared. The big question at the time, the election, was enriched by many details relating to the ruinous fall of the Chigi family, 'from rulers to vassals'. The writer is also clearly in favour of the antinepotist policies of the new pope and of his 'modest' behaviour, which was such a contrast to that of his predecessors. The rhythm of the narrative is often urgent, the language basic and the tone emotive, especially so when it is striving to show the actions of the dead pope's family in a bad light. The author does not spare the reader even the most horrifying details about the death of Alexander VII, nor does he hide his satisfaction when reporting the misfortunes of the former pope's brother, Mario. In the sheet dated 28 May 1667, which gave the news of the pope's death, he wrote that the Chigi 'were beginning to swallow bitter pills'. Don Mario had been attacked by the people, the façade of his palace covered in mud

[31] BM, ms. it., cl. vi, cod. 232 (5698), 28 May 1667.

and his servants maltreated. 'In all these days', adds the writer, 'various pasquinades have been fixed on the statue of Pasquino which only speak of popular unrestrained rancour with no wisdom or good sense, so are not worth mentioning.'

> Don Mario squawks that he doesn't understand why he is so hated by the people, he can't ignore things now, saying that his defunct brother's pontificate was a very unhappy one, because there was famine, plague, floods, arms and continuous transfers of big money to the Emperor and to the Venetians who were fighting the Turks, all of which money has been milked from the apostolic coffers.

The same tone continued the following week. On 23 July, it was reported that Cardinal Chigi had a temperature, 'only the effect of immoderate gorging on *starnotti* [small grey partridges], pistachio sorbets and on what Sanazzaro says is harmful in youth and shameful in old age; therefore his life will be short'. But it was not the cardinal whose life proved short. On 19 November the death of his brother Mario was reported: Don Mario Chigi died 'as he had lived, with no confession, communion or extreme unction. One could say the same of him as was said of Bonifatio Ottavo: he ruled like a lion, lived like a wolf and died like a dog.' And the reporter went on to describe the public jubilation at this death.[32] On the other hand, the antinepotistic activities of the new pope were systematically reported, indeed amplified, despite the fact that during the conclave itself the possibility that he might be elected had not been reported with much enthusiasm. There was a reference to him on 18 June 1667 when the writer noted: 'it is no longer the right time to have empty-headed popes'.

Everything was seasoned with colourful details and it really didn't matter how irreverent these were. The descriptions of how the various cardinals entered the conclave are curious: for example, Bonelli 'with ridiculous affectation accentuated the burden of his years, walking bent over, mournfully, and supported in a way that makes it seem he is most afraid of tripping where there is nothing to trip over'.[33]

This ironical and somewhat disrespectful tone can also be found elsewhere. In 1665, when describing the problems of Cardinal Imperiali, 'chief and *condottiere*' of the *squadrone volante*, which was then in crisis, it was reported that 'he was once the factotum of nepotism and of the court' but that since the French 'caught the chief red-handed, it seems that he no longer walks with the usual Genoese arrogance'.

---

[32] For the attacks on the morality of the Chigi family see L. von Pastor, *Storia dei papi dalla fine del Medio Evo*, Rome, 1932, vol. XIV/1, pp. 329–30.

[33] BM, ms. it., cl. VI, cod. 232 (5698), 4 June 1667.

However, it was noted that he got about a lot, now in the palace, now with the Queen of Sweden, now with the cardinals 'of his party, and the *squadrone volante* has now become the chickenhearted squad'.[34]

Another weekly collection, dated 1682, is full of annotations about life in Rome and the controversy with the Gallican church. It also has an abundance of details about the various positions assumed from time to time by the curia, and every opportunity or pretext is exploited to attack the Jesuits, sometimes merely touching them with the weapon of irony but other times hitting out at them with sarcasm. This is how the election of General Charles de Noyelle, on 11 July 1682, is recounted:

> It has been many years since the headquarters of the good father Jesuits last saw such a marvellous, amazing function as that on Sunday morning – the opening of the Jesuit conclave (a function which, I dare say, is more famous and more important than that which is held in order to elect a new pope, since in the conclave that elected Innocent II there were only sixty-six people enclosed to choose and crown the candidate while in this one there were more than 400 ravens, come from all over the world to put themselves in a cage in order to elect a black being from Brussels, a monarch for the Jesuit band). The great election was won by the Vicar General, Father Carlo Noyella, a Fleming, an important man by dint of both his birth and his merit. For thirty years he has been continuously in Rome, occupying a series of important posts within the Order, and amongst these he has most recently been the much-applauded Vicar General of the illustrious company, so that his election is acclaimed by every voice, by every voter, as never has been seen before; and they'll do it all the faster, those despots, when they find themselves shut in on bread and water, their stomachs not being accustomed to such rigours.[35]

It is obvious that it was not the sheer vivacity of the Roman *avvisi* that contributed most to helping them circulate freely, since it was perfectly possible that a sheet from Rome might be copied in (for example) Venice, and only from there would it fly off around the rest of Europe – and often, through other channels, return to Rome.

In March 1690, Don Antonio Ottoboni, a relative of the pope, complained about a Roman sheet, produced in Venice, that was circulating in the city and which contained news about his family. The sheet talked openly about the pope's intention to provide his relatives with large incomes, just as his predecessors since Urban VIII had always done. It also described the licentious musical performances some cardinals had taken

---

[34] *De gli avvisi di Roma della corrente estate del 1665*, c. 40v. On the *squadrone volante* see Gianvittorio Signorotto's chapter in this volume.

[35] BM, ms. it., cl. VI 459 (12103), *Mercuri 1682*, Rome, 11 July 1682.

part in. The pope and his family asked the Venetian authorities to intervene because

> as regards the writers in Rome it is extremely difficult to trace them, espe-
> cially as all correspondence is carried out under false names, pseudonyms,
> because of the sanctions which are very severe here. Furthermore, those
> who practise this damned profession of writing false and titillating infor-
> mation are usually men of a certain sphere and of high rank who, in order
> to hide themselves, make every sheet they send out pass through many
> hands; and if they have to put a name to letters for correspondence or
> whatever they usually use false names, which only serve to send the letter
> out and back, but the real people do not appear, neither can they be found,
> or if they are then they are not the right person.

Thus they hoped to be able to trace the Roman corespondent with the
help of the Venetian correspondent. But the state inquisitors, into whose
hands the matter was put, could find no culprit. The Venetian reporter
responsible did give a name, Pietro Filippo, but it was a very common
name in Rome. There was even a servant of the Venetian ambassador
with the same name; he was, however, proved innocent of the charges
without a shadow of doubt.[36]

This was not an unusual case; neither was the continuous passing of
news items back and forth between Venice and Rome in any way unusual.
Cardinal Flavio Chigi paid annually for a regular supply of *avvisi* from a
famous Venetian reporter, Domenico Marchesatti, who was a civil lawyer
in one of the Republic's magistrates courts. Marchesatti regularly sent
information to other important public figures, including the Duke of
Savoy and the historian Girolamo Brusoni.[37]

Giovanni Quorli, who produced newsletters for a multitude of ambassadors and aristocrats all over Europe, was active in Venice in the middle
of the seventeenth century. He offered his clients sheets from London,
Cologne, Antwerp, Paris, Vienna and Rome. He was a subject of the
papal states, born in Gubbio, but had been 'bandito di forca da Firenze
e di galera da Roma' ('banished from Florence and for the galleys in
Rome').[38] For many years he ran the most flourishing *scrittoria* (writer's
workshop) in Venice, a true news agency which gathered news from all

---

[36] ASV, Inquisitori di Stato, b. 166, 18 March 1690, letters from the state inquisitors to
the ambassador Giovanni Lando; b. 475, 11, 18 and 25 March, 1 and 15 April 1690,
letters from Ambassador Lando. The 'guilty' *avviso* from Rome of 4 March 1690 was
enclosed with the dispatch of 18 March.

[37] BAV, Archivio Chigi. Corrispondenze, b. 32, letters from Domenico and Giambattista
Marchesatti to Cardinal Flavio Chigi; ASV, Inquisitori di Stato, b. 566, 5 and 19 July
1677.

[38] Ibid., b. 638, 11 September 1656. On Quorli see Infelise, 'Professione reportista'.

over, organized it and sent it on. The adventurous vicissitudes of his life had taught him how to ply his trade. He was also very good at selecting the right news. As regards the Romans, even though he had no scruples about selling even the most satirical and irreverent sheets from his workshop, he realized only too well that it was better to leave 'material which might interest the inquisition' alone. But he was also able to assess who could supply the best news at the best (lowest) prices: he wrote 'For twenty-five *giuli* [silver coins] I had [...] what the ambassador in Rome has, good, well-thought-out, political material, without "fangs" and titillating concepts, without errors and which one could call a satire rather than an *avviso*'.[39]

Thus the connection with embassies comes up again. Clearly, diplomatic offices were among the nerve centres for the editing and distribution of news.[40] Ambassadors would meet regularly with the gazetteers, both to obtain new *avvisi* and to spread specific news items through the sheets. Thus the relationship worked in the interests of both parties, as well as offering a means of controlling and checking on flows of information. In 1663 the Venetian ambassador, Basadonna, alarmed, warned of the possible political consequences of the incorrect information currently circulating in Roman reports concerning Venetian attitudes towards the pope and France. Information had been put out by the Roman writers, whose news was regularly recorded by the ambassadors of other powers:

> This week, among other things, there is news that the Senate has denied the pope free passage through the Republic and has decided to take up arms in Italy so as to join with the French. This type of people are always wide of the mark because, with no basis, they merely collect the news from the *piazza* and have no other aim than to fill their sheets; but everywhere one can see that they do not enter by mistake into the affairs of their own country about which the world supposes them to be well-informed and so gives them the benefit of the doubt. It doesn't matter if they tell lies about Flanders, Germany or Turkey, but let them abstain from comments on Venetian affairs! This is even more necessary because those who then write to palaces write their dispatches on the basis of these reports, which are thus confirmed and have the worst possible effects.[41]

Hence the *avvisi* often ended up conditioning the contents of ambassadors' dispatches and could even influence the actions of courts. On

[39] ASV, Avogaria di Comun, Miscellanea civile, b. 233, fasc. 13.
[40] See e.g. the events surrounding Monsignor Jacopo Amidei, who came and went freely in the palace at Venice and who used to procure *avvisi* for priests who were 'in the government'. He was involved in a murder trial in 1635. ASR, Tribunale criminale del Governatore. Processi, vol. 33.
[41] ASV, Inquisitori di Stato, b. 473, 24 February 1663.

the other hand, discrepancies between the contents of a gazette and the contents of an official dispatch could cause problems for diplomats since, as the Venetian ambassador noted, 'because of these gazettes they do not know what information to give to their Sovereigns when writing, because they may describe an event in one way and the gazetteers in another, which could cause a minister to fall without knowing why'.[42]

By the middle of the century printed *avvisi* were becoming more common and a new chapter was opened. The printed gazette meant that it was no longer only courts, men in power and other restricted groups that were concerned. The general public, too, was demanding information, and at times this was provided. Every imaginable type of this new form of information could be found in seventeenth-century Italy. For example, in Milan and Turin the governor and the court gave permission for one single sheet, strictly controlled by the government, to circulate. In Genoa, two such sheets were permitted, one sympathetic to the French, the other to the Spanish. However, in Venice, and very probably in Rome too, there was no printed gazette. The rare examples headed 'Rome' that have survived were probably editions printed in Florence and based on hand-written public sheets.[43] During the second half of the seventeenth century, however, the situation in the rest of the country was very different. All major urban centres in Umbria, the Marches and Romagna had their own weekly printed sheet, which was compiled on the basis of hand-written manuscripts from Venice and Rome.

As already mentioned, the printed gazettes did not entirely replace hand-written sheets: the latter continued to be indispensable for many courts and chancelleries. The hand-written sheets were less subject to censorship, could be written and produced faster, and could be personalized for individual clients. The printed sheets, on the other hand, were standardized, the same for everybody. Hence it was only natural that the contents should be different, even when they spoke about the same events – even, indeed, when the source was the same hand-written *avviso*.

Direct comparison between the two forms can prove interesting, especially if it is possible to ascertain whether the printed sheet was derived

---

[42] Ibid., b. 661, 1 March 1693.

[43] There seems to be no foundation for the idea that there was a printed gazette in Rome in the seventeenth century. All the printed *avvisi* in the archives of the Vatican Secretary of State which are headed 'Rome' have always turned out to have been sent from the nuncio in Florence (ASV, Segreteria di Stato. Avvisi, f. 23a). Furthermore, it would seem that a printed sheet, headed 'Venice', came from the same printing house in Florence (see f. 101). For further information on the Florentine gazettes see M. A. Morelli, 'Gli inizi della stampa periodica a Firenze nella prima metà del XVII secolo', *Critica storica*, 3 (1968), pp. 288–323.

directly from the hand-written version. When evaluating the editing of news items we must not forget that a gazetteer who wrote for printing often simply did not have the time to make major changes to the manuscript sheets he received: the work of compiling and composing the gazette was always done frenetically, probably directly in the printer's workshop. Thus the gazetteers often preferred to limit themselves to assembling, somewhat haphazardly, whatever the hand-written sheets offered, recopying some passages word for word and eliminating others entirely, with little regard for the overall intelligibility of the sheet.

In Foligno, by the end of the century, there were two weekly gazettes written and edited on the basis of hand-written sheets from Rome. In this case, the large collection of *avvisi* held by the Secretary of State in the Vatican has made fruitful comparison possible. Overall, the printed gazettes offer less information than the sheets they are based on. Many facts and events have been cut out, others hastily summarized – either in order to shorten the times required for editing or in order to avoid problems with the censors.

One example, a communication from Rome dated 5 March 1695, gives the news that Rinaldo d'Este has renounced his office of cardinal in order to ensure that there will be a successor to the Duchy of Modena. The hand-written *avviso* from Rome presents the news in these terms:

> On Saturday evening Monsignor Maraciani (*sic*), minister to Cardinal d'Este, Duke of Modena, renounced his office as cardinal to the pope in the name of this sovereign, because he had to change his status in order to ensure the succession of his line. There is no doubt that he has not done this in order to set up house with the widow, the Princess of Parma, and as His Holiness has accepted this renunciation in private, it will soon be done again at a public function, in the usual way, at the next Consistory to be held.

However, the printed version reads:

> Rome 5 March. Mons. Marciani minister in this court to sig. card. Este Duke of Modena until last Saturday, has in the name of his highness, put his resignation from his cardinal's office in hands of the His Holiness. He has been obliged to do this, to change his status, by his family, in order to ensure the succession to his noble house, and as His Holiness has accepted this request in private there will soon be a public function, following the usual forms, during the next consistory which will be semi-public.

In the same edition there is another item of news that concerns Cardinal d'Este: the printed version says he 'had asked permission to confer three abbacies, one on each of the two Cardinals Barberini and the third on Abbot Grimani'. But in the hand-written version there is a detail of considerable importance: the Cardinal d'Este 'has asked, as Duke, permission to confer two abbacies on the two Cardinals Barberini his cousins, but has had some difficulty with the other, which he would like to give to Abbot Grimani'.[44]

The fact that one text was derived from the other is clear, just as is the type of news it was judged wiser to omit from the printed version: it was better not to pass on unverified news about those in power. Editors of the printed sheets had to avoid any dangerous items, items which could cause problems for those in power and alarm a public that was much wider than the usual readership reached by the hand-written newsletters. Thus they offered 'sweetened', more innocuous, news. In the printed versions, news of a political nature appeared only in the briefest possible way, without a hint either of any background or of compromising details. Often the gazetteers would limit themselves to reporting the arrivals and departures of eminent persons, troop movements and battles.

These examples are minimal and more cases should be found for comparison. It is, however, clear that by the middle of the seventeenth century, printed gazettes were introducing a new factor into political life: public opinion, which by the following century was beginning to acquire substantial weight and influence. Since it is generally accepted that this informed public had considerable influence on events during the Age of Enlightenment, there is surely good reason to trace its seventeenth-century origins.

[44] This comparison of texts is based on the *avviso* from Rome of 5 March 1695, a c. 25, and the Foligno gazette, no. 10, 9 March 1695, both in ASV, Segreteria di Stato. Avvisi, f. 58 cc. 25–6.

HEGEMONY OVER THE SOCIAL SCENE
AND ZEALOUS POPES (1676–1700)

RENATA AGO

The growth in the number of studies on the Roman curia,[1] of which the present book is an example, has increasingly shed light on the specific characteristics of a court in which the sovereign was elective and elderly and, therefore, destined to reign for a short – sometimes very short – period of time. Although pontiffs, like other European sovereigns, could consider themselves superior to everyone else, this was not true of their families or, in particular, their heirs. Indeed, after the death of a pope, his relatives were, as it were, downgraded from their status as members of a reigning house[2] to that of simple nobles. Moreover, the election of a new sovereign often meant open season for the settling of old scores, invariably at the expense of the deceased pope's nephews and more faithful relations.

The movements and divisions of the curia's internal factions had to conform to this particular configuration. As Reinhard has explained,[3] the composition of these antagonistic factions in the court reflected the transitory nature of the title of 'reigning family', which could only be boasted by a single house, and the fact that it would soon be handed over to another. This made any triumph over rival factions extremely fragile, and effectively ensured that the next victory would go to the coalition of groups which had been defeated in the previous conclave.

In the seventeenth century, the most sensational settling of old scores was surely the one involving the younger relatives of Urban VIII Barberini; but Mario Rosa has pointed out that even Cardinal Ludovisi

---

[1] See M. A. Visceglia, 'Burocrazia, mobilità sociale e patronage alla corte di Roma tra Cinque e Seicento. Alcuni aspetti del recente dibattito storiografico e prospettive di ricerca', *Roma moderna e contemporanea*, I (1995), pp. 11–54.

[2] On the relatives of popes as members of a reigning house, see the explicit reference in R. Ago, *Carriere e clientele nella Roma barocca*, Rome and Bari, 1990, pp. 67–8.

[3] W. Reinhard, *Freunde und Kreaturen: 'Verflechtung' als Konzept zur Erforschung historischer Führungsgruppen. Römische Oligarchie um 1600*, Munich, 1979. See also Maria Antonietta Visceglia's chapter in this volume.

had to organize an 'advertising campaign' in order to maintain his image as an honest and unselfish man. Gregory XV's warning to his nephew demonstrates the tactics and behaviour which characterized the pontifical nobility. The main advice – and practice – was to marry into the families of other important cardinals. From the Borghese to the Barberini to the Chigi, there was not one house of foreign origin which did not adhere to this strategy, preferably choosing a Roman family or a family with a solid Roman heritage.

These well-known phenomena, however, have always been inspected with a very 'curial' eye: the members of the curia, the cardinals, are the object of nearly every study on Rome.[4] Thus all the light that has been shed on the College of Cardinals has left the city of Rome in the dark. The focus on the clergy has diverted historians from analysing the role and function of laymen, the internal mechanisms of the city's nobility and its competitions. Nonetheless, the desire and need to marry into a Roman family demonstrate that the greater social context in which the curia existed, that of all the Roman aristocratic families, played an important role and that its relevance was clear to everyone.

Furthermore, many of the studies I have mentioned share a basic theoretical assumption: the explanation of the internal dynamics running through the Roman curia is to be found in the system of patronage and the categories of friendship, loyalty and other related concepts. What has been barely studied, however, is the concept of court society in its true Eliasian sense of a particular social configuration in which the high nobility – the court nobility – strive to emphasize their distinctness from the rest of society. The sovereign backed his court nobility in this challenge, but at the same time similarly emphasized the distance between himself and his nobles. The peculiarity of Roman society fits this interpretative model perfectly. In theory at least, due to his court of ecclesiastics, the pope had a discretionary power to grant or withhold which was far more powerful than that of any other temporal monarch. Thus, the competition surrounding appointments to the College of Cardinals may be interpreted as the equivalent of the contest for the privilege of attending a *lever du roi*. Moreover, the ability of many pontiffs to keep every candidate waiting until the last minute was simply a clear manifestation of how they could exercise their sovereignty. On the other hand, the rhetoric of pretence – the idiom in which competition and uncertainty are expressed – found fertile ground in Rome even earlier than in Paris. Indeed, court protocol was profoundly indebted to curial and ecclesiastical ceremony.

---

[4] See Visceglia, 'Burocrazia, mobilità sociale e patronage'.

Papal power, however, was threatened by a structural weakness that could not be fully compensated by the ability to grant or withhold favours at will. The papal sovereign may have been the precursor of absolute power, but this was not enough to save his family from being drawn into the circus of rivalries and alliances which exist in any urban society. Thus, notwithstanding his double nature as a temporal and spiritual sovereign, the pope, as head of his family, often had to come to terms with the other aristocratic families.

Recent studies have actually reduced the range of the pontiffs' absolute power, at least with regard to their relations with the city and citizens of Rome. Laurie Nussdorfer's research has revealed, for example, quite a different picture of the municipal authority from the prevalent one according to which the Roman magistracies were deprived of power from the beginning of the sixteenth century, the onset of an irreversible decline. From a practical point of view, the role of the Campidoglio in the administration and direction of the city of Rome remained important throughout the seventeenth century and beyond. From a symbolic point of view, the Capitoline Hill, its stairway, the square and the Palazzo del Senatore and the Palazzo dei Conservatori upheld their central position in public ritual, whilst the pontiffs and their families took care to insert their names and insignia among the symbols of the *Senatus Populusque Romanus.*[5]

Even the continuous conflicts over precedence between the Roman feudal lords and the pontifical nobility may be considered as a sign of the bitter struggle for pre-eminence, which at the end of the seventeenth century had still not been definitively secured by the pope's relatives.

Other episodes and circumstances, however, may be given as examples of the spirit of collaboration that existed between the pontiff and the Roman aristocracy. Negotiations and agreements brought the two parties closer together and diminished the asymmetry of their respective positions. The effects, however, were substantially analogous to the unresolved conflicts on precedence. This is what emerges, for example, from a significant part of the period's building activity and, in particular, from the position of certain roads and squares that attributed powerful features of symbolic representation to the reigning family and its allies. Thus, the rebuilding of the Piazza di Trevi was the result of an agreement and collaboration between the Barberini family and Ambrogio Carpegna, who gave Borromini the task of making this visible to everyone. The project was 'a symbol of what the

[5] L. Nussdorfer, *Civic Politics in the Rome of Urban VIII*, Princeton, 1992.

relationship between the Barberini family and the older aristocracy should ideally be like'.[6] If Alexander VII's grandiose urbanistic policy was meant to affirm and represent the ideal of the absolute pre-eminence of the church and the exemption of its state and sovereign from dealing with 'privates',[7] his successors opted for a less ambitious strategy of cooperation with the aristocratic families. The renovation of the Piazza Campitelli is therefore an example of the convergence of interests between the Albertoni family, the order of the Chierici Regolari di S. Maria in Portico, and the Capitoline authorities, and was crowned by the intervention of Clement X Altieri, a close relative of the Albertoni family.[8]

As is natural, the relationship of interdependency, rather than dominion, which bound the pope to the Roman nobility emerged even more clearly in dramatic circumstances, such as when the mobilization of allies was indispensable for mutual survival. One such episode was the 'Castro' War, in which the Roman knights participated with renewed pride as they at last had the opportunity to demonstrate their prowess in battle. This was clearly manifested by Pietro della Valle, who was happy to be 'for once among people of my same profession, among knights and soldiers, that is, rather than among robes [i.e. magistrates] that do not suit me'.[9]

An even more dramatic episode occurred when the Colonna constable deployed his soldiers in defence of the statue of Urban VIII on the day of the pope's death. This constable's loyalty may have been that which any general owes to his deceased sovereign, but in the eyes of contemporaries his gesture seemed inspired by family feeling, considering that his daughter had married Taddeo Barberini.[10]

The pontifical sovereign was thus an absolute monarch who was far more dependent on his nobility than other monarchs. Unlike the royal monarchies, which were never disrupted,[11] the pontifical sovereignty was continuously exposed to interruptions between the death of one pope and the proclamation of the next. During these periods, known as 'vacant see' (*sede vacante*), the College of Cardinals, the municipal authorities, the great aristocracy, and (in a steadily less formalized manner) the representatives of foreign powers and others, without access to or liberated

---

[6] J. Connors, 'Alliance and Enmity in Roman Baroque Urbanism', *Römisches Jarbuch für Kunstgeschichte*, 25 (1989), pp. 207–94.
[7] See R. Krautheimer, *The Rome of Alexander VII*, Princeton, 1986.
[8] See Connors, 'Alliance and Enmity'.
[9] ASV, Fondo Della Valle – Del Bufalo, b. 53, 10 October. 1642.
[10] See Nussdorfer, *Civic Politics*.
[11] See E. Kantorowitz, *The King's Two Bodies*, Princeton, 1957.

from the decision-making summit of power and hierarchical organization, experimented with different arrangements of the relationships which bound them to one another.

It is not surprising that it was precisely during the periods of 'vacant see' that jurisdictional conflicts broke out between the Capitoline magistracies (a direct emanation of the patrician citizens) and the governor of Rome (a prelate nominated by the pope), as well as between the governor of the *Borgo* (a curia ecclesiastic) and the conclave marshal (who, due to an ancient privilege, was always a member of the Savelli feudal family).[12]

The relationship between Roman society and the curia is thus far more complex than the simple concept of pontifical absolutism. There continued to be wide margins for manoeuvre for the more or less formalized – and corporate – clienteles that formed around every great aristocratic family.

Similar traits can be found on the more informal plane of hegemony over the cultural and festive scene. During the pontificate of Urban VIII, the Barberini family steadily advanced to occupy the centre stage, although one of the greatest collectors and patrons of the period was the 'private' lay noble Vincenzo Giustiniani.[13]

The same policies as were practised by individuals and their families to promote themselves through magnificent 'society life' were also pursued by Pope Innocent X, who bought the houses surrounding his family palace and incorporated them behind its new façade. Not content with this, he also had part of another building demolished because it spoiled the symmetry of the place, and transformed the church of St Agnes into his family chapel. Piazza Navona practically became the Pamphilis' own square.[14] However, the apex of urbanistic magnificence was achieved during the pontificate of Alexander VII, who organized both St Peter's Square and the entire area around the Quirinale. Rome's splendour had to compensate for the defeat of the Holy See in Münster where, notwithstanding all his efforts, the Chigi papal nuncio had been unable to avoid the 'defeat of the Catholic powers by their Protestant enemies'.[15]

Emulating the measures adopted by his predecessors, Alexander VII's cultural policy also included far more frivolous events. The arrival of Queen Christina of Sweden in Rome, for example, provided the excuse

[12] See Nussdorfer, *Civic Politics*.
[13] See F. Haskell, *Patrons and Painters*, 2nd edn, New Haven, 1980.
[14] See L. von Pastor, *Storia dei Papi*, 20 vols., Rome, 1908–34, vol. XIV/I.
[15] See Krautheimer, *The Rome of Alexander VII*.

to arrange celebrations in her honour, but also to exalt the magnificence of the host.[16]

The death of the Chigi pope led to a decline in the splendour and pomp of the Roman court. His immediate successors reigned for short periods or were too old to follow his example. The most important fact, however, is that during the last decades of the century St. Peter's chair was occupied in quick succession by two austere prelates who were fierce enemies of nepotism and their predecessors' temporal celebrations.

All studies of court society have emphasized the importance and function of the sovereign's presence at the apex of the social scene. The Renaissance and early baroque popes were perfectly aware of the significance of their role. The most austere pontificate of the baroque age, that of Innocent XI Odescalchi, allows us to measure the opposite effect: to see what happened to the scenario when the sovereign and his family withdrew from it.

As is predictable, contemporary chronicles of the age tell us that the competition among the great families, brought about by the void at the centre of ceremonial life, became far more heated. Nonetheless, since we have to deal with a festive scene and court, we must first identify the space that contains and delimits them.

In Rome there is no actual place that may be defined as a court, nor is it possible to identify one particular pontifical residence or even one which was preferred by the sovereign. Therefore the term 'court' was extended, both by contemporary chronicles and by the great jurist de Luca, to embrace all of the people who orbited around the pope and had access to him. Thus, the court was made up not only of curia prelates, but also of lay men and women. Its physical environment incorporated all of the city areas which were involved in the daily life of the pontiff and of his courtiers.

If we are to understand the concept of 'court' in the latter sense, we might say that the construction and enlargement of the Quirinale, and its use as a pontifical residence in the summer and autumn, expanded the space of the Roman court from what it had been up to the sixteenth century. Thus, from the beginning of the seventeenth century, this space was delineated by the two pontifical residences, the Vatican and the Quirinale, which were situated at the two extreme ends of the inhabited area of the city. The third papal building, St John Lateran, became central only on account of the functions that the pope performed there as Bishop of

---

[16] See von Pastor, *Storia dei papi*, vol. XIV/1, pp. 351–2, but also M.-L. Rodén, *Cardinal Decio Azzolino, Queen Christina of Sweden and the Squadrone Volante: Political and Administrative Developments at the Roman Curia 1644–1692*, Ann Arbor, 1992.

Rome, but it did not have any influence on the urbanistic development of the city of Rome.

As Krautheimer and Connors have shown,[17] the territory thus delimited became the object of fierce competition. It acquired forms and meanings as a result of the continuous power struggles which pervaded the social hierarchies. However, this space also gave meaning to and organized the internal order of Roman court society.

A sign of this process was the attraction exerted by the new pontifical palace, the Quirinale, and in particular by the urbanistic policy that exalted its presence in the context of the city.[18] It was certainly not by chance that the parish with the greatest concentration of high-class homes at the end of the seventeenth century was that of S. Vincenzo e Atanasio in Trevi, while the new noble residences were concentrated around the Via del Corso.[19]

Besides the popes' approach, however, there was also a policy of space management by 'private' individuals, although the scale of its activity depended on the circumstances.

By 'private individuals' I mean principally, though not exclusively, the great noble families. Significant roles were also played by various religious orders, as well as by the confraternities which were under the patronage of cardinals who were, in turn, related to the great families. We can therefore consider these confraternities as belonging to the social sphere of the great aristocratic families.

The occupation and management of space took place primarily through the construction and enlargement of patrician palaces by old – but also, and especially, by new – families, as well as through the construction and enlargement of churches by religious orders, confraternities, cardinals and lay nobles. The objective was always to make the façade of their palaces stand out from the rest on the same road or square. If it was not possible to project the façades forwards, they could always push the neighbouring houses backwards.[20] The success or failure of these construction policies were seen, and experienced, as a confirmation or confutation of their families' prestige. Family palaces and churches became the focal points of the city, providing the opportunity and the location for ceremonial and festive competition between the members of the court.

---

[17] Besides the works already mentioned, see J. Connors, *Borromini and the Roman Oratory*, Cambridge, 1980.

[18] See Krautheimer, *The Rome of Alexander VII*.

[19] Archivio del Vicariato di Roma, Parrocchia di S. Vincenzo e Atanasio in Trevi, Stati delle anime. See also Ago, *Carriere e clientele*.

[20] See Connors, 'Alliance and Enmity'.

This type of competition was far more important than its apparent frivolousness would seem to indicate. In our case, for example, it was part of the long-standing rivalry between the pontifical nobility and the old Roman feudal households. The Ottoboni Archive contains an order of precedence which openly conforms to the text by Gerolamo Lunadoro, mentioned by Maria Antonietta Visceglia,[21] and clearly shows the distance that separated the Roman feudal families from the pontifical families and the mass of 'other barons':

Order of Precedence[22]
Senator of Rome
Ambassadors of France and Spain
Auditor camerae
General Treasurer
Six Patriarchs
Head of the Orsini family / Head of the Colonna family
Participating protonotaries
Barons of the Colonna, Orsini, Savelli and Conti families
Heads of the pontifical houses
Ambassadors of Bologna, Ferrara and Malta
Judges of the *Rota*
Dignitaries of the Apostolic Chamber
Other barons
Presidents and agents of the serene princes
Chancery officers and non-participating protonotaries

We get the same impression from the description of an Easter ceremony which was attended – from a special lodge which only they were entitled to enter – by the Duchess of Bracciano (Orsini) and the Princess of Paliano (Colonna), because the other Roman ladies were 'unwilling to accept this disparity of treatment, notwithstanding the long-standing possession [of this privilege] by the two Colonna and Orsini families'.[23]

In general, the predecessors of Innocent XI all thought that the monopoly of power should be pursued in part through the control and centralization of artistic and cultural production, of ceremonies and social events, and had therefore been very active in these fields. Now however

---

[21] G. Lunadoro, *Relatione della Corte di Roma, e de riti da osservarsi in essa* ..., Rome, 1615, cit. in M. A. Visceglia, 'Il cerimoniale come linguaggio politico: su alcuni conflitti di precedenza alla corte di Roma tra Cinquecento e Seicento', in M. A. Visceglia and C. Brice (eds.), *Cérémonial et rituel à Rome (xvie-xixe siècle)*, Rome, 1997, pp. 117–76.
[22] BAV, Ottob. Lat., n. 2719.
[23] BNCVE, Fondo Vittorio Emanuele, ms. 787, 24 April 1683.

the pope locked himself away in an ascetic and austere life, leaving festive occasions to the lay nobility, who competed to affirm their excellence and modify the hierarchies of prestige.

Even ceremonies that were more closely related to the pontiff, such as the distribution of Confraternita dell'Annunziata dowry coupons to marrigeable girls, were boycotted or, at least, avoided by the pope. On 25 March 1684 the ceremony, which was traditionally presided over by the pontiff, was headed by the senior cardinal, as the 'pope no longer attends, probably because he never liked to'.[24]

Nonetheless, the pope was well aware of the symbolic value of such ceremonies. By refusing to legitimate with his presence the initiative of the Confraternita dell'Annunziata, Innocent XI was probably not imposing himself simply as an austere pontiff, but rather as a 'prince' who wanted to reduce the prerogatives of single groups in order to favour a more impersonal and universal conception of sovereignty. An analogous emphasis of his role as a sovereign clearly emerges from his relationship with foreign powers. During the 1683–4 presentation of the Chinea (the white horse) to the pontiff, for example, 'the ministers of Spain . . . would have liked the pope to excuse them from the horse ride through Rome this year, but His Holiness is resolute about it'.[25] The skirmish continued:

> The Viceroy of Naples does not want the Chinea to be presented in the Consistory chamber, as it does not seem right to the Spaniards that while the ambassador is on his knees, the Camerlengo cardinal will observe the ceremony sitting down. Since the prince does not want to introduce anything which will displease the Spanish court and as there is the example set by other popes who received it in bed, though with the assistance of the Camerlengo, he would like to do so again, or otherwise in another public place such as the chapel . . . but the pope does not want to be in bed as he says that that is only when he is ill or not well.[26]

Thus the pope continued to insist that the Spaniards present him with the Chinea 'with less formality, in the Consistory chamber'.

Innocent XI was intransigent in his defence of the privileges of the Apostolic See and was perfectly aware of the value of such ceremonial acts, which safeguarded a hierarchical order, or perhaps modified it in favour of Rome (the ambassador kneeling, the Camerlengo cardinal seated).

The same struggle is revealed in the granting of exemptions from customs duty to the ambassadors of foreign powers, or of extra-territorial status for the roads surrounding their palaces, the so-called *quartieri*: 'The pope wanted the new *barigello* from Ravenna to take possession

---

[24] Ibid., 28 March 1684.   [25] Ibid., 10 July 1683.
[26] Ibid., 15 January 1683.   [27] Ibid., 22 January 1683.

of Piazza di Spagna by passing through it with his party, but he did so with reluctance, keeping close to the houses opposite the royal palace'.[28] A few years later, the same treatment was given to France: the governor's *birri* had to walk through Piazza Farnese.[29]

Thus, it is evident that the pope sought to affirm the independence and full jurisdiction of the Holy See in order to avoid the formation of a hierarchy among the Catholic powers, with one prevailing over the others. However, the fact that no festive celebrations were given by the pope or his relatives, the complete lack of interest in culture and art and the complete withdrawal from the social scene left an empty space which was soon occupied by 'private individuals'.[30]

Innocent XI would have liked to extend his own austerity even to the 'private individuals'. From the beginning of his pontificate he forbade theatrical representations, carnival games and shows, and even the new French fashions which had been replacing the more austere Spanish ones.[31] However, the pope did not have the power to enforce his edicts and compel his nobles to respect them. The proclamation against fashions – according to a 1683 account – 'declared that even family heads would incur excommunication and arbitrary penalties, but the Colonna constable declared that he could not oblige the princess of Paliano, his daughter-in-law, nor her Spanish damsels to observe it and could do nothing more than attach the edict to their door'.[32] Games and theatrical representations were not interrupted either: according to one account, 'in the garden of Queen Christina many knights performed the noble game of the *biscia* under the supervision of the Colonna constable in order to make up for its austerity during the past carnival . . . Her Majesty looked on from a balcony, along with eight cardinals'.[33] A month later, in the Clementine College, there was 'a beautiful ball . . . with fencing and horsemanship'.[34] Similar edicts, with analogous violations, continued throughout the pontificate of Innocent XI, while the competition for pre-eminence continued unhindered.

We have already considered the case of the two ladies. Even the presentation of the Chinea was an issue which developed due to the demands of the Colonna constable, who was 'thinking about . . . participating

---

[28] Ibid., 27 November 1683.

[29] See von Pastor, *Storia dei papi*, vol. XIV/2, pp. 255–6.

[30] This is also important from a documentary point of view, because the absence of the pope and his relatives gave the chronicles room to record the doings of the 'private individuals', and thus provide us with information about them.

[31] See von Pastor, *Storia dei papi*, vol. XIV/2, pp. 21–4.

[32] BNCVE, Fondo Vittorio Emanuele, ms. 787, 11 December 1683.

[33] Ibid., 22 April 1684.   [34] Ibid., 13 May 1684.

unexpectedly in the ride and taking the place that he claimed in relation to the papal guards'.[35] The Borghese prince, who had initially been put in charge of leading the ceremony, 'decided to retire without ending the celebration, so as not to jeopardize his situation with respect to the quarrel that he and the other heads of the pontifical houses had with this constable. The Spanish faction in the college of Cardinals, however, immediately summoned and urgently sent a courier to Naples'.[36]

In the end, the constable had the upper hand and the Borghese prince was forced to give up the lavish ride, on which he had already spent thousands of *scudi* 'in order to show his generosity and magnificence'. 'As no form of agreement was reached between the Colonna constable and the Borghese prince, the extraordinary ambassador to the Catholic King . . . the celebration was suspended, to the utter dismay of the populace, in a quite unprecedented way'.[37] A little later, there was even a rumour that the Chinea would be presented by the Duke of Paliano, the son of the constable, 'who will have deserved his honour and the Borghese prince will have lost his. That will serve as a lesson to all the other princes of this state, who will never receive a similar charge from the court of Spain.'[38] Thus, 'these politicians talk about the Borghese prince, who is going to uphold France and marry his son to a French lady . . . It was Cardinal d'Estrée who visited this prince and . . . immediately these spiteful politicians decided that the intention was to make him pro-French.'[39]

Thus, the competition for precedence between the two houses threatened to develop into a clash between a 'French' faction and a 'Spanish' faction – or, at least, to be represented as such. Although with regard to true political acts, pope Innocent XI seemed determined to maintain the status quo between factions and valiantly defend his own prerogatives, the absence of the pope and his family from the festive scene allowed the clash to be transferred to that plane, on which one group dominated the others. On the social scene, in fact, the Colonna family were the undisputed leaders, so much so that the prince of Butera, ambassador extraordinary of the Viceroy of Naples, 'although . . . he was a relative of the Borghese prince, and notwithstanding the offers that he received, accepted those made to him by the Colonna constable, who was to receive him in Marino'.[40]

The worldly pre-eminence of the constable was due to his privileged relationship with Spain, although it often turned to his disadvantage. In January 1684, the rumour began to spread that he would not be participating in the famous horse ride together with the Borghese prince 'since

---

[35] Ibid., 26 June 1683.   [36] Ibid.   [37] Ibid., 3 July 1683.
[38] Ibid., 11 September 1683.   [39] Ibid.   [40] Ibid., 23 October 1683.

if he wants to participate he will have to meet the prince [the ambassador extraordinary] without obtaining the [place at his] right hand, or
the [right to use the] secret staircase that was the point he demanded'.[41]
This was surely interpreted as a sign that the protest sent to Madrid by
the Borghese prince had been successful, but in reality the constable had
never had the privilege of the right hand, as we know from the instructions given by the King of France to the Duc de Créqui, who was on his
way to Rome.[42]

Nonetheless, the prestige of a person was based particularly on his or
her being one of the last representatives of the 'true' Roman aristocracy.
By the end of the seventeenth century the autochthonous feudal families
were almost all either extinct or in decline. The only two families who
had survived and were actively present on the scene were the Orsini and
the Colonna. These two families were divided by ancient rivalries that
were expressed in the urban space and are still inscribed in the topogra-
phy of Rome. The residence of one family was on the western side of
Rome, towards the Vatican, while the other resided in the eastern part,
between the Campidoglio and the Quirinale. Although separated by their
rivalry, the Orsini and Colonna families were united by their prestige, by
their pre-eminence over all other aristocratic families. Only members of
the reigning family could claim precedence over them. Thus the absence
of the pope's relatives could only lead to the further growth of their prestige and encourage them to wield their influence by forming a greater
following and strengthening their clientele. Furthermore, since the Orsini
and Colonna families were (as we have seen) traditionally loyal to France
and Spain respectively, the supremacy of one of the two families may
have had consequences that must be evaluated most carefully, including
the possibility that the Colonna supremacy was secretly encouraged by
the pope, who was in conflict with Louis XIV on the issue of the *régale*
and on the declarations of the Gallican clergy.

Having absented himself from the festive scene without succeeding in
ending its pomp, the pope had in effect yielded its resources to his nobles.
His austerity had thus become contradictory with regard to the policy
of safeguarding his sovereign prerogatives, which in other matters he had
pursued with such zeal.

[41] Ibid., 8 January 1684.
[42] *Recueil des instructions données aux ambassadeurs et ministres de France*, vol. VI: *Rome*,
Paris, 1888, pp. 104ff., *Instruction au duc de Créqui* (1662): the King of France ordered
his ambassador in Rome not to offer his right hand to the Orsini duke because the
Spanish ambassador had not offered his to the Colonna constable. The ambassador's
wife, in turn, did not offer her right hand to the constable's wife, Maria Mancini,
Mazarin's niece.

In contrast with Innocent XI's anti-festive rigour, the new atmosphere created by the accession of pope Alexander VIII was immediately perceived by contemporary observers. The Colonna, Orsini and Borghese families disappeared from the scene, which became the territory of the Ottoboni family.

From the day of his election, the new pope gave an honorary role to his very young nephew Peter. On 8 October , the chronicles report that 'His Holiness sent Don Pietro, his nephew, to visit the Sacred College to thank them for the honour they had given to his uncle'.[43] On November 12, the young man was made a cardinal:

> That night [the Pope] appointed him vice-chancellor and decided that at the first Consistory he would declare him legate to Avignon, Umbria and Marca and general superintendent of the ecclesiastical state, so that he will be able to enjoy an income of 100,000 *scudi*. Right after the promotion, cannon shots were fired from the castle as [was the tradition] with every dominant cardinal. This event had not taken place for twenty-two years, since Cardinal Rospigliosi.[44]

The young cardinal-nephew did not hesitate about fulfilling his role. After a few weeks, the arrival of a new ambassador and the appointment of new cardinals provided him with the opportunity to affirm his ceremonial and worldly position, as well as to eliminate members of other families from the scene. During the reign of Innocent XI, the ambassador extraordinary of the Polish king, who had come to announce the liberation of Vienna, was welcomed by the Barberini family, 'private individuals', who had distinguished themselves by their magnificence. The princess had donated a 'box full of Spanish gloves, phials of different scents, a beautiful miniature painting with six fans embroidered in gold, and pearls to be presented to the Queen of Poland in her name'. [45] The cardinal and the Barberini prince had also loaded the ambassador with gifts for himself and his king. The reason behind all this generosity did not escape chroniclers: 'And why do the gifts of this court seem in excess?' said one *avviso*. 'Some believe that it was not without a specific purpose, and as this king has already received the right to nominate cardinals, like the other monarchs, we may believe that all this courtesy is in favour of the Barberini abbot, who wishes to receive a cardinal's robe'.[46]

In 1689, Pietro Ottoboni refused to tolerate his rivals in this field and reserved to himself the privilege of receiving the Portuguese

---

[43] BNCVE, Fondo Vittorio Emanuele, ms. 788.
[44] Ibid.   [45] Ibid., ms. 787, 16 October 1683.
[46] Ibid., 9 October 1683.

ambassador and leading him to the pope. The young man demonstrated the same vivacity in celebrating the newly elected cardinals, who 'when the celebration ended, were conducted to Cardinal Ottoboni's apartment, where he held a sumptuous banquet with music'.[47]

The arrival in Rome of other members of the pope's family sparked the usual competition among Roman noblewomen for the presentation of the nicest gift, 'of which the Ruspoli Marquise could boast'.[48] But it was the Ottoboni who provoked this competition and reaped its benefits. The young cardinal was able to crown his civic career and surround himself with a magnificent court, becoming the generous and cultured promoter of one of the most lively musical venues of his age.

The pontificate of Alexander VIII, however, lasted less than a year and his successor, Innocent XII, adopted the style, as well as the name, of the previous Odescalchi pope. The last twenty years of the century were characterized, practically without interruption, by the austere and non-worldly policies of these two pontiffs.

These frivolous skirmishes can certainly not be seen as the cause of the decline of papal power, nor was Rome ever the scene of dramatic transformations. Nonetheless we must not forget that, in the opinion of the interested parties, the victories achieved in this field – as well as the losses, inflicted or suffered – led to variations in prestige that were capable of modifying the internal hierarchies of the nobility. Such a change could, in turn, influence the relations between the entire body of the nobility and the 'prince'. Furthermore, if it is true that the curia represented the prototype of court society and that the spiritual sovereignty of the pope played an important role in this process, the Roman lay and ecclesiastical nobility tended to portray itself as a true court society. They emphasized the temporal nature of the pope's authority,[49] even using lay titles such as 'prince' or 'lord' in their conversations with and letters to ministers and officers.[50] However, as the context was specifically a court society, an ensemble made up of interdependent people and rules of government and behaviour, hegemony over the social scene was no less important than other central positions, and the absence or withdrawal of a sovereign from this stage could lead to an imbalance in the entire system.

Historians stress that Innocent XI was the inspiration behind the bull against nepotism, while Innocent XII was the pontiff who actually adopted this measure. These two popes should, therefore, be consid-

---

[47] Ibid., 2 November 1683.   [48] Ibid., 26 November 1689.   [49] See note 2.

[50] Besides these there was the title 'Our Lord' which, compared to the more spiritual 'His Holiness', offers the advantage of combining the religious principle with the feudal one.

ered the masterminds of the first serious attempts to liberate the church from the fetters of worldliness. Historians have never inquired, however, into the relationship between their austerity and the political culture of their age; into what influence the temporal quality of pontifical power could have exercised on its far more familiar spiritual nature.

What has been referred to as Innocent's 'turning-point' – which was immediately disputed by his successor – actually corresponds to a vigorous attempt to 'moralize' the ecclesiastical hierarchies and their lifestyle. However, the contrast between the pontificates of Innocent XI and of Alexander VIII does not merely express two diametrically opposed conceptions of the church and its clergy.[51] The analogous discrepancy between the nature of the governments of the Odescalchi pope and the Ottoboni pope, which we have examined in its festive and mundane aspects, also shows the great differences in their two concepts of sovereignty and its practice. Indeed, this distance reflects the two approaches to politics – the art of good government versus the reason of state – that pervaded political thought in the early modern age.[52]

The fundamental issues of this debate emerge very explicitly from two pamphlets that appeared around 1680, one by de Luca, auditor to pope Innocent XI, and the other written by a rather obscure antagonist belonging to the same curial sphere.[53] Experience, wrote de Luca, teaches that the court is 'a wolf that devours the greatest and best substance [of the principality], or in truth a leech which, in order to grow fat and stay alive, sucks out all the body's blood'. Thus, 'a governor who is liked and approved by the court will govern the principality badly', while anyone who tries to do his best for the principality will cause hostility in the court because he will have to 'do away with useless and unnecessary positions and eliminate the use of gifts, corruption and venality, and prevent the illicit introduction of so many exemptions'. This, however, is the only way in which to achieve the 'good politics of a true, good prince, who distinguishes himself from a tyrant by being principally interested in the well-being of his subjects, before his own and that of his private sphere'.[54]

---

[51] See C. Donati, 'La Chiesa di Roma tra antico regime e riforme settecentesche (1675–1760)', in G. Chittolini and G. Miccoli (eds.), *Storia d'Italia*, Annali 9, *La Chiesa e il potere politico*, Turin, 1986, pp. 721–68.

[52] See M. Viroli, *Dalla politica alla ragion di stato. La scienza del governo tra XIII e XVII secolo*, Rome, 1994.

[53] The Vaticani Latini manuscript mentioned in the following note is anonymous, but other versions of the same text are attributed to Abbot Elpidio Benedetti (see A. Lauro, *Il cardinale Giovanni Battista De Luca. Diritto e riforme nello Stato della Chiesa (1676–1683)*, Naples, 1991, p. 200). On Benedetti see *DBI*, vol. VIII, pp. 250–1.

[54] ASV, Vat. Lat. 8194, cc. 234r–242v, *La nemicitia tra la Corte e il Principato/ discorso di Mons. De Luca uditore di Innocenzo XI*.

De Luca's words, and the very idea of structural antagonism between a small number of courtiers and the whole state, unmistakably echo the Florentine civic humanist tradition, with its emphasis on the nobility of politics and political action. This includes the actions of prince in an open dispute with the 'reason of state' theoreticians, and the art of government, the main aim of which is the conservation and expansion of the governor's power.[55] However, equally plain is the espousal of an absolutist concept of the sovereign's prerogatives, which tends to exalt his separation from the rest of the political body. This is even more evident when these reflections are applied to the court within the greater framework of de Luca's argument on the Christian prince and his relations with his nobles, in which he openly echoes Richelieu.[56] In both cases, the greatness and good nature of the prince depend on his perfect compliance with the principle of justice, a principle that must prevail over all others.[57]

The very prosperity of the nation, replies de Luca's antagonist, requires the great to be great, and while 'it is true that luxuries are detrimental to families', this is not true of the whole country, which can reap advantages from a greater circulation of money.

> The prince must be very careful to treat the principality as a principality and not as a private house, since some small savings can cause damage to many and do little for the public good . . . It is self-evident that a decrease in the income of the rich only deprives the poor of a great source of money. The catastrophic state of our age, with its universal drop in income that has even impoverished rich households, deserves the attention of our zealous prince, who should look for ways to fight such calamities . . . Depriving Rome of the decorous and splendid presence of the many missing cardinals' courts not only deprives many gentlemen of an honest and necessary lifestyle: does it not also weaken the prelacy?[58]

A man who wants to 'perform with great princely sentiments' must not upset the natural social hierarchies, denying 'those who have undertaken a career in order to increase their fortunes through toil and merit' their rightful reward of income and honour. It is the splendour of the court which makes a prince great, and the humiliation of the former entails the humiliation of the latter.

[55] See Viroli, *Dalla politica alla ragion di stato*; see also J. G. A. Pocock, *The Machiavellian Moment. Florentine Political Thought and the Atlantic Republican Tradition*, Princeton, 1975.

[56] See G. B. de Luca, *Il principe cristiano pratico*, Rome, 1680, pp. 649–52, in which de Luca advises the prince to ensure that no noble becomes too 'great'.

[57] Ibid., p. 218.

[58] ASV, Vat. Lat. 8194, cc. 94r–97v, *Risposta alla scrittura intitolata La nemicitia della Corte col Principato, e riconciliatione d'essi*. The idea that the increase in consumption played a key role in the entire economy is accepted by some students of this period's politics and 'economy': see J. A. Schumpeter, *History of Economic Analysis*, vol. 1, New York, 1954.

Using perfect court logic, which fits neatly into the long tradition of considerations and warnings on the Roman curia, Benedetti points out the dangers that had already been denounced a century earlier by Commendone: only a few exceptional men love virtue for itself, and therefore it must be adequately rewarded, otherwise 'the court will be doubly damaged, as it will not only be deprived of good men or, at least, of men who follow the path of virtue, but will also give each the chance to turn his projects and ambitions elsewhere'.[59] Moreover, if it is true that Rome 'is the republic of every Christian, it is more that of those who toil for it'.[60] The justice of the prince is tempered by his other virtues, prudence and liberality.

De Luca and his antagonist use the same idiom to describe a sovereign's qualities. Both of their texts contain some of the commonplaces of humanist politics: the exaltation of 'virtue', the necessity of 'merit' and the condemnation of 'abuses'.[61] Nonetheless, although both set out with a common vocabulary, they end up reflecting the two different viewpoints – that of the prince and that of the courtier – from which court society can be observed and, therefore, the two different ways in which justice and injustice can be understood. Drawing on the classics, de Luca makes a clear distinction between commutative and distributive justice. While the former belongs to civic government, to the administration of a state which can in no way avoid or fail in its duties, distributive justice is the prerogative of sovereignty.[62] Court culture tends to ignore this distinction in order to emphasize, as Benedetti does, the fact that 'toil and merit' must be proportionally rewarded. Thus, what de Luca considered a prerogative of the prince is turned into an essentially hierarchical quality, a manifestation of the natural order of persons and classes of persons.[63] Court society demands its privileges, which are 'right' because they are 'natural'.

At this point it becomes clear what was really at stake. The reform project of Pope Innocent XI and his councillor de Luca was not limited to the spiritual restoration of the church, but was simultaneously and inextricably directed towards a transformation of the state, through the retrieval of the humanist virtues of the good prince and the triumph of justice over prudence. In its distributive form, which is a monopoly of the sovereign, justice does not forbid the introduction of differences among

---

[59] G. F. Commendone, *Discorso sopra la corte di Roma*, ed. C. Mozzarelli, Rome, 1996, p. 59.

[60] Ibid., p. 60.

[61] On the methodological aspects of this issue see J. G. A. Pocock, *Virtue, Commerce and History. Essays on Political Thought and History, Chiefly in the Eighteenth Century*, Cambridge, 1985, pp. 1–34, 'Introduction: The state of the art'.

[62] De Luca, *Il Principe cristiano*, pp. 231–2.

[63] ASV, Vat. Lat. 8194, cc. 94r–97v, *Risposta alla scrittura*.

subjects by rewarding the best. Nonetheless, the just prince tolerates no abuses. Reason of state, the art of preserving the principality, which is founded on prudence, seems to suggest that it is better not to make enemies of the powerful, but rather to safeguard one's nobility, as it is the immediate referent of sovereign power. Thus, it seeks its theoretical justification in the defensive invocation of a rigid hierarchical order in both the religious and the political fields.

For Innocent XI and his theoretician de Luca, the withdrawal of the pope from the festive scene was only the first act in a long war against both civic and spiritual corruption. The privileges and abuses which they sought to oppose were not only those of the ecclesiastical hierarchies, but also those of the entire court according to the definition I have tried to give.[64] The entire social structure which depended on the court was threatened by these projects. However, as a temporal and elected sovereign, the pontiff was an integral part of a structure which was not going to accept its dissolution without a struggle.

Thus Roman court society was in no way original. During those same years, at the end of the seventeenth century, an analogous opposition between the 'virtue' of reformers and the 'corruption' of the establishment animated the political debates of other European countries.[65] Those establishments, like the Roman court, were not particularly willing to let themselves be 'reformed'. Nonetheless, the social context was favourable to a theoretical reflection in the tradition of civic humanism. In Rome, however, the debate was sluggish due to a scarcity of interlocutors.

---

[64] And frequently even more than the court, as is shown by the case of the appointed offices (*provisionati*) of the Holy Office. See A. Prosperi, *Tribunali della coscienza. Inquisitori, confessori, missionari*, Turin, 1996, pp. 180–5.

[65] See Pocock, *The Machiavellian Moment*; idem, *Virtue, Commerce and History*.

INDEX